World Recession and the Food Crisis in Africa

Edited by
Peter Lawrence
Lecturer in Economics
University of Keele

REVIEW OF
African
Political Economy

James Currey

LONDON

James Currey Ltd
54b Thornhill Square, Islington
London N1 1BE

Book trade orders for edition published
by James Currey Ltd:
J.M. Dent & Sons (Distribution) Ltd
Dunhams Lane, Letchworth, Herts SG6 1LF
or Third World Publications (Co-op) Ltd
151 Stratford Road, Birmingham B11 1RD

British Library Cataloguing in Publication Data
World recession and the food crisis in Africa.
1. Africa   Economic conditions   1960–
I. Lawrence, Peter
330. 96'0328   HC800
ISBN 0-85255-309-9
ISBN 0-85255-304-8 Pbk

To the memory of
Jitendra Mohan

Typesetting by Selina Cohen in association with
Oxford Publishing Services, The Old Toffee Factory
120a Marlborough Road, Oxford OX1 4LS
Printed in Great Britain

Table of Contents

Contents

Part Three – The food crisis and famine in Africa · 157

Preface

The chapters comprising this volume were initially presented as papers to the *Review of African Political Economy* Conference, entitled *The World Recession and the Crisis in Africa*, which took place at the University of Keele, England, in September 1984. Over 50 papers were presented to the conference. The publication of all of them would have required either excerpting each of the papers doing justice to none, or publishing a relatively coherent selection and thereby leaving out many good contributions. The latter course was chosen. Most of the papers have been revised by their authors for this book and I have written a general introduction and attempted to give some coherence to the volume by writing short introductions linking the articles in each section. Because many of the articles rely on the same sources, I have produced a common bibliography at the end of the book.

Thanks are due to all the contributors for responding quickly to my requests for revisions and to my own editorial input. Thanks are also due to Robin Cohen for helpfully suggesting that the book should focus on the food crisis, to Catherine Fitzmaurice who helped compile the bibliography and gave constant encouragement and advice, to James Currey, Ingrid Crewdson, Keith Sambrook and Clare Currey for getting the book so speedily to press, to Selina Cohen for her swift and expert setting of some highly variable copy, to the Department of Economics at Keele for co-sponsoring the conference and providing logistical support, and to Sylvia Beech, Pam Davenport and Jayne Braddick for executing that support so efficiently. Finally, on behalf of the ROAPE editorial working group, I should like to thank the Swedish Agency for Research in Developing Countries (SAREC) and the British Academy for helping to fund the costs of bringing over speakers from Africa and North America to the conference. Their contributions are well represented in this volume.

The 1984 conference was for many, the last occasion to meet and talk with Jitendra Mohan, a fellow editor of ROAPE, who died six weeks after the conference took place. This book is dedicated to his memory.

Peter Lawrence
Keele, 1986

Notes on Contributors

Peter Lawrence is a lecturer in economics at the University of Keele, England.

Giovanni Arrighi is professor of sociology at the State University of New York at Binghamton.

Bob Sutcliffe teaches economics at Kingston Polytechnic, England.

Frederick Nixson is senior lecturer in economics at the University of Manchester.

Yusuf Bangura lectures in political science at Ahmadu Bello University, Zaria, Nigeria.

Barry Munslow and his colleagues are based at the Centre of African Studies, University of Liverpool, England.

Laurence Harris is professor of economics at the Open University, Milton Keynes.

John Loxley is professor of economics at the University of Manitoba, Winnipeg.

Ajit Singh teaches economics at the University of Cambridge, England.

John Sender and *Sheila Smith* teach economics at the University of Cambridge and the University of Sussex, respectively.

Kighoma Malima is Minister of Economic Planning in the Tanzanian Government.

Werner Biermann works in the Economic Research Bureau, University of Dar es Salaam, Tanzania.

Jumanne Wagao is head of the Economics Department at the University of Dar es Salaam, Tanzania.

Dirk Hansohm works at the University of Bremen in the Federal Republic of Germany.

Philip Raikes is a member of the Institute for Development Research, Copenhagen.

Brooke Schoepf is based in Massachusetts and has taught and researched in Zaire.

Bjorn Beckman and *Gunilla Andrae* teach at the University of Stockholm, Sweden and at the Ahmadu Bello University in Zaria, Nigeria.

Eskor Toyo teaches economics at the University of Calabar, Nigeria.

Rudo Gaidzanwa teaches sociology at the University of Zimbabwe.

Roger Leys is a member of the Institute for Development Research, Copenhagen.

Meredeth Turshen teaches at Rutgers University, New Jersey, USA.

Lionel Cliffe and *Ray Bush* teach politics at the University of Leeds, England.

Valerey Jansen is a research student in the Department of Politics at the University of Leeds, England working on women and birth control policy in Namibia.

Introduction
World recession and the food crisis in Africa
Peter Lawrence

Africa's crisis and the world recession

By any estimation, sub-Saharan Africa (SSA) is in a state of profound economic, social and political crisis. Growth rates have declined sharply since 1973 in all sectors and have been outstripped or matched by rising population growth rates (Sutcliffe, Chapter 2). Food production per capita has fallen over the last decade by up to 15 per cent in some countries and by 6 per cent over the whole of the region. Cereal imports have risen by 117 per cent and food aid by 172 per cent (World Bank 1985, Annex Table 6). Industrial growth rates have been very low or negative as industries dependent on scarce foreign exchange for imported inputs have had to close down. Foreign exchange has become scarcer as export revenues have declined. The resultant increases in balance of payments deficits have resulted in recourse to borrowing. While many third world countries have shifted their structure of exports away from dependence on primary products, sub-Saharan Africa has made little progress in this direction. As borrowing has increased to finance payments deficits, the burden of servicing the debt has increased; this demand for funds is competing with that for imports urgently required to maintain industry and services. Although there has been some improvement recently, in 1983 almost 20 per cent of export revenue of middle-income Africa went to debt service compared with a level of 14.5 per cent for low-income Africa (World Bank 1985: Annex Table 16).

There is little sign of improved prospects for African economies in the second half of the 1980s. The International Monetary Fund (IMF), which was cautiously optimistic about world recovery at the beginning of 1985 (IMF 1985: 1), has more recently offered a gloomier prognosis for 1986 and beyond. In particular, developing country export volume growth is expected to be 0.25 per cent in 1985 compared with 8.5 per cent in 1984, the year of recovery, leading to a further reduction in developing country imports. Lower growth of world trade and of the industrialised economies than in 1984 is also predicted (*Financial Times* 7 October 1985). Although this still constitutes a recovery from the depths of the 1980 recession, it is both slower than that which occurred after 1974–5 and which brings real GNP to only a percentage point or two above the level obtaining in 1979 (IMF 1985). None of this can be of any comfort to sub-Saharan Africa. In any case, 1984, a year of 'recovery', resulted in a growth rate of only 1.5 per cent for SSA, so that the likelihood of sustaining, let alone increasing, this rate is poor.

The facts of SSA's economic crisis are generally undisputed and Sutcliffe lays out their stark reality in this volume. The severe drought which has affected many areas of this region at varying times during the last two decades has further curtailed food production and caused the deaths of millions through starvation and/or malnutrition, or a combination of both, and caused a severe strain on the balance of payments as food imports have had to be increased. The root causes of Africa's crisis and the nature of effective solutions are not at all as clear and are the subject of considerable debate, as we shall see in this volume. However, even the IMF and the World Bank have been forced to admit that Africa's crisis is not only the result of 'shortcomings in policies' but also of 'a less favourable export structure' and of 'prolonged drought' (IMF 1985: 69). The issue that lies at the heart of the debate is the degree to which IMF/World Bank market liberalisation and incentive policies lead to the continuation of this less favourable export structure and excessive vulnerability to the behaviour of the wider world economy. An assessment of policies proposed requires a clear view of what has caused the world 'recession', 'depression' or 'crisis' and what the interrelationship is between the African economies and the world economy.

Recession, depression and crisis

Crisis is a much overused word. At its extreme, it has connotations of systemic breakdown, but more generally it can refer to a moment or a specific time period in the history of a system at which various developments of a negative character combine to generate a serious threat to its survival. In this sense the slowdown of world economic growth evident in the 1970s and 1980s exhibits several negative characteristics which when combined could lead to a systemic breakdown of capitalism, but which could equally be viewed as a serious, but resolvable, threat to survival, or even a temporary, though lengthy, pause in capitalism's as yet unfulfilled purpose of world development. The use of the word 'recession' in the title of the conference and of this book constitutes a suspension of judgement as to the nature of the current phase of world economic development rather than any certain view as to the way in which the world economy will resolve its inherent rivalries and contradictions. We can perhaps justifiably refer to 'crisis' in two respects: first, as regards the world economy, in the accumulation of debt by third world countries and in their inability to repay; and secondly in the evident failure of African states to feed their populations. In the worst sense of debt crisis, many African countries have avoided this by virtue of having insufficient collateral to obtain loans, as Sutcliffe points out (Chapter 2). As regards the food crisis, we have witnessed the breakdown of economies, the overthrow of governments and the mass starvation and death of whole communities. The extent to which we can link these two developments – world recession and Africa's food crisis – relates very much to the theoretical framework adopted to explain the way in which world economic development and underdevelopment has unfolded.

In search of a theory

Leaving aside for the moment the question of the relationship between capitalist development and third world underdevelopment, it is clearly important to understand what governs development at the centres of capitalism. Here we are faced with several theories, not all of which are mutually exclusive. Essentially the question is what governs the rate of capital accumulation. Clearly the major determinant of the rate of accumulation is the rate of profit, and most theorising concerns the determinant of this rate (Arrighi, Chapter 1; Kay 1975; Glyn and Sutcliffe 1972). Ultimately, the rate of profit is determined by the relationship between changes in wages and changes in productivity. This latter factor is a function of the rate of technical progress, as well as the efficiency of production organisation. The current wave of innovation based on microtechnology has yet to generate widespread productivity gains and high rates of economic growth, and therefore make inroads into the exceptionally high levels of unemployment.

Hence we would appear to be in a period of restructuring and relocation of manufacturing industry in which both the state and international economic organisations have assumed a key regulatory role. We have seen this particularly in older 'heavier' industries of steel and coal, but such production regulation and restructuring has occurred in automobiles too. It leads to the removal of inefficient (i.e. low profit rate) enterprises and the survival of those which can compete.

However, the depression which such restructuring brings to markets makes recovery slow. Company failure leads to increasing unemployment and in such an economic climate investment is discouraged because there appears to be little prospect of expanding markets. The result is stagnation or very slow growth, not enough to mop up the higher levels of unemployment. The resolution of such a depression depends upon a combination of productivity gains and substantial reductions in the rate of growth of real wages, so that the cheapening of mass consumption goods can lead to an expansion in sales. The development of cohesive working classes with well-organised trade unions has reduced the possibility of pushing down real wages. Hence those who remain in work enjoy higher than ever living standards while the unemployed drift into poverty, giving potential to social and political dislocation. However, it seems clear that were productivity to rise at substantially higher rates than in the last decade, the upward pressure on real wages, and therefore unit labour costs, could be more than matched by the downward pressure on unit costs resulting from very much higher levels of productivity. So that even if the IMF and World Bank 'monetarist' view, that real wage rigidities in labour markets have been the real cause of high unemployment in Europe were the case, real wages could still rise without leading to higher unemployment, as would appear to be the case in Japan (*The Economist*, 21 September 1985). Only in the USA, with its weaker labour organisation, did real wages fall, and the US has limited the rise in unemployment since 1980 and enjoyed relatively high growth rates, but this has been based on lower productivity increases than in Western Europe and Japan. So, it can still be argued that the relative strengths of labour and capital have indeed been decisive in determining the course of economic decline and recovery in the developed world. It is clear, however, that these adverse developments have hit some developed capitalist countries harder than others. The ability of Japan to survive the recession relatively unscathed gives support to the role of productivity gains induced by advanced technology, although Japan is also characterised by different forms of social organisation and public provision, which limit unemployment levels.

The need for increasing competitiveness in international markets, in which Japan has been singularly successful, despite a strong currency, is a reflection of intercapitalist and/or imperialist rivalries and the so-called crisis of hegemony of the US. At the heart of this is the role of the US in attempting to preserve hegemony over the world economy (Arrighi, Chapter 1). There is little doubt that the recovery of the world economy as well as the resolution of the international debt crisis has been hindered by the high US interest rates resulting from its high budget deficit. The forcing up of international interest rates has hindered European investment recovery. At the root of the US budget deficit is its military spending, which might have engineered a Keynesian style economic recovery in the US, but which has not helped recovery elsewhere. Indeed it has led to fears of a renewed US military involvement abroad with consequences for the world and US economy similar to those which occurred during and after the Vietnam War. The US therefore still seeks to dominate the world economy and does so by inhibiting recovery in rival economies and by seeking to dominate militarily. In this way it is clearly anxious to limit the degree to which Western Europe and the Soviet Union could become economically integrated to the exclusion of the US itself. Its concern with Central America and with Southern Africa also reflects the degree to which it seeks to reduce European influence in these regions. So the length of this recession can partially be adduced to the ways in which the US tries and generally succeeds in maintaining its hegemony over Europe and Japan in the face of Europe's expansion eastward and to the South.

The new imperialism

This brings us to the character of the world economic system in the late twentieth century. International capitalism springing from national bases brings a system of oligopolistic competition crossing national boundaries and operating increasingly in a *world market*. While national and continental rivalries for a world hegemony push in one direction, the drive for the maintenance and growth of capitalism as a system pull in the other. Transnational corporations, international organisations and military alliances are expressions of this tendency to unify in the face of threats to the system in its own interests. Given its effective control over the IMF and the power of its own transnationals as well as the worldwide exercise of military power, the USA retains its hegemonic position in the alliance of developed capitalist states, in spite of increasingly powerful challenges from Europe and Japan.

Nevertheless, economic rivalries between the main centres of capitalism and the continuing military rivalry between the two great power blocs has spread into the third world over the last four decades leading to a new imperialist division into spheres of influence and competition. The perceived need of each power bloc to preserve its influence and defend its own sphere has led to the mushrooming of military bases, the spread of military alliances, and the massive build-up of the arms trade with the third world. Here US hegemonic interests have been challenged, most notably in Indochina, but also in the Middle East and Latin (mainly Central) America. Both the USSR and Europe have been active in seeking to replace the US, especially in Africa, where British and French capital and culture have traditionally held sway. It is now clear that this struggle to establish military superiority, always led by the USA, has dramatically biased third world expenditure by governments towards the military sector and further begun to bias the character of industrial development (Shindo 1985). This has been particularly evident in Ethiopia, but has also begun to affect most of the African continent, with the continuing existence of wars in which each side is backed by one or other superpower.

This increasingly crude form of neo-imperialism has tended to overshadow the relatively more subtle ways in which capitalist centres determine the course of economic development or underdevelopment in the third world. In the case of SSA, the continuing dependence of most economies on export markets for primary commodities, often controlled by those buying for the large food- and mineral-using corporations, is the main form of external domination. The need for capital investment, foreign aid and capital borrowed on the commercial money markets, are equally means by which the unequal interdependent relationship of industrial centres of accumulation and underdeveloped suppliers of raw materials is maintained.

All of this is well enough known and well documented. But two questions are raised

4

by this general view of neo-imperialist economic domination. The first is how far this domination is resisted or reinforced by the ruling strata of third world states; the second is how far within this system of domination it is possible for the dominated economies to gain anything by playing the system in order to get a better deal within it.

This is not the place to enter into a discussion of underdevelopment theory. Some discussion of this will be found elsewhere in this volume (Andrae and Beckman, Chapter 18) and in any case there is a voluminous literature arising out of the 'dependency debate' (Brewer 1980; Warren 1980; Beckman 1981; De Palma 1978). However, it is increasingly clear that the character of domestic class relations and the balance of political forces within the ruling strata play the key role in determining the degree to which external economic interests are well represented. Also, in Africa, as elsewhere in the third world, the military and its civilian political allies exercise a dominant role in the process of reinforcement of, or resistance to, external economic domination. The means of securing military supplies from one or other great power bloc, or even on the private market, will clearly influence the character of external economic relations. Alliances between national and international capital and between international capital and the local state act as a vehicle for continued external domination. All of these determining elements have had differential effects. It is not universally true or false that international capital's expansion has retarded the development of the third world. What seems to have been decisive has been the strength of the local state and its ability to encourage or organise capital accumulation. Clearly international capital is attracted to third world centres of accumulation and to economies where the conditions for rapid capital accumulation are created. In other cases, the risks of investment will be safeguarded by the various profit securing practices (such as transfer pricing) for which transnationals are so frequently attacked.

The IMF and the World Bank

Acting as financial regulator and guardian of this increasingly complex world system is the IMF. The papers in this volume on the role of the Fund and the World Bank draw attention to these institutions' regulatory functions. The central question is in whose interests this regulatory function operates. There would appear to be agreement here that the IMF and the World Bank are policing the international system largely in the interests of maintaining and expanding this system. Within that function, the power of the USA in terms of voting rights and rights to appoint key functionaries is a means of maintaining US hegemony within the system. Nevertheless both IMF and World Bank become arenas for rivalries between nation states, where that hegemony is challenged or reinforced.

The Fund and the Bank have taken on the role of an international state machine, custodian of financial stability, controller of balance of payments stability, examiner of nation states' economic policies, issuer of certificates of financial respectability and coordinators of world economic policy, all heavily influenced by the prevailing 'monetarist' orthodoxy. It is in the attaching of conditions to the granting of IMF balance of payments support, World Bank structural adjustment loans, or simply the seal of respectability, that these institutions have come in for considerable criticism. While it is hardly surprising that lending institutions should want to lend in the knowledge that there is a good chance that the loans will be repaid, it is the general prescriptions offered, rather than the principle of conditionality itself, which have come under fire. It has of course been argued that general prescriptions are not offered (Bird 1982), but this is clearly negated by the contents of the 'Berg Report' (World Bank 1981b) which does make general prescriptions for sub-Saharan Africa (Loxley,

Chapter 7). These prescriptions can be broadly conceived as consisting of the gradual elimination of subsidies, reduction of state expenditure, reduction in the size of the state sector ('privatisation'), import liberalisation and the devaluation of the national currency.

The arguments surrounding the validity of these prescriptions are to be found in the second part of this volume. However, it ought to be common sense to see that not all policies will be appropriate for all countries and those who emphasise the diversity of African economies are surely right to do so (Allison and Green 1983a, 1985). Nevertheless, agricultural decline, industrial stagnation and low or negative growth in foreign exchange earnings from primary commodities is common to most of SSA and does have its roots both in policies which governments followed in the 1960s and 1970s and in declining prospects for primary commodities, discernible long before that. It is in this context that the vexed question of devaluation should be seen, this often being the sticking point in the acceptance of Fund or Bank lending packages. Given what we know about the relative price elasticities of exports and imports (and that is very little because of the difficulties of estimation), balance of payments improvement may only occur if there is a substantial resulting drop in import expenditure, because export revenues are unlikely to increase (Godfrey 1985). However, precisely because of the import substitution industrialisation policies adopted by African governments in the past, this is what is unlikely to occur, except by force of necessity, that is to say, sheer inability to pay, compelling countries to block imports. Hence devaluation may paradoxically have the effect of inducing an internally-oriented development strategy of industrial development. It is because of this likely effect that we can expect ruling strata in Africa to resist such packages, as their implementation may well undermine their close relationship with international capital and therefore, their domestic power base. What the debate around the Fund and Bank packages still lacks is a satisfactory explanation of why some governments accept and others resist conditionality, an explanation based on the politics of economic decision-making and therefore on the competing and coalescing interests of the various political forces operating in the state arena.

Nevertheless, if nothing else, the debate on the technicalities of the IMF-World Bank programme does draw attention to the need for further research into the responsiveness of producers to price changes, the responsiveness of world demand to changes in commodity prices and indeed the factors which determine these prices. Questionable assumptions are continually made about producer price response and much of the debate about the cause of Africa's agricultural decline hinges on this question, and on the responsibility of state pricing policies, and it is to this question that we now turn.

The food crisis and famine in Africa

State policy towards agriculture is at the heart of the debate about the cause of Africa's inability to feed its growing population. The papers in the third part of this volume both present recent data on the drought and on food supply, but also attempt to situate the empirical studies in some overall theoretical framework. Many show the strong influence of the work of Sen (1981) which makes a clear differentiation between drought and famine and emphasises individuals' ability to secure food supplies being dependent on economic position, their set of entitlements based on exchange, production, labour or inheritance, or a combination of some or all of these. However while these distinctions are important, they cannot be allowed to divert discussion away from the question of why food supply has been unable to keep up with demand. There are several explanations for this, all of which would appear to have varying degrees of validity, and the most widely put forward is that of poor agricultural pricing policy. Here it is argued that squeezing producer prices in order to maintain a cheap food policy resulted in lower deliveries to state marketing organisations. The problem with this approach is that changing policy will at any stage be inflationary and risk political upheaval (Seddon, Chapter 15), so that an increase in state subsidy will be the only measure to square the circle. However, this results in an increasing state budget deficit, supportable only by borrowing. In this sense, the expenditure by the governments on subsidies would be better spent on researching new varieties, building upon local drought resistant strains, and thus offer farmers the prospect of higher incomes through higher, technology-induced, productivity, allowing them to expend the same effort on achieving a higher level of output. This of course requires the reorientation of state policy towards the poorer sections of the peasantry, but recognising in the short run the economic value of the family farm and building whatever forms of co-operation are required for advance on this known and accepted structure.

The history of state intervention in rural development in Africa has been little short of disastrous (Heyer *et al.* 1981). Successive schemes incorporating transformation and improvement have not yielded the expected results. Lack of attention to ecological and economic detail, unfamiliarity with the pre-existing production relations and systems, over-mechanisation, failure to supply key inputs, and sheer managerial incompetence have left a trail of unfinished or abandoned initiatives. Attempts to 'diffuse' technical improvements through the agency of agricultural field officers have met with little success given the poverty of resources, both of personnel and of credit and agricultural inputs, allocated to these tasks. Encouragement of large-scale capitalist agriculture in countries where these interests are powerful in the state arena, has further marginalised the peasantry, thus deepening their impoverishment (O'Brien, Chapter 16; Schoepf, Chapter 17).

The net result of state policies has been to worsen the economic situation of the peasants, either by driving them off the land altogether, or by forcing them increasingly to produce for the market at prices controlled by the state. The development of parallel markets, smuggling to neighbouring countries where prices are higher, or simply 'retreating into subsistence', are different responses peasants have made to increased coercion. What they have not done is to increase output.

The belief that this complex picture is to be resolved by incentives begs the question of the nature of the incentives. The readily available supply of consumer and producer goods at affordable prices is more important than the relative price level itself. The ability to supply the goods is an indicator of the degree of success of the industrial and the export sectors. The failure of African industrialisation and the drain it has exerted on foreign exchange is just as important a set of factors in explaining the decline of agriculture on the continent, as the factors specific to agriculture, outlined above (Nixson, Chapter 3).

There are obviously longer term explanations too. Colonial policy emphasised export cash crops and downplayed food output for the domestic market as a potential export revenue earner. Nomadic pastoralists, whose vast numbers of cattle might have been developed into an important source of meat, were encouraged to settle and produce 'real crops'. These policies have often been extended to the present by the post-colonial governments. Labour migration to the mines and plantations placed certain regions of the continent in a cycle of ecological damage that generated declining soil fertility through over-cultivation, as the male migrants left the women and the old behind and the clearing of new land was neglected. The latter two aspects of policy in particular were responsible for the further degradation of the land as overgrazing and desertification of already arid areas by intensive 'mining' of the soil left its mark.

Out of the crisis

This volume, like the Conference itself, has little to say about ways out of the crisis. The various policies proposed by the international organisations do not convince as general solutions to the crisis, although they may contain some answers to specific problems and should not be dismissed out of hand. However, these policies do not solve the immediate problems of plant operating at below capacity, of shortages of necessary inputs, of low productivity in agriculture, and of declining terms of trade for primary products. And these problems affect countries throughout the continent whatever their declared politics. While it may be the case that collectivist and democratic methods of achieving higher growth rates in agriculture are superior to the competitive individualism advanced by the new orthodoxy, those declared socialist states in Africa have yet to demonstrate this superiority. Likewise, the socialist character of nationalisation in African states is also open to serious question (Bolton 1985), as is the overall strategy pursued by socialist governments in Africa.

State agricultural policy has to give independent smallholders of all sizes a rationale for increasing output which fits in with their family requirements. Necessary forms of co-operation will arise out of that as have forms of labour exchange in the past. There is nothing magical about the establishment of a co-operative for its own sake. And there is little point in trying to 'plan' agriculture by trying to control, and impose production targets on, the peasantry. State industrial policy has to attend to the consumption needs of the rural majority of the population as assiduously as it courts the politically powerful and numerically small high-income urban minorities.

Ultimately, it is at the meeting point of the state and the peasantry that the problem would appear to lie. All panaceas for Africa's agricultural ills have failed to explain why good and appropriate policies are not pursued, why government bureaucracies take charge and insist on over-asserting their power over those they control. The cure for many of these agricultural ills lies at the political rather than the economic level, although attention has to be paid to the question of economic incentives, and the related issues raised by IMF and World Bank prescriptions (Loxley, Chapter 7; Raikes, Chapter 14; Smith and Sender, Chapter 9). But until peasants are able to challenge the power of the state, to clip its wings, and to assert their own interests through independent organisations, recommendations as to economic policy, from whatever source of expertise such advice may come, will not be implemented.

However, the advice continues to pour in. Africa's persistent food crisis has led to the mobilisation of millions of dollars of aid for famine relief. International and governmental organisations have contributed less than enthusiastically. In general, they are falling in with the IMF and World Bank view that development aid should only go to those countries which demonstrate a willingness to implement 'appropriate' domestic economic policies. The Bank and the Fund both believe that they are winning the argument and that countries are adjusting to the realities of their economic condition (World Bank 1984; IMF 1985). The evidence that this process of adjustment is sowing the seeds of Africa's economic regeneration is sadly lacking. The prospects for a period of prolonged growth of the developed economies are equally lacking. The crisis, and the struggle of Africa's poor for survival, continues.

PART ONE

The world recession and the African economies

This section begins with an analysis by Giovanni Arrighi (Chapter 1) of the differences between the current Depression, or B-phase, and earlier Great Depressions. The recurrent combination of high unemployment and high inflation – stagflation – is partly a consequence of what economists refer to as an upward shift in the 'Phillips' curve. This curve plots the relationship between changes in wage rates and changes in unemployment rates, such that as unemployment rises, wage rate increases, and therefore the general rate of inflation, are also depressed. A trade-off between inflation and unemployment is therefore suggested. However, more recently it has been argued that there has been a shift of this curve outwards, such that the same levels of unemployment are consistent with ever higher rates of inflation. In its 'monetarist' form, the argument is that attempts to reduce the unemployment level by reflation will simply lead to the same, or higher, levels of unemployment at higher inflation rates. The existence of stagflation, according to Arrighi, is the result of two distinguishing features of the current depression. The first is the slower rate of productivity growth, while the second is the failure of the money wage rate increases to stay below the rate of productivity growth. As real wage growth exceeds productivity growth, profits are squeezed, and can only be recovered in the short run by price increases. Manufacturing industry is increasingly vulnerable to selective strikes, as the division of labour becomes more complex, thus exerting a further upward pressure on wage rates. This 'impasse' leads manufacturing industry out into the 'periphery', indicating the peripheralisation of industry as much as the industrialisation of the periphery. Africa, with the exception of Nigeria and South Africa, has largely been left out of this process of the relocation of manufacturing, and its prospects for developing a strong manufacturing base are poor.

Bob Sutcliffe (Chapter 2) provides a descriptive overview of the crisis which complements Arrighi's theoretical approach. Noting the economic diversity of Africa's economies, he nevertheless finds many common features uniting Africa's recent economic experience. He lays particular emphasis on the growth of the urban population, the decline in investment and the increasing scale of indebtedness. He suggests that Africa is going through a period of 'secular economic decline' with the erosion of 'even a minimum rate of 'internally financed capital accumulation'. Yet there is much fertile land and mineral wealth that ought to secure the future of the continent, but the lack of serious changes in political direction suggests that solutions to the crisis are unlikely to appear in the near future.

Fred Nixson (Chapter 3) continues Sutcliffe's story with respect to Africa's industrialisation and especially its development of a manufacturing capacity. He notes

Africa's relatively low share of manufacturing in Gross Domestic Product (GDP), and the decline in manufacturing growth rates. Nevertheless, although manufacturing is more important to African economies than it was a decade ago, it has still failed to provide the expected impulse to overall growth of the African economies. In particular it has failed to mix successfully with the agricultural sector and to satisfy this sector's need for incentive goods to generate increased output. Nixson looks at different recent explanations for the poor performance of Africa's manufacturing sector and concludes that neither the neoclassical or 'world crisis' perspectives are a substitute for much needed case studies of the interaction between world crisis and manufacturing decline.

The two papers which follow deal with the crisis as it has affected two important African regions. First Yusuf Bangura (Chapter 4) presents an analysis of Nigeria's crisis and the various explanations of and solutions for it which have been advanced, especially from inside Nigeria. It also serves as an introduction to debates which have taken place, especially on the Nigerian 'Left'. While recognising the usefulness of some 'official' explanations, for example, world recession and oil price decline, he goes beyond this to expose some of the structural contradictions of the Nigerian economy which when taken together with external factors have caused the crisis. He rejects the 'contractocracy' school view that corruption is the cause and settles instead for the orthodox Marxist view that the crisis is one of accumulation set 'against the background of combined and uneven development' and that this is rooted in the process of surplus extraction begun under colonial rule and continued by the ruling Nigerian bourgeoisie. He then documents the ways in which people have responded to and resisted government policies which reinforce the power of the bourgeoisie and argues that solutions to the crisis reside in a strengthening of 'democratic and mass political organisations' with a 'clear programme' to eliminate 'capitalist property relations' as opposed to the bureaucratic and 'technicist' solutions advanced by much of the Left.

In their paper, Munslow et al. (Chapter 5) set out the crisis in the countries belonging to the Southern Africa Development Co-ordination Conference as one with several dimensions – colonial inheritance, labour reserve economies, destabilisation by South Africa and vulnerability to disease and drought. Their paper puts together the data currently available on the SADCC states, and analyses their economies on a sectoral basis, looking at industry, transport, agriculture, mining and energy. They note both the low level of development of much of SADCC, but equally the high potential if members can co-ordinate policies. The overriding influence and power of the South African military machine tends to overshadow unifying developments between the politically heterogeneous SADCC states. However, a regional strategy of self-reliance is seen by the authors as a viable strategy for survival.

1

The current depression in historical perspective

Giovanni Arrighi

One of the most striking characteristics of the current Great Depression or B-phase (understood, quite simply, as a relatively long period of widespread and persistent economic difficulties) has been the fact that high and persistent unemployment has overall not brought the rate of growth of money wages down to a level below or equal to the level of the rate of growth of productivity. To be sure, a short-term trade-off between rates of unemployment and rates of growth of money wages has been observed in most core countries and interpolated by various versions of the Phillips curve. However, the most significant aspect of this relationship (and the one that has engendered much controversy) has not been its short-term stability but its medium and long-term tendency to shift upwards: the tendency, that is, for the same rate of growth of money wages to be associated with progressively higher levels of unemployment (or, conversely, for the same rate of unemployment to be associated with progressively higher rates of growth of money wages). Indeed, it would seem from the experience of most core states in the 1970s and early 1980s that there is no 'feasible' rate of unemployment that can bring down (and keep for more than a few years) the rate of growth of money wages at the same level as the rate of growth of productivity.

In part, this is a consequence of the upward shift in the Phillips curve. In part, however, it is the consequence of another tendency whose significance has been fully revealed in the course of the current B-phase: the tendency for increasing unemployment to be associated with a slow-down in the growth of productivity. That is to say, unemployment has not only tended to be less efficient than previously (or than one would have expected from the short-term Phillips curve) in bringing down the rate of growth of money wages. In addition, it has tended to push down the rate of growth of productivity so as to make generally impossible (and not just 'unfeasible') the attainment of some rough equality between the two rates. The 'task' of keeping the rate of growth of *real* wages in line with productivity over the medium-to-long-run, so as to prevent or loosen the squeeze on the rate of profit, has thus been fulfilled mainly by price inflation and the adaptive monetary policies that have sustained it.

This pattern of behaviour differs sharply from that of previous B-phases. Let us focus on the last two: that of 1873–96 (in many ways representative of nineteenth century B-phases in general) and that of the interwar years, and let us refer to the former as Great Depression I (GD I), to the latter as GD II, and to the current B-phase as GD III.

In GD I and in GD II increasing unemployment was not associated with a slow-down in the growth of productivity, which in some countries even increased.

Furthermore, rates of growth of money wages not only fell rapidly with increases in unemployment but in most countries became negative. The responsiveness of money wages and productivity to changes in unemployment levels was greater and more uniform during GD I but, with the qualifications to be made presently, it could still be observed in the interwar period (Phelps Brown 1968; Maddison 1982).

Given this pattern, even small increases in unemployment were sufficient to depress the rate of growth of money wages below that of productivity. As a consequence, whatever the immediate causes of B-phases, overproduction tendencies were bound to develop or deepen. These tendencies, however, materialised quite differently according to the kind of response they prompted from capitalist enterprises and it is in this respect that GD I and GD II differed sharply not only in relation to the current B-phase but also in relation to each other.

In GD I, the response was an intense price competition that more than counteracted the fall of money wages. The intensity of the response differed from country to country, being much stronger, for example, in the UK and the US than in France and Germany. By and large, however, it tended to raise real wages in step or at times even faster than the increase in productivity. Overproduction tendencies were thereby more or less automatically translated into a squeeze on the rate of profit without any dramatic and persistent curtailment of output and employment.

The asymmetry with the current GD is striking. In both B-phases, price changes tend to bring the rate of growth of real wages in line with the rate of growth of productivity. In GD I, however, the equilibrium is brought about 'from below': falling prices increase the rate of growth of real wages to match the rate of increase in productivity. In a sense, the squeeze on the rate of profit was the outcome of intense inter-capitalist competition. In GD III, by contrast, the equilibrium is brought about 'from above': rising prices reduce the rate of growth of real wages to match the rate of increase in productivity. In a sense, the squeeze on the rate of profit is the outcome of the imperviousness of money wages to labour market regulation (Glyn and Sutcliffe 1972; Arrighi 1978; Phelps Brown 1973, 1975).

Before I turn to interpret this difference, let me briefly outline the specificities of GD II. As already mentioned, labour market behaviour in GD II was analogous to that typical of GD I in the sense that rates of growth of money wages were sufficiently responsive, and rates of growth of productivity sufficiently unresponsive, to increases in unemployment for there to be a feasible rate of unemployment capable of depressing the rate of growth of money wages below that of productivity. The analogy, however, was far from perfect.

In the first place, there probably was a difference in the extent to which the above was true: much higher levels of unemployment (supplemented by a greater dose of extra-economic coercion) seem to have been necessary to produce the same outcome in GD II as in GD I. The unreliability and scantiness of data for the earlier period, combined with the difficulty of gauging ex-ante relationships from ex-post data may cast some doubts on this difference. The second difference, however, was unmistakable: the tendencies in question were far less uniform among the main core states or would-be core states and between the first and the second decade of the B-phase than they had been in the course of GD I.

Thus, in the 1920s, the previous pattern of high unemployment elasticity of money wages and low unemployment elasticity of productivity could be clearly observed only in some countries. The main instances were the UK and the US where unemployment brought about a decrease in money wages but left the rate of growth of productivity unaffected. Only in Britain, however, did prices fall sufficiently to raise real wages more or less in step with labour productivity. In the US too prices fell, but they left real wages trailing far behind a rapidly increasing productivity.

In other countries, the previous pattern was no longer observable. In Germany, France and Italy, for example, unemployment failed in the course of the 1920s to bring the rate of growth of money wages below that of labour productivity. As in GD III, the adjustment came 'from above' through price inflation, but in Italy and France, unlike what has generally been happening in the course of GD III, inflation overshot the mark and kept the rate of growth of real wages well below that of productivity. Only in Germany did inflation fail to bring real wages in line with productivity.

The picture that emerges is one of fragmentation of the core zone of the world-economy into disparate national labour market patterns, some of which reproduced the pattern of GD I while others seemed to prefigure those of GD III. All we can say in general is that, in the first decade of the B-phase, the intense price competition that in the course of GD I promptly and generally translated overproduction tendencies into rising real wages and a squeeze on the rate of profit were largely absent and heavily lopsided in their effects. This contributed to make overproduction tendencies more explosive and to make them materialise, in the second decade of the B-phase, in generalised curtailments of both production and employment which were on a scale without precedent in previous B-phases.

The open outbreak of an overproduction crisis in the 1930s restructured the nationally fragmented labour market pattern of the 1920s. In Germany and Italy, both money wages and prices fell producing a close to zero rate of growth of real wages while the growth of productivity accelerated. In France, where the growth of productivity also accelerated, the same outcome resulted from positive but drastically reduced and roughly equal rates of growth of money wages and prices. In Britain and the US, prices continued to fall (at a slower rate than in the 1920s in Britain, at a faster rate in the US) but money wages rose (faster than productivity in the US and more slowly than productivity in the UK).

In sum, the labour market pattern of the interwar years was far less linear and uniform than in either GD I or GD III. In many ways, it looks like a transitional pattern that retained some aspects of the earlier and prefigured some aspects of the later patterns. In what follows, I shall therefore focus on the transition from the 'deflationary' pattern of the late nineteenth century to the 'inflationary' pattern of the current B-phase, bringing in the interwar period only to the extent that it helps in explicating that transition.

The transition from a deflationary to an inflationary pattern of labour market regulation has often been traced to changes in the pattern of competition in products or labour markets, and to changes in government policies related or unrelated to changes in the pattern of competition. The development of monopoly capital (or of oligopolistic competition), the parallel or autonomous development of trade union power, and the parallel or autonomous development of 'lax' monetary and budgetary policies are the typical ingredients (variously combined according to political preferences) of the interpretations most commonly offered in the relevant literature.

In my view, these interpretations leave out of consideration significant aspects of the transition or do not convincingly relate the transition to the long-run dynamic of capitalist accumulation. More specifically, interpretations that emphasise the transformation of capitalist competition from an atomistic to a monopolistic or oligopolistic pattern tend to ignore the fact that this transformation has not been as linear as they assume. For monopolistic and oligopolistic practices were far more widespread and entrenched in the war and interwar years than they have been in the

1970s and 1980s. As a consequence, their relevance in explaining tendencies that have fully materialised only in the latter period is necessarily very limited. Moreover, as witnessed by the interwar experience, there is no necessary connection between monopolistic and oligopolistic practices and the 'inefficiency' of unemployment in bringing the rate of growth of money wages in line with that of productivity. Only temporarily in Germany in the 1920s and, on a more lasting and solid basis, in the US in the 1930s, were there any serious symptoms of such inefficiency.

This does not mean that the demise of atomistic competition has not been an important factor in the transition. It does explain, for example, why the nineteenth-century pattern, based on intense and prompt price competition as the main force keeping the rate of growth of real wages and of productivity in step with each other, was progressively undermined and eventually superseded. For the spread of monopolistic and oligopolistic practices makes the adjustment through falling prices far less automatic and more dependent on an autonomous increase in money wages – autonomous, that is, from labour market conditions. But there is no reason or evidence for supposing that the spread of monopoly and oligopoly in the products market will in and by itself promote such an autonomous growth of money wages.

It is to fill this gap that trade unions and state budgetary and monetary policies are brought into the picture in many accounts as the main explanatory variable of the imperviousness of money wages. The role of unions and governments in building all kinds of rigidities in the labour market and in imposing upon capital and society at large at least some recognition of the fact that labour is a fictitious commodity can hardly be denied. Yet, there is very little evidence that unions and state policies are the main culprits (or heroes) of wage inflation.

When both unions and governments have displayed a propensity to use their power to affect labour market conditions, they have done so by attempting to protect levels of employment rather than by promoting increases in money wages out of step with increases with productivity. While there are thus very few instances of 'pay explosions' initiated or even encouraged by unions and governments, one can think of a great many instances of unions and governments jointly or separately bent on containing pay explosions in an attempt to protect employment levels or just to contain inflationary pressures. Whatever might have been the situation during the previous A-phase, unions and governments in the 1970s and 1980s have been mainly reacting to labour market conditions that were not of their own making. They were reacting, that is, to conditions that were primarily the outcome of world economic tendencies outside of their control, on the one hand, and of 'spontaneous' outbursts of industrial conflict, on the other. It is in these two directions, particularly the latter, that the main explanation of the inflationary regulation of contemporary labour markets has to be sought.

It has been my view since the early days of the current B-phase that in order to explain a transition that has stretched over a century or more we should resort to some secular trend of capitalist accumulation. Three such trends seem to me to be particularly relevant: the widening proletarianisation of labour, the deepening division of labour and the increasing mechanisation of labour processes. As hinted by Marx long ago, whatever their short and medium-term effects, these three secular trends are bound in the long run to provide labour's bargaining power vis-a-vis capital with a different and more solid basis than the one originally provided by the ownership and control of the means of production. And this transformation in the basis of labour's bargaining power is bound to be reflected in the way political and economic actors behave and states and markets operate.

Briefly stated, the argument runs as follows. Widening proletarianisation, by depriving labour of alternatives to wage employment, undermines the 'original' bases of its bargaining power vis-a-vis capital. At the same time, however, it tends to equalise the conditions from which workers compete for jobs and, since subsistence has to be increasingly derived from wage incomes, it tends to make wage claims more rigid. In particular, protracted and high levels of unemployment will tend to inflate the wage claims of those still employed to compensate for the losses of jobs by other members of their households. But how can labour enforce these increasingly rigid and higher wage claims in the face of a secular downward trend in bargaining power? The answer to this question is that no such downward trend need be assumed if proper account is taken of the effects of the other two secular trends on labour's bargaining power.

The growing division of labour and increasing mechanisation of labour processes that accompany and characterise capitalist accumulation deepen some of the effects of proletarianisation but, most importantly, create a new basis for labour's bargaining power in the 'hidden abodes of production'. The deepening of the effects of proletarianisation are well known and need not be repeated here. As for the creation of a new basis for labour's bargaining power, suffice it to say that the division of labour, by increasing the interdependence and connectedness of work roles and the weight of indirect costs, makes capital vulnerable to work stoppages or passive resistance by any and every disgruntled group of workers. And this vulnerability is further enhanced where the damages inflicted by any interruption or slowdown in the labour process is compounded by the growing organic composition of capital that generally accompanies increasing mechanisation (Arrighi and Silver 1984).

It follows that while widening proletarianisation inflates and makes wage claims more rigid, deepening division of labour and mechanisation provides labour with a power base from which to enforce these claims. These are obviously long-term trends subject to a whole variety of countertendencies which makes it difficult to pin them down over short periods of time within individual industries, countries or regions. However, when they are put in historical perspective they provide a plausible explanation of the transition over the last century from a predominantly deflationary to a predominantly inflationary pattern of labour market regulation.

Lack of space and time prevent me from dealing with such issues as why the transition started when it did and why it unfolded so unevenly, particularly in the first half of this century. All I can say here is that the transition started when it did mainly because it was at the end of the nineteenth century that world capitalist expansion through new incorporations of land and peoples reached its limits, forcing capital into more intensive patterns of production and accumulation. At the same time, the transition has been bound up with a switch from one world-hegemony to another and the struggles among would-be hegemonic powers that have characterised the switch have enhanced the inevitable unevenness of the transition (Kindleberger 1973).

The foregoing interpretation of changes in patterns of labour market regulation over the last three B-phases, while focused on core zones of the world-economy, has important implications for an understanding of core-periphery relations. One such implication is that the shift in the locus of industrialisation from core to more peripheral zones of the world-economy which has characterised the 1970s is probably the outcome of long-run structural trends rather than a conjunctural phenomenon (World Bank 1983). That is to say, it might very well be a consequence of the impasse of capitalist accumulation in core zones due to an overextension and overdeepening of proletarianisation, division of labour and mechanisation in those zones.

As a matter of fact, the relocation of industry towards peripheral and semi-peripheral zones of the late 1960s and of the 1970s can be interpreted as an intensification and generalisation of a tendency already observable in the previous A-phase: the emigration of capital towards zones of the world-economy endowed with less rigid labour supplies. The emigration of US capital to Western Europe, for example, was a key factor in the reproduction of the command of core capital over labour and, therefore, in generating and sustaining the postwar boom in capitalist accumulation on a world scale.

By the mid-1960s, however, capitalist accumulation had induced changes in the labour processes and social structures of Western European societies that, by inflating wage claims and enhancing labour's bargaining power in the workplace, undermined the viability of further accumulation in the region. The attainment of this situation, signalled by the wave of industrial conflict that ran through Western Europe between 1968 and 1973, meant that capitalist accumulation could take off again only through an enlarged decentralisation drive toward other, more peripheral regions of the world-economy.

In the past 15 years or so, this decentralisation drive has been constrained and shaped in various and changing ways by the crisis of US *formal* hegemony (Arrighi 1982). In the mid 1970s, the sharp increase in world liquidity associated with highly inflated oil rents, expansionary US monetary policies, and close to zero real interest rates artificially boosted the process for a few years. In the early 1980s, the curtailment of oil rents, tighter monetary policies in many core countries, and record-high real interest rates in the US have combined in bringing about a sharp deceleration.

Assuming that the world monetary system is sturdy and flexible enough to withstand this kind of swing in world monetary management and that the 'toy' will not break before the US government has learned to rule the world *informally*, we can expect the process to resume in one form or another and to further shift the locus of industrialisation towards peripheral and semi-peripheral zones of the world-economy. In itself, however, the resumption of the process will not eliminate either its spatial unevenness or its overall tendency to reproduce the core-peripheral structure of the world-economy.

Spatial unevenness in the 1970s meant that industrialisation and growth outside of the core zone was largely concentrated in national locales that offered some relatively optimal combination of the following conditions: (i) a privileged (by geography or politics) access to elastic labour supplies at a relatively low wage rate; (ii) a privileged (again, by geography or politics) access to markets large enough to warrant the use of modern mass production techniques; (iii) the presence of private or public entrepreneurs capable of promoting and efficiently 'servicing' industrial growth; (iv) a stable political regime capable of reproducing the above conditions over some length of time.

All the success stories of growth and industrialisation of the last two decades can be shown to have or have had at the 'right time' a strong competitive advantage (vis-à-vis other non-core locales) in two or more of these conditions, and no strong comparative disadvantage in any of them. One important reason why Africa (with the partial exception of Nigeria but including South Africa) has largely been bypassed by the process is that very few (Nigeria being one of them) of its national locales had a strong comparative advantage in any of the above conditions, while most locales had strong comparative disadvantages in two or more of them. The more recent socialisation of its labour force to wage employment, the less extensive development of proto-capitalist entrepreneurship, the more fragmented nature of its economic space, compounded by political balkanization, put Africa at a disadvantage in competing for industrial relocation vis-avis the labour-rich East and Southeast Asian locales and the market-rich large Latin American countries.

In addition to the spatial unevenness of peripheral industrialisation due to differences in natural endowments and historical heritage, the process in question has built-in elements of a zero-sum game. The states that were quick in seizing the opportunities offered by 'core de-industrialisation' were, so to say, Schumpeterian innovators who reaped the temporary but often substantial benefits of early 'peripheral industrialisation'. The states that were slow in seizing the opportunity, if and when they tried to do so, far from reaping any benefits, were saddled with all the burdens of peripheral industrialisation.

As a matter of fact, this is precisely one of the mechanisms through which the core-peripheral structure of the world-economy is reproduced through the relocation of industrial activities. As argued earlier on, industrial activities are being relocated because they are no longer profitable in the labour market conditions of the core zones. But the more they are relocated the more peripheral they tend to become in terms of their capacity to generate and appropriate surplus because of the growing competition among and from peripheral locales in carrying them out. Under these circumstances, industrialisation is more a symptom of the downgrading of industrial activities to peripheral status than a symptom of the upgrading of the countries and regions that experience it to core status.*

Yet, however peripheral and peripheralising, industrialisation further revolutionises social relations in peripheral and semi-peripheral zones. By so doing, it leads to a partial duplication of patterns of conflict and labour control previously experienced by core zones: as proletarianisation, division of labour and mechanisation spread in the peripheral and semi-peripheral zones, patterns of industrial conflict and conflict resolution typically associated with those processes also tend to develop. The continuing peripheral and semi-peripheral status of the new loci of industrialisation, however, necessarily limits the extent of the duplication. Patterns of labour control that presuppose core status (such as the upgrading of the core labour force through the relocation of industrial activities towards more peripheral zones) obviously cannot be duplicated in the peripheral zones themselves. And as the conditions of relocation are progressively undermined by relocation itself, the social context of political struggles will tend to be transformed in core and peripheral states alike.

*The validity of this assessment is supported by the fact that the narrowing of the gap between the degree of industrialisation of core and peripheral countries implicit in the data provided by the World Bank has been matched, according to the same source, by a widening gap of their GNP per capita.

2

Africa and the world economic crisis

Bob Sutcliffe

Definition and explanation

Such a title raises three questions of interpretation, the first of which is what is meant by
'Africa'? It refers here to the continent as a whole, excluding South Africa and the
northern countries with a Mediterranean coast. This is a definition which is frequently
used in African studies but that does not make it a particularly logical one. This
aggregate of countries is not in any real sense an economic region.

It is hard, and to some extent arbitrary, to delineate economic regions. But if this
were done in Africa then one of them would undoubtedly be South Africa plus those
Southern African countries which are peripheral to and in some ways economically
dependent on it. The problems and economic dynamics of those countries are largely
missed by the way I have approached the subject here. More than this, many of the
important features of economies in Africa, as anywhere else, can only be identified by
looking at them in a much more disaggregated and much more qualitative way than I
am able to do. Sub-Saharan Africa may be a more homogeneous category of countries
than 'the third world' but it encompasses countries with a range of national income per
head as calculated by the World Bank of from nearly $4,000 (Gabon) to $80 (Chad) – a
difference of about fiftyfold (though the great majority lie between $200 and #500 on
this rather dubious scale); countries whose exports have grown by 7 per cent a year or
more in the years of crisis since 1973 and countries whose exports have declined by 7
per cent a year or more; countries that pay nearly one-third of their export earnings in
debt service and countries who pay nothing.

Averages and aggregates of a large number of countries can easily conceal the
divergent realities which go to make them up. Many of the empirical generalisations
which follow, therefore, should be seen more as hypotheses about what might be
discovered by closer, more appropriate examination, than as facts. I do not want to
suggest from the aggregates and averages which I use in this paper that there is a typical
sub-Saharan Africa country, or that averages are very meaningful; but I do conclude
that, with suitable case by case qualifications, there seems to be a set of extremely
widespread experiences and problems; that there seems to be a peculiarly African
economic story in the last decade or so; and that this story is a tragic one.

To define 'the economic crisis' is even more problematical. While there is an
enormous amount of agreement among political economists that there is – and has been
for some years – a major economic crisis of the world capitalist system, there is also a
declining amount of agreement among us about the nature of that crisis. It is argued by
different writers that the roots of the crisis are to be found in the process of capital

accumulation, in the labour market, in the labour process, in the monetary system, in the imbalance of the competitive strength of the major capitalist powers, in the limitations of consumption and so on. The crisis is variously conceived as something which characterises the capitalist system as a totality, as something which simultaneously characterises its leading countries, or something which is associated with relations between classes or nations within the system. Of course, these different approaches are not always mutually exclusive; many of them have common elements or overlap. Despite the theoretical diversity, there has been considerable common ground about what are the salient empirical manifestations of the world capitalist crisis. There does seem to be some general agreement that a major and historic boom for the world capitalist system, concentrated in its advanced countries but profoundly affecting also many of the underdeveloped ones, took place in the 1950s and 1960s and has since been replaced by a period, or succession of periods, of a qualitatively different character. The average rate of growth of total production declined and became more erratic. Cycles became longer and profits and capital accumulation fell markedly. A sharp inflationary spiral developed to be followed by more rigid monetarist controls which intensified the pressures towards slump. The world monetary system became severely unstable. The minimum level of unemployment went sharply upwards. The relative prices of world commodities shifted radically – oil rising and many tropical products falling. That at least is some broad empirical definition of the crisis.

But to continue the definitional problems which come from my title, we also require an interpretation of the interrelations between the world crisis and the economic conditions and performance of African countries. There are several ways in which this interrelation could be seen, each of which may be partially true.

First, it could be argued that the economic problems of African countries in the years of the world crisis are nothing new but a continuation of trends which have existed in the whole of the post-war or post-independence periods and which spring from Africa's economic dependency.

Secondly, Africa could be seen as the passive recipient of shocks and influences from the outside. The major economic events of the world of the last two decades have not originated in Africa. Most African countries, for instance, have been obliged to endure the rise of import prices resulting from the oil price shocks. Only two, albeit including the largest, have been significant oil producers: and the effects, even to them, of the oil price increase have been ambiguous to say the least. For the importers the increase in the oil price affected not only the cost of oil but also of oil-related products such as agricultural fertilisers, of which Africa, however, uses startlingly less than the rest of the third world. In addition the prices of imported manufactured goods rose inordinately during the inflationary bouts in the developed countries. At the same time slower growth and worldwide depression have induced declines in the prices of raw materials, which have had a disproportionate effect on the continent which more than any other remains an exporter of primary products.

The problems experienced by African countries in weathering the storm have been acute partly because of the lack of economic flexibility which is part of extreme economic backwardness; most African countries lacked the resources which might have allowed them to break into some of the world markets which continued to expand. This very fact made them, in the eyes of the international banks, less creditworthy; and so another form of alleviation of the storm was not available to them.

Even as limited debtors African countries have suffered further external shocks: the drying up of new loans after the debt crises of the early 1980s; the rise of interest rates; the rise in the international value of the dollar (in which most debts are denominated) has meant that underdeveloped countries are increasingly being forced to repay money which they have never borrowed. In practice African countries after 1973 were obliged to impose policies of austerity and internal demand reduction much more rapidly and intensely than was necessary for other countries of the third world which were able either to borrow, or to export manufactures or to substitute more imports. Although Africa produces only 1.2 per cent of the Gross Planetary Product and accounts for an even smaller proportion of world trade, lower demand in Africa fed back into the world economy and helped marginally to contribute to world stagnation. A great deal of the economic travail of African countries can be explained in terms of these vicious international economic circles, which African countries experienced largely as passive sufferers. If we add to the metaphorical climatic influences the literal ones, in particular prolonged drought, then it would be tempting to interpret Africa's crisis as something wholly external in origin in which the role of Africa is that of helpless victim. The present economic situation could be seen as the combined result of long-term secular effects of imperialism suddenly boosted by the impact of world capitalist crisis.

So, an approach to the economic crisis of Africa which sees it as part of a world economic condition allows the present position to be understood in two ways – as the result of long-term underdevelopment, using dependency theory, and as the result of short-term vulnerability to a world economic disaster, using some of the international aspects of crisis theory.

Partial insights can be gained from these approaches but it seems to me very doubtful that they can explain everything we want them to. Neither seems able to account for more than a small part of the following phenomena: the economic and ecological effects of drought, the decline of agriculture, the prevalence of famine, the nature of the African ruling class and its economic privileges, and the extent of internal and international military conflict within the continent. Yet all of these diverse factors have had an important bearing on the special virulence of Africa's experience of the world epidemic of economic crisis.

If we attempt to reduce the explanation of these phenomena to economics, or to the inescapable consequences of imperialism then we will miss important aspects of their origins and also fail to understand their specific nature. To put it a little more concretely, a war between African states or a major famine are of necessity influenced by the imperialist domination of Africa. But that domination does not entail permanent and universal war and famine; so such events require their own specific explanation. And once they occur they possess their own laws which most political economy is not very well developed to understand. We are better equipped to explain a general polarisation process in the abstract than we are to explain its specific manifestations.

This is only to state but not at all to resolve what seems to be a challenge to political economists: whether in our work we can make a real contribution to overcoming the truly cataclysmic situation of many of Africa's peoples and communities today. The more concrete and specific papers in this volume are a response to that challenge. As a backdrop to them, the rest of this paper aims to present a broad overview of macroeconomic trends in sub-Saharan Africa as a whole in the years of economic pestilence since the early 1970s.

A picture of economic decline

The following overview of the recent macroeconomic experience of Africa derives almost entirely from widely available figures published by the World Bank. My analysis of these is not based on any recent personal experience of Africa, and it passes over altogether the probable deficiencies of the quantitative data. For these reasons it does not purport to undertake any of the necessary specific and qualitative analysis of Africa's economy.

The Gross Continental Product of sub-Saharan Africa in 1983 was about $158 billion – around one half of US military spending in that year. Divided among a population of 393 million this gives an average continental income per head of about $400. The 22 Africa countries in the World Bank category 'low-income countries' have average incomes of $220, making them among the poorest nations on earth (see Table 2.1).

TABLE 2.1 Selected indicators to compare Africa with all developing countries

Country group	Per capita income 1983 ($)	Adult literacy 1980 (%)	Life expectancy 1983 (M)	(F)	Female primary school enrolment 1982 (%)
Sub-Saharan Africa	400				
Low-income	220	38	46	49	56
Middle-income	700	35	48	51	81
All low-income countries	260	52	58	60	77
All middle-income countries	1,310	65	55	59	99

Table 2.2 shows that the recent growth of production in African countries, especially in the poorest ones, has been much lower than in the rest of the world.

TABLE 2.2 GDP growth rates (average annual percentage change)

Country group	1960–73	1973–80	1981	1982	1983	1984
Developing countries	6.3	5.5	3.3	1.9	2.0	4.1
Low-income	5.6	5.5	4.0	7.2	7.2	6.6
Sub-Saharan Africa	3.5	2.7	1.7	0.7	0.7	1.6
Middle-income						
Oil importers	6.3	5.6	2.0	0.8	0.7	3.3
Sub-Saharan Africa	5.6	3.6	6.9	−1.0	−1.8	−2.1
Industrial market economies	4.9	2.8	1.4	−0.3	2.6	4.8

African countries have the highest death rates (on average 18 per 1,000) in the world. Africa also has, by a wider margin, the highest birth rates (49 per 1,000). These have not, as in other continents, appreciably fallen in the last 30 years. The net result is that, contrary to widespread belief Africa is the continent with the fastest rate of growth of population, now over 3 per cent per year.

For 30 years Africa has had, as it is expected to have for the next 20 years at least, the fastest rates of growth of any continent of both urban and rural population. Because urban and rural social and economic problems depend in part on the growth rate of the population they are more intense than in any other continent, quite irrespective of the world economic crisis. And in terms of its available economic resources Africa is the least equipped continent to deal with them. Between 1950 and 1980 African towns and cities grew at the astounding rate of 7.0 per cent a year (implying a doubling in size every 11 years). The rural population was continuing during these years to grow at a rate of 2.5 per cent a year.

The net result of the lowest growth rates of production and income along with the highest growth rates of population in the world is very low growth or decline of average income (GNP per head). For a long time the average inhabitant of Africa has been getting steadily poorer.

TABLE 2.3 Growth and decline of GNP per head: 1965–84

	1965–73	*1973–80*	*1980–84*
Low-income economies	3.0	3.1	3.6
Sub-Saharan Africa	1.3	0.0	−2.1
Middle-income economies	4.6	3.1	−0.8
Sub-Saharan Africa	2.0	0.5	−3.8

Other statistics confirm the low growth record shown in Table 2.3. During the whole period from 1965 to 1983, 13 countries in the world had a negative rate of growth of GNP per head; 8 of those were in Africa. Between 1974–6 and 1981–3, 19 out of 31 African countries showed a fall in food production per head. For the whole continent food production fell by an average 1.1 per cent a year during the decade of the 1970s. Also during the period 1973–83 of the 12 underdeveloped countries which had a negative rate of growth of aggregate industrial output, 7 were in Africa (see Table 2.8 for details).

In most African countries the proportion of the labour force working in industry has risen. But in most cases this does not seem to have indicated any significant industrialisation since there seems to have been a substantial increase in manufacturing production in only a few countries. Ten African countries experienced a decline in the value of manufacturing production per head of population during the 1970s.

Reliable figures are not available about changes in income distribution in Africa. Many observers testify to a worsening of distribution between classes and areas over the last two decades. So, given that even the average living standard appears to be declining, that of the more luckless sections of the population must in some cases be falling quite precipitously as they are obliged to make do with a diminishing slice of a shrinking cake.

When the figures for national income are disaggregated into the shares of consumption, savings and investment, then a more long-term, less static picture of Africa's impoverishment emerges. In response to falling incomes in low-income Africa the share of consumption in the national income rose from 87 per cent in 1965 (already much higher than for other underdeveloped areas) to 94 per cent in 1983. Correspondingly, the share of gross savings fell from 13 per cent to under 6 per cent. Given the structure of production, the distribution of income and economic policies, Africa has become too poor to finance internally even a minimum level of capital accumulation.

Gross investment was maintained during the 1970s at around 15–16 per cent of the national income although this is much lower than in the rest of the underdeveloped world. Even to finance this relatively very low level of investment Africa as a whole has been plunged into a situation of resource deficit (investment *minus* domestic savings) equal to 5–8 per cent of continental income. This has to be financed by imports of capital from outside. Hence Africa is the part of the third world most dependent on external finance (see Table 2.4 and Table 2.8 for details).

TABLE 2.4 Structure of demand and resource gap (% of GDP)

Country group	1965			1983	
	All		Africa	All	Africa
Low-income countries					
Consumption	85		87	82	94
Investment	21		15	26	16
Savings	19		13	24	7
Resource gap (I-S)	−2		−2	−2	−2
Middle-income countries					
Consumption	79		81	79	81
Investment	21		17	22	22
Savings	21		16	21	17
Resource gap (I-S)	0		−1	−1	−5

External payments and debt

The years of economic crisis have, with a very few exceptions, produced disaster for the exports and balance of payments of African countries. This is closely associated with the exceptionally high concentration of African exports in primary products (see Table 2.8). Since 1973 demand for these products and their prices have fallen substantially as a result of the decline in growth and the series of major recessions in the advanced capitalist countries. In some countries supplies have been disrupted as well by war and other causes. For 10 years from 1973 Africa's exports declined by about 5 per cent a year. Table 2.5 shows the growth and decline of merchandise trade from 1965 to 1983. In the first half of the 1980s the current account balance of payments deficit of low-income African countries was running at between $4.6 billion and $6.4 billion. It was financed almost entirely by flows of funds from government sources in the advanced countries. The net flow of direct foreign investment to these countries was negligible and the flow of private bank lending had eventually in 1984 become negative. Africa, in particular its poorest countries, was considered by the banking community as too much of a 'credit risk' to obtain the mixed and ambiguous blessing of private banking credit. For other countries the 'debt crisis' tends to mean that they are too

TABLE 2.5 Growth and decline of merchandise trade: 1965–83

Country group	Average annual growth rate (per cent)			
	Exports		Imports	
	1965–73	1973–83	1965–73	1973–83
Low-income countries	1.5	0.9	−2.0	1.4
Sub-Saharan Africa	2.4	−4.0	2.3	−2.2
Middle-income countries	5.9	−0.4	8.3	4.1
Sub-Saharan Africa	6.9	−5.8	6.5	8.2

much in debt to the banks. Africa's debt crisis is in a sense the opposite – it has been scarcely able to get into private debt. Table 2.6 shows the decline in private debt as a share of the total.

TABLE 2.6 Low-income Africa's debt and debt servicing

	1974	1984
Ratio of debt to GNP (%)	23.8	54.5
Ratio of debt to exports (%)	99.5	278.1
Debt service ratio (%)	8.6	19.9
Ratio of interest service to GNP (%)	0.7	2.1
Total debt outstanding and disbursed ($ billion)	7	27
Private debt as per cent of total (%)	39.3	18.4

African countries are given a low credit rating by international bankers. Out of 107 countries the highest African state (according to a recent article in *International Investor*) was Nigeria, ranking 46; then came Ivory Coast (61), Gabon (66) and Cameroon (68). Of the bottom ranking 12 countries, 8 were African.

The total debt of African countries is estimated to be about $80 billion, rather more than one half of the gross continental product. This means that the average African country is less indebted, relatively and absolutely, than countries in many other parts of the world, especially in Latin America. It is a dubious advantage since it has meant that the adjustment to the various external shocks of the last decade (such as the increase in the oil price) has had to be met in many African countries not through borrowing which, even if it creates long-term problems, at least cushions instant impact. In Africa the effect of such shocks has been transmitted much more directly and immediately to the people in the form of enforced declines in living standards. Many Africans have paid an awesome price for not living in 'creditworthy' countries, for being inhabitants of countries which the world capitalist system in an era of crisis has been able to marginalise.

But the poverty of many African nations is so acute that even a small amount of debt payment and interest can be inordinately burdensome. So paradoxically Africa is less indebted than elsewhere but even more burdened by debt. In addition, since all individual African countries are such small debtors by world standards, they possess none of the limited 'debtors' power' which some Latin American and East European nations can muster to hold their creditors at bay.

Africa thus exemplifies the plight of the extremely poor through the ages: you can have a debt crisis without being deeply in debt. Despite the fact that the whole continent has hardly more total debt than a number of single countries in other parts of the world (Mexico, Brazil, Argentina, Poland) its nations have had to make a record number of standby loan and rescheduling agreements with the IMF, the Paris Club (consisting of the main creditor nations) and to admit the ubiquitous carpetbaggers of debt rescheduling and stabilisation schemes, the investment and merchant bankers. Anyone who has spent time in the waiting rooms of African airport lounges will know them as peopled with a large number of white middle-aged men wearing expensive lightweight suits and ties. These are likely to be IMF officials and investment bank executives, mostly 'earning' in one day an amount which is many multiples of the average incomes of Africans in one year.

Between 1979 and 1982 African countries altogether negotiated 45 standby agreements and extended Fund Facilities with the IMF. African countries have been forced into more repeat agreements with the IMF than any other continent; this was because the initial agreements so often failed to achieve their economic targets. By 1982, 36 African countries had been forced to appeal to the IMF for assistance and thereby agree to operate economic policies dictated by the IMF. Also, again in the years since 1979, the rescheduling negotiated with the Paris Club of creditors has been disproportionately with African countries. Table 2.7 identifies those countries whose debt with the Paris Club has been rescheduled.

TABLE 2.7 African countries rescheduling public and publicly insured private debt with the Paris Club

1976	Zaire
1977	Sierra Leone, Zaire
1978	Gabon
1979	Togo, Sudan, Zaire
1980	Sierra Leone, Liberia
1981	Central African Republic, Liberia, Madagascar, Senegal, Togo, Uganda, Zaire
1982	Madagascar, Malawi, Senegal, Sudan, Uganda
1983	Central African Republic, Liberia, Malawi, Niger, Senegal, Sudan, Togo, Zaire, Zambia
1984	Ivory Coast, Liberia, Madagascar, Mozambique, Niger, Sierra Leone, Sudan, Togo, Zambia

Four countries have also had to reschedule private non-insured debt:
Togo and Zaire (1980), Sudan (1981), Liberia (1982)

The debt crisis has also opened the way to another group of white men in suits and ties arriving at the airport, ostensibly to advise the governments of African countries how best to deal with the IMF and the Paris Club. These are the various firms of investment bankers, in particular Lazard Frères, Lehman Brothers, Kuhn Loeb, and S.G. Warburg. These firms have advised the governments of Zaire, Gabon, the Ivory Coast, Senegal, Togo, Congo, Mozambique and Nigeria. (Lazard Frères is also the company which has supplied the expertise for the 'rescue' of New York City and the rationalisation of the British steel and coal industries – in the form of Messrs Felix Rohatyn and Ian MacGregor.) In addition the firm of Morgan Grenfell has advised Sudan, Uganda and Zimbabwe; and Samuel Montagu has advised Zambia. So Africa's impoverishment is at least making someone wealthy.

Africa's crisis

For the world capitalist economy as a whole the years since 1973, or even before, have been years of economic pestilence. A disproportionate number of the most stricken countries have been in Africa. The macroeconomic evidence seems to suggest that the experience of Africa during these years has not merely been quantitatively worse than that of most other countries but that it is to some extent a qualitatively different experience. It seems to consist not of troubled, erratic and crisis-torn growth, but rather a period of secular economic decline. The consequences of the decline are all the more tragic because it began from such a low economic level. The basis for even a minimum rate of internally financed capital accumulation has been eroded. Countries depend increasingly for day-to-day survival on subventions, with the inevitable attached conditions, from outside. In many places this is an economic environment which not only fails to sustain capital accumulation but is increasingly failing even to support human life.

Both the common and the differential economic experiences of African peoples and countries during the current economic crisis are part of a very complex process of polarisations which has characterised the world economy in the last two decades. It is a process which I do not believe is yet very widely understood. I think that it calls into question a number of the assumptions which most of us have held about the functioning of imperialism and about economic crisis.

Polarisation has taken place not around one axis alone but around several. The most significant polarisations have probably been within the third world rather than between it as a whole and the imperialist countries. The tragedy of Africa today is that much of the continent is on the relatively disadvantaged side of virtually every one of the polarisations which is taking place. Access to economic resources is being reduced and the physical environment, the fertility of the soil, the means of production and the lives of its inhabitants are being destroyed.

The prospects for a significant alleviation of this situation through a trickle-down of benefit from the recovery of the world capitalist economy do not at present look very favourable. Its solution seems to depend on change within the continent itself. An examination of recent evidence could easily induce fatalism about the possibility of real changes. But we should not lose sight of the facts that Africa, despite its debt crisis, has very few debts; despite its food crisis has an abundance of potentially fertile land; and despite its economic decline is rich in natural resources and human capacities. A solution to crisis may be socially and politically difficult. But it is surely not materially impossible.

TABLE 2.8 Sub-Saharan Africa: national and aggregate economic data, 1973–83

Country	GNP per head 1983 (US$)	Growth of GNP per head, 1965–83 (annual %)	Growth of industrial output 1973–80 (annual %)	Domestic Saving minus domestic investment 1983 (% of GDP)	Index of food production per head 1981–3 (1974–6 =100)	Debt service, 1983 as % of GNP	Debt service, 1983 as % of Imports	Growth of exports 1973–83 (annual %)	Exports which are primary products 1982 (%)
Chad	80[a]	..	..	..	101	0.1	0.6	-3.4	..
Ethiopia	120	0.5	2.6	-9	106	1.4	11.5	1.4	99
Mali	160	1.2	0.2	-19	106	1.3	6.1	5.1	..
Zaire	170	-1.3	-2.0	2	93	2.9	..	-8.7	..
Guinea-Bissau	180	..	..	..	..	..	..	..	..
Burkina	180	1.4	5.1	-27	100	1.3	..	1.7	85
Malawi	210	2.2	4.2	-9	101	4.5	20.3	2.8	88
Uganda	220	-4.4	-10.1	-3	91	1.9	..	-8.0	92[b]
Burundi	240	2.1	8.3	-14	97	0.7	..	..	..
Niger	240	1.2	10.9	-14	122	5.6	..	19.0	98
Tanzania	240	0.9	0.2	-12	103	1.5	..	-4.6	87
Somalia	250	-0.8	1.1	-22	72	1.2	13.1	7.3	99
Rwanda	270	2.3	..	..	114	0.3	2.6	2.6	..
Central African Republic	280	0.1	1.0	-13	94	2.7	11.3	3.8	74[b]
Togo	280	1.1	2.6	-19	99	6.3	16.8	3.5	85
Benin	290	1.0	6.9	-14	95	2.5	..	-1.4	..
Gambia	290	1.4	..	..	..	4.0	..	..	..
Guinea	300	1.1	6.7	2	85	4.0	..	..	..
Ghana	310	-2.1	-7.0	-3	65	1.9	14.2	-6.4	..

Madagascar	310	-1.2	-1.8	-10	90	4.9	..	-4.3	93
Sierra Leone	330	1.1	-2.9	-7	98	0.9	7.2	-5.3	..
Kenya	340	2.3	5.3	-2	86	5.5	20.6	-4.8	86
Sudan	400	1.3	6.7	-16	94	1.2	11.2	-1.5	98
Mozambique	..	..	..	..	68	..	..	-8.3	..
Low-income average	220	-0.2	0.6	-8	94	5.4	14.5	-4.0	91
Senegal	440	-0.5	6.1	-13	71	1.9	..	-1.3	81
Lesotho	460	6.3	..	-106	76	1.9	2.5	..	..
Liberia	480	0.8	-1.5	-5	92	3.2	6.6	8.9	98
Mauritania	480	0.3	..	-29	102	5.0	10.0	9.7	..
Zambia	580	-1.3	-0.3	-1	74	4.0	12.6	-0.3	..
Ivory Coast	710	1.0	7.4	-2	108	12.9	31.0	7.1	89
Zimbabwe	740	1.5	..	-3	79	8.1	31.6	..	..
Nigeria	770	3.2	0.3	0	98	3.1	18.6	8.9	..
Cameroon	820	2.7	13.7	10	84	3.1	13.9	3.9	93
Swaziland	870	2.6	..	..	..	..	..	..	..
Botswana	920	8.5	..	..	..	..	..	..	..
Congo, Peoples Republic	1,230	3.5	12.7	-11	99	12.2	20.5	4.4	94[b]
Gabon	3,950	3.2	..	..	..	..	..	..	..
Middle-income average	700	1.9	1.0	-1	93	4.2	19.7	6.9	..

Notes: [a] 1982 [b] 1981

Sources: World Bank, 1984a and 1985. Most of the data in the text comes from the same sources and from Callaghy, 1984.

3

The crisis of industrial accumulation in Africa: an overview[1]

Frederick Nixson

The main objective of this paper is to summarise Africa's record of industrialisation (principally that of the sub-Saharan economies) over the past quarter of a century and to discuss a number of analyses that have attempted to 'explain' Africa's industrial performance. No single or principal explanation of performance is advanced. Rather, emphasis is placed on the complexity of the problem of evaluating industrial performance, the relative paucity of research in this area, and the dangers of generalisation from the experience of one or a small group of economies to the continent as a whole.

Industrialisation: a statistical overview[2]

Data on rates of growth of manufacturing output are given in Tables 3.1 and 3.2. The data in Table 3.1 are 'distorted' by the inclusion of South Africa, but even with the inclusion of that country, the rate of growth of manufacturing production in sub-Saharan Africa was less than the average for all LDCs. The data in Table 3.2 permit a more detailed examination of the record. The non-arid low income sub-Saharan economies achieved a relatively high rate of growth of 9.3 per cent per annum during 1960–65, but the rate of growth fell steadily in each succeeding five-year period. The middle-income oil importers maintained acceptable (although by no means outstanding) rates of growth until the mid-1970s, and thereafter suffered a decline. The growth of manufacturing output in the sub-Saharan middle-income oil exporters fluctuated widely – they experienced rapid growth during 1965–70, significantly slower growth during 1970–75, with an upturn (although not to the levels reached in 1965–70) during 1975–80. The low-income sub-Saharan semi-arid economies (Chad, Somalia, Mali, Burkina Faso, Gambia, Niger and Mauritania) achieved a respectable rate of growth during 1965–70, but stagnated throughout the 1970s.

The data in Table 3.2 also show that during the 1970s, the ratio of manufacturing growth to GDP growth fell dramatically for the low-income economies and to a lesser, but still significant extent for the middle-income oil importers. As Steel (1984) notes, the manufacturing sector, far from playing the role of a 'leading sector' in the development effort, became a lagging sector in the 1970s, especially in the low-income economies.

In spite of this poor growth record, however, the share of manufacturing in GDP rose between 1960 and 1980 (Tables 3.3 and 3.4). It reached nearly 10 per cent for

TABLE 3.1 Selected economic indicators, by region (Annual percentage change)

Region	Growth of GNP		Growth of GNP per capita		Growth of agricultural production		Growth of manufacturing production	
	1960–70	1970–81	1960–70	1970–81	1960–70	1970–81	1960–70	1970–81
Sub-Saharan Africa[a]	4.7	3.6	2.1	0.9	2.3	1.4	8.3	4.9
East Asia and the Pacific	7.3	6.7	2.1	3.1	4.6	3.6	10.3	9.4
South Asia	4.3	3.8	1.9	1.5	2.5	2.6	6.5	4.9
Latin America and the Caribbean	5.5	5.0	2.6	2.6	3.2	3.4	6.5	5.8[b]
All developing countries	5.8	5.5	3.5	3.1	3.0	2.7	8.1	7.3[b]

Notes: [a] South Africa is included in the Sub-Saharan group.
     [b] 1970–80
Source: UNIDO (1983: Table V.I., p. 101)

TABLE 3.2 African manufacturing output growth and ratio to GDP growth, five-year periods 1960–80 (% per annum at constant 1970 prices)

Country grouping	Manufacturing output growth				Ratio of manufacturing growth to GDP growth			
	1960–65	1965–70	1970–75	1975–80	1960–65	1965–70	1970–75	1975–80
Low-income sub-Saharan								
Semi-arid	4.8	9.7	1.8	0.4	1.5	4.0	1.1	0.1
Other	9.3	6.0	2.4	−0.2	2.7	1.6	1.4	neg.
Middle-income sub-Saharan								
Oil importers	7.5	7.6	7.7	4.2	1.6	1.7	1.5	1.2
Oil exporters	3.7	15.9	6.6	11.5	0.8	3.1	0.8	2.3
Sub-Saharan Africa, total	7.3	8.4	5.3	4.4	1.7	1.9	1.0	1.2
North Africa	6.2	5.6	5.6	11.7	1.8	0.9	1.4	1.6

Source: Steel (1984: Table 5, p. 32)

low-income sub-Saharan Africa, equivalent to that in all low-income LDCs excluding India and the Peoples Republic of China. The middle-income sub-Saharan oil importers raised the share of manufacturing in GDP to 14.0 per cent in 1980, in comparison with 23 per cent of all middle-income oil importing LDCs (Table 3.4).

TABLE 3.3 Comparative indicators of industrial performance in Africa (%)

Indicator	Africa	Other developing regions
Share of manufacturing in GDP[a]		
1960	7.1	16.0
1970	8.6	18.7
1980	9.7	21.2
Rates of growth of manufacturing per annum, at constant (1975) prices		
1960–65	8.5	7.0
1965–70	7.3	7.8
1970–75	5.5	7.7
1975–80	6.3	6.0

Note: [a] Percentages are averages weighted by the value of MVA (US $) in each country.
Source: UNIDO (1983: Table V.2, p. 102)

TABLE 3.4 Manufacturing share of GDP, sub-Saharan Africa and other groupings, 1960, 1970 and 1980 (% of group GDP)

	Current prices			1980 in constant 1970 prices
	1960	1970	1980	
Low-income sub-Saharan Africa	6.3	9.0	9.6	8.3
Middle-income sub-Saharan Africa				
Oil importers	10.0	13.1	14.0	15.3
Oil exporters	5.0	4.8	4.9	5.9
Sub-Saharan Africa, total	6.8	8.6	8.2	9.0
North Africa	15.0	14.2	13.4	19.2
All low-income economies	12		15	
(excluding China and India)	(8)		(10)	
All middle-income oil importers	23		23	
All middle-income oil exporters	13		16	
Industrial market economies	30		27	

Source: Steel (1984: Table 6, p. 34)

Table 3.5 gives data on the share of manufacturing in GDP for individual African economies (North and sub-Saharan) for 1980. Given that Swaziland appears to be more industrialised than Nigeria on this criteria, the point that the data on industrialisation and the resulting structural change must be interpreted carefully and cautiously once more requires emphasis.

TABLE 3.5 Africa: share of manufacturing in GDP in 1980

Less than 5%

Angola	Guinea-Bissau
Botswana	Lesotho
Congo	Libyan Arab Jamahiriya
Gambia	Namibia
Guinea	Reunion

5–10%

Algeria	Niger
Benin	Nigeria
Cape Verde	Sierra Leone
Chad	Somalia
Comoros	Sudan
Equatorial Guinea	Togo
Gabon	Uganda
Ghana	United Republic of Cameroon
Liberia	United Republic of Tanzania
Mauritania	Zaire
Mozambique	

10–15%

Burundi	Mali
Central African Republic	Rwanda
Ethiopia	Tunisia
Ivory Coast	Egypt
Kenya	Burkina Faso
Madagascar	

Above 15%

Mauritius	Swaziland
Morocco	Zambia
Senegal	Zimbabwe

Source: UNIDO (1983: Table V.4, p. 104)

Table 3.6 presents data showing Africa's share in world manufacturing production and manufactured exports. There was a slight increase in its share of world manufacturing production (from 0.73 per cent in 1960 to 0.97 per cent in 1980) but it was still very small. (Latin American and Asian economies have also increased their shares – (Steel 1984: 37).) Africa's share in manufactured exports was never large (0.48 per cent in 1970) and it fell consistently throughout the 1970s to reach 0.36 per cent in 1980 (Table 3.6). UNIDO (1983: 105) notes that the African economies have been unable to alter the composition of their exports in favour of processed goods and that it can be confidently inferred from the available data that the major cause of African industrialisation has been import substitution.

TABLE 3.6 Africa's share in world production and exports of manufactures, selected years (%)

Year	Output	Exports[a]	Exports as fraction of output
1960	0.73	—	—
1965	0.79	—	—
1970	0.83	0.48	0.58
1972	0.81	0.41	0.51
1974	0.83	0.39	0.47
1976	0.84	0.28	0.33
1978	0.87	0.29	0.33
1980	0.97	0.36	0.37

Note: [a]SITC 5–8 less 68
Source: UNIDO (1983: Table V.5, p. 105)

Table 3.7 gives information on the share and rate of growth of the labour force in the industrial sector (which includes mining, construction and public utilities, as well as manufacturing). Although there has been an increase in the share of the industrial sector in the total labour force over the period 1960–80, the various African groupings remain below the averages for all LDCs.

Comprehensive data on structural change within the manufacturing sector are not available for all African countries but most observers agree that the process of industrialisation in Africa has not as yet been accompanied by significant changes in the structure of manufacturing industry.

Steel (1984: 40–44) presents data for nine economies which demonstrate a major orientation towards the production of consumer goods in general, and export processing activities, food products and beverages in particular. UNIDO (1983: 105–7) analyses data on changes in the industrial structure of four major African economies (Algeria, Egypt, Morocco and Nigeria) which together accounted for 60 per cent of African manufacturing value added in 1979 (excluding South Africa). The industrial structures of these four economies are more complex and diversified than those of the smaller, low-income (mainly sub-Saharan) economies and highlight the changes in structure that are to be expected as industrialisation proceeds – a fall in the share of consumer goods (especially food, beverages and tobacco) and a rise in the share of intermediate goods (chemicals, petroleum products) and capital goods (metal products, machinery and equipment).

'Explaining' the industrialisation experience

In this section we will briefly consider a number of analyses of Africa's overall and industrial performance and return to a consideration of some of the substantive points that they raise in the next section of this paper.

The World Bank (Berg) report is concerned with explaining sub-Saharan Africa's overall performance and devotes relatively little attention directly to the experience of

TABLE 3.7 Share and growth of labour force in industry[a] by country group, 1960–80 (%)

Group	Industry share of labour force			Industrial labour force growth (% per annum)	
	1960	1970	1980[c]	1960–70	1970–80[c]
Low-income sub-Saharan Africa					
Semi-arid	3.4	5.2	9.6	5.9	8.0
Other	6.1	7.8	9.6	4.2	4.2
Middle-income sub-Saharan Africa					
Oil importers	5.6	7.1	9.0	4.5	4.9
Oil exporters	10.2	14.1	18.8	4.7	4.4
Sub-Saharan Africa, total	6.8	9.0	11.7	4.5	4.6
North Africa	13.0	18.2	27.3	4.7	6.8
All low-income economies	10	n.a.	15		
(excluding China and India)	(8)	(10)[b]	(11)		
All middle-income economies					
Oil importers	16	17	22		
Oil exporters	13		21		
Industrial market economies	38	39	38		
Non-market industrial economies	31	38	45		

Notes: [a]Includes manufacturing, mining, construction and public utilities
[b]Excludes China but includes India
[c]Projections
Source: Steel (1984: Table 7, p. 36)

industrialisation. The tenor of its approach is well captured in the following quotation: Africa's disappointing economic performance during the past two decades reflects, in part, internal constraints based on 'structural' factors that evolved from historical circumstances or from the physical environment. These include underdeveloped human resources, the decolonization and post-colonial consolidation, climatic and geographic factors hostile to development, and rapidly growing population. . . .Growth was also affected by a set of external factors – notably adverse trends in the international economy, particularly since 1974. . . .The internal 'structural' problems and the external factors impeding African economic growth have been exacerbated by domestic policy inadequacies, of which three are initial. First, trade and exchange-rate policies have overprotected industry, held back agriculture, and absorbed much administrative capacity. Second, too little attention has been paid to administrative constraints in mobilizing and managing resources for development. . . .Third, there has been a consistent bias against agriculture in price, tax, and exchange rate policies. (World Bank 1981b: 4).

The standard neoclassical critique of import-substituting industrialisation (ISI) is presented in the Report (Chapter 7), focusing largely on alleged 'distortions' in factor and product markets but considering all issues such as market size, population density,

34

wages and productivity, management costs and capital and infrastructure costs, as they relate to the industrialisation strategy chosen.

Overall, an agriculture-based and export-oriented development strategy is recommended for the remainder of the century. It recognises that African economies have not yet begun to export manufactured goods to any significant extent but it nonetheless argues that an important potential for manufactured exports exists (p. 94). The standard neoclassical policy package is advanced to achieve these objectives: correction of overvalued exchange rates; improved price incentives for exports and for agriculture; lower and more uniform protection for industry; reduced use of direct controls (p. 30).

In a piece of work closely related to World Bank (1981), Acharya divides a sub-sample of sub-Saharan African economies into two groups – 'étatist' and 'market oriented' (p. 118). The 'étatist' economies (Ghana, Sudan, Tanzania, Zambia, Guinea) are characterised by high levels of state ownership and intervention, policies of rapid Africanisation, 'forced' industrialisation and inward-looking production priorities. The 'market oriented' economies (Ivory Coast, Kenya, Malawi) as the name implies, have placed, *inter alia*, relatively greater reliance on the market, have shown a greater willingness to let the pace and character of industrialisation be governed by market forces and have viewed external trade and investment as a source of gains.

It is hardly necessary to add that, given the neoclassical perspective adopted, it is argued that the 'market oriented' economies have performed better than their 'étatist' counterparts on virtually all counts. With respect to the industrial sector, Acharya points to a variety of causes of inefficiency – lack of competitive pressures, uncertain and chaotic quantitative import restrictions, scarcity of management cadres, policy discrimination against small-scale enterprises and the special problems of parastatal enterprises (p. 134). He concludes that 'The nub of this sorry story is not that sub-Saharan Africa economies should not industrialise, but rather that certain kinds of costly errors and "non-solutions" should be soft-pedalled' and some 'positive actions' supported (Acharya 1981: 134). Examples of the latter include the development in the longer-run of a manufactured export capacity, the encouragement of small-scale industry and the reform of the parastatal sector.

A more balanced, less rigidly neoclassical explanation of the causes of sub-Saharan Africa's poor industrial performance is presented by Steel (1984). It concerns itself more with the structural changes that accompany ISI and it is less sanguine about being able to divide, in some objective sense, the industrial strategies of the sub-Saharan African economies into state versus private investment categories (p. 60).

The paper is particularly concerned with the low level of capacity utilisation typical of the manufacturing sector in many African economies. It suggests that the underlying causes of this problem relate to the dependence of production on imported inputs and the excessive growth of productive capacity relative to the growth of import capacity (and in some cases, relative to the size of the market) (p. 53).

The policy proposals are basically similar to the World Bank's, although the need for greater sub-regional trade flows and industrial planning are also recognised as important preconditions for successful and self-reliant industrial development, especially in the strategic intermediate and capital goods sectors (p. 73).

In an attempt to investigate quantitatively the sources of economic stagnation in sub-Saharan Africa, Wheeler, analysing time series data for the period 1960–80, concludes that there exists an extremely close relationship between movements in export prices and average performance – 'Movements in the terms of trade and international conditions of demand seem to have been a very powerful impact on the general growth experience of African states through their impact on foreign exchange earnings' (Wheeler 1984: 3).

He then attempts to investigate empirically the effect of environmental and policy variables on economic growth on a cross-country basis for the period 1970–80. The environmental variables (terms of trade, degree of political and military stability, share of non-oil minerals in export revenues, average export diversification) are dominant, although the impact of the policy variables (real effective exchange rate, import allocation policy, ability to preserve balance in the trade accounts) is not insignificant. In particular, great weight is attached to the ability to maintain flexibility in import structures in the face of foreign exchange shortages in order to maintain imports of intermediate manufacturing and agriculture inputs.

Wheeler concludes that 'ideological labels' are not of fundamental importance in evaluating the performance of African states. Specific policies were of importance in determining outcomes but 'countries from across the ideological spectrum seem ranked randomly on most of the policy measures' (p. 17).

Critique

The four studies briefly summarised above are all, to a greater or lesser extent, within the neoclassical analytical framework. Clearly, for the neoclassical economist, 'policy matters' and it is crucial to the neoclassical argument that some African economies have pursued 'correct' policies and as a consequence have achieved a certain degree of economic success.

This is most clearly highlighted in Acharya's (1981) distinction between the 'unsuccessful' 'étatist' economies and the 'successful' 'free-market economies'. Given that it is extremely difficult to distinguish, in some objective sense, between such groups of economies (are the differences in state intervention in the two groups of economies differences of degree or kind, for example?), one may be forgiven the suspicion that 'being successful' automatically places an economy in the 'free market' grouping, rather than vice versa.

The question of economic policy does, however, appear to pose a number of problems for non-neoclassical economists. Too often, the response of the latter is to reject outright a document such as (for example) the Berg Report because it is within/comes from a different paradigm. A more useful and productive approach would however be one that was more selective – what is there in the neoclassical critique and its associated policy measures that may be relevant or useful to those approaching the problem for a different analytical/ideological perspective (an issue raised in Chapter 9 by Smith and Sender)?

Three issues can be briefly touched on which are relevant to the main concern of this paper: the relationship between agricultural and industrial development; the experience of import-substituting industrialisation (ISI) and, the potential for the export of manufactured goods.

Agricultural and industrial development

A central theme of the Berg Report is the failure, for a variety of reasons, of the agricultural sector to grow rapidly:

agricultural output is the single most important determinant of overall economic growth and its sluggish record of recent years is the principal factor underlying the poor, economic performance of the countries of this region. (World Bank 1981b: 45).

The Report advocates what it calls 'an agriculture-oriented development strategy with industry in a supporting role' (p. 95). It emphasises that this does not mean that Africa must forgo industrial development:

Long-term industrial growth might, in fact, be higher with this approach. Although agriculture would be the driving force, industry would still grow faster than agriculture. In fact, agricultural incomes will stimulate demand for products from a number of industries – textiles, metal manufactures, building materials, and light consumer goods – that could be produced relatively efficiently in most African economies. Efficient industries generate their own momentum. And then export possibilities are opened up and the local market for intermediate goods widens. (World Bank 1981b: 95).

Taken out of its wider context, there is surely little in the above quotation with which the majority of development economists of all persuasions would disagree.[3] We no longer talk of industry *versus* agriculture, but rather emphasise the linkages and complementarities that exist between the two sectors. We also recognise the possibility that industrialisation may in some sense 'fail' because of a government's inability or unwillingness to 'transform' the agricultural sector.

The experience of ISI

It is not our intention to produce yet another survey of the experience of ISI (see Nixson 1982 and the references cited therein). Nevertheless it is necessary to point out that there is much in the neoclassical critique of ISI that is of value, and its insights can enrich an analysis located within a very different framework. We need to explain why so much installed capacity in the manufacturing sector is underutilised, why the industrial sector is usually so inefficient, highly protected and made to withstand international competition, why it is over-diversified and so dependent on imported product and process technology? The neoclassical critique provides neither a sufficient nor a convincing answer to these problems but it does provide a part of the answer and it must be recognised as such.

Export-led industrialisation

Another major theme of the Berg Report is the need to encourage export-led development. With respect to the export of manufactured goods, the report notes that 'Neither the past record nor newly uncovered special advantages suggests that concentration on exports of labor-intensive manufactures is a promising strategy for most of Africa' (p. 94). It goes on to argue that an 'important potential for manufactured exports does exist' (p. 94) and that 'for many African countries export production will have to play a more important role in overall economic growth' (p. 95); hardly a highly contentious statement!

This aspect of the Report has attracted much criticism (see for example, Loxley 1984). Bienefeld (1983) has quite rightly pointed to the heterogeneity of the NIC phenomenon and the strategic role that the state plays in export-led industrialisation (contrary to the generally anti-state bias of the Report). Godfrey (1983) emphasises the problems associated with the expansion of manufactured goods exports and argues that the rate of increase in manufactured exports implied by the arithmetic of the Banks' strategy is totally unrealistic (Godfrey 1983: 44).

Both Bienefeld and Godfrey refer to possible agents of export-led industrialisation (the state and TNCs respectively) and this is a point which deserves emphasis.

Export-led industrialisation does not occur as a result of wishful thinking. There must be institutions, classes or individuals that are able to export manufactured goods and benefit economically from such a strategy. The agent of export-led industrialisation may be the state, indigenous capitalists or TNCs, or some combination of all three – joint ventures between foreign and local capital and/or parastatal enterprises, for example. If such export-oriented group or class alignments do not exist, it is, of course, hardly likely that the neoclassical policy of 'getting prices right' will in itself bring them into existence.

The critics of Berg are thus right to focus on the simplistic policy recommendations but we need to go further and consider the process of class formation and class alignments in individual African economies. Simply to assume that, in the near future, there is no possibility of an export-oriented entrepreneurial group emerging (backed, by necessary macro, sectoral and enterprise level policies and with full state support) is to substitute crude prediction for careful analysis.

Conclusions

The experience of industrialisation in (mainly) sub-Saharan Africa is by no means wholly negative. The colonial 'inheritance' of the majority of African economies was not conducive to rapid industrialisation, but in spite of that initially adverse situation, significant growth and diversification of the manufacturing sector has been achieved. The rapid growth achieved by many economies in the 1960s did not, however, continue into the 1970s and many African economies began to experience the classic symptoms of the slowing down of the market-based ISI model (Nixson 1982; for a contrary assertion see Sender and Smith, Chapter 9).

The explanation of the industrialisation experience must obviously encompass both internal and external factors, assuming for the sake of simplicity that such a clear-cut distinction can be made. Most authors have recognised the importance of the variety of factors that will determine industrial performance[4] and both neoclassical and structuralist/neo-marxist writers recognise the interaction of both internal and external factors.[5]

However, having thus identified the importance of locating the analysis of the problem within an historical, international context, most analyses within a broadly neoclassical framework emphasise policy, i.e. internal, factors, as being of greatest significance. Analyses, on the other hand, which reject the neoclassical approach, usually begin with the 'global crisis' (Loxley 1984a) and tend to downgrade internal, policy issues. A largely unproductive debate thus ensues between those emphasising 'external' and those emphasising 'internal' causes of the crisis.

It is surely the case that a more complete understanding of the overall problem must take into account the historical evolution of the individual LDC region, the international environment and the ways in which the LDC is articulated with that environment, domestic socio-economic and political structures within the LDC itself (and the way that they in turn were and are influenced by historical, external factors as part of the process of dialectical development), the strategies and policies pursued by the LDC itself, and, importantly, the way in which external factors are 'internalised', the way, that is, that external forces 'filter through', or are mediated by, internal structures. Without a recognition of the latter point, LDCs are all too often seen as the helpless victims of a hostile international environment, prey to forces beyond their control and lacking any dynamic of development of their own.

Industrialisation cannot be divorced from the development of the other sectors of the economy, in particular the agricultural sector. Related to this point is the argument that the capacity of sub-Saharan Africa to earn or otherwise acquire foreign exchange must be expanded in order to sustain the higher level of imports required for structural transformation (a point emphasised here by Sender and Smith).

The agricultural sector must be regarded as a prime earner of foreign exchange and thus we appear to be arguing that the possibilities for industrialisation largely depend on external factors beyond the control of the individual LDC – conditions in international commodity markets, the implementation of protectionist policies within the developed capitalist economies, etc. In reality, the problem is more complex. 'External' performance is influenced by internal policy measures and the selection and implementation of 'internal' policies is constrained by 'external' factors. Equally, the specificity of each country's historical experience and the (perhaps highly individualistic) characteristics of its particular incorporation into the international economy need also to be given their due weight. The analysis of the interaction between 'internal' and 'external' factors within specific historical situations must be considered a priority for future research.

NOTES

1. I would like to thank Philip Leeson for his comments. The usual disclaimer applies.
2. Caution should be exercised when considering and comparing statistics on Africa. Apart from accuracy and coverage, the important points to note are: do the data relate to Gross National Product (GNP) or Gross Domestic Product (GDP)?; are they for total or *per capita* income?; are they in current or constant prices?; what time period is covered?; what is the country coverage? – do the data relate to Africa as a whole or only sub-Saharan Africa?; if the data relate only to the latter, are South Africa and Namibia included or excluded?
3. cf. Sutcliffe (1971: 72): 'To give priority to something does not necessarily involve the expenditure of more than a very small amount of time or money. Matters of priority can be small or large. To give "priority" to agriculture does not imply that investment, employment, output or productivity in agriculture should grow *faster* than in industry or that public investment in agriculture should be greater than that in industry. . ..It is quite possible that if the aim of a government was to encourage the maximum growth of industry within ten years, then for the first five years most attention would be devoted to agriculture, which could thereby more effectively provide raw materials for industry and demand for its products. . .."Priority" to industry here appears to imply "priority" for agriculture; "priority" is thus robbed of any operational meaning.'
4. Steel (1984) for example refers to the interaction between four sets of factors: the initial conditions, the economic, political and climatic environment, the strategy of industrialisation adopted and the policies used. The first two are seen as external factors, outside of the control of the policy makers.
5. Acharya (1981) emphasises the point that '. . .initial conditions (which are themselves a cumulation of past history) exercise substantial influence on subsequent feasible development paths' (p. 117).

4

The Nigerian economic crisis[1]

Yusuf Bangura

Nigeria is experiencing its most profound economic crisis in its post-independence history. Currently, it has been observed that about six million able-bodied Nigerians are unemployed; the prices of most essential commodities have skyrocketed; some of the goods are even difficult to find. Massive government expenditure cuts have been introduced; a wage freeze has been announced; the domestic value of the naira has deteriorated; the balance of payments is in a chronic deficit and various anti-democratic laws have been passed to impose some 'order' on the lifestyles of people.

What are the causes of the crisis? This paper attempts to review the major explanations that have been offered. First, we shall examine the official explanations of the crises. Secondly we shall analyse the 'third option' explanations of 'contractocracy', mismanagement and fraud and their relationship to underdevelopment theory. Thirdly, we shall attempt an empirical study of the roots of Nigeria's crisis within the context of the process of combined and uneven development. In the last two sections we shall go on to examine the official policies that have been implemented or recommended to contain the crisis, the popular responses of the working people to these policies and some of the alternative strategies from the Left.

Official explanations and neoclassical economic theory

The official explanations are derived from neoclassical economic theory. These have been modified, however, to take account of the specific Nigerian context. The following interlocking factors have been offered by government agencies as the causes of the crises:
(a) The general worldwide recession;
(b) The world oil glut and Nigeria's dependence on a single commodity;
(c) Low productivity and high wages;
(d) Unregulated government expenditure;
(e) Low savings and low investments, coupled with low sectoral linkages.

Both the ousted civilian administration and the Federal Military Government have given considerable prominence to the world recession which has affected Nigeria's foreign exchange earnings (Bangura 1984). Usually, the oil glut argument, Nigeria's dependence on a single commodity and the recession go together. This was first articulated by ex-President Shagari in his April speech to the National Assembly introducing the Economic Stabilisation Act, and reinforced in many subsequent policy statements. The maiden speech of President Buhari quite clearly recognised the mismanagement factor as a major cause of the crisis. However, subsequent statements and policies of the government while not abandoning the mismanagement thesis placed a lot of stress on the oil glut, the world recession and the disarticulation of the economy as explanations of the crisis. Since the Federal Military Government does not seek to challenge property relations but to introduce some rationality and discipline in the allocation and management of the country's resources, it cannot but accept and articulate the structural explanations of the ousted regime; this is because its quarrel with the ousted regime is mainly on the indiscipline and mismanagement of the economy that the latter exhibited.

Since both regimes accept the centrality of capitalist relations in managing the economy, the arguments of oil glut and recession are usually linked with the problems of low worker-productivity, high wages and excessive government expenditure. The argument is usually made that wages are too high for the level of productivity generated, and that workers are lazy and inefficient; hence the inauguration of the *Ethical Revolution* by Shagari's administration and the *War Against Indiscipline* by the Federal Military Government. Furthermore, it is argued that the federal and state governments have been forced to spend too much money on social services and other public projects which have become a burden on the economy. Certainly some of the official explanations offer some insights into the problem. For instance, it is true that the price of oil has suffered in the oil market and that this has led to a reduction of revenue for the federal and state governments which has affected public projects and private companies that manufacture goods with a high import content. It is also true that the world capitalist economy has been experiencing a prolonged recession since the early 1970s and this has affected the terms of trade of Nigeria's principal commodities.

However, on their own, these two explanations do not go far enough. Quite apart from the ideological smokescreen which they offer the policymakers to present the crisis as an 'international' conspiracy requiring the patriotic sacrifice of all Nigerians, when such official arguments are offered they do not take account of the fact that oil revenues for 1974–6, for instance, usually regarded as the boom period, were about ₦12 billion compared with ₦24 billion for the depression years of 1980–2. Furthermore, it has been shown that under the NPN administration the country experienced its highest receipt of revenue from oil, ₦53.48 billion, which was 55 per cent of the total receipts for twenty years (*National Concord*: 6 October 1983). Yet the country suffered its worst economic crisis under that administration.

Even if less revenue was recorded during the depression years and more in the boom period it would still be superficial to tag an explanation of crises onto oil prices, for one would then have to explain why the prices fell in the first place and what accounts for the high level of dependence on a single commodity and on the international economy. If the world recession caused the crisis, the official explanation is saying that a crisis (at the global level) caused a crisis (at the national level). We have still not explained what caused the crisis; for it assumes that the Nigerian economy is external to the world economy, a recipient and not an actor in the development of the world economy. As we shall try to demonstrate later, the oil glut certainly exposed the underlying structural contradictions of the Nigerian economy.

Similar problems are encountered with the general neoclassical explanations themselves. Here we are dealing with a methodology which stays at the level of market relations. Although it is able to capture some of the contradictions between sectors of a capitalist economy, it is not able to bring out the totality of the social relationships that condition the savings and investment pattern of the economy. This is because the methodology does not recognise fundamental conflicts in production and the way in which working class surplus is used to provide an incomes structure which is skewed against the latter. The struggle for the control of surplus by the various arms of the bourgeoisie and the state against the working people, which is central to capitalist production and crises, is not brought out by the static, equilibrium-oriented Keynesian models of savings and investment (Ekuerhare 1983).

TABLE 4.1 Economic performance of Nigeria's biggest three banks

Bank	Total assets (N thousand)	Turnover gross earnings (N thousand)	Profits (net after tax) (N thousand)	Dividends (N thousand)	Deposits current bank other a/c (N thousand)	Loans and advances (N thousand)
Union Bank						
1980	1,825,362	138,942	20,788	6,532	1,624,586	931,654
1981	2,567,166	201,817	29,801	6,532	2,318,280	1,395,593
1982	3,182,226	284,838	32,623	8,165	2,853,545	1,654,710
First Bank						
1980	2,610,887	126,633	17,967	10,754	2,141,980	1,039,239
1981	2,641,547	209,598	28,402	11,004	2,262,066	1,339,420
1982	—	—	—	—	—	—
UBA						
1980	1,715,883	124,699	20,036	6,362	1,576,225	864,836
1981	2,518,970	176,835	22,715	6,389	2,407,218	1,161,294
1982	2,826,935	232,195	26,602	8,003	2,548,230	1,519,426

Source: Wilmot (1983); derived from *Business Concord* 18 March 1983

In the specific Nigerian context, it has been shown that the wage bill does not consume more than 5 per cent of the gross domestic product so that workers cannot be held responsible for the shortcomings of capitalism. Furthermore, if productivity of workers is low, as the official explanations maintain, it certainly does not explain the huge amount of profit which many companies continue to make in Nigeria even in the period of austerity. Similarly with public expenditure. There is no doubt that this has expanded over the years from ₦3 billion in the Second National Plan of 1970/71 to ₦82 billion in the Fourth Plan of 1981. Much of it is geared towards the enrichment of a few individuals as the projects are either inflated in cost, badly done or abandoned. But, surely, the rise of public expenditure is associated with the crisis of *laissez-faireism*. Capitalism needs an interventionist state to regulate the level of demand and to accommodate some of the economic and political demands of the dispossessed; without it the naked forces of capitalist exploitation would be exposed; but the expansion of public expenditure limits the surplus necessary for expanded accumulation – a contradiction. A rise in public expenditure cannot, therefore, be held as the cause of the crisis for it protects the very unstable character of modern capitalism. Without it the entire capitalist edifice would come down crumbling under the pressures of working-class demands (Gough 1979).

TABLE 4.2 Comparison of pre-tax profits of major firms in 1981 and 1982

Company	Pretax profit (1981 N thousand)	Pretax profit (1982 N thousand)	Difference (N thousand)
Leventis Motors	7,886	8,760	874
Leventis Technical	3,700	3,330	−370
Leventis Stores	1,710	2,011	301
John Holt	8,370	13,030	4,660
Roads Nigeria Ltd	4,156	5,866	1,710
Thomas Wyatt	1,940	1,280	−660
Nigerian Breweries Ltd	16,977	23,000	6,023
G. Cappa Ltd	2,012	4,577	2,565
Agip Nigeria Ltd	9,872	11,937	2,065
SCOA	6,525	11,538	5,013
Total	15,000	16,600	1,600
Incar	1,579	2,448	869
Intra Motors	5,764	7,462	1,698
Flour Mills Nigeria Ltd	20,103	17,082	3,021
Dumex Nigeria Ltd	8,613	9,841	1,228
UTC Nigeria Ltd	36,358	39,664	3,306
Glaxo Nigeria Ltd	6,850	7,374	524
Nigerian Bottling Company	13,626	18,672	5,046
African Plywood Ltd	15,088	16,715	1,627
Van Leer Container Nigeria Ltd	4,350	5,184	834
Texaco	16,084	12,232	−3,854
Mobil Oil	16,518	17,281	761
Costain (W.A) Ltd	1,525	1,798	273
Northern Nigeria Flour Ltd	5,197	1,773	−3,424
STEYR	2,500 (after tax)		

Source: *Liberation News*, February 1983; also derived from *National Concord*, 23 October 1982. Wilmot (1983)

Underdevelopment theory and third option explanations

Next we examine what I have described elsewhere as 'third option' explanations (Bangura 1984) – explanations which eschew rigorous class categories, structural relationships and the internal dynamics of the Nigerian economy, but which instead focus on corruption, mismanagement and the role of the middle strata of the economy. The essence of these explanations has been captured by the single word, *contractocracy*, which has been defined as 'government for contractors, by contractors and of contractors' (Usman 1984a). Sections of both the Left and the Right share parts of these positions with the Left concentrating on contractocracy and the Right on the problems of mismanagement and indiscipline. At bottom, of course, the two sets of explanations are not fundamentally different, despite arguments to the contrary (Usman 1984b), because the 'contractocracy school' is saying that the crisis has been caused by (i) proliferation of contractors, middlemen and consultants; (ii) the inflation

43

of contracts sometimes to the value of three or four times their worth in other developing countries; (iii) the shoddy execution of the projects or in many cases their complete abandonment after mobilisation fees have been collected; (iv) the looting of public funds; (iv) the repatriation of profit; and (v) the general mismanagement of the economy (Usman 1984a; Mohammed 1984).

Although sections of the left have been quite effective in pushing these positions, such as the *Green Paper* which followed the workshop on the State of the Economy held at the Ahmadu Bello University, Zaria in December 1983, the communique of the *State of the Nation* conference organised by the Department of Political Science, ABU in December 1983, the Academic Staff Union of Universities conference on the *State of the Economy* in April 1984 and the Annual Conference of the Nigerian Political Science Association on *The State and Society* held in May 1984, it is now very clear that even the policy-makers, members of the business community and the general public have also embraced most of these ideas as the explanations of the crisis (National Economic Council 1983).

The Federal Military Government, for instance, has been waging a campaign against corruption, indiscipline, the inflation of contracts and mismanagement. The maiden speech of General Buhari was quite emphatic on the mismanagement/contratocracy thesis:

It is true that there is a world-wide economic recession. However, in the case of Nigeria, its impact was aggravated by mismanagement. We believe that appropriate government agencies have good advice but the advice was disregarded by the leadership. ... This government will not tolerate kickbacks, inflation of contracts, over-invoicing of imports etc. Nor will it condone forgery, fraud, embezzlement, misuse and abuse of office, illegal dealing in foreign exchange and smuggling. (*National Concord*, 21 January 1984).

It is quite true that contractors, middlemen and consultants have expanded over the years, particularly during the oil boom. Such an expansion is consistent with the development of capitalism where specialisation intensifies as commodity production expands.

The point of course has been made that the activities of these business people are corrupt. If only contracts have not been inflated, public funds looted and repatriated and projects abandoned Nigeria would not have faced a crisis. Again it is true that the contract system has been abused in Nigeria. Many public servants, politicians, private business companies and individuals have been implicated in the on-going probes. For instance, three senior civil servants in Benue State have been dismissed following the recommendations of a panel which probed the ₦3.2 billion chalk deal and other irregularities in some local governments between 1980 and 1983 (*New Nigerian* 25 June 1984). It has also been reported that three former politicians in Bendel State confessed to sharing ₦146,000 public funds from the Delta Boatyard Company which was unable to pay salaries for eighteen months (*The Guardian* 10 February 1984). Some pricing experts have maintained that seven fertilizer contracts awarded by the NPN administration for which foreign exchange had been transferred were inflated by $6.8 million (*The Guardian* 19 January 1984). In the area of debts probes it has been established that many fraudulent devices, such as forgeries of such documents as bills of lading, import licences and letters of credit, have been used. It has been pointed out that some of the companies obtained the co-operation of their foreign partners to stuff sawdust, sand and grass into containers and then shipped them into the country – this is, after the companies had obtained the import licences. Three companies were said to have illegally transferred $5.4 million, $3.3 million and $1.9 million respectively in this way (*National Concord* 23 January 1984).

In the Niger State contract probes, it has been alleged that the ex-deputy governor of Niger State approved the payment of ₦1.3 million to a contractor as customs charges on goods imported for the state water board without examining the contract document (*New Nigerian* 20 June 1984). It has also been reported that the same deputy governor of Niger State confessed that he was misled into approving a ₦99 million contract for the Niger State Water Scheme to Bi-Water. Only 30 per cent of construction work has been completed on the scheme, even though ₦93 million has already been spent (*New Nigerian* 1 June 1984).

Furthermore, various ex-state governors have been sent to prison with terms ranging from 12 to 22 years. For instance, ex-Governor Onabanjo was jailed for 22 years for receiving a ₦2.8 million kickback from Bouygues Nigeria Ltd for the construction of the Great Nigeria Insurance Company. This was paid into the accounts of the Unity Party of Nigeria. Ambrose Ali, ex-governor of Bendel, was jailed for 22 years for helping the UPN to get a ₦983,000 kickback from public contract funds (*The Guardian* 20 June 1984). Sabo Bakin Zuwo, ex-governor of Kano, received 20 years for accepting ₦100,000 from one Valentin Pargov, a projects manager of Electro Impex Ltd before awarding the contract to the company (*New Nigerian* 21 June 1984). Aper Aku, ex-governor of Benue, was jailed for 15 years for buying #10,000 and #10,500 at different times in 1983 (*New Nigerian* 11 July 1984). Adamu Atta, ex-governor of Kwara, received 21 years for diverting ₦2 million from government funds (*National Concord* 11 July 1984). Jim Nwobodo was jailed for 22 years on a two-count charge of misappropriating ₦5.8 million public funds (*New Nigerian* 22 June 1984).

There have also been revelations of abandoned projects. For instance, it was reported that work has stopped on 12 projects worth more than ₦100 million in Sokoto (*New Nigerian* 10 February 1984). Work at the Ajaokuta Steel Complex has also come to a halt. It is reported that ₦2.8 billion has so far been sunk into the project. Construction work on three dams in Kano, Niger and Bendel states has stopped. The three dams are worth about ₦65 million (*New Nigerian* 16 February 1984). Also projects worth more than ₦11 billion are said to have been grounded in Gongola, Borno and Kano states. The work came to a standstill after the contractors had collected mobilisation fees. It has also been reported that the Minister of the Federal Capital Territory ordered the arrest of six contractors. These are said to have collected mobilisation fees without doing the work. Thirty contractors, some of whom had collected mobilisation fees had abandoned the housing projects costing about ₦2,281,000 (*The Guardian* 22 February 1984).

Such stories of inflated contracts, abandoned projects and shady deals continue to dominate the news items in the national dailies. They actually give us a graphic picture of the corrupt nature of the Nigerian bourgeoisie. Certainly no discussion of Nigeria's crisis will be complete without an exposition of this phenomenon. However, to focus on corruption and the exchange strata of the economy and hope that a comprehensive explanation of the crisis will be derived from there is to deny that the contract system and corruption are integral parts of the process of bourgeois class formation and the development of capitalism in Nigeria.

It is interesting to note that the contractocracy school shares a common affinity with Underdevelopment Theory in its conception of the Nigerian state, the process of class formation, the nature of the bourgeoisie and the solutions to the problems of underdevelopment. The Nigerian state is conceived as compradorial whose character is defined by the dependent nature of the bourgeoisie; a class which is seen as incapable of performing the historic role of transforming the productive forces (Osoba 1978; Turner 1976; Usman 1979). This is because as a creation of the metropolitan bourgeoisie, the Nigerian bourgeoisie is quite content to play the role of junior partners, restricting itself to the role of importers and exporters, contractors and consultants, thus allowing the foreign bourgeoisie to reap maximum benefits from the stagnation and impoverishment of the economy. Why imperialism should not be interested in widening the basis of its surplus by expanding certain sectors of the economy is never fully confronted by this school. The indigenisation decrees, the multi-billion naira agricultural projects and the construction of the new federal capital, Abuja, are seen as providing the basis for the emergence and expansion of this parasitic class. Instead of recognising the objective and concrete self-interest of this class in capitalist development which has a common interest with imperialism to defend and expand capitalism in Nigeria, they are rather seen as robots, transmission belts and errand boys of imperialism who have no permanent and 'independent' stake in the survival of capitalism in Nigeria (Beckman 1982).

Like the *ad hoc* and shifting positions of the classical underdevelopment theoreticians, they recognise some of the developments that have occurred in the economy through import-substitution, but dismiss them as insignificant and as having plunged the country into further dependence and underdevelopment. The state is central in tying the economy to the dictates of the metropolitan bourgeoisie by utilising the petro-naira to develop a local bourgeoisie which lacks autonomy and resourcefulness. This it does through inflated contracts, the open looting of public funds and the corrupt transfer of capital to foreign accounts.

There are several dissimilarities, however, between classical Underdevelopment Theory and some of the leading theoreticians of the contractocracy school in Nigeria. Classical Underdevelopment Theory sees the major problem emanating from imperialism which effects its influence through subordinate and weak domestic allies. Although they condemn the local bourgeoisie for having betrayed the national interest, they very often support them in some of their recommendations on how to improve the bargaining strength of the third world nations (Emmanuel 1972). The theoreticians of the contractocracy school have tended to contradict themselves on these issues. On some occasions they find themselves in total agreement with the classical position; but at other times they tend to see the main enemy as the *Northern Oligarchy* (Abba *et al.* 1983; Bello 1983; Mustapha 1984). With specific reference to the current crisis they have identified the NPN administration which has a relationship with the Northern Oligarchy as the main enemy (Usman 1982). They hold the view that the Shagari administration was capable of solving or preventing the crisis but let the nation down because of ineptness and subservience to outside forces. There is thus a dilemma for this school, which on the one hand supports the central propositions of Underdevelopment Theory in seeing the state and the national bourgeoisie under the administration of the NPN as dependent and neocolonial, but, at the same time, sees this class as capable of transforming the economy if it had wanted to because of the legal instruments at its disposal:

As the Chief Executive of the Federal Government, Head of the Nigerian State, and Commander-in-Chief of the Armed Forces, as the federal media organs continuously remind us, he certainly has, in his hands, all the legal powers, instruments, institutions, and the machinery with which to curb this drain on our external reserves. He controls the Central Bank of Nigeria; and in addition, by virtue of the Federal Government's majority shareholding, he also effectively controls all the major commercial banks operating in this country.

The Federal Ministry of Commerce which alone issues licences for imports is controlled by him; while the customs Department and the Nigerian Ports and Airports Authority, which control the physical movement of the goods into the country are all agencies of the federal government, under his authority and his control. So, both directly, the President has the power, the machinery, the institutions and the instruments to curb this drain on our foreign reserves. (Usman 1982; 36–7)

Some of them even argue that the world capitalist economy has nothing or very little to do with the crisis:

Let us not engage in empty opportunistic rhetorics and jargons such as the argument that the nature of our crisis in Nigeria is totally part of the world imperialist crisis within a neocolonial formation, and that is why free education is not possible or that haraji, poll tax and hospital fees are being reintroduced. Those who advance this argument are double agents, double agents because they want to divert attention and delay action until the outbreak of a 'world revolution'. While it is true that part of our problem in Nigeria as in any neocolony is capitalist exploitation, added to that in the specific case of Nigeria is the entrenchment of 'contractocracy', the direct and indirect stealing of public wealth. If the latter is arrested, the resources we have in Nigeria can provide us with meaningful free education at all levels. For only if a society is well prepared and fully armed can it fight capitalist exploitation and eliminate imperialism. An illiterate society is most ill-prepared for this. (Modibbo 1984: 20)

Part of the confusion of the Contractocracy School stems from a parochial and opportunistic type of political practice which identifies political struggles with the struggles against particular individuals outside the social forces that condition their behaviour.

The crisis of Nigeria's political economy: uneven development

It should be obvious by now that all economic crises have a direct relationship with the accumulation process and are therefore manifestations of the crisis of accumulation. But it is against the background of combined and uneven development that we can understand the way the other contradictions have manifested themselves in the Nigerian economy.

The Nigerian economy was incorporated into the capitalist world economy through the activities of giant trading companies like Unilever, and its subsidiary United African Company, John Holt, SCOA and the colonial state. Colonialism dissolved the multiple pre-capitalist socio-economic systems and connected them to a wider, centrally-controlled imperialist system. The colonial state imposed a specific system of division of labour on the economy, forcing it to specialise in the export of selected raw materials and the importation of manufactured commodities.

The surplus from the agricultural and mineral commodities was expropriated by the giant trading companies and the industrialists of Europe who needed these commodities as raw materials. Although colonialism provided the basis for the subsequent expansion of the domestic market, the link between this market and the external sector was skewed in favour of the latter, especially as the domestic industries that would have formed the basis for the expansion of domestic capitalism in Nigeria were crushed; this created the conditions for the disarticulation of the economy – a situation underdevelopment theory has well documented.

Despite its external orientation and the tendency for colonialism to block the productive forces, the internal economy itself was not static. The economy was undergoing its own motion in terms of class formation, contradictions and struggles.

Apart from the educated petit bourgeoisie which emerged to help man the colonial state apparatus, many Nigerians also began to move into the intermediate strata of the economy by acting as middlemen between the colonial trading companies and the peasants, buying the commodities from the latter and selling at a high price to the trading companies. Later, when the marketing boards were formed, these people consolidated their positions as licensed buying agents for the boards, thus occupying a definite position in the intricate system of the colonial extraction of surplus from the peasantry. It was this class which was later to lead the struggle for indigenisation and to co-operate with transnational companies in joint industrial and commercial schemes (Mustapha 1983). There was also a proletarian class being formed in the tin mining areas, the railways, ports and other service industries. This class of workers and the peasantry were later to join the petit bourgeoisie to decolonise the society.

The colonial economy had its own contradictions, the principal one being the exploitative and oppressive relationship between the metropolitan ruling class, the giant colonial companies and the colonial state on the one hand and the colonial working class and the peasantry on the other. This led to a series of industrial actions and peasant uprisings in the colonial period. But the colonial economy also prevented the educated petit bourgeoisie and the bourgeoning merchant class from realising their full potentials: thus their unflinching opposition to colonialism (Mustapha 1983).

However, because the nationalist struggle had mainly a petit bourgeois orientation the material roots of the colonial system were not destroyed. Against the background of the worldwide collapse of British power, the British policymakers made frantic efforts to impose their stamp on the decolonisation process by trying to win the confidence of the educated class and the merchants to establish a diarchal system which would guarantee specific British interests. The principal ones during this period were the protection of British capital, symbolised in the emphasis which British policymakers placed on the defence of the pound sterling. This called for a very complex trading and financial system in which the colonies were forced to curtail their imports from non-sterling areas, to give preference to British goods, to produce special commodities that would earn dollars and would meet Britain's needs in raw materials, and the export of commodities to the US to earn dollars. Such earnings were centralised under a common dollar pool controlled by Britain. These measures were supplemented by the colonial monetary exchange standard in which the currencies in Nigeria and other African colonies were tied to the British pound on a one-to-one basis, with the surplus invested in British short and medium-term securities (Bangura 1983).

The nationalists accepted the broad principles of these arrangements; this made their specific demands of Africanisation and share-participation in industry and commerce easy to meet. In fact some of the large companies had even taken the lead in Africanising the top echelons of their companies and moving from simple trading activities into manufacturing (Hopkins 1973; 273–7). Although the tight budgetary and monetary policies were later revised, the seeds for the consolidation and expansion of capitalism had already been planted; the revision did not take, therefore, a root and branch opposition to imperialism but one of indigenising the capitalist institutions which had developed, thereby giving the Nigerian policymakers and the nascent bourgeoisie extra powers to relate much more effectively with imperialism.

The initial development of the Nigerian bourgeoisie was fuelled by the surplus from agricultural production, with the economy depending on agriculture for about 70 per cent of its foreign exchange and 66 per cent of its gross domestic product (Teriba *et al*. 1981: 18). The indigenised administrative state system which followed the constitutional changes of the 1950s which called for the regionalisation of the commodity boards became an important vehicle for the siphoning of public funds, the financing of massive government projects and the conspicuous importation of consumer goods. This led to a serious crisis in 1955/6, just after the Korean war boom. The decline of the prices of Nigeria's key commodities reduced the state's revenue; this fell far short of the expanding cost of government expenditure, the high cost of the import bill and the foreign exchange requirements of the local and foreign companies.

The crisis of 1955/6 had deeper structural roots. For it signalled the secular collapse of the agrarian basis of capital accumulation as the earnings from agriculture in the gross domestic product dropped from 61 per cent in 1964 to 18 per cent in 1982 (Abdullahi 1983). This produced a series of crises in the 1960s, thus exposing the fragility and instability of Nigeria's political economy – a product of the uneven development of capitalism.

The push for indigenisation was, therefore, not as intensive in the first decade of independence as it came to be in the post-civil war period. Apart from the crisis which the economy was experiencing, the material basis of comprador business was very limited as it seemed to be content with such moderate policies as occupying top management posts in the civil service and business, having limited shares in foreign companies and expanding trade contacts. The civil war did, of course, transform the wealth of some of the individuals that were acting as intermediaries between the warring factions and suppliers of wanted commodities. But, by and large, the capacity of this class to push for radical indigenisation was limited.

The end of the civil war and the quadrupling of oil prices were to change all this. The massive increase in oil prices not only changed the agrarian basis of capital accumulation to that of crude petroleum but also reinforced and expanded the structure of import-substitution industrialisation which had started in the immediate post-Second World War period. Petroleum's share of total export earnings which was only 10 per cent in 1962 rose to 82.77 per cent in 1973. The price of crude oil which already tripled between 1973 and 1974 'jumped from $11.7 per barrel in 1974 to $40 per barrel in 1980' and the production of crude oil reached 2.05 million barrels per day by 1980. Thus the revenue accruing from crude petroleum jumped from ₦4.733 billion in 1975 to ₦9,825 billion in 1981 (National Economic Council 1983).

This unprecedented increase in oil revenues led to a massive expansion of planned capital expenditure in subsequent national development plans. Whereas the second national development plan of 1970–74 was only ₦3 billion that of the third plan was ₦30 billion and the fourth plan of 1981–5 was ₦82.5 billion. The availability of such massive funds increased the tempo of economic activity and led to the formulation and implementation of the indigenisation decrees of 1972 and 1977.

The activities of the middle strata of the economy multiplied by leaps and bounds to meet the extraordinary demands of foreign companies, the state and local producers for the expansion of the domestic market and the creation of new investment outlets. The contract system became firmly established, pervading the entire system of project formulation and implementation and other commercial transactions. The ownership of the Nigerian economy by Nigerian businessmen, politicians and civil servants rose from 7 per cent in 1966 to 42 per cent in 1976 (*Financial Times* 1980). Many projects were executed by the state which drew the attention of foreign and local capital. There was the massive infusion of capital into the iron and steel complex, the funding of various infrastructural projects by federal and state governments, the construction of the new capital, Abuja, and the implementation of the World Bank agricultural projects. All these projects acted as a conduit pipe for the siphoning of much of the state funds into private accounts.

TABLE 4.3 Development in prices and government revenue from crude oil

Year	Production (million barrels per day)	Export (million barrels per day)	Posted Price ($bn)	Revenue to government (billion naira)
1975	1.785	1.713	13.7	4.733 (1975/76)
1976	2.067	2.013	14.0	5.498 (1976/77)
1977	2.085	2.030	15.5	6.177 (1977/78)
1978	1.897	1.827	14.9	4.809 (1978/79)
1979	2.302	2.210	33.0	10.100 (1979/80)
1980	2.054	1.940	44.4	9.489 (Apr-Dec)
1981	1.440	1.227	42.5	9.825[c]
1981	1.294	0.991[a]	39.0[b]	5.161[c]

Notes: [a] For the first nine months
  [b] For the first eight months
  [c] Estimates only
Source: National Economic Council (1983)

However, the extent of industrialisation was quite minimal, representing only about 8 per cent of the GDP, even though the rate of growth of the manufacturing sector in the 1970s was about 15 per cent. Most of the industries are simple assembly and packaging enterprises which contribute very little to local value added. Most of the industries have a value added of less than 15 per cent with animal feed (13.9 per cent), spirits, distilleries and beer (14.6 per cent), textiles (10.9 per cent) and transport equipment (9.7 per cent) occupying the top category. The capital goods sector was conspicuously underdeveloped (Ekuerhare and Ihuema 1984). This pattern of industrialisation was entrenched by the profligate administration of the NPN which liberalised imports in the March 1980 budget and set in motion an expanded public expenditure programme (*Financial Times* 1980). This was against the background of the deflationary policies introduced by the outgoing Obasanjo administration in 1978 to check the strains which had started to appear in the economy as a result of the tumbling of oil prices by 16 per cent in 1977 and the 40 per cent rate of increase in imports in the same period.

Food imports more than doubled between 1976 and 1978/9 and more than doubled again in 1981 when they exceeded ₦2 billion. The importation of manufactured goods increased by nearly 50 per cent between 1976 and 1978/9 and nearly doubled again by 1981 when the figure was as much as ₦2.6 billion. Similarly the importation of machinery and transport equipment increased by 12 per cent between 1976 and 1981 (National Economic Council 1983). Added to this was the substantial increase in the importation of capital equipment and raw materials. Capital imports increased by about 156 per cent between 1974 and 1977 and by 28 per cent between 1978/9 and 1981 and raw material imports increased by 110 and 100 per cent respectively. By 1981 both capital and raw material imports had reached a level of ₦5.7 billion. With the tumbling of oil prices leading to a decline in oil revenues from ₦10,000 million in 1979 to ₦161 million in 1982, a crisis was bound to occur, exposing the fragile political economy.

TABLE 4.4 Imports by end-use at current prices

	1974	1975	1976	1977	1978	1979	1980	1981
Consumer goods								
Non durable								
Food	166.4	353.7	526.7	912.6	1,004.1	1,040.1	1,416.8	2,198.3
Textile	31.5	81.3	65.0	38.9	41.9	73.2	92.4	202.6
Others	173.6	353.5	476.7	612.1	720.5	705.8	567.4	822.0
Durable	68.5	191.3	282.0	421.7	370.2	380.7	473.7	674.1
Total	400.0	979.8	1,350.4	1,985.3	2,136.8	2,119.8	2,550.3	3,897.0
Capital goods								
Capital	490.1	1,136.6	1,515.0	2,129.8	2,595.5	1,576.9	2,228.7	2,661.3
Transport equipment	124.9	371.1	729.6	1,012.5	1,233.8	988.7	1,770.2	1,818.7
Raw material	519.3	903.0	1,094.0	1,543.0	1,880.0	1,115.7	2,166.9	3,038.5
Fuel	55.4	100.2	175.0	128.6	156.7	116.4	173.4	187.2
Total	1,189.7	2,509.9	3,513.9	4,813.9	5,866.3	3,799.7	6,339.2	7,705.7
Passenger cars	97.0	220.3	261.0	297.4	350.1	169.7	206.1	1,316.6
Grand Total	1,726.7	3,710.0	5,125.0	7.096.6	8.353.2	6,169.2	9,095.6	12,919.6

Official policies and subordination

There has been, in Nigeria, an intricate blend of Keynesianism and monetarism (with an increasing bias towards the latter) coupled with specific solutions which are peculiar to the Nigerian experience. The Economic Stabilisation Act of 1982 relied heavily on a combination of import restrictions, monetary controls and fiscal policies. For instance, all unused import licences were recalled for review; capital projects not yet started were deferred; and the issue of licences to import vehicles was suspended. The basic travel allowance (BTA) was reduced from ₦800 to ₦500 and the business travel allowance reduced from ₦3,000 to ₦2,500. Compulsory advanced deposits ranging from 50 to 250 per cent were imposed on a wide range of commodities. There was also an increase in government decreed interest rates of 2 per cent, a reduction of government expenditure and restrictions on the external borrowing by state governments. Monetary and credit guidelines were established for industries, development finance institutions and general commerce (The President 1983). Most of these policies were given a non-partisan endorsement by the National Executive Committee Council's expert Committee Report on the *State of the Economy* which was prepared by Federal government representatives and the economic advisers of all 19 state governments of the federation under the chairmanship of Dr J.S. Odama, the special adviser to the government in the Vice President's office (National Economic Council 1983). Most of the recommendations of this Report were endorsed by the Government's White Paper on the State of the Economy.

These policies were reinforced in Shagari's National Day Speech of October 1983 and the budget speech which followed it in December 1983. In the National Day Speech notice was given of the determination of the government to reorder and reappraise priorities with a view to curtailing public expenditure. Also revealed was the government's intention to implement the recommendations of the various commissions on the privatisation of parastatals, a standard IMF recommendation (*National Concord* 6 June 1983).

It is not surprising, therefore, that the December pre-coup budget of the federal government showed a decrease in recurrent expenditure of ₦107,070,210 which was roughly 3 per cent of the corresponding figure of ₦3,833,606,790 for 1983. The capital expenditure sector also experienced a decrease of ₦1.931 billion which is approximately 29 per cent of the 1983 figure of ₦6.59 billion. The credit guidelines which prescribed an overall ceiling as well as the sectoral distribution of credit for commerce and merchant banking were retained. Deposit interest rates and lending rates, with the exception of those for agriculture, were raised by about 2 per cent. This was presumably to stimulate domestic savings, promote capital formation and discourage consumption which might escalate the inflation and the payments deficit (*The Guardian*, 31 December 1983). The government also announced its intention to reduce the level of subsidy provided by the government on certain goods and services. This was to have affected petrol and food prices, if implemented, something the IMF had been urging the government to do. The budget ignored devaluation, but the government insisted on continuing talks with the IMF for a ₦1.7 billion loan to offset part of the deficit.

The leadership of the NPN presided over the most irresponsible and profligate government in Nigeria's history. The various connections of the NPN leadership to the agencies that have inflicted the crisis on the nation made it difficult for the government to impose even the kind of fiscal and monetary discipline on the economy which it had prescribed. For instance, the import deposit schemes and the regulation of import licences not only bureaucratised the import system but also increased the level of corruption, nepotism and politicisation which has always been associated with the procurement of import licences in Nigeria. Import licences went to party stalwarts and their agents who in many cases have little or no connection with industry and commerce (Abubakar 1983). Many well established companies were forced to buy these licences on the black market, forcing the Managing Director of the United Africa Company to threaten the government with the closure of the company.

An extensive campaign was waged by the Manufacturers Association of Nigeria for a revision of the Economic Stabilisation Act, especially as it related to 'import deposits which the Association claimed reduced the cash flow of small and medium-sized companies. Through its connections with powerful senators such as David Dafinone and the submission of persuasive memoranda to the Senate Committee on Banking and Currency (Senate 1982) the MAN was able to get the National Assembly to amend the Act with a view to review periodically the effectiveness of the measures taken by the President under the Act. This was vetoed by President Shagari (*New Nigerian* 1 November 1983).

The measures that were taken to contain the crisis further deepened it. A large number of factories collapsed during this period. A poll conducted by the MAN showed that by 31 July 1983 a total of 101 companies had within a period of 12 months closed for a period of between seven and twelve weeks involving a labour force of 20,000 workers (*Business Concord* 21 October 1983). At least 5.93 million Nigerians are now unemployed (*Business Concord* 8 June 1984). The building and construction industry which employs an estimated 418,000 lost at least 150,000 workers between 1983 and June 1984. The employment of textile workers fell from 200,000 in the 1970s to 80,000 in December 1983. About one-third of the textile mills have temporarily closed down while the remaining two-thirds are operating at between 30 and 40 per cent capacity. Some are operating on a three-day week. According to the National Union of Textile Garment and Tailoring workers, all this is 'in addition to about 10,000 workers that have been forced on compulsory leave ranging from six weeks to three months and more . . . [and] another 6,000 working between 3 and 4 days a week' (*National Concord* 5 July 1984).

Furthermore, the price level of many basic commodities rose astronomically as manufacturers failed to get import licences; middlemen took advantage of the situation by hoarding commodities and hiking prices. Coupled with this was the non-payment of salaries. Since the various governments found it difficult to impose a wage freeze, they simply refused to honour their civic responsibilities of paying salaries on time. A loan of ₦537 million had to be given to the various state governments just before the August 1983 elections to enable the state governments to pay arrears of salaries, wages and allowances to workers to stem the threat of industrial action by the Nigerian Labour Congress (NLC) (*New Nigerian* 5 August 1983). The point should be made that the poor economic record of the government forced it to sharpen its repressive state instruments by rigging the election, imposing a de facto single party dominant government on the electorate and by increasingly relying on the notorious 'Kill and Go' military police to intimidate and harass opposition groups, parties and individuals.

It was against this background that the coup of 31 December 1983 took place which was essentially a coup of senior army officers (*The Guardian* 22 January 1984) who were worried about the dangers associated with the bankrupt policies of the government and the possibilities of economic collapse and political instability (*National Concord* 2 January 1984). The military certainly rode on the crest of the popular opposition to the corrupt, wasteful and indisciplined NPN government. Some of the policies which the NPN government wanted to, but could not, implement because of its powerful clientele were to be implemented by the Federal Military Government (FMG).

The Economic Stabilisation Act of April 1982 was renewed by the FMG in January 1984; talks with the IMF were resumed, and the government announced prompt payment of salaries. In line with the general thrust of curtailing public expenditure the revised recurrent expenditure of ₦6.07 billion represented a reduction of 17 and 15 per cent respectively over those of 1983 and of the 1984 draft estimates of the ousted NPN administration. The capital expenditure for the 1984 fiscal year has been put at ₦3.93 billion. When compared with the 1983 figure of ₦6.59 billion and that of the 1984 draft estimates of ₦4.66 billion, there is a decrease of ₦2.66 billion and ₦0.73 billion which represents 40.3 and 15.6 per cent respectively (*National Concord*, 11 May 1984). Business travel allowances were abolished, the BTA was reduced to ₦100 and the home remittance of expatriates reduced from 50 to 25 per cent. The compulsory advanced deposits were abolished and all invisible items of imports put under specific import licences. This has gone some way to satisfy the objectives of MAN. Reduction of subsidies and the privatisation of parastatals already accepted by the NPN government were shelved, and external borrowing by state governments terminated. The government further announced its intention to amend the Nigerian Enterprises Promotion Decree to enable non-Nigerians to own up to 80 per cent of large farm projects. Import duties on agricultural machinery and farm projects were abolished and duties on wheat and tea reduced. Interest rates for deposits and lending, apart from those of agriculture, were adjusted upwards ostensibly to encourage savings and reduce consumption; workers in the public sector were told not to expect pay increases, but instead were to receive all arrears of their salaries, allowances and bonuses.

The FMG backed up these measures with a sudden change of the currency which resulted in a rigid naira-squeeze from 25 April to 6 June. This was meant to kill a lot of repatriated naira and some of those buried in undisclosed quarters in the country which are believed to have made the implementation of any monetary policy impossible. In practice since there was a discrepancy between what the Central Bank initially printed and the amount that was to have been replaced, a serious liquidity crisis hit many companies and homes (Mawuli 1984). The exercise enabled the government briefly to regulate the spending habits of the people by crudely rationing legitimately-earned salaries and wages through the banks, sometimes at such ridiculous amounts as ₦20 and ₦50 per person. Bottlenecks developed, bureaucratisation in the banking and commercial sectors intensified and the distribution networks almost collapsed as the recycling of naira through the banks became questionable since business people were not sure about the possibility of withdrawing their money when they wanted it. This forced the Central Bank to pump more money into the economy in order to correct the imbalance.

Most of the policies of the FMG are not fundamentally different from those of the ousted NPN government. These policies, as we have seen, are derived from the neoclassical economic theory of capitalist crisis-management. This should not be surprising because even the FMG believes 'that appropriate government agencies have good advice but the advice was ignored by the leadership (*National Concord* 2 January 1984). The differences are at the level of detail; namely more/less public expenditure; reduction/cancellation of Business Travel Allowances; mild reduction/massive reduction of BTA; modifications/cancellations of import deposit schemes; retention/reduction of home remittance; proposed cancellation/retention of subsidies; appeal for wage freeze/mandatory wage freeze, etc. All these policies are within the framework of the liberal solutions of regulating the level of demand; they do not constitute an attack on the structure of property relations that inform the structure and character of demand.

The one major area of difference is the attack by the FMG on the undisciplined contractors, middlemen, civil servants, politicians and foreign companies that have swindled public funds. Steps have been taken to recover some of the looted money from those that could not escape to Western Europe and the US; probes have been established and some civil servants and politicians have been jailed. The plan of the FMG seems to be one which gives primacy to agricultural and industrial production, the optimum utilisation of raw materials, a rational contract system and a disciplined labour force. Such measures have been backed by several draconian decrees limiting press freedom, insulating public officers from critical public scrutiny, dismissing public officers without recourse to appeal, etc. Amidst all this, the economic situation continues to deteriorate through loss of jobs, spiralling inflation and a freeze in wages.

Popular responses and alternative solutions

Popular responses and left-wing solutions have been conditioned by two major factors. The first is a short-term response intended to prevent the bourgeois state from resolving the crisis on the backs of the peasants and workers. Resistance here refers mainly to the opposition of students, wage-workers, academics, petty commodity producers, the unemployed and the peasants, to the stiff official policies of retrenchment, wage freeze, curtailment of subsidies and government expenditure, devaluation, special taxes and educational levies and the procurement of the IMF loan. Although the ranks of the workers have been depleted and their finances stretched, some popular resistance has been demonstrated at various levels.

Popular resistance was much more effective and intense under the administration of the NPN. For instance, the threat of a national strike in 1981 forced the federal government to raise the minimum wage to ₦125. Also the Academic Staff Union of Universities was able to wage a protracted industrial struggle against the government over the revision of salary scales, deteriorating conditions of service and the funding of the universities with a measure of success in some of the demands, particularly the ones relating to increases in salaries and the delinking of the academic salary scale from the general civil service scale. Attempts by the government to suspend the USS scale barely a month after its introduction was met with stiff opposition resulting in the reconfirmation of the government's acceptance of the Cookey Commission Report and its White Paper. Similarly, even though the NPN administration threatened to raise fees, the combined opposition of the various student bodies under the leadership of the National Association of Nigerian Students (NANS) helped to stall such attempts.

The situation has been a bit different under the regime of the FMG. The FMG has been very effective in using the 'NPN squandermania' as a perfect alibi to introduce policies that seriously affect the ordinary people. Thus its constant calls for sacrifice, discipline, unity and support for government policies. Where the Shagari administration hesitated in introducing a complete freeze on wages, the FMG introduced the policy of promising to pay wages on time and demanded from the workers the commitment not to ask for higher wages. Salaries and wages were in fact cut for certain categories of workers in some states. Where the NPN government hesitated to lay off workers in the public service, the FMG and the various state governments have retired various categories of workers and a decree has even been passed making it impossible to challenge such decisions. During the NLC convention in Enugu, the FMG made it clear to the delegates that it would not tolerate any pay rises and industrial action. In some Northern states, poll and cattle taxes were reintroduced and many state and federal institutions introduced tuition fees. The wage freeze has now been confirmed by the government (*New Nigerian* 11 August 1984).

Popular resistance to these measures has not been very effective. For instance, the attempt by the Plateau State NLC to resist the policy of retrenchment was met with stiff opposition from the state government. Fearing further dismissals and stern measures, the union was forced to retract its stand of a possible industrial strike and to co-operate with the government 'in finding ways of solving the fiscal crisis of Plateau State'. The mass retrenchment of workers in both the public and private sectors has curtailed the funds of the various unions and has made it difficult to sustain protracted strikes. The same fate befell the pilots of Nigeria Airways who embarked on an industrial action early in 1984 to complain about poor conditions of service. The authorities used the big stick by dismissing them *en masse* and forced them to return to the negotiating table and reach an acceptable resolution with the management. The petty traders and road-side mechanics were also unable to put up any effective resistance to the destruction of their kiosks and work-places that followed the ban on street trading by various state governments.

In the case of NANS, however, they were partially successful in boycotting classes to protest against statements from government officials that free education could not be sustained in Nigeria. This forced the FMG to announce that tuition fees would be free in all federal government institutions; many of the student leaders were detained, however, in line with lecturers suspected to be sympathetic to their cause; furthermore the government has announced the withdrawal of subsidies for student meals; this is likely to increase the cost of education in the country (*New Nigerian* 11 August 1984).

Some measure of success has been achieved in the campaign against the removal of subsidies from petrol which was recommended by the IMF and accepted by the Shagari administration. The resistance to public expenditure cuts has not, however, been quite effective, mainly because the Left and other mass-based unions have not paid serious attention to this area until very recently when the NANS tried to make it a big issue in one of their campaign strategies against cuts in educational subsidies and allocations (NANS 1984). This is because of the populist tendency which has pervaded the Left's perception of public expenditure under the regime of Shagari as an area which has simply provided a basis for enriching the coffers of a few public servants, politicians, contractors and other business groups. Even though there is a general opposition to the withdrawal of government funds from public services (NLC 1983), the whole package of public expenditure cuts has not been responded to in a systematic and effective way. More attention has instead been given to wage cuts/freeze and retrenchments.

Perhaps the one area where popular opposition has been quite effective in checking the orientation of the government is the demand for devaluation and the loan from the IMF. Surely, the talks with the IMF have not been suspended and the value of the naira has been fluctuating in the foreign exchange market. However, the press, student organisations, ASUU, the NLC and other left organisations have waged an unceasing campaign against the IMF as the fountain of the policies of repression, further crises and imperialist domination. Although most of the policies which the IMF would have recommended have actually been implemented, the government seems to be very concerned about accepting wholesale the IMF package.

The solutions to the crisis must, therefore, take into account these specifically imperialist-induced problems of unequal development and the quest for a complete transformation of the social relations of production. The problem here is how the national and class objectives are articulated in a situation where the oppressed classes and the Left do not control state power and are in fact being threatened with extinction through the obnoxious state policies of mass retrenchment, inflation and wage freeze.

It is obvious that certain policies which advance national objectives could work against the short-term interests of the oppressed classes. Take for instance the whole question of food importation. As Beckman and Andrae have shown in the case of wheat, its continued production in Nigeria is not only uneconomical from the point of view of climatic conditions and comparative costs but it also pushes the country deeply into the 'wheat trap' (Beckman and Andrae, Chapter 18). This increases the debt problems of the country and its dependence on American agri-business. But wheat is necessary for making bread which has become a standard food item for the broad masses of the people, including the working class, the civil servants and the urban petit bourgeoisie of traders and mechanics. The government has, therefore, found it difficult to curtail the importation of wheat. In fact in the recent FMG budget, the duties on wheat were removed specifically to make 'bread cheaper' for Nigerians (*National Concord* 11 May 1984). In periods of rising prices, retrenchment of workers and the disappearance of commodities it certainly would be difficult for the working class to accept open-ended national objectives without substantial concessions to them from the state and clear alternatives that would satisfy their long-term interests.

Similarly, if we take the issue of productivity and raw materials, the emphasis of government has been on the need to curtail wages and to give specific assistance to companies to utilise fully the resources for greater productivity. The argument usually is that if workers do not make such sacrifices, industries would fold up bringing more hardship to workers, their families and the general productive capacity of the country. This is well demonstrated in the crisis at Kaduna Textiles Limited (KTL). The textile industry has been facing severe problems, stemming mainly from shortages of raw materials, spare parts and poor management. The KTL stopped production for over three and a half months between the end of June and the middle of October 1983 (*New Nigerian* 24 January 1984). Workers were forced to go on compulsory leave for this period with 50 per cent pay in July, 75 per cent pay in August and 75 per cent pay in September. At the end of the compulsory leave, the management persuaded the union to accept 50 per cent of their basic earnings while production fully resumed on the basis that although they had received some raw materials, they still had cash flow problems. The union, on behalf of the workers, agreed to work fully and to receive only 50 per cent of their earnings while the remaining 50 per cent would be regarded as compulsory savings to be paid to the workers in March 1984. An agreement reached on 28 October 1983 stipulated that full payment of salaries and allowances would be restored in January 1984. The crisis erupted when the management refused to honour the agreement but proceeded to ask the workers to accept half pay for another indefinite period (*New Nigerian* 30 January 1984).

The 3,600 workers refused the offer, and in an open rally summoned by the Managing Director, the workers booed and jeered at the management, demanded full payment of their salaries and decided to call on the governor of the state to help in resolving the crisis. It was at this point that the police intervened, beat up some of the demonstrators, and arrested 22 of them. Three thousand workers were later dismissed by management, and made to go through an intimidating screening process for re-employment.

This crisis shows the problems involved in trying to resolve capitalist crises with supposedly national objectives of company-viability. Workers were concerned about their short-term livelihood; they therefore co-operated with management to accept cuts in the salaries. Management took advantage of this and tried to extend this indefinitely with the hope of reaping maximum profit. Non co-operation, of course, would have earned them the sack and would have led to the closure of the company. From the short-term perspective it made some sense to accept part payment, but this acceptance played into the hands of capital which wanted to institutionalise it on a more permanent basis. This shows the limitations of isolating the 'national' objectives from the existing structure of property relations; for the pursuit of national objectives at any given time affects the various classes differently. The challenge before the Left is how to make sure that the legitimate national demands of sectoral linkages, use of local raw materials, appropriate technology and the development of an effective capital goods industry does not hamper the struggles of the working class and other oppressed groups for a radical transformation of the economy.

Unfortunately the various solutions from the Left have either been too abstract (Ake 1984; Toyo 1984) or not well formulated to take cognisance of the class struggle. Very often the national objectives have been confused for socialist objectives (Usman 1984a; Abba 1984). For instance the National Workshop on the State of the Economy held at Ahmadu Bello University produced a Green Paper which was supposed to be a rejoinder to the White Paper on the Odama Report on the state of the economy. It was actually a bold attempt to show the evasive character of both the White Paper and the Report on the state of the economy in their diagnoses and solutions to the crisis, and contributed to the raising of popular consciousness on the rapidly deteriorating state of the economy, especially with regard to mismanagement. But by accepting the format and procedures of the White Paper it became a prisoner of that Report and a mere protest document, especially in the area of fundamental restructuring of the economy. It is not surprising that most of the solutions turned out to be bureaucratic and technicist, calling for the nationalisation of foreign trade, the destruction of the contract system and its substitution by direct labour (The Green Paper 1983).

The point needs to be emphasized that it is necessary to respond to the specific policies of the state by shifting the burden of the resolution of the crisis, such as retrenchment, wage freeze, and curtailment of public expenditure from the backs of the working people. This general thrust which calls for the strengthening of democratic and mass political organisations needs to be supported by a clear programme of resolving the national problems of imperialist domination within the context of the general class struggles for the elimination of capitalist property relations.

NOTE

1. I am grateful to colleagues and students for their comments and criticisms following the debate I had with Dr Yusuf Bala Usman on the Nigerian economic crisis. The present paper has built on the paper on 'Overcoming some basic misconceptions of the Nigerian economic crisis' and the joint paper with R. Mustapha and S. Adamu on 'The deepening economic crisis and its political implications'. This is an edited version of a longer paper prepared for the ROAPE Conference.

5

The world recession and its impact on SADCC

Barry Munslow, Peter Phillips, Steve Kibble,
Phil O'Keefe, Paul Goodison and Paul Jourdan

The world recession has exerted its influence throughout and in many similar ways upon different parts of the globe. However, each region and nation state has its own specific circumstances mediating these effects. In southern Africa these specific regional characteristics have tended both to complicate and to intensify the general crisis. Undoubtedly the most important factor has been the bitter regional confrontation precipitated by the continued existence of the white minority apartheid state of South Africa and its colony, Namibia. South Africa is the dominant power in the continent, whether measured in terms of economic strength, technological development or military might, and its influence is felt overwhelmingly in the southern African region.

The economic dominance of South Africa has been built upon, and has deliberately reinforced, the relative weakness and dependence of the surrounding countries. Its emergence as a 'sub-imperialist power' was not always perceived to be in the interests of the imperialist powers themselves, especially Britain. However, the nature of South Africa's rise has for a long time attracted capital from the capitalist centre seeking high profits. The huge volume of western foreign investment has reinforced the existing apartheid state and has produced and perpetuated an increasing dependence and underdevelopment in most of the SADCC countries, which have served as vast labour reserves, dependent on the employment in South Africa of large numbers of their inhabitants. In addition, many of the countries are dependent on South Africa for most imported goods and access to the sea. Of course, there are great differences between, on the one hand, the relatively small degree of economic dependence of Tanzania and Angola and, on the other, the high levels of dependence, of the BLS countries (Botswana, Lesotho, Swaziland), Mozambique, Malawi, Zimbabwe, and Zambia, although these differ markedly in degree. The situation of the labour reserves has changed substantially in recent years, not as the result of development in the SADCC states but rather of South Africa's declining demand for foreign labour. SADCC states have been deprived of their own labour for many decades and developed a degree of dependence on forces beyond their control that is extraordinary, even by third world standards. Drained of labour and largely ignored for most of the colonial period as places worthy of substantial social or economic infrastructural investment, the SADCC countries are some of the poorest and least developed in the world; despite the presence of vast 'natural' resources. Their economies were in no position to face any kind of contraction in the world economy, let alone one so sustained and as severe as this current one, whose costs are so clearly being specifically transferred onto the developing countries.

South Africa's GDP alone is more than twice that of the nine SADCC states combined; it has higher marketed agricultural output, industrial production, energy consumption, rail line and tarred roads. With regard to skilled labour and technological capacity, there is simply no comparison at present.

These facts hold certain implications for individual and collective options within SADCC which we shall later discuss. But we are concerned for the moment with the specific nature of the crisis in southern Africa. Whilst there is most definitely a *regional* crisis, this derives both from the general crisis and the particular historical developments in the southern Africa cone, most notably South Africa's economic domination and politico-military aggression. This has both exacerbated and conditioned the effects of the general crisis on the SADCC states. This is true at the economic level, but also at the levels of political manoeuvring, ideological manipulation and military strategy which form the component parts of a complex regional confrontation.

Western capital's response to the general crisis took on a more aggressive stance from the beginning of the 1980s, although there is no deep-seated uniformity, and significant divisions exist within the West. Criticism of the South African regime from the new right wing governments in the US, Great Britain and Germany diminished, with a renewed emphasis on security of investments, access to raw materials and geopolitical concerns with the struggle against Soviet influence. South Africa was effectively being embraced as an ally with a recognition of its important role within the region. Its importance outweighed concerns in the West about the sensibilities of the SADCC states, the OAU in general, or wider international opinion. Indeed, the very success of South Africa's policy with its diplomatic breakthrough in the signing of the Nkomati Accord with the government of the Peoples Republic of Mozambique made such western support to South Africa all the easier to give. It was only the widespread upsurge of popular struggles in South Africa and the international media attention given to these that was responsible for a limited backing-off from such a hardline stance. The Free South Africa movement in the United States was particularly effective in forcing President Reagan to do a 'U-turn' and impose limited sanctions. This was accompanied, however, by a more aggressive stance towards Angola, with moves being taken to increase support to rebel forces.

The possibility that the SADCC might emerge as a serious competitor to South Africa in attracting new investments has, for the present, disappeared. When crisis hits South Africa, it is of major concern to capital and western governments, as the large unconditional loan from the IMF to South Africa indicated. The smallness of the SADCC economies makes it inevitable, especially in crisis, that capital's interest will remain predominantly in South Africa. The current intensity of the world crisis and the recent ideological and political shifts at the centre reinforce this tendency. In the latter part of 1985, the collapse of the Rand and the freeze on repayments automatically had a serious effect on a number of the SADCC countries (*Africa Economic Digest* 7 September 1985).

In this context, key western governments' economic interests and fundamental political and ideological positions have given South Africa a freer hand to embark on one element of its total strategy – the offensive against its neighbours, particularly those posing the greatest political and ideological threat, and aiming to back this up with increased economic independence. As President Machel of Mozambique has commented, 'The western countries witnessed our destruction passively not concerning themselves with the violence used against our people' (MIO *News Review*

37: 84). The offensive has, of course, been partly an attempt to destroy the African National Congress, but both South Africa's purposes are served by direct or covert military action. There are signs now that the destruction and instability that South Africa and its surrogates have created has gone too far as the West requires a degree of stability, economic growth and social coherence in the region. But whatever the case, the effects on some of the SADCC economies have been disastrous.

The historical legacy of colonialism and the rise of a major sub-imperialist state is reflected throughout the region. The West's regional interest long ago centred on South Africa to the neglect of the rest of the region, except in so far as the supply of labour was concerned. The settler economies of some anglophone countries gained a degree of independence and profited from their subordinate role. The structures that developed in both anglophone and lusophone southern Africa ensured that capitalist agriculture and industry, overshadowed by South Africa and unable to attract sufficient investment, were based on the super-exploitation of labour and, more than usually, on extraction at the expense of development and reinvestment. Agriculture in many areas visibly deteriorated, as a result of labour shortages, land alienation and state discrimination. What emerged as a result of South Africa's rise and the interests of the western powers was an entire regional economic structure, extraordinarily dependent upon both a regional centre and the western capitalist core.

The definition of *Crisis* has to be multidimensional and it is here conceived of in its southern African regional context. It results from a configuration of:

1. the inheritance of a political economy shaped by colonial rule and a distorted pattern of regional development;
2. the all-pervasive influence of the world recession;
3. development strategies which do not successfully address the problem of transition (be it capitalist or socialist) in migrant labour reserve economies dependent upon the remittances of wage labour earnings from capitalist production relations;
4. the direct or indirect effects of economic, social and political destabilisation orchestrated by South Africa; and
5. vulnerability to disaster as a result of the above (by drought, flood or other calamity).

Amongst the most important effects of this crisis and its most obvious manifestations are:

1. the rural crisis of social reproduction;
2. a crisis of developmental strategy; and
3. a political crisis of legitimacy.

Assembling the necessary data upon which to begin one's analysis is a precarious undertaking for a variety of reasons. The first of these is the unreliability of the national data sets available, not least because this reflects the weakness of the state's capacity, the importance of subsistence, and therefore not easily recordable production, and the political and economically important weight attached to the statistics, which may lead to conscious distortions. Secondly, it is our contention that the severe effects of the world recession only became truly apparent from 1979 onwards. The run of figures to 1986, therefore, becomes of crucial importance. This is neither readily available nor easily comparable.

Before attempting to compile a table illustrating the extent of the current economic crisis across all nine SADCC states, let us examine the major economies of the region in turn.

Turning first to Angola, we have here the only oil producer in the region, which is the best economic asset any country could have, so it seemed, following the post-1973 oil price hike. But the oil price proved volatile and the burdens of South African destabilisation and an overly optimistic and indeed unrealistic development strategy counteracted this. Turning first to the balance of payments, total reserves fell from 10,920 million kwanza (1 US dollar = 30 kwanza) in 1978 to 3,467 million kwanza in 1981, only slightly rising to 3,667 million kwanza according to the preliminary figures for 1982 (Bhagavan 1986). Debt servicing (as a percentage of debts to exports) increased from 9.5 to 17.4 per cent between 1980 and 1981. Over the same period the overall balance went from 3,215 million kwanzas to minus 4,989 million kwanzas.

Angola, along with Tanzania, has one of the economies with the least degree of dependence on South Africa. This is why, given its socialist orientation and strong support for SWAPO and the ANC, it was the subject of the most intensive assault, both directly by the South African military occupation of the southern border region and by massive levels of support given to Jonas Savimbi's UNITA movement. Estimates of the economic cost of the South African military invasion of 1975–6 and the destabilisation in the 1976 to 1981 period, totals to a staggering US$7,614 million, or more than twice the GDP for 1980 (Bhagavan 1986). The sheer financial costs do not even begin to illustrate the social costs, which include the displacement of almost three-quarters of a million people by the middle of 1981 (UNDRO 1982) and thousands dead and injured.

In Zimbabwe, GDP declined in real terms by 2 per cent in 1982, by 3 per cent in 1983 and possibly by a further 2 per cent in 1984. Given a population growth rate of 3.5 per cent a year, this means that GDP per head fell 15 per cent in three years (*Financial Gazette* 3 August 1984). From a positive net reserve balance of Zimbabwean $68 million in 1981, the reserve position declined to minus Z$162 million in 1983. This position was only sustainable by a Z$160 million IMF standby facility in 1983. However, prospects improved with the good harvest of 1985, and a real growth of 5 per cent was expected (*Financial Times* 21 August 1985).

In Mozambique, where similarly to Angola, South African destabilisation has been orchestrated on a huge scale, natural disasters have also wreaked their toll and costly mistakes in development policy have been made. The country's economy was closely tied in with, and dependent upon, that of South Africa, leaving small room for manoeuvre, and economic destabilisation was savagely used by Pretoria. Table 5.1 summarises some of these costs to the economy. The current balance in 1980 was minus 9 billion meticais (b.m.), 1981 minus 11.55 b.m., and in 1982 minus 10.77 b.m. Increasing bottlenecks were caused by foreign exchange shortages. Although there are some signs of a reduction in the current account deficit, this is essentially the result of an increase in external grants and the invisible trade surplus. The value of exports is only half that of 1980 or just over. Imports have had to be cut back, and this inevitably creates numerous bottlenecks. Sums expended on equipment are not rising as one might expect. Instead, the cost of raw materials imports rocketed, especially of crude petroleum. The increased expenditure on petroleum reduced possibilities for importing other much needed raw material. There has also been an increase of expenditure on consumer goods. A vicious cycle has been created as export production is highly dependent on imported inputs, hence a downward spiral has ensued with the situation worsened by deteriorating terms of trade. To give only a couple of examples to illustrate the latter point: almost two and a half times as much cotton had to be exported in 1981 than in 1975, in order to purchase one truck; over the same period, more than three and a half times as much sugar had to be exported to purchase one gallon of crude oil. Global Social Product rose in total only 11.6 per cent over the period 1977–81,

TABLE 5.1 Estimate of direct losses and reduction of income, 1978–83

Description of Actions	Meticais (millions)	US Dollars (millions)
1. Effects of colonial economy devastated by war, distorted, highly dependent and in recession	n.a.	—
2. Economic sabotage and abandonment of enterprises, equipment and vehicles of settlers who abandoned the country	n.a.	—
3. Southern Rhodesian sanctions and aggressions, March 1976–February 1980	16,479	556
4. Damages from Limpopo/Incomati river floods in 1977	1,099	34
5. Zambezi river flood damages, 1978	2,095	64
6. Effects of non-declared war by the apartheid regime against People's Republic of Mozambique	131,986	3,796
6.1 Reduction of railway-port traffic, 1975–83	8,460	248
6.2 Non-integral fulfilment of the agreements on miners by South Africa from April 1978	91,289	2,647
6.3 Reduction of official number of the Mozambican miners in South Africa	19,252	568
6.4 Direct aggressions and those carried out through armed bandits in 1982/8	12,985	333
7. Direct damages from drought in the South and Centre of the country in 1982 and 1983	6,200	154
8. Effects of the increase in oil prices from 1975	34,069	819
9. Reduction in the export income due to drought, deterioration of international terms of exchange 1980–82, and actions of bandits armed by the South African regime	3,659	131
10. Total 2–9	195,587	5,554

Source: National Planning Commission, Peoples Republic of Mozambique, *Economic Report*, Maputo, January 1984.

barely keeping pace with the population increase. But it fell 6.9 per cent in 1981–2 and continued to fall further thereafter (PRM National Planning Commission 1984). In 1982 Global Social Product was given as 90.7 billion meticais (32 meticais – 1 US$) and this fell to 76.5 billion meticais in 1983. The decline continued and economic activity fell by 20 per cent in 1985 compared with the previous year (MIO 1985).

At 1980 prices, per capita GDP in Tanzania fell 6.6 per cent in 1981 and an estimated 7.8 per cent in 1982. The deficit on current account (in US$ million) was 350 in 1979, 530 in 1980, 280 in 1981 and an estimated 300 in 1982 (Lloyds Bank 1984). External debt rose 12.7 per cent per annum from 1978 to 1982.

In Zambia, GDP per capita fell a dramatic 11.5 per cent in 1979, 0.2 per cent in 1980 and 3.9 per cent in 1981 (Lloyds Bank 1983). Deficit on current account (US$ million) was 566 in 1980, 654 in 1981 and 600 in 1982. By 1981 external debt was US$ 2,293.8.

In Malawi, GDP per capita fell 2.2 per cent in 1980, 3.2 per cent in 1981 but showed a small estimated positive growth in 1982 of 0.4 per cent (Lloyds Bank 1983). Deficit on current account was (US$ million) 76.5 in 1981 and an estimated 117.6 in 1982.

If we try now to produce comparable figures for some, if not all, of the SADCC countries, then with the foregoing country data, they vividly emphasise the desperate and deteriorating position of the SADCC countries as a whole. Turning first to examine the terms of trade, comparable figures for only five of the countries are possible, because the BLS countries are in the South African Customs Union, and Zimbabwe underwent 15 years of sanctions. Table 5.2 provides the data on net barter terms of trade and income terms of trade.

TABLE 5.2 SADCC terms of trade

| | *net barter terms of trade (1975=100)* | | |
	1960	*1970*	*1979*
Malawi	115	99	85
Mozambique	90	88	75
Tanzania	98	103	102
Zambia	115	227	100
Angola	60	68	113
	Income terms of trade (1978=100)		
	1960	*1970*	*1979*
Malawi	40	83	112
Mozambique	89	167	32
Tanzania	118	154	104
Zambia	99	238	91
Angola	30	93	102

Source: World Bank 1983a, Annex Table 13

According to the World Bank, the terms of trade of low income African countries have continued to decline since 1979, and the terms of trade between manufacturers and non-oil commodities (i.e. SADCC exports, apart from Angola) have moved sharply in favour of manufactures (World Bank 1983a: 28 and 30). An idea of the trend, is given by Tanzania's estimated 50 per cent fall in external terms of trade between 1977 and 1982, in fact mostly since 1979 (Green 1983: 111) and a 14 per cent nominal decline in Zambia's copper exports value between 1979 and 1981. Some countries have, of course, fared better. Angola has benefited from rising oil prices, though it has consequently suffered a fall in terms of trade since 1979. Zimbabwe had a one-off large improvement in terms of trade when sanctions were lifted. Botswana's diamonds exports have different trends on world markets than most commodities. Mozambique's terms of trade, however, have fallen disastrously in just two years, 1980–82, by 24 per cent (UNIDO Country Report 1984).

It is not, therefore, at all surprising that the deficits on balance of payments present a similarly gloomy picture, as shown in Table 5.3. Again, figures are not comprehensive and comparable for the same years.

TABLE 5.3 Balance of payments of SADCC countries (in current US$ million, unless otherwise stated)

	1979	Current Account Balance 1980	1981	1982	
Angola	−5,430	−1,030	−18,469	−6,200	(in million kwanzas, 30= 1US$, 1982 is preliminary)
Botswana	36.7	−79	−272		
Malawi	9.0	67.2	−76.5	−117.6	
Mozambique		−9,000	11,550	−10,770	(in millions of current Meticals; 1US$ = 38 MT
Tanzania	−345	−534	−278		
Zambia	− 11	−566	−654	−600	(1982 is provisional)
Zimbabwe	−73.9	−156.7	−439.6	−532.9	(millions of current Zimbabwean dollars)

Notes: Lesotho's 1979 balance on current account before debt payments was US$22 million. Swaziland had a balance of trade on visible exports and imports of – E 221.58 million (when E 1 = 0.9US$ approx.) in 1982.
Sources: Lloyds Bank Group Economic Report on Botswana (1983); Malawi (1983); Tanzania (1984); Zambia (1983); and Zimbabwe (1984); UNIDO (1984); Bhagavan (1986); World Bank (1981b); Appendix, table 17 (Lesotho); Central Bank of Swaziland, *Quarterly Review*, March 1984

For the seven countries where we have obtained figures for several years, it is noticeable that the only countries to have kept their deficits fairly stable, were already in a desperate situation. It suggests that they have been forced to reduce imports below those essentials for consumption and maintaining production, whereas previously they had continued to import these, borrowing in the hope of an upturn in world demand for exports etc. Since 1979, the position of Botswana, Malawi, Zambia and Zimbabwe has deteriorated rapidly.

The desire to maintain imports has contributed to a rapid growth of debt in the SADCC countries (see Table 5.4). combined with the deterioration in the terms of borrowing which we presented earlier, and which were especially severe for Africa, this has resulted in a position where much of the export earnings of SADCC countries are already accounted for in servicing the debt; in other words, it flows straight back to the centre.

We have not been able to obtain reliable figures for the debt service ratio for Mozambique. However, UNIDO estimates (UNIDO 1984: 12–13) that Mozambique's external debt, *excluding* debts to centrally-planned economies, was, in April 1983, US$3,200, or Œ27Œ times the estimated value of exports for the whole of 1983. Only if the average interest payable on this debt is less than 3.5 per cent per annum will current exports cover interest payments quite apart from repayment of the principal. The ratio, therefore, must be several hundred per cent. It is perhaps not surprising to

TABLE 5.4 SADCC debt-ratios (payments on public debt as per cent of exports of goods and services)

	1979	*1980*	*1981*
Angola		9.5	17.4
Botswana	1.6	1.7	1.5
Lesotho	0.9	1.4	2.9
Malawi	15.9	18.5	24.5
Swaziland	2.7	3.2	3.6
Tanzania	7.5	8.8	20–30[a]
Zambia	18.0	22.2	24.0
Zimbabwe	1.2	2.6	4.4

Note: [a] Estimate
Sources: Angola: Bhagavan (1985); others: World Bank, 1983: Statistical Annex, Table 4

find that Mozambique has joined the IMF and has undertaken complex debt rescheduling discussions following the visit to the country by the Paris Club fact-finding mission in May 1984.

The evidence from this collection of data indicates that the position of SADCC countries as a whole is among the worst in the world in terms of how they are affected by the accumulative effects of the recession and the regional crisis. South African destabilisation has directly affected Angola, Lesotho, Mozambique, Zambia and Zimbabwe, not least by the financing of armed bands to operate in these countries. The blockade of Lesotho at the beginning of 1986 which precipitated the coup against Chief Jonathan and the installing of a government more amenable to South Africa's dictates, was an extreme indication of this process. Indirectly it has affected even the most conservative of the SADCC states, Malawi and Swaziland, interrupting their imports and exports, and thereby damaging their economies. The drought has had a devastating effect on several of the countries. Table 5.5 shows the cereal supply position as of March 1984. In the concluding section of this chapter, we will try to argue that the extent of the crisis offers renewed prospects for regional co-operation, but implies a rethink of both national and regional development strategies given the myriad constraints which close down certain options. But we now turn to the sectoral issues.

Sectoral issues

We will now briefly outline some of the key issues and problems in the main sectors of SADCC activity: industry, transport, agriculture, energy and minerals.

Industry

The restructuring of industrial production that took place in the world in the late 1960s and the 1970s did not substantially benefit sub-Saharan Africa. In 1980, this region accounted for only an estimated 1 per cent of world manufacturing value-added (UNIDO 1981: 31). Within the region, low income countries contributed an even smaller proportion, and the growth rate for all low-income industrial output (we use industry and manufacturing interchangeably, to include mineral and agricultural

TABLE 5.5 Cereal supply position in SADCC countries with abnormally high cereal import requirements (quantities in thousand tons)

Country	Cereal production forecast (1983)	Total import needs (1982/3 or 1983)	Total imports (est.) 1982/3 or 1983	Total import needs 1983/4 or 1984	Total needs covered March 1984 (000 tons)
Angola	350	350	303	290	219
Botswana	14	150	150	160	150
Lesotho	120	160	160	180	156
Mozambique	330	400	254	550	447
Swaziland	45	75	75	110	74
Zambia	990	310	247	270	168
Zimbabwe	1,425	50	50	180	84
Total	3,274	1,495	1,239	1,740	1,298

Sources: Estimates based on the latest available official and unofficial information collected through the FAO Global Information and Early Warning System

In 1982, Malawi's industrial output fell 4.4 per cent (Lloyds Bank 1983), and that of Mozambique 13.64 per cent (UNIDO 1984). The industrial exports of Swaziland fell 20 per cent in 1982/3, and those of Tanzania 40 per cent in 1981 and even further in 1982 (Lloyds Bank 1984). Tanzanian industry is now operating at around one-quarter of capacity, down from 70 per cent in 1978, whilst most Zambian industry is operating at between 25 and 50 per cent of capacity. Zimbabwean industrial output fell 8 per cent between 1981 and 1984 (*Financial Times* 21 August 1985). Cuts in foreign exchange allocations have significantly reduced capacity utilisation since then. For almost all SADCC countries, predictions were that industrial output would continue to contract at least in the short term.

Not only is industry a small proportion of GDP in most SADCC states and dominated by the other productive sectors, it is also extremely structurally weak. The share of heavy industry is 34.2 per cent in industrial output for the SADCC as a whole; only in Zimbabwe (49.2 per cent) does heavy industry account for more than 30 per cent of all industrial output (Peet 1984: figures for various years). By contrast, heavy industry accounted for 64.5 per cent of all world industrial output and 54.8 per cent of processing but to *exclude* mining, construction, and energy and water) was the lowest for the third world between 1960 and 1975 (UNIDO 1979: 30). Central Africa had the lowest industrial growth rate of all Africa during the 1970s, an annual average of only 2 per cent (UNECA 1981: 56). The SADCC region as a whole is low to middle income, with industry forming a small part of GDP. Table 5.6 gives the annual growth of industry and its contribution to GDP compared with all other productive sectors; that is, agriculture, mining, construction, and electricity, water and gas.

Comprehensive post-1979 figures for SADCC industry are not available. However, the data we have obtained suggests that a major contraction is occurring in most countries' industrial sectors as a result of the crisis. This contraction itself is contributing to the severity and intractability of the regional crisis.

TABLE 5.6 Industrial growth rates and industry's contribution to GDP

	Industrial sector average annual growth rate (%)	1979 % of GDP	Other productive sectors (% of GDP)
Angola	−12.0	3	68
Botswana	n.a.	4.2	47
Lesotho	10.2	2.0	49
Malawi	6.7	12.0	51
Mozambique	−5.8	9.0	51
Swaziland	n.a.	22.0	32
Tanzania	3.6	9.0	58
Zambia	0.4	16.0	40
Zimbabwe	2.8	25.0	26
All	1.3	13.0	48

Note: n.a. = not available
Sources: World Bank 1981a: Annex, Tables 2 and 3; Peet 1984

developing countries output in 1975. Zimbabwe accounts for 37.5 per cent of total SADCC industrial output and *54* per cent of its heavy industry.

The wide consensus on the importance of industry for development, and the consensus among many radical commentators on the central role of heavy industry for SADCC development and economic independence, would appear to be justified on the basis of these figures – but we will go on to question this as providing a viable strategic guideline in the immediate crisis and under the given constraints. Light industry currently dominates, based on the processing of local mineral and agricultural products for export and domestic consumption. Industrial output is geared to luxury demand rather than supplying the population with essential goods. The causes of such an uneven development can be traced to the political economy of colonialism and the emergence of South Africa as a sub-imperialist regional power. In South Africa, and on a much smaller scale, Southern Rhodesia, poles of growth developed, draining the surrounding areas of labour, expanding their own infrastructure and industrial capacity at the expense of other countries and their own 'black' rural areas.

The SADCC industrial structure exhibits a high dependence on imported inputs, even in Zimbabwe. In addition, industrial growth within the present structure depends on the prosperity of the agricultural and mining sectors (directly and through their effects on employment, foreign exchange and GDP), and on world demand for processed exports. Industrial activity in the SADCC is not at present dictated by the real needs of the population, but by the profitability of foreign and local capital and by the conditions in the world economy.

With the exception of Angola and Mozambique, the crisis in southern Africa has only become acute in the last five years, with increased South African aggression, renewed global recession, and the adoption of monetarist/deflationary policies in the capitalist centre. The effects on industry in the SADCC have been catastrophic for some countries, though comprehensive data is not available for a thorough comparative evaluation. Part of the cause has been sabotage and destruction by South Africa through the MNR in Mozambique and UNITA in Angola. For most SADCC countries, industry has contracted 'consequentially', through the world recession's effects on other economic sectors and GDP, a consequence that is, of industry's weakness and dependence in the SADCC countries economic structures.

We argue that the urgent priority in the current crisis is *physical survival*. This being so, it is necessary to direct policy and planning towards the immediate satisfaction of basic needs, combined with a development strategy that will ensure *future* basic needs through regional self-reliance. This means that the priority for industry is to: 1) provide the essential inputs for agricultural production and 2) manufacture essential consumer goods that will satisfy the needs of the rural population, thereby providing a stimulus for them to produce and market an agricultural surplus.

In the context of world industrial excess capacity, export-led industrialisation can have little chance of success. A similar argument holds for import-substitution strategies which, in addition, require high import spending and do not generally cater for essential goods. In the light of the crisis, short-term measures must be adopted in industrial development. However, these should not be seen as simply bridging the gap until changed external conditions allow resumption of import-substitution and export-orientation. On the contrary, these short-term measures must be capable of creating the basis for a long-term strategy of self-reliance in which demand is determined by mass needs and increasingly converges with production that is democratically controlled and employs physical and human resources available within the region. We do not see this as an 'option' but as the only way forward *in the current crisis*.

Transport

Along with other major sectors of the economy, the issues facing the SADCC countries in the transport sector derive from the combined effect of structures inherited from colonialism, South African domination, and the severe nature of the general and regional crises.

The transport systems inherited from colonial rule resulted directly from the nature of the colonial involvement and from the emergence of South Africa as a sub-imperialist power. Transport systems were constructed, as the SADCC has noted, 'based on the concept of creating subsidiary systems to that of South Africa'. Railway lines radiated out from South Africa as the 'interior' was 'opened up', in the search for raw materials and settlers' search for gold and good land. Mozambique's transport 'network' in fact comprised several isolated rail-port routes serving the landlocked British colonies for transit to the sea and neglecting Mozambique's own need for transport. The construction of tarred roads was minimal, concentrating on linking the settler population centres to one another and to the major areas of mining and commercial agriculture. In short, transport has developed according to the existing or intended needs of foreign and settler capital, both creating and responding to economies that were and remain highly trade-dependent. Transport links between SADCC countries are very poor, except where the external trade of one passes through another, and even at the national level the transport systems do not contribute to an integrated economic structure, but rather reinforce the uneven development that characterises the region. Most of all, most of the rural population does not have access to *efficient and reliable modes* of transport.

South Africa now has 65 per cent of the tarred road mileage of southern Africa, and

60 per cent of total African railway track. Six of the SADCC states are land-locked, and five of these are heavily dependent on the South African ports, railways and roads for the movement of their exports and imports. This gives South Africa power over SADCC economic prosperity and development, and in the context of acute food shortages, over the physical survival of many citizens of the SADCC states. It makes transport the sector in which SADCC dependence on South Africa is most marked, most visible and most critical. As a result, at its inception, SADCC gave the transport sector clear priority for regional co-operation and appeal for foreign aid. The formation of the Southern African Transport and Communications Committee (SATCC) reflected this priority.

The present level of transport dependence is not just the result of the transport infrastructure created under colonialism. It also derives from the general and regional crises. Economic decline and lack of foreign exchange have led to serious underinvestment in transport in several countries in recent years. Liberation struggles added to (or preceded) this deterioration, but most important has been the identification by South Africa of the transport sector as vital in ensuring its continued regional domination. The attacks by South Africa and its surrogate groups on railways in Mozambique and Angola are the most obvious demonstrations of the aim of maintaining transport dependence, but other tactics have been used, such as withholding imports, slowing exports, withdrawing loaned engines, rolling stock, technical staff, and so on.

The result of these factors has been that the SADCC transport infrastructure is incapable of operating at anywhere near the level of installed capacity, and therefore unable to fulfil its primary function of serving economic structures geared to trade. Only intensive use of South African routes enables the landlocked SADCC states to maintain their levels of trade, and the earnings from transit trade, on which the Mozambican economy had become so dependent, have been severely depressed.

The present transport infrastructure reflects the SADCC states' position in the international division of labour, as exporters of raw materials and processed primary products to the capitalist centre. Though it reflects patterns of trade, it also plays a vital role in reinforcing and perpetuating them. Therefore, SADCC's focus on the existing infrastructure contains the danger of prolonging or deepening SADCC's exploitation and underdevelopment, whilst reduction of dependence on South Africa in this way threatens to replace it with an increased structural dependence on the capitalist centre. The dilemma is that survival in the present crisis and scarcity of resources suggests the best use of existing economic capacities, i.e. to concentrate on exports, whilst such a strategy is not confronting the causes of current economic problems in SADCC states.

Of all sectors, transport has been the best supported by Western donors so far (although still representing only about one-quarter of the required foreign exchange) and it is useful to consider why this is so. The SATCC projects offer Western governments easier access to a number of raw materials and the prospect of future 'market penetration'. For many TNCs operating in the SADCC states, improved transport promises increased profits, and for contractors in the transport sector, tied aid gives large contracts during a severe domestic recession. Unfortunately, such advantages lead to the conclusion that donor support would have been lower if SATCC projects had concentrated on smaller national and intra-regional transport links.

Agriculture

With few exceptions agriculture in the SADCC countries has fared no better than in the continent as a whole. The latest World Bank report indicates that in recent years, per capita income and output are both lower than in 1970, hence 15 or more years of development have effectively been lost. The extended period of drought ensured poor harvests, and this even affected South Africa, normally a net food exporter, which in 1984 had to import some four million tons of staple foods at a cost of 800 million rand (*Financial Times* 8 August 1984). SADCC estimates suggest that given current trends in population growth and food production, whilst the region was 95 per cent sufficient in home-grown foods in 1979–81, it will only be, in the words of the Minister responsible for food security within SADCC, 'a terrifying 64 per cent by the turn of the century' (Norman 1984). Present grain imports of 1.8 million tons will have to rise to over 8 million tons to cover such a deficit. The agriculture sector is by far the most important of all; it is the most complex and least amenable to abbreviated treatment and here we will only touch on certain key issues for discussion.

The essence of the agricultural crisis for many of the SADCC states is the culmination of the historical development of a regional sub-system based on the creation of migrant labour reserves. These subsidised the reproduction of the labour force and thereby permitted higher levels of capital accumulation to occur. At the same time earnings from off-farm income were important both to establish and to maintain the peasant family farming unit. Recession, transformations in the organic composition of mining, manufacturing and agrarian capital, the upheavals caused by socialist transition in Angola and Mozambique, and the regional confrontation with South Africa have severely restricted the wage-labour earning opportunities for many households. Wage earnings for many peasant families have declined and the poorest families in the rural areas are usually found to be those with no off-farm income at all, especially female-headed households. Yet the wage rises of the 1970s meant that those families with well positioned wage labourers are better off; hence there is evidence of a process of greater rural differentiation taking place, yet this remains a fluid situation (Murray 1981; First 1983).

On the other side, sales from cash crop production have been constrained by depressed world prices and the too low producer prices fixed by many SADCC governments in an attempt to follow a cheap food policy for the urban areas. In many cases the problem is further compounded by an absence of goods for peasants to purchase; hence there is a double disincentive to market surplus production and a withdrawal by the peasantry into subsistence production.

This double squeeze upon the peasantry in the context of the bitter regional confrontation creates an enormous vulnerability to hazard, be it drought, flood or cyclone. Many deaths have occurred as a result – particularly in southern Mozambique, southwest Zimbabwe and in central and southern Angola. Underlying the malaise of agriculture is a crisis of social reproduction (see Bush, Cliffe and Jansen, Chapter 23).

There is a growing disparity between the returns to agriculture and the returns to migrant labour which is likely to prove a major impediment to agricultural development initiatives. This is probably best illustrated if we explore the Swazi experience with the early stages of its Rural Development Areas Programme. In the case of Swaziland only 18 per cent of homesteads have no member in wage employment. The expectation of employment is firmly established in most Swazi families, and as long as jobs are available they will be sought. This expectation and the added security it can bring – as it is a regular weekly income not subject to the vagaries of the weather – is a major factor in the operation of the RDAP. Since 1976/7, 45 million emalangeni (2.14 emalangeni = £1 sterling) has been spent on the RDAP which is the equivalent of 1,691.7 per household or 198.2 per person. The return to this investment in terms of production has been disappointing. Yields have remained static and well below attainable possibilities. Effectively, farmers are producing just enough to satisfy their own consumption needs. Fewer hectares were being planted as a result of increasing productivity, through applying more fertiliser and using higher-yielding hybrid varieties. The time saved is then invested in off-farm income earning. In 1980/81 3 per cent less production was achieved than in 1979/80, but on 22 per cent less land. If the yields in the former years had been achieved on the greater area of land previously planted, Swaziland's maize gap would have practically closed. Low productivity is not an intrinsic feature of the peasant system but is a contextual feature determined by the level of support given to the peasant sector both directly and indirectly, and equally important, the alternative income-earning opportunities in the wider society, which in the context of southern Africa cannot fail to take into account the overbearing influence of the dominant regional economy, South Africa.

, The scissors effect of low producer prices coupled with rising input costs is contributing to the withdrawal of peasant producers from the official economy and the massive burgeoning of parallel markets – most noticeably in Tanzania, Zambia, Angola and Mozambique. Governments have to consider whether there is less of a danger in paying higher producer prices necessitating a rise in food prices, or by continuing to keep these artificially low causing acute shortages on official markets with astronomical prices on parallel markets. Both the equity and the efficacy effects of the latter course are highly questionable. Not least because in the two extreme cases of Angola and Mozambique, there is both a breakdown in rural urban linkages plus a strain on the worker-peasant alliance (which is meant to provide the class base of support for the regime) and a return to barter trade with currency becoming virtually worthless.

Peasant producers in many areas have been deprived of the best land by a policy of giving priority to commercial, plantation or state farms and these have commanded the overwhelming majority of state support, investment, access to inputs and transportation routes and back-up research. In Zimbabwe in particular, but also in Swaziland, the issue of land reform looms large on the agenda. It is not in the interests of the regional, national or even peasant economies, for the highly productive and *efficient* amongst these three forms of production unit to be abandoned. A section of the white commercial farmers in Zimbabwe make a substantial contribution to food production and export earnings. Yet some are inefficient and there is strong evidence of the underutilisation of good arable land (Weiner *et al*. 1985). Generally a greater emphasis on support to the peasantry is required and this requires a rethinking of the relationship of the state with the peasantry (Bernstein 1981; Cliffe and Munslow 1985).

The importance of the surplus-producing commercial farmers was clearly shown by the contrasting ability of the Zimbabwean and Mozambican states to keep alive their populations during the drought of 1982–3. The Zimbabwean state kept two and a half million people alive over the worst of the drought period, and relief supplies only finished in April 1984. This was the result of predominantly commercial farm produced surpluses stored from the excellent 1981 harvest of the 'Mugabe rains'. The Mozambican state had no such surpluses to call upon. But a further difference was also the level of destabilisation engendered from South Africa. External food aid arrived in the Mozambican ports, but it was mainly MNR activities, plus limited storage facilities and transportation problems which prevented the relief getting through to many parts of the south of the country. Tens of thousands died whilst others made their way to neighbouring countries seeking refuge. It would be hard to overestimate the negative effects on rural development and agricultural production of the successful South African destabilisation policy. The Nkomati Accords held out, albeit only briefly, a prospect of peace, to enable the government of Mozambique to implement its changed policy emphasis following the Frelimo Fourth Party Congress of 1983, which rightly stressed support to family and co-operative production and a reduction of the state farms. The latter have been broken down into smaller more manageable units with some being turned over to peasant production and others to joint ventures with agricapital, which at least has the managerial ability and track record to produce food and export surpluses, with a political voice which can be raised within those circles that are actively engineering destabilisation and which may have some influence to restrain it – that at least is the hope and the thinking within government circles. The evidence to date suggests that economic rationale will not outweigh Boer ideology.

The recent Zimbabwean case has illustrated the capacity of the peasants to produce, when given the necessary incentives and state support. The percentage of maize sold to the Grain Marketing Board by communal farmers expanded from 14 per cent in 1981, to 23 per cent in 1982, to 25 per cent (the worst drought year) in 1983, with the figures for 1984 (*The Herald* 6 September 1984) showing 35 per cent of commercial maize deliveries coming from communal and resettlement peasant farmers (but overwhelmingly the former). Deliveries in 1985 were even more spectacular. These figures indicate that Zimbabwe's dependence on the commercial farm sector in maize production is decreasing. Bratton (1983) reminds us that co-operative endeavours can also be successful in encouraging production, especially in the purchasing of inputs and in marketing. Furthermore, most governments fail to identify a crucial element of rural production by their consideration of women's labour as non-productive (Ong 1985). The role of women in the labour reserve economies has to be considered. This is essential in particular, for the successful formulation of an agricultural and an energy strategy.

In Zimbabwe, recent research has suggested that labour shortages have constrained the area of land cropped by the peasantry (Callear 1983). There is also evidence that cropped areas (and yields of course), are higher in better rainfall areas. This indicates that peasants are allocating more labour time in areas where returns per unit input are higher and illustrates that the reproduction squeeze has different effects on households and sub-national regions depending on the role of the state vis-à-vis the peasantry; the importance of off-farm versus on-farm income in overall reproduction; and the environmental and capital constraints towards achieving more on-farm income through increased yields. National level variations, along with internal policies, have increasingly been influenced by South African destabilisation and the process of decolonisation. No agricultural strategy can work where links between town and country are severed, extension workers cannot get into the rural areas and marketing facilities are grossly inadequate. Although the agricultural stagnation in Tanzania and Zimbabwe is clearly not caused by external aggression, death as a result of starvation in Mozambique and Angola is. Peace is not going to resolve the region's agrarian crisis but it will certainly alleviate it.

Energy

The SADCC countries face a double energy crisis, deriving on the one hand from higher oil prices and on the other from increasingly rapid depletion of wood resources. This has an immediate effect on living conditions as well as serious consequences for economic and social development.

The energy crisis in SADCC is characterised by special features related to the historical development of class and gender relations and economic structures. It has also recently displayed a unique feature in the identification of energy as a strategic sector in the regional confrontation (Munslow and O'Keefe 1984).

Earlier in this chapter, we drew attention to the disastrous balance of payments position of most SADCC states. Despite supplying a very small part of total energy demand, oil imports account for a large proportion of the foreign exchange earnings of the SADCC countries (Angola is excepted). The bulk of this oil is used in transport. Demand reductions therefore require either technical conservation (usually involving large capital outlays) or restrictions on transport, especially private cars (which has incalculable consequences in some countries). However, since Angola could produce enough oil to meet SADCC's needs, and refining capacity is almost sufficient (though not of the required 'mix'), oil could provide a perfect opportunity for SADCC planning and co-operation (Simoes 1984). Indeed, Angola has already offered to supply all SADCC's oil needs. The crucial problems are agreement on price, transport, and most seriously, the method of payment.

Along with oil, SADCC has such large resources of coal, hydroelectric power and solar potential, and wood, as well as natural gas (with much of the region yet to be carefully surveyed) that the talk of a crisis seems absurd. However, to transform potential into actual supply requires the combined action of capital and labour. This action needs to be promoted by economic motive and/or political will.

The political economy of colonialism, which has largely conditioned present structures, has meant that energy developed only where this was itself profitable or where energy was necessary for the profitability of capital in other sectors. Energy supplies were not brought into existence to meet the real needs of the population. As a result, the growth of the energy sector has been highly uneven. 'Commercialised' energy has not been supplied at the right places, in suitable form or at affordable prices to meet mass needs. Most people still depend on 'traditional' fuels, predominantly fuelwood. The result of regional structures has been highly uneven and unbalanced energy systems in the SADCC countries, reflecting and perpetuating international and internal power relations. These systems are extremely vulnerable to shocks and indeed contain contradictions which make crisis inevitable, in a way similar to the crisis inherent in the reserve labour system.

This brings us to the second aspect of the energy crisis – depletion of wood resources, deforestation, and increasing local wood scarcity. In the labour reserve system, with 'traditional' energy sources performing a parallel function to that of subsistence agriculture such a crisis of wood supplies is inevitable. It has been exacerbated by several factors. Firstly, the increasing 'costs' of rural and peri-urban energy supplies have been hidden, requiring greater unpaid labour time by women, but also the increasing commoditisation of a formerly free good. This increased labour burden has fallen overwhelmingly on women, who are neither a major political force nor of great concern to urban-based, male-dominated authorities. The problem is complex, local, and emerges only gradually. It has therefore been largely ignored until fairly recently, but increasing population pressure and no access to other energy sources have now caused a situation in which wood-harvesting is faster than annual incremental growth, and stocks thus decline, setting in train a downward spiral in wood supplies (see O'Keefe and Munslow, eds 1984, for detailed case studies of all nine SADCC countries). Serious local shortages have become very common, rural people are reducing energy consumption with detrimental effects on health and nutrition. Local shortages threaten to become widespread deforestation, with enormous implications for soil erosion, flooding, water retention and soil fertility. This aspect of the energy crisis, therefore, threatens the environment as a whole, endangering subsistence farming, large-scale agriculture, and causing rapid desertification. It is these dangers, more than the extra labour burden on women of longer hours collecting wood, which have forced the government to attend to the rural energy crisis.

Minerals

With the exception of petroleum in Angola, diamonds in Botswana, Angola and Tanzania, and gold in Zimbabwe the SADCC minerals/metals fall into the worst hit, non-fuel and non-precious group (see Tables 5.7 and 5.8).

TABLE 5.7 SADCC: Principal exports
(percentage of total exports)

Country		Principal exports	
Angola	(1983)	oil	84
		diamonds	8
		coffee	5
Botswana	(1984)	diamonds	66
		copper-nickel malte	8
		meat	7
Lesotho	(1981)	diamonds	40
		wool/mohair	18
Malawi	(1984)	tobacco	52
		tea	25
		sugar	7
Mozambique	(1983)	prawns	24
		oil products	18
		cashew and oil	15
		tea	14
		cotton fibre	7
Swaziland	(1982)	sugar	33
		chemicals	17
		wood pulp	15
		fruit	10
		electronics	5
Tanzania	(1982)	coffee	30
		cloves	18
		cotton	12
		cashew	6
		sisal	6
Zambia	(1984)	copper	84
Zimbabwe	(1982)	tobacco	20
		gold	15
		ferro-alloys	8
		asbestos	6
Namibia	(1981)	uranium	30
		diamonds	23
		other minerals	15
		meat	7

Sources: Economist Intelligence Unit 1984; IMF (1986)

TABLE 5.8 SADCC, South Africa, Namibia, Zaire: production of major minerals
1982

Mineral/Metal	SADCC Total	Proportion of western world (%)	South Africa	Namibia	Zaire
Gold (metric tons (mt))	13.8	1.4	664.3	—	4.2
Nickel ('000 mt)	31.2	8.0	205.0	—	—
Copper ('000 mt)	573.0	9.0	207.0	49	503.0
High carbon ferro chrome ('000 mt)	200.0	12.0	570.0	—	503.0
Diamonds (carats)	9,470.0	28.0	8,850.0	1,010	1,000.0

Sources: US Bureau of Mines, *Minerals Yearbook*, 1982; *Metal Statistics* 1972–82

Most SADCC metals/minerals have declined in real value over the last 15 years and dramatically declined in both export value and volume since the onset of the present world crisis (see Tables 5.9 and 5.10). The causes for this are manifold, but the most important are the following three. First, unlike petroleum and tin which have strong producer organisations (OPEC and the ITC) to combat attempts by the developed countries to export their crisis to the periphery, in the form of declining terms of trade (manufactures vs commodities) the SADCC minerals (see Tables 5.7 and 5.8) are 'unprotected'. The worst cases are copper and nickel which in 1983 were worth 46 and 36 per cent respectively of their 1970 unit value (Shearson American Express 1984).

TABLE 5.9 Change in export prices in developing countries (average annual % change)

	1965–73	1973–80	1981	1982	1983
Metals and minerals	1.6	5.6	−12.0	−3.0	−2.2
Fuels	6.7	24.7	10.5	−26.0	−14.5

Source: World Bank 1984: Table 2.7

TABLE 5.10 Change in export volumes and value of exports in developing
countries, 1965–83

	(average annual % change)					Value of exports	
	65–73	73–80	1981	1982	1983	1965	1981
Metals and minerals	6.3	5.9	2.6	−2.1	−1.9	4.5	26.9
Fuels	6.4	−1.3	−21.9	5.1	6.1	7.3	165.1

Source: World Bank 1984a: Table 2.9

In addition, Western consumption dropped 9 per cent for copper and 25 per cent for nickel between 1979 and 1982 (see Table 5.11). The SADCC region accounted for 9 per cent of copper and 8 per cent of nickel production in the western world in 1982 (see Table 5.8).

TABLE 5.11 Western world metal consumption (production), 1976–82

	1976	1977	1978	1979	1980	1981	1982
Aluminium (t million)	14.0	14.5	15.3	16.2	15.6	15.1	14.7
Lead (t million)	3.9	4.2	4.2	4.2	3.9	3.8	3.8
Copper (t million)	6.4	6.8	7.5	7.2	7.2	7.3	6.8
Zinc (t thousand)	4.2	4.2	4.7	4.5	4.5	4.4	4.2
Tin (t thousand)	184	174	178	178	167	156	146
Nickel (t thousand)	488	459	524	584	527	474	439
Gold (+)*	869	972	980	961	946	962	971
Silver (+)*	7,769	8,357	8,381	8,431	8,157	8,721	9,054

* Mine production   t – metric ton
Sources: Metallgesselschaft, 1983, p. 16–62; Shearson, American Express, 1984, Table 3.3

Diamonds, on the other hand, have a TNC marketing monopoly, the De Beer's Central Selling Organisation (CSO), which has managed to maintain the real value of diamonds except for the diamond crisis of 1980/1 when the CSO temporarily lost control of the price as a result of excessive speculation by diamond buyers. Diamond production increased in volume from 41 million carats in 1977 to 57 million carats in 1983 (*Engineering and Mining Journal* March 1984: 90) and the CSO sales increased by 27 per cent from US$1,257 million to US$1,599 million from 1982 to 1983 (De Beers 1983; 1984). From the end of 1968 to the end of 1983 the real value of rough diamonds increased by 57 per cent (Ousey 1984). The second reason is that precious metals/minerals benefit from speculation provoked by the economic uncertainty prevalent at the onset of crises, which does not apply to the non-precious metals whose prices drop rapidly with falling industrial demand.

This brings us to the third, developing country-specific, dynamic. Mineral exports for many third world economies are the major means of earning hard currency, so when the unit value of their mineral(s) declines, they attempt to increase their production and sales so as to avoid cutting back on vital imports. In this way supply often increases or remains constant during periods of falling demand resulting in an oversupplied 'buyers market' and low prices. These lower prices provoke a further increase in production to maintain foreign currency flows by the third world producers which again results in lower prices, and so the downward spiral continues.

As a result of falling foreign exchange earnings aggravated by high interest rates stemming from the OECD crisis, third world mineral economies have 'extensive loans to pay off and their need for foreign currency is so great that production must continue unabated' (Shearson/American Express 1984: 5), resulting in oversupply and lower prices. In addition, mining tends to be capital intensive, requiring large imports of capital goods which with the prevailing low prices is often financed by loans, increasing debt servicing commitments. Other hard currency costs such as the mining TNC's profit repatriation or management fees and expatriate salaries are common for third world mining industries.

Conclusions

We are fully aware of the extreme limitations imposed by a chapter which purports to cover nine widely diverse countries, across all sectors, in a few pages and at a time of extreme and complex crisis. This offering is only intended as an initial contribution to such an endeavour, and represents work in progress. If at times we have placed the arguments in a rather simplified and overtly stark form, this has been with the aim of shifting the terrain of debate to a full and deep appreciation of the extent of the crisis among the SADCC states which all indicators suggest will only deepen in the short term.

We have described a situation in which the SADCC countries essentially face a struggle of survival and this has to be the starting point from which any analysis and prognosis begins. We have argued that survival refers not only to governments faced with a disintegration of legitimacy and the collapse of development strategies, but to the physical survival of the population. In fact, the reality is more complex and more differentiated. Just as the uneven development of capitalism contributed to the domination of South Africa, so the rest of the region manifests dependence and domination within itself. The different level of crisis and its different forms are noticeable between SADCC states and within individual ones.

This important qualification of our argument is one factor hindering a co-ordinated regional response to the crisis. Just as important are the different ways SADCC states analyse the crisis and draw conclusions for a strategy which itself is aimed at different long-term objectives. Intra-SADCC structural and political differences may soon be overshadowed by the threat posed by the crisis to all SADCC governments, but different analyses and objectives will continue to obstruct agreement on and, implementation of, a regional strategy for survival. They will be most important when attempts are made to conceptualise the integration of short-term strategy into long-term development.

Although the crisis is less acute in some countries, and some can expect improvements in aid, foreign exchange, investments, agricultural output, etc. *somewhere in the future*, the strategy for survival must not be simply a regional variation of crisis management, reliant upon an inability of the capitalist core to resolve its reverse problem of agrarian *over*-production, hence facilitating food aid. If this were so, it would begin to collapse as soon as conditions improved for some members. Even ignoring the plight of certain SADCC countries, this would only perpetuate the structural position which has rendered the crisis so acute. If we accept that capitalism will have recurrent crises and that the centre will be able to transfer most of the costs of recovery onto dependent countries then the highly dependent and underdeveloped nature of *all* SADCC countries will mean severe and recurrent crisis for them too.

We would argue that the freedom of South Africa and Namibia will not on its own, alter this vulnerability to capitalist crisis in the long term. It will, however, fundamentally change the prospects for regional self-reliance. However, the SADCC states cannot afford to wait on this event. Currently, it appears that the South African regime will be with us for some time albeit in modified form. The crisis does not, as has been argued, simply present an *opportunity* for self-reliance and the reduction of dependence, but rather creates the *necessity* for this. The crisis has simultaneously interrupted and altered some aspects of dependence, whilst clearly manifesting its disastrous consequences. It demonstrates how vital it is for all dependent economies, whether their governments are embarked upon a socialist or capitalist path, to reduce

· this dependence. Riding out global recession in order to re-establish, and strive marginally to improve, one's position in the international division of labour effectively destroys all planning. The duration and severity of the general crisis, and the magnitude of South Africa's offensive, have demonstrated this most clearly since the late 1970s.

We have a situation in which the domestic and international dimensions of the SADCC economies have demonstrated first, their incapacity to supply the basic needs of the people in certain conditions; and secondly, that their persistence will guarantee the periodic recurrence of such conditions. The structures and motives of economic activity, therefore, have to be geared to ending the situation. Seen in this way, integration of a survival strategy with a longer-term development strategy becomes less of a problem. Indeed, the two become largely complementary.

Small, dependent economies face severe difficulties in achieving a *rapid* transformation from dependence to self-reliance. Speed is essential, since critical conditions cannot be expected to disappear simply with a year of good rains. The crisis of survival by no means results from natural phenomena. In the short term, a larger economy (SADCC) can supply more goods, technical skills and capital, as well as diversifying transport routes, access to aid and investment.

How is SADCC to respond *collectively* to the crisis? Currently, despite its successes, it has understandably taken the line of least resistance. This has resulted in SADCC programmes which are an uneasy synthesis of national programmes and action under the SADCC umbrella which essentially consists of appraising and supporting *nationally-devised* projects within a very broad interpretation of the word 'regional'. If genuine regional self-reliance is to advance, coherent and precise *regional* plans must be drawn up. Efforts were made in this regard at the annual SADCC Conference in Harare in 1986, when sectoral Five-Year Plans were presented. National planning can then take place within the objectives of these plans. It could be remarked that this would immediately founder on the twin rocks of economic and political diversity. However, such plans need not be ambitious; it is better to have limited but substantive regional plans to which all members can agree, than highly ambitious objectives that are incapable of translation into concrete policies.

A regional strategy of self-reliance will include certain measures that entail losses to members. This will be more true if and when conditions improve. Immediate survival policies that contribute to future *self-reliance* mean that the pattern of production of goods in SADCC must change, since it has patently failed a large number of the people of the region to date. Therefore, expansion of existing production and full utilisation of existing structures can only be a priority where the contribution to basic needs and/or increasing self-reliance is clear. If scarce resources are allocated to maximising existing output potential in all productive sectors, there are unlikely to be any funds to invest in new productive capacity, directed towards basic needs and self-reliance. There are obvious political and economic dangers in deliberately allowing the output of various goods to decline or collapse, but unless the risks are taken, it is difficult to see how and where economic restructuring can begin.

A similar argument can be applied to the role of private capital and to policies towards foreign investment. Real need does not interest capital unless it is allied to the wherewithal to purchase output, which is clearly lacking for many people in the region. At present, it is neither politically nor economically on the agenda for SADCC states to take over private operations. On the other hand, those companies producing luxuries or using substantial foreign exchange with no net benefit can no longer be supported, either by subsidies, foreign exchange allocations, etc. Where they are producing essential goods, government help in recovery can be made conditional on a variety of demands, such as government shares, regulation of profit margins, direction of new investment, use of local resources etc.

In the situation of desperate foreign exchange shortage which is the most obvious effect of the recession, it can be argued that any new foreign investment is welcome. We cannot agree with this. In the first place, how much of the benefits will remain in the region? Secondly, which groups will receive these benefits, and what effect will this have on class and gender relations? Finally, how far will this investment fit a strategy of increased self-reliance, rather than deepening the existing structures of dependence? The last question is so important, that it might even mean the rejection of some offers of aid. A united SADCC policy towards foreign investment and aid is an urgent priority. Otherwise, 'self-reliance' could be reduced to isolated projects in subordinated areas, while more powerful economic forces move economic structures in the opposite direction.

Even when the immediate crisis of survival subsides, the SADCC countries are mostly likely to face chronic shortages of domestic investible funds. The generation of a growing surplus is unlikely to come from industry in the medium-term, especially as this industry is to be re-oriented to producing essentials, not profits. Surplus from the mining sector is beset with difficulties related to the dominant position of foreign capital. Realistically, only the agricultural sector can provide a substantial surplus in the short and medium-term. Hence, development becomes complementary to survival, since agricultural growth is also the central feature of a strategy to survive the crisis. Agriculture must therefore be recognised as the *de facto* leading sector in the SADCC; similarly the rural population must be the subject of crisis management. Such an argument leads to the conclusion that (in the near future) the bottom line in national and regional planning must be sectoral and sub-sectoral contribution to (i) an increasing locally-marketed agricultural surplus, and (ii) provision of the basic needs of the rural population.

Finally, we would like to end with SADCC's own appraisal of the crisis and the role of regional co-operation: 'The crisis has rendered the region poorer and more dependent than it was in 1980, but it would certainly be in an even worse position without the co-operation which has taken place among SADCC member states. In fact the crisis has served to underline the validity of the objectives of seeking economic liberation through regional co-operation and self-reliance' (SADCC 1985).

PART TWO
The IMF, the World Bank and Africa

The chapters in this section examine the role played by the International Monetary Fund and the World Bank in Africa. In particular, the authors are concerned with the validity of the policy prescriptions advanced by these two institutions, and with the feasibility of the alternative policies advanced by critics of Fund and Bank policy. The key issue is that of conditionality, the principle of insisting on the implementation of a particular set of policies before granting balance of payments support (IMF) or structural adjustment loans (World Bank). The authors in this part are not concerned with the ethics of conditionality, but rather with its rationale and with the likely effectiveness of the policies recommended. In Chapter 6 Laurence Harris argues that the role of the IMF is that of constructing a free market economy based on multilateral economic relations. The original force behind such a role was United States economic expansion to replace British imperial domination. Now, however, in attempting to construct an international economic system based on capitalist market relations, the IMF is representing not just the interests of US capital but rather the general interests of capital in operating within a system where it is possible to accumulate. Concentrating as it does on balance of payments support, the IMF is able to integrate African economies into the logic of this wider system, although as a consequence of the uneven development of world capitalism, Africa is a long way behind economically.

In Chapter 7 John Loxley takes a similar view to that of Harris on the IMF as an institution policing the world economic system, and helping to fulfil the profit objectives of capital. He then questions the effectiveness of IMF policies on their own terms and finds such policies, as pursued in Africa, ineffective. He then goes on to look at World Bank conditionality and the characteristics of structural adjustment loans. He finds that the conditionality attached to such loans has features common to each country 'package' and is critical of the policy measures contained therein, doubting their relevance to the problems, especially of food supply, faced by Africa. On the other hand, he argues against totally rejecting the Bank's diagnosis. Using the example of the Structural Adjustment Programme for Tanzania of 1982, he suggests that there is an alternative stabilisation programme which can be advanced and which does try to protect the interests of the more oppressed sections of the population. However, he notes that external financial support was not forthcoming, thus forcing Tanzania to reconsider the orthodox Fund-Bank package.

In Chapters 8 and 10 Ajit Singh and Kighoma Malima are strongly critical of the policies advanced by the IMF and the World Bank. Again they rely for much of their evidence on the policy as it relates to Tanzania, a country which has the reputation of resisting the medicine of these institutions. Both authors are scathing in their criticism of devaluation as a policy option, but are equally critical of other policies advanced as being irrelevant to the circumstances of the case. Singh traces the problems which countries like Tanzania face to the structural characteristics of their economies, and sees the solution in a more effective and self-reliant industrialisation, while Malima, endorsing this view, accepts the need for adjustment to the new conditions operating in the world economy, but questions the speed with which such adjustment is expected to be carried out.

In Chapter 9 John Sender and Sheila Smith are sharply critical of the positions taken up by those on the Left advocating alternative economic strategies. They query many of the generally accepted wisdoms on the Left, but while refusing to denounce many of the policy prescriptions criticised by Singh and Malima, are also very critical of the Fund and the Bank. They argue that neither institution has any conception of the state and of the political forces ranged in the state arena, and therefore are unable to explain the economic policies which have been pursued by different regimes other than in terms of 'mistakes'. They are critical of the pessimism of these institutions and regard the prospects for increased food production and sustained rates of import substitution industrialisation as not nearly as poor as presented by the Fund and the Bank.

The final two Chapters in Part Two are concerned with detailed accounts of the impact of IMF and World Bank policies on the economic behaviour of, once again, Tanzania, and of the Sudan. For Werner Biermann and Jumanne Wagao in Chapter 11, Tanzania's open economy makes it subject to capitalist regulation. They see the policy pursued as a nationalist populism intended to unite the different interest groups and classes behind the state. They root the failure of Tanzanian agricultural and industrial development in the 'unchecked growth of bureaucracy'. The resistance to IMF proposals is an attempt to get better terms to preserve the role of the bureaucracy and the state, while it maintains a popular base. The more recent acceptance of the economic liberalisation measures, documented in detail here by the authors, is seen as a shift by the ruling strata in the state towards 'reliance on the metropolitan bourgeoisies'. Dirk Hansohm's account in Chapter 12 of the effect of IMF and World Bank policies in the Sudan tends to confirm Loxley's view that such policies have not had the desired results. He concludes that the policy pursued by the government, that is the IMF stabilisation policy, 'failed to attain its own targets' or 'to achieve improvements in economic structure', indeed it reinforced the distorted character of the latter, and worsened the very balance of payments it was meant to improve, thus throwing the country further into the arms of the IMF and the Bank.

6

Conceptions of the IMF's role in Africa

Laurence Harris

In the 1970s and 1980s the principal and most prominent role of the International Monetary Fund has become lending to third world states experiencing shortages of foreign exchange, and, as part of this, prescribing economic policies for them. Within this general development, African countries have become increasingly important borrowers so that by the beginning of the 1980s Africa had become one of the IMF's principal concerns. From 1973 to 1979 the increase in African states' borrowing occurred mainly under special credit lines designed to finance balance of payments deficits due to increased oil prices, temporary shortfalls in export receipts or to provide 'soft' credit from the proceeds of the Fund's sales of gold. But from 1979 African countries have become prominent borrowers under the 'regular' system for borrowing under 'stand-by' or 'extended' arrangements which are tied to prescriptions and conditions on the borrowing state's actions. Of the total amount of IMF credit committed to all countries under such arrangements, African countries accounted for 30 per cent in 1979 and 1980 whereas they accounted for only 3 per cent over 1970 to 1978 (Kanesa-Thasan 1981: 20–24).

Africa has, therefore, come to the forefront of controversy over the role of the IMF. Its public manifestation has ranged from riots in Sudan and Morocco over policies arising from IMF loans (1981 and 1982) to open confrontation between the Tanzanian state and the IMF in protracted on-off negotiations. The prognosis of the IMF and independent writers is that Africa, and particularly sub-Saharan Africa, will continue to become an increasingly significant debtor to the IMF and, as a result, political conflicts over the Fund's role are likely to increase.

In this paper I am concerned with the ideologies at play in that context, the conceptions of the Fund's role that inform debate. I begin by outlining and appraising the conception of its role that the IMF itself promulgates in Africa (section 6.1) bearing in mind that this does not necessarily coincide with the internal ideology of the Fund. In section 6.2 I assess the concept of the Fund underlying the work of market-oriented critics such as Killick's work for the Overseas Development Institute, while in section 6.3 I consider an alternative framework which provides a firmer underpinning for African states and movements in the politics of dealing with the IMF.

This paper concentrates solely upon the conceptions of the Fund with regard to one of its activities, the attaching of conditions to its loans, defining these broadly to include the preconditions for loans and the formal and informal requirements to be met in the course of the loan itself. But it should not be forgotten that the Fund's activities in Africa are more extensive than that.

The Fund perspective

The IMF attaches substantial conditions to the loans it provides a member state beyond that state's first tranche of credit or some special types of loans. Thus, in 'upper tranche' borrowing, conditions attach to the stand-by arrangements the Fund makes with a borrower; as the name implies these stand-by arrangements, once agreed, commit the Fund to 'stand-by' to provide credit up to specified limits over a specified period – a year was formerly the norm – as long as the borrower satisfied specified conditions. Similar conditions apply to funds provided under the IMF's Extended Fund Facility. The imposition of such conditions has not always been part of the IMF's practice but the policy was developed in its first decades and has been modified at intervals (Horsefeld 1969; IMF 1981). Systematic information on the conditions imposed is not available, for the details of each country agreement are secret. However, information about the conditions some borrowing countries have faced has been publicised by non-IMF sources (Killick et al. 1984; Girvan et al. 1980), a survey of IMF officials (Killick et al. 1984), and summaries of the broad character of such conditions for borrowers in general or as applied to a range of countries in one region which the IMF itself has produced (Zulu and Nsouli 1984).

The IMF's own statements on the character of these conditions give a clear indication of the Fund's official rationale for establishing them and, hence, of its rationale for its own role in relation to borrowing states.

The names the IMF gives to the packages of conditions it attaches to a loan are 'stabilisation programme' and 'adjustment programme' which express the IMF's underlying conception that its role is to help borrowers to return to some norm. The member state needs funds because of some temporary deviation from a stable position, or some disturbance to which it must adjust; stability needs to be restored and, once this is regained, IMF credit and conditions will no longer be needed. The conception has been modified in the 1980s for in the face of the intractable problems that the increasing numbers of African borrowers seemed to face, it was recognised that a return to a stable position 'may call for a succession of adjustment programmes supported by the Fund' (Kanesa-Thasan 1981). But the basic conception that the need for adjustment or stabilisation is essentially temporary, albeit spanning more than the normal period of one programme, remains.

That terminology does not specify what it is that is to be stabilised. The rationale of the IMF at its foundation was that stability in member countries' balance of payments was the objective to be achieved under the Bretton Woods mixture of fixed but adjustable exchange rates. Fundamental disequilibria would be overcome by negotiated exchange rate changes while temporary disequilibria would be ridden out with loans from the Fund (Gardner 1980). But the conditions attached in recent decades to stand-by and extended loans to third world countries have embraced a wide range of policies that themselves take on the appearance of the things to be stabilised: domestic credit, government borrowing, and overseas debt being particularly prominent (Killick et al. 1984). In the IMF's perspective these are not themselves the objects of stabilisation but are instruments to be used to achieve higher level objectives such as balance of payments stability, a stable rate of economic growth, or greater stability of the price level.

The Fund's statements of the objects of stabilisation programmes treats them as a hierarchy with some objectives being only means to an end, but the ultimate end has varied over time. Stabilisation of the balance of payments has, at times, been replaced in public statements by the aim of achieving stable growth with targets such as control of credit expansion, stable price level and balance of payments stability itself presented as means to that end. Thus, the Director and Deputy-Director of the IMF's African Department, surveying 21 adjustment programmes operating in Africa in 1980/1 wrote:

While the Fund provided resources to support appropriate adjustment programmes, a primary concern of the African countries that adopted such programmes was the achievement of a sustainable level of economic growth. However, the key to such sustainability was the establishment of domestic and external financial stability. . . . Accordingly, in the general design of these programmes, the three basic and interdependent objectives were to promote economic growth, to reduce inflation, and to improve the current account position of the balance of payments over the medium term. . . . Considerable emphasis was given to economic growth in the programmes under consideration; most aimed for an increase in economic growth during the programme year (Zulu and Nsouli 1984).

and, reviewing the same programme:

Fund programmes, by emphasising the re-establishment of domestic and external financial stability, can contribute to putting a country on a sustainable growth path (Zulu 1983).

However, the Fund does not always present growth as the overarching objective. Officials note that:

objectives are not infrequently in conflict (for example, a reduction in the payments imbalance will make growth more difficult to achieve) (Kanesa-Thasan 1981b).

so that balance of payments stability cannot be seen as a key to growth. In that context, the principal objective is seen as balance of payments stability with growth a subordinate goal:

From the Fund's perspective, (an adjustment) programme should meet the objectives of achieving within a reasonable period of time a viable payments position. *The purpose is therefore essentially* to achieve a current account deficit that could be sustained by capital inflows, at a level and on terms compatible with the country's development prospects, and without resort to restrictions on trade and payments for balance of payments reasons *and without undue sacrifice to growth prospects* (Kanesa-Thasan 1981b).

The different emphasis partly reflects the differences within the IMF between the regional departments responsible for particular countries (such as the Africa Department) and the Exchange and Trade Relations Department with responsibility for the elements of adjustment programmes irrespective of which member country is involved. It is an institutionalised conflict between flexibility and individually negotiated conditions in the face of local circumstances on the one hand and the pursuit of uniformity and an IMF rule on the other. And the regional departments' public pronouncements and internal stance give a greater role to the borrowing states' own interest in growth compared to balance of payments stability.

But the inconsistency between pronouncements giving priority to growth and those which put the balance of payments first reflects more than a conflict between two interest groups. It reflects the fact that these objectives themselves are not adequate to specify the IMF's role in full; they do not recognise the wider role that the IMF is supposed to have for the system as a whole and these two aims themselves cannot be adequately specified without acknowledging it.

The system-wide role of the IMF is the obligation to develop and maintain 'multilateralism' in international payments to complement multilateral trade in contrast to the bilateral treaties, autarkic arrangements, and imperial blocs that characterised international trade and finance in, for example, the 1930s. Multilateralism was the ideology promoted by the US State Department at the IMF's foundation, for representing internationally expansionist US capital it was seen as a principle which would open up the protected markets of the British Empire and remove the protection the Sterling Area gave to the City of London's financial domination (Gardner 1980; Block 1977). Although that original impetus lost its force in the postwar years as US dominance was quickly consolidated, the commitment to multilateralism has been basic to the IMF since its foundation. Thus the objectives of an adjustment programme cannot be reduced to the particular country's growth and/or its balance of payments stability, for the IMF has the promotion of a world system of multilateral trade and payments as a general objective and, hence, as an objective within its adjustment programmes.

Indeed, the explicit aims of adjustment programmes, growth or balance of payments stability for the particular country, cannot be properly specified independently of this systemic objective. 'Growth' is a meaningless objective unless its qualitative dimensions are specified, balance of payments stability cannot be defined without specifying its character and its components, and the commitment to multilateralism is what informs the IMF's concept of these objectives. Or, rather, the IMF's commitment to a particular form of multilateralism is the key: it is the idea of multilateralism as a system where international trade and finance are determined by market forces rather than by state regulation, and this is rationalised on the grounds that market forces allocate world resources according to comparative advantage. Thus, the growth objective in adjustment programmes does have more specific qualitative dimensions, for the IMF conceives a country's sustainable growth as that which can be reached when trade and production are developed in accordance with international (and domestic) market forces. Growth means growth of production in the sectors dictated by the market, with the decline of other sectors and the distribution of income that results. Similarly, the commitment to an international system based upon multilateralism gives substance to the objective of balance of payments stability. This is defined as a current account deficit that can be sustained by capital inflows, but the definition only gains content when we consider what type of capital inflows are assumed. The free market multilateralism objective implies that, apart from some World Bank loans, the relevant capital inflows are market fund attracted by market-determined interest rates; thus, the definition of balance of payments stability means a limit to the current account deficit determined by these forces.

In its presentation of the objectives of adjustment programmes in Africa the IMF does not make explicit its role with respect to the international system, so the growth and balance of payments objectives are conceptually empty and thus easily presented in the contradictory manner I have noted. Nevertheless, the IMF's free market multilateralism objective does have a counterpart in its conception of the role of adjustment programmes for the individual state. The emphasis on freeing external trade and payments from state intervention is common in the Fund's view of African programmes as in the passage already quoted ('without resort to restrictions on trade and payments') and in statements regarding loan conditions in general (Guitian 1981). The 1980/81 African programme reviewed by the Fund viewed the liberalisation of trade and payments as an incontrovertible desideratum that could be achieved if exchange rates were devalued:

Restrictions had usually been imposed in response to rising imbalances; without such control, there would have been, at the prevailing exchange rate, a shortage of foreign exchange in the country and pressures on the exchange rate. Such restrictions were thus symptomatic of the need for adjustment. All programmes, therefore, attempted to deal with the underlying imbalances in order to enable the country to reduce the restriction.
The exchange rate ... is a major instrument in the adjustment process. The appropriateness of the exchange rate level, therefore, was carefully reviewed in the context of (these African) programmes. . . In several cases, exchange rate action was taken. A notable example is Somalia, which devalued its currency by 150 per cent in domestic currency terms during 1981–2 (Zulu and Nsouli 1984).

Generally, the liberalisation of controls over foreign trade and payments was accompanied by similar internal measures, raising prices that had been administratively controlled and taking similar action with regard to interest rates. Thus restoration of market forces has meant raising prices and interest rates toward the levels that market forces would have generated earlier in the absence of controls. The ideology in support of this policy conceived the deviations from market prices that African states' interventions had induced as distortions: 'The growing distortions contributed significantly to the slowdown in economic activity' (Zulu and Nsouli 1984). Thus, the norm is taken to be a world economy regulated by market forces working through prices; this norm is conducive to growth, state policies which interrupt these processes are undesirable, and the stable growth and balance of payments position at which adjustment programmes aim are subject to the overriding objective of integrating the economy into a market-regulated world economy.
  Thus the IMF's conception of its role with respect to African, and other third world, borrowers, its conception as presented in its publications, is internally flawed because it focuses on the aims for the particular country whereas these are in fact conditioned by the Fund's role in regulating the international capitalist economy as a whole. This conclusion, however, can be questioned on two counts.
  First, the IMF's defenders can point to its frequent assertions that it has no bias against socialist development programmes. For example, in the context of African adjustment programmes, Fund officials claim:

the Fund takes into account the particular circumstances of members, including their social, political, and economic priorities (Kanesa-Thasan 1981a).

On this view the fact that adjustment programmes require restrictions on state spending and borrowing is seen as a consequence of macroeconomic policies to control credit creation, and these policies in turn are seen as necessary and politically neutral in the light of the simple macro-theory first developed by the Fund's research staff (the Polak Model) and subsequently widely adopted as the monetary theory of the balance of payments (Polak 1957; Polak and Argy 1971). Similarly, the emphasis adjustment programmes place on replacing state controls over trade and payments by greater reliance on prices, exchange rate and interest rate flexibility is justified by the assumption that the price system is optimal and arguments that, for example, the administration of controls wastefully absorbs skilled personnel. But these arguments in support of the Fund's political neutrality are themselves the sharpest indicators of the fund's commitment to promoting a market-oriented international economy structured around capitalist relations, for the premises, the optimality of the price system and the validity of the Polak model, are themselves ideological. The IMF's claim to political neutrality is undermined by the absence of a recognition of what socialist 'social, political and economic priorities' would entail. Thus, in a passage quoted above, the IMF's African Department, saw import restrictions only as 'symptomatic of the need for adjustment', as having been adopted out of necessity because an inappropriate exchange rate caused foreign exchange shortages. Without recognition that such controls have to be adopted as an essential part of a socialist programme in order to achieve political control over economic forces (irrespective of the level of the exchange rate) the Fund's claim to respect socialist policy choices amounts to nothing more than neutrality with regard to the name of the governing party.

Second, critics of the IMF adopting the perspective of classical Marxist theories of imperialism argue that its role and policies are determined by the interests of US capital or a section of it and have been since its foundation (Block 1977). At one level this contrasts to the view taken here that the IMF's overriding role is the support of an international system based on free market forces and capitalist relations rather than the support of one particular block of capital's expansionary interests. The importance of US capital's expansionist aims for shaping the IMF at its foundation is well established, but it is wrong to believe that these interests have a direct stake in the type of policies that each borrowing state has to adopt. Indeed, the pursuit of free-market policies does not always benefit US capital or any other single country's capital in the borrowing state, for it can lose the protection previously given by an interventionist but friendly state. However, the free-market orientation of adjustment programmes does benefit international capital in general, rather than a particular part, to the extent that its operation requires mobility and freedom from intervention from potentially nationalist states. In this it should be noted that, first, different types of international capital have a greater interest in mobility and free markets than others; financial capital, for example, more than industrial capital. And, second, in seeing the main consideration behind IMF adjustment programmes as the integration of the individual economy into a capitalist world economy based on free market forces, it should be recognised that this is an attempt to *construct* such a world economy. The international economy is not a free market economy where trade and capital movements are dictated by relative prices, market interest rates and free exchange rates. Although such variables do have a major influence they do so within a framework where market forces are fractured and controlled by states and multinational corporations, and this absence of laissez-faire has been the rule since the beginning of the capitalist world market. Thus, the IMF's objective, reflected in the conditions imposed on borrowers and requiring them to 'liberalise', is not so much to return those countries to a normal relationship with the international economy, it is not in fact to correct 'distortions' from the norm or, in the wider view, to maintain a free market international system. It is, instead, to construct such a system.

Reformers' conceptions

The political controversies over the role of the IMF and the structural shift, from 1971, in the character of the postwar international economy have encouraged the development of plans for reforming the Fund's operations regarding loans to third world states (Dell and Lawrence 1980; Killick 1984). Killick and his collaborators' reform plans are based on an extensive analysis of the IMF's character and role. The types of reforms proposed and the question of whether any reforms of lending practice are feasible at all depends on the reformers' underlying conception of the IMF. The proposals for reforms on the conditionality attached to third world loans have, in the main, been limited and would not fundamentally affect the Fund's mode of operation; the reason is that the reformers largely share with the Fund the same basic conception of its role and position as presented above.

Many of the reforms that commentators have recommended in recent years are brought together in the 'real-economy approach' promulgated by the Overseas Development Institute (ODI) team under Killick. Under this heading they recommend that IMF stabilisation programmes should envisage adjustment over the medium term rather than the attainment of specific targets in the short term and that, while restraining aggregate demand, they should concentrate on improving the balance of payments through increasing the economy's supply potential, specifically the supply of tradeable commodities, rather than concentrating solely on demand management. At this general level they also emphasise the need to design adjustment programmes that are politically acceptable to the borrower, greater flexibility in Fund programmes, and, in monitoring the borrower, a switch from rigid and quantified performance criteria to broad 'review clauses' on the borrowing state's overall performance (Killick 1984).

The authors of these reform proposals give a specific example of the type of programme that it would imply for Kenya if the real-economy approach were applied to that country in mid-1982. The package would include limits on state spending, restriction of state borrowing from the banks, restriction of domestic credit expansion, raising interest rates, devaluation, reducing the coverage of price controls and of controls over imports and exports. Thus, the programme for Kenya would be very similar to the typical adjustment programme the IMF already applies in Africa in association with stand-by agreements, or rather, given the 'real-economy approach's' emphasis on medium-term adjustment, similar to the programmes associated with the IMF's extended fund facility. This is despite the fact that the author's study of Kenya's experience with IMF programmes in the 1970s and 1980s showed them to have been largely unsuccessful (Killick et al. 1984).

The specific, but hypothetical programme this school suggested for Kenya is similar in its details to a typical IMF programme and the general principles of the reforms they suggest for IMF loan conditions also mark no new departure from IMF practices. The general principle of extended length for adjustment programmes was adopted by the IMF as long ago as 1974 when it introduced the extended fund facility as a source of medium-term credit. The principle of not specifying conditions as rigid quantitative performance criteria has already operated *de facto* to a significant extent since the IMF has interpreted the criteria flexibly in several cases allowing latitude to some borrowers on a discretionary basis. And the principle of emphasising increases in supply of tradeable commodities together with demand restriction rather than relying solely upon demand management has been a prominent aspect of the IMF's own programmes in the 1980s. Thus, in the context of adjustment programmes adopted by African states the IMF has written:

Since most of the African countries under consideration faced, and continue to face, deep-rooted structural problems, the programmes generally emphasised supply-oriented policies designed to bring about structural change, and financial policies aimed at reinforcing the structural adjustment process and limiting the growth in demand. (Zulu and Nsouli 1984)

The emphasis on supply-side policies is in general terms, but the instruments the IMF relies on to influence supply are relative prices of all kinds which are seen as the main and legitimate influences on resource allocation. Thus the IMF's supply side policies encompass devaluation, to improve the allocation of resources toward production of tradeables, increases in interest rates to improve the allocation of resources toward saving, as well as increasing the producer prices and decreasing subsidies of basic commodities. Supply-side policies for the IMF means, therefore, only an increased role for market forces in the allocation of resources, and the ODI's team has the same orientation in the programme it postulates for Kenya. Both the IMF in its African programmes and the ODI reformers' example associate their price oriented supply-side programmes with a laissez-faire role for the state and an incomes policy to restrain real wages.

The similarity between these reformers' adjustment programmes and the IMF's own relates to the coincidence between the two groups' conception of the IMF's position and role.

The ODI writers see the IMF's essential function as stabilisation and interpret that in terms of achieving equilibrium on the borrowing state's balance of payments. Like the IMF, in its Exchange and Trade Relations Department's publications at least, the balance of payments is given priority. Consideration is given to growth in the secondary sense that balance of payments policies should be designed so as to minimise their short-term and medium-term harm to growth and that overcoming balance of payments problems is a precondition for future growth in the long term. But the IMF's role is seen as facilitating medium-term adjustment and the balance of payments has priority.

As in the IMF's own conception, balance of payments problems are seen as arising from particular events which have disturbed the norm of balance of payments equilibrium. The issue for them as for Dell and Lawrence (1980) who, nevertheless, draw different implications is whether the disturbance emanates from internal events such as over-expansionary financial policies or from external events such as the declining terms of trade faced by many third world countries in particularly sharp form since the early 1970s. Either way, in the view of both the ODI and IMF, the role of IMF programmes is to adjust the economy so that the balance of payments deficits may be a structural characteristic of their position in the international division of labour. They consider that the decade after 1974 saw 'large and *persistent* deficits on current account becoming commonplace' and locate the principal causes as the 'oil shocks' of 1973/4 and 1979/80. They see them simply as a symptom of 'an imbalance between aggregate demand and aggregate supply capacity' and susceptible to policies on aggregate demand and aggregate supply as an 'adjustment designed to restore equilibrium' (Killick 1984). The principal cause may have been external ('oil-shocks'), but aggregate demand and supply have to be adjusted because they are out of balance in the sense of being inappropriate to the country's position in a world with 'post oil-shocks' terms of trade. The ODI team present this as a regrettable but unavoidable necessity. In their 'real economy' programmes for countries such as the Kenyan example, other sub-Saharan African countries, or, indeed, for any:

the chief burden must fall upon consumption. This is an unwelcome fact, since we are writing about countries with generally low average incomes and many people living in absolute poverty. But . . . we see no alternative to austerity. This is the sharp end of the truth that the adverse movement in the terms of trade suffered by most oil-importing ldcs represent a transfer of real income from them to their suppliers. (Killick 1984)

Once the adjustment to this transfer has been made, equilibrium in the balance of payments will have been restored and will only be at risk from the danger of further disturbances.

The ODI teams' perspective on the character of balance of payments deficits, their financing, and the role the IMF can and does play in assisting individual states is, therefore, similar to the Fund's own perspective. At the same time they share with the Fund a single-minded focus of attention upon the adjustment of the borrowing state's own individual economy instead of considering the manner in which Fund lending policies to individual states bear upon the Fund's role in the maintenance and construction of the international economy. Although the ODI authors acknowledge their omission of 'the Fund's wider role in overseeing the conduct of the international financial system as a whole' they treat it as a separate issue so that stabilisation programmes can be analysed in terms of the economy to which they apply. The only way in which the international capitalist economy enters their analysis is as the locus of one major source of disturbances to a country's balance of payments equilibrium, such as the oil price rises of the 1973/4 and 1979/80 periods. Even there the conception of the international system is weak. It sees the international economic system as a system of prices and the resulting monetary flows, relating the rise of persistent deficits to changes in the terms of trade rather than to changes in the international division of labour.

The effective omission of the international system from the ODI's analysis of the IMF's role means that they are unable to locate properly or appraise the IMF's emphasis on market forces in its individual country adjustment programmes. Instead of understanding them as a manifestation of the IMF's main role, the maintenance and construction of a market-based international economy, the authors consider them as policies applying to individual countries that, case by case, are neutral and technically efficient. Entwined with this is a view that the IMF is politically neutral and certainly not pro-capitalist or against socialist forms of economic organisation, but the basis for this view is limited. Taking a pluralist view of the influence of lobbying within the Fund on the formulation of stabilisation programmes and loans which favour some third world countries rather than others, the authors argue:

However inequitable this is, it cannot accurately be generalised as a pro-market, anti-socialist bias ... The political-strategic considerations are too complex for outcomes to be fitted neatly into such a simple scheme. In addition to Yugoslavia, Manley's Jamaica was for a time among the beneficiaries of political lobbying ... The charge of an anti-socialist bias has also been made more difficult to sustain by the fact that such countries as China, Hungary, Poland and Vietnam have joined (or applied for membership) in recent years. (Killick 1984)

This assessment can be questioned in its own terms, but the relevant point for the present is that it considers the question of the IMF's stance without recognition of its principal role as promulgator and guardian of a free international market. Indeed, the absence of a conception of how this role manifests itself in generally promoting market forces within countries' adjustment programmes leads the authors to single out Chile after 1975 as an exceptional case where 'short-term stabilisation goals were part of a long-term strategy to transform the economy to accord more closely with free market forces'.

I have concentrated upon the conception of the Fund and its role employed by the ODI team, but other reform proposals are also limited by adopting a similar conception. Dell and Lawrence (1980) focus on stabilisation programmes assuming that assistance in the attainment of equilibrium of the country's balance of payments is the IMF's principle role. Their criticism of the IMF stems from their examination of the causes of the disequilibrium; their emphasis on the external causes of disequilibrium (such as the oil price) leads to recommendations for low conditionality and long adjustment periods in IMF programmes. Since their conception of the IMF's role does not differ fundamentally from the conception promulgated by the IMF or from the ODI team's, their reforms are limited; although they differ from the ODI on the strength of the conditions that should be imposed, their recommendations for change are similar. And the critical assessment of the IMF by Stewart and Sengupta (1982) is based upon a similar theoretical position leading, again, to reform proposals that are not well founded.

The IMF and Africa: towards a conceptual framework

The increased importance of African states as recipients of the IMF's 'upper tranche' and 'extended fund facility' credit, and the expectation that this trend will continue in the late 1980s, makes Africa critical for the IMF and the IMF critical for Africa. Much comment on the IMF is directed toward proposing reforms in its lending practices, but here I have an aim which is both more limited and relevant to a wider range of actions. It is to outline a conceptual framework for understanding the IMF's role; it is a framework which can inform actions toward the IMF whether those actions consist of African states' negotiations for loans or membership, the formulation of development plans, or political and economic debates in Africa. There are four key points regarding the IMF's role.

First, the principal role and characteristic of the IMF is a responsibility for the construction and maintenance of an international economic system based upon capitalist forms of production and exchange. Constructing an environment in which market forces operate without state restraints, and profit is accumulated by private capital is, therefore, central to this role.

This overriding objective underlies Article 1 of the IMF's Articles of Association. Written as the international economic relations of the capitalist (and socialist) world were being reconstructed and reshaped after the disruption of the 1930s and the Second World War, Article 1 gave the IMF a central role 'in the establishment of a multilateral system of payments', a system based on free markets with 'the elimination of foreign exchange restrictions'. The growth of the international economy on this basis was seen as the priority, with the development of national economies flowing from it, for the IMF was 'to facilitate the expansion and balanced growth of world trade, and to contribute thereby to individual states" growth and development. Although the founders' orientation at that time was toward the fractured economic relations of the advanced capitalist states, the same priority toward the international system and the construction of an international market system characterises the IMF's role today although the focus has shifted toward the third world and, now, towards Africa.

Second, the construction of such an international system requires the IMF to have leverage over the national economies within it, for the rules of the international system rest upon the policies and rules of national states. The Fund's ability to operate on these rests on its role regarding member states' balance of payments. In this system, countries' external payments represent a real constraint on policy, and the Fund's role in providing balance of payments finance enables it to operate on these constraints so that they exert pressure towards the adoption of national policies which contribute to a market-based international system rather than hinder it.

Thus adjustment programmes cannot be seen simply or primarily as aimed at balance of payments equilibrium; their aim is to integrate the national economy into a particular international system with the need to finance the balance of payments being a key lever to enforce these programmes. Moreover, the balance of payments has this key role because it appears as an objective and inescapable constraint but, in fact, it is a relatively ill-defined mesure and open to debate and redefinition. Losses or shortages of foreign exchange are the real constraint upon third world states, but on the IMF's definition of balance of payments equilibrium a country may be far from reaching equilibrium (because, for example, its foreign trade and capital movements are subject to permanent quantitative controls) and yet not be losing foreign exchange.

Although 'balance of payments equilibrium' is not the main objective but a means towards constructing the international economy, it ranks above 'economic development' in adjustment programmes. The latter cannot be counted as an objective or even as a means towards achieving the overriding international objective despite the fact that the IMF's African Department presents it as a principal aim. Instead, the logic of the IMF is that it is regarded as an automatic outcome of the construction of a market-based international system (hence IMF descriptions of adjustment programmes' contributions to supply-side development summarise measures only designed to improve the price system).

Third, the origins of African countries' balance of payments (or foreign exchange) problems are rooted in the uneven development of production which is inherent in the international economy of capitalism. For example, the basic source of the increased payments problems of African and other states in the 1970s and early 1980s was exceptional shifts in the international division of labour and the fact that within a capitalist system they require an international economic crisis to effect and consolidate them. It was such a world crisis rather than the price of oil that depressed African countries' export earnings in that period.

This contrasts with the perspective taken by the IMF and the critics reviewed here. For them the source of balance of payments problems is located in the realm of exchange, trade and money rather than production. In that perspective balance of payments problems are caused either by the state's irresponsible financial and spending policies (in the traditional IMF emphasis upon 'internal' causes) or by the OPEC states' increases in the price of oil in the 1970s (in the critics' emphasis on 'external' factors). And they see these problems as the results of specific policies or agency; hence they are problems susceptible to remedy by the correct policies put forward by another agency, the IMF (or, in the view of its critics, by different policies that should be promulgated by an 'enlightened' IMF).

Since the balance of payments problems are symptoms of the uneven development of productive forces which is, in itself, an inherent characteristic of the system, the idea of balance of payments equilibrium, achievable through policies acting on money and prices and thereafter sustainable through freeing market forces to determine exchange rates, interest rates and prices is invalid. Instead, deficits and surpluses on states' balance of payments (however defined) can be seen as the norm under capitalism and the financial flows they entail be treated as one element in long-term development plans as a whole.

Fourth, the international division of labour reflected in African states' balance of payments reflects not simply an uneven development of productive resources (a lower degree of mechanisation in some countries for example); it also reflects differences in the organisation of production. Economic relations in African countries are based upon modes of production which differ from, say, those in advanced capitalist countries. Balance of payments figures or losses of foreign exchange hide these differences for, appearing as a summary indicator of 'economic health', they reduce everything to the monetary measures appropriate to a capitalist world market instead of to the economic relations actually obtaining within the economy.

Presenting the balance of payments as the crucial indicator of an economy's health and operating on it as the IMF does is an important aspect of its role. It rationalises the imposition of policies that assume the particular economy is wholly a capitalist economy which is structured around market relations, or would be if the state allowed it, and thereby rationalises policies which attempt to construct such market relations. The IMF's assumption that economic relations in third world countries are essentially no different from advanced capitalist economies' mode of production is explicit in the simple analytic model its Research Department has developed as the basis of stabilisation programme's macroeconomic policies. The only difference it allows between developing and developed countries is the assumption that the latter have developed financial markets with interest-elastic demand functions for money and investment functions (Polak and Argy 1971). Similar assumptions of homogeneity in models of production are implicit in the writings of the Fund's critics. However, some critics do have a partial and distorted recognition of the differences in so far as they consider 'supply rigidities', or 'short-run inelasticities of supply' as reasons for stabilisation programmes to allow for longer periods of adjustment (as in the ODI study). Similarly, Stewart and Sengupta have a notion that adjustment programmes harm growth in 'many low-income countries' if they have 'small manufacturing sectors and few private entrepreneurship in growth and the shortage of this input in economies such as those of sub-Saharan Africa than a recognition that such economies have quite distinct forms of organisation (Stewart and Sengupta 1982).

In sum, then, the IMF's role is the construction of an international economic system based on market relations and the private accumulation of capital; in carrying out that role a particular conception of the balance of payments gives the IMF leverage for influencing national economies toward a mode of operating required by that international project; the balance of payments position upon which it operates is itself the outcome of structural forces working on the international division of labour; and the latter is bound up with differences in the mode of production. These considerations bear upon all the IMF's operations and, particularly the conditionality it applies on loans to African and similar states. But how do they bear upon the question of power, class interests and imperialism?

The Arusha Initiative analyses the IMF's role in similar terms to those adopted here and links it to the power of imperialist interests, for the IMF's role in constructing a market-based international system is seen as an expression of those interests (*Development Dialogue* 1980). The Arusha Initiative recognises that the IMF's 'analytical approach and policy prescription ignore the structural and and inevitable nature of payments disequilibria that result from the development process for 'structural change generates imbalances'; that the basic aim of its founders was international, 'to provide a stable basis for economic relations within the capitalist world'; and that as part of this enterprise its role is to promote 'the free play of national and international market forces' and capital.

Correctly, the Arusha authors see this as reflected in and a reflection of the class interests of particular sections of capital for 'Money is power. . . . An international monetary system is both a function and an instrument of prevailing power structures.' In the Arusha view multinational corporations in general benefit from an international economy free of national restrictions; banks and financial capital benefit from such freedom (especially in the context of volatile currency markets); and, within each national state, the IMF allies itself with and supports local capitalist interests against state control.

The IMF's role in supporting the interests of capital is illustrated by the exceptions to the IMF rule of reducing state intervention in markets. On the international scale the IMF exerts no leverage against the protectionism of advanced capitalist countries. Within national economies, stabilisation programmes require state intervention to increase rather than decrease in one sphere, namely the labour market; for while subsidies to hold down the prices of basic goods are rejected, incomes policies to hold down wages are regularly included in stabilisation programmes so that the distributional balance in the waged employment sector is tilted from real wages towards profits. Thus, the construction of a market-based international system is conditioned by interventionism to protect profitable accumulation. Within this framework the IMF programmes in Africa can be assessed.

7

IMF and World Bank conditionality and Sub-Saharan Africa

John Loxley

There is little evidence to support the contention of the IMF that its programmes are effective in restoring growth and balance in low-income third world countries. A recent study by the author has shown that the economic performance of low-income countries in terms of balance of payments, growth, inflation, savings and investment in the 1970s was no better for countries with IMF programmes than for those without (Loxley 1984b). At the same time an IMF internal report revealed that the Fund's record in SSA was particularly bleak with performance falling well short of targets. Thus, growth targets were reached in only 5 out of 23 African programmes, inflation targets in only 13 out of 28 and trade targets in only 11 out of 28 (IMF 1983). The evidence also indicates that IMF programmes have not led to an inflow of bank credit to low income countries (Loxley 1984b).

The studies in question throw no light on the explanations for this record which, in terms of the IMF's own objectives, can be regarded only as a poor one. The Fund argues that governments were either not committed enough or not strong enough to implement programmes properly, but that the situation would have been worse without even partial implementation. Critics of the Fund, on the other hand, have argued that Fund conditionality is inappropriate in economies with economic structures like those of SSA countries. They would argue that demand restraint and exchange rate and related price adjustments would not quickly lead to a switching of expenditures from domestic consumption to exports or to domestic production from imports, on account of the low degree of substitutability of traded for non-traded goods – i.e. few exports are consumed locally and few imports have local substitutes. It also takes time to expand agricultural or mineral exports production in response to price stimuli but IMF programmes rarely allow for this (Crockett 1981; Helleiner 1983). In addition, the promotion of manufacturing exports requires much more than the correct price stimuli; there must first of all be a reasonably well developed manufacturing sector and then an ability to penetrate competitive foreign markets which requires marketing contacts and product quality. Few SSA countries could meet these requirements and certainly not within the one year time frame which characterises most IMF programmes.

Since 1981 the IMF has been pursuing a distinctly more monetarist approach to problems of global instability. It has shifted its policy emphasis much more in the direction of third world countries *adjusting* to their crises and reduced their access to low or non-conditional *financing*. It has moved away from three-year to one-year programmes with a greater emphasis on *demand* restraint and on what has been described as 'shock treatment'. While recognising that low-income countries face peculiar structural difficulties in adjusting their economies, and therefore, could benefit from large inflows of concessional assistance to facilitate adjustment, it does not believe it should be the source of that assistance. This position stands in stark contrast to the one adopted by the IMF in the 1974/5 crisis and even as recently as 1980/81 when the Fund greatly expanded cheap, concessional, financing to third world countries. The pronounced shift of policy is a reflection of the ascendancy of monetarist thinking in the USA and Europe and its extension to the international arena. The Fund's reluctance to issue more unconditional financing, along the lines of the SDR for instance, is also a reflection of the revival of the centrality of the US dollar in international finance, a role which many would see as being an essential aspect of Reaganomics and not merely a bi-product of it (Loxley forthcoming).

Thus, the IMF has emerged from the most recent global crisis as policeman of third world economic policies. It has, however, few powers of enforcement relying on the state in borrowing countries to suppress any domestic political opposition to adjustment policies. The only sanction the Fund has for non-compliance is the withdrawal of credits and the withholding of its 'good housekeeping seal of approval' from governments borrowing from it. This leverage is often inadequate to persuade governments to adhere to IMF austerity measures in the face of domestic opposition but, as the balance of payments crises of African governments worsen and as alternative financing sources become exhausted, the danger exists of SSA governments resorting to increasingly more repressive measures in an attempt to comply with IMF directives.

Critics of Fund conditionality have evolved two extreme alternatives. On the one hand some argue that the Fund should lay down no other criteria than the prompt repayment of its credits (Williamson 1983; Killick 1983; Dell 1981). This is the minimalist position which argues that the IMF has no business dictating economic and social policy to sovereign governments. At the other extreme lies the argument that conditionality must be focused more on relieving economic policy bottlenecks and on correcting institutional weaknesses so as to make possible greater supply responses. The conditionality which the World Bank is seeking to enforce is of this latter type.

World Bank conditionality

The blueprint for the conditionality attaching to Structural Adjustment Loans (SALs) to SSA is the Bank's report *Accelerated Development in sub-Saharan Africa* (The Berg Report), published in 1981. The basic premise of this report is that 'domestic policy issues are at the heart of the crisis'. Written just before the recent global recession, the Berg Report played down external shocks as a cause of SSA's woes and instead emphasised overvalued exchange rates, inappropriate pricing policies, excessive state intervention and costly import substitution internationalisation as the culprits. The prescription followed logically from the diagnosis. The internal terms of trade must be shifted back towards the rural sector and, especially, in favour of exporters; the activities of the state must be trimmed and private enterprise encouraged in many areas of the economy. Urban real wages must be cut back and charges should be levied for state-provided services. Resources should be channelled into regions with high growth potential and focused on large successful farmers. Industries should also be geared to export promotion. The Report made the case for a doubling of aid in real terms to SSA by 1990 to facilitate adjustment and argued that if this target were met and if its proposed adjustment measures were taken, accompanied by effective family planning programmes, then per capita incomes could grow by as much as 2.1 per cent per annum in the 1980s.

The Berg Report met with widespread criticism for failing to assign sufficient weight to external factors in SSA's problems and for its unqualified espousal of export oriented growth (Allison and Green 1983a; Loxley 1984a). The global recession and its negative effect on the demand for SSA exports, the terms of trade, private foreign investment and official aid flows, provided a telling and timely commentary on the wisdom of Berg's advice. Preoccupied with the need for export promotion, the Report failed to address the critical food supply situation in SSA which had begun to manifest itself by that time. This prompted one observer to comment that the economic strategy proposed by Berg 'would probably be a recipe for starvation' (Green 1983a). The Report was also roundly condemned for its biases in favour of private enterprise over state involvement, for advocating a shift in income distribution from labour to capital and for promoting growth over equity. Some were also quite uneasy over the Report's recommendation that the World Bank should play a more important role in co-ordinating bilateral donors and that both bilateral and multilateral aid flows should be made conditional upon the acceptance by SSA governments of World Bank conditionality.

A follow-up report to 'Accelerated Development' was published by the World Bank in 1983 (World Bank 1983b). This gave greater weight to external shocks, avoided Berg's emphasis on promoting rural differentials through progressive farmer schemes, addressed food problems more explicitly and, above all, recognised the severe political constraints on adjusting SSA economies in the 'desired' direction. Otherwise the policy recommendations paralleled closely those of the Berg Report.

World Bank SAL Conditionality embodies the policy emphases discussed above. Table 7.1 summarises the content of the programmes adopted by the six SSA countries which have, to date, accepted SALs. It is readily apparent that the Bank's concerns go well beyond those of the IMF and reach down to the very micro-level foundations of the

TABLE 7.1

	Ivory Coast I	Ivory Coast II	Kenya I	Kenya II	Malawi I	Malawi II	Mauritius I	Mauritius II	Senegal	Togo
TRADE POLICY										
Tariff reform and imports liberalisation			x	x			x	x		
Export incentive and improved institutional support	x	x	x	x	x		x	x	x	
RESOURCE MOBILISATION										
Budget policy			x	x	x	x			x	x
Interest rate policy			x	x	x	x				

	Ivory Coast		Kenya		Malawi		Mauritius		Senegal	Togo
	I	II	I	II	I	II	I	II		
Strengthening of institutional capacity to manage external borrowing	x		x	x	x	x	x	x	x	x
Public enterprise financial performance		x			x	x			x	x
EFFICIENT USE OF RESOURCES										
Public investment programme revision and review of structural priorities	x	x	x		x	x	x	x	x	x
Pricing policy: • Agriculture	x	x		x	x	x	x	x	x	x
• Energy				x	x		x	x		x
Incentive system: • Industry		x	x	x	x	x	x	x	x	x
Energy conservation measures				x						x
Energy – development of indigenous sources				x			x			x
INSTITUTIONAL REFORMS										
Strengthening of institutional capacity to formulate and implement public investment programme	x	x	x	x	x	x		x	x	x
Institutional efficiency of public sector enterprises	x	x			x	x	x	x	x	x
Improved institutional support in agriculture (marketing etc.)	x	x			x	x	x	x	x	x
Institutional improvements in industry and sub-sector programmes		x			x	x	x			

Notes: I = First SAL Programme II = Second SAL Programme *Source*: World Bank (1984b) economy. World Bank structural adjustment programmes typically provide for extensive institutional and policy reform with the main focus being on allowing world prices a much greater say in the economies of SSA. Other emphases are extending the scope of operations of the private sector and the strengthening of the administrative and technical capacities of the public sector.

Advocates of World Bank-type conditionality claim it is superior to that imposed by the IMF because it avoids the use of a few blunt macro-policy instruments and of inappropriate 'pin-point targetry' of macro performance indicators. It also concentrates on supply stimulation rather than demand restraint.

In reality, however SALs are almost invariably advanced only to countries already implementing an IMF programme and hence World Bank conditionality does *not* substitute for IMF conditionality but, rather, consolidates it. There is no conflict between the two forms of conditionality; one complements the other. The two institutions share the same strategic objectives for third world countries and their conditionality is the instrument for achieving these objectives. They have a written agreement not to disagree publicly about the policy advice each gives and while disputes still arise, these tend to concern the degree to which adjustment efforts need be undertaken and not the *direction* or *type* of adjustment being undertaken.

Leverage and alternative approaches to structural adjustment

The double layer of conditionality implicit in current IMF/IBRD balance of payments assistance is indicative of a growing degree of outside leverage over government policies in SSA. While it is true that no government is compelled to borrow from these institutions, it is equally true that the severity of the crisis in SSA since 1981 leaves most governments with few alternatives. Rehabilitation and revitalisation of SSA economies after the disastrous terms of trade, export volume and capital inflow situation of 1982 requires, at a minimum, a significant injection of foreign exchange and the IMF and IBRD are virtually the only sources available. This renders SSA governments particularly vulnerable to leverage by these bodies. What is more, in the case of the World Bank, this leverage is being exercised, as a matter of explicit Bank policy, even where countries have not negotiated balance of payments assistance in the form of SALs.

The Bank is applying leverage also through its project lending which, of course, unlike IMF and SAL lending, is an on-going feature of World Bank activities in SSA. In addition, the Bank is becoming increasingly active in the field of donor co-ordination. Since SSA countries are highly dependent on both multilateral and bilateral aid flows the potential threat to national sovereignty implicit in a series of World Bank-led donor cartels is obvious. Donors do not, of course, generally acknowledge this threat. Closer co-ordination of aid effort has an appeal when aid resources are scarce and when the broader environment in which aid is being administered is difficult. At the same time recipient governments have generally abdicated responsibility for aid co-ordination – sometimes because of staff constraints, occasionally to prevent the emergence of a collective donor position on economic policy.

While some SSA governments oppose the idea of donor leverage on economic policy, it appears to be a key feature of the World Bank's proposed 'Joint Programme of Action for sub-Saharan Africa'. It seems likely that this programme will consist essentially of Bank initiatives to achieve closer donor co-operation and co-ordination, a larger Bank staff presence in SSA and greater IBRD/IDA input into agricultural research and project preparation. The Bank is likely also to take steps to encourage greater foreign private investment in SSA and to give SSA priority in IBRD/IDA lending. It appears to be appealing for additional annual aid flows of up to $2 billion per annum, but it is not clear where these funds will originate. If the package emerges in this form it will mirror quite closely the recommendations of the Berg Report. Conditionality and donor leverage over SSA economic policy will be strengthened considerably, especially since the additional aid flows would be placed in a special fund and be made available *only* to SSA governments pursuing acceptable adjustment programmes.

The clear trend towards increasing use of leverage over economic policy in SSA does not require a conspiratorial explanation. The IMF and World Bank's model of accumulation, as it has evolved over the past five years, is well-publicised and has an underlying theoretical rationale which is both clear and reasonably coherent. Critics of the Bank and Fund have generally failed to develop an alternative which has these qualities and often opposition to prescribed programmes derives from narrow class or sectional interests with a stake in the 'status quo'. In this situation, donors can make a persuasive case that they would be both remiss and irresponsible if they did *not* exercise leverage. The question that arises, therefore, is what scope exists for SSA countries designing adjustment programmes that address the very real problems they face at the same time avoiding the shortcomings of the IMF/IBRD approach. The Tanzanian experience would suggest that it *is* possible to design a programme which restores macro-balance and growth while at the same time preserving a degree of equity in income distribution *and* a commitment to a strategy of national economic integration. That experience also highlights, however, the crucial role of foreign exchange flows in such a strategy – flows which have not been forthcoming in Tanzania's case.

The starting point for the drawing up of alternative approaches must be the recognition that a good deal of the diagnosis of the IMF and the World Bank has substance, even if one might use broader political economic explanations for the emergence and nature of the problems. SSA governments have undoubtedly pursued policies which have had an anti-rural bias and this has contributed to declining rural surpluses and, in some cases, total production. Investment resources have been used unproductively so that while the rate of investment in SSA has been in excess of 20 per cent on average, growth rates have been relatively low. The export sector has been neglected and there has been a failure to recognise that this sector, traditional or otherwise, would have to be relied upon for many years to assist economic transformation. There has also been in many SSA countries an explosion of unproductive bureaucratisation and the expansion of state control and intervention to the very micro-level of the economy with serious implications for the surplus and efficiency. In rejecting IMF/IBRD prescriptions it is important not to reject out of hand the whole of their diagnosis.

Alternative strategies would, therefore, have to address these problems and the Structural Adjustment Programme for Tanzania did so (Tanzania 1982). It provided for a significant shift in purchasing power towards the rural sector but (unlike IMF prescriptions) only *after* provision had been made for incentive goods to be produced and distributed up-country so that farmers would have *real* and not simply monetary incentives. It provided therefore, for a phasing in of adjustment policies *after* the receipt of emergency balance of payments support. The SAP provided also for the postponement of most investment projects and a concentration instead on rehabilitation and on the utilisation of existing capacity. At the same time, however, it also provided for the maintenance of a portion of investment resources in projects than would further convergence or national economic integration. Provision was made for *gradual* alignment of the exchange rate – in the face of opposition which bordered on religious fanaticism – but did so in a way that protected minimum wage earners through wage adjustment. Subsidies on urban food supplies were cut for 'luxury' items but retained and frozen for maize flour. Recurrent budget expenditures were cut back in the areas of defence and administration, and parastatal overheads were surcharged and reduced. At the same time the imposition of user fees on basic needs services (for example education) was resisted while basic needs expenditures were protected and actually expanded in real terms. Foreign exchange was to be allocated among three priority areas with a view to its having an immediate positive effect on the production of (i) basic essentials; (ii) export earnings through the expansion of selected products; and (iii) recurrent budget revenue. Domestic credit to productive sectors was to rise to make expansion possible. Aid donors were requested to reduce project aid and to switch to the provision of import support to facilitate the implementation of SAP. The programme also argued for a *reduction* in dependence on aid and for the Tanzania government to take decisive and pre-emptive action in the direction of co-ordinating aid donors. Food marketing arrangements were liberalised to permit easier local trade and to reduce the role of the state buying agency to that of buyer of last resort and provider of emergency food relief. Co-operatives, community corporations or, failing them, small private traders were to be encouraged to fill the gaps. Measures were also taken to improve the efficiency of parastatals, in one version of SAP, by greatly extending workers control.

SAP, therefore, recognised the need to expand foreign exchange earnings, improve production and efficiency but at the same time it avoided shock treatment and a commitment to (i) a long-term strategy of all-out export promotion; (ii) the promotion of capitalism; and (iii)- the drastic reduction of living standards of poorer urban workers which underlies IMF/IBRD programmes. As Cheryl Payer has noted, SAP clearly had a different class orientation from orthodox adjustment programmes (Payer 1983).

While much of the SAP has been implemented, the failure of Tanzania to obtain an emergency infusion of foreign finance has meant that several critical components have had to be abandoned. Also, the commitment by the state to some key provisions has been questionable. Foreign exchange shortages have prevented the restoration of growth and the use of idle capacity. As a result, the government seems to have failed to retain some of the redistribution measures originally proposed. Producer prices have risen significantly without goods being first made available in the stores; the exchange rate movements have been slower than recommended so that increased grower prices have led to budgetary imbalance; attempts to rectify this imbalance have resulted in the removal of maize flour subsidies; expanded workers' control was rejected. It is also not clear to what extent basic needs expenditures have been protected and parastatal overheads and defence spending reduced. It appears, however, that investment in projects furthering national economic integration has all but ceased and that the failure to negotiate a short-term foreign exchange infusion has undermined several key aspects of SAP that differentiated it from orthodox packages. As the crisis in Tanzania becomes more protracted, the danger of the government succumbing to external pressures becomes more real and what little remains of progressive policies becoming eroded.

It would be wrong, however, to regard the pressures against a more gradual, equitable, convergence – oriented strategy as emanating entirely from outside the country. There is a good deal of internal support for IMF/IBRD type strategies, mainly from sections of the managerial elite and from would-be capitalists who see their interests being served by an opening up of the system. As current adjustment efforts falter, one can expect pressures from those sections of society to become stronger.

The Tanzania case demonstrates that the design of alternative stabilisation and structural adjustment programmes to those proffered by the IMF and IBRD is possible; but more importantly, it demonstrates that these alternatives may not be feasible, even assuming a commitment to them by the state (on which point Tanzania's record is quite chequered), because of the limited financing options available to SSA.

For those who believe that SSA needs a period of unfettered capitalist accumulation, this conclusion will not be a cause for concern. For those who, like the author, believe that alternative strategies are desirable and, in countries like Tanzania and Mozambique still have a degree of domestic support, the question of their practicability in the current global context remains unanswered. For most of SSA the question of designing alternatives does not, regrettably, arise. Most SSA governments will be pressured in the years ahead to transform their economies along IMF/World Bank lines and will attempt to do so if only because their foreign aid lifeline will be contingent upon those efforts.

8

A commentary on the IMF and World Bank policy programme[1]

Ajit Singh

Introduction

The current world economic crisis has had a devastating effect on the African economies (see Chapter 2). Largely as a result of adverse external factors the trade deficit of the non-oil developing countries in Africa has moved from a small surplus in 1973 to an enormous deficit of nearly $6 billion in 1982. Similarly the current account deficit for these economies has increased 6-fold over the period 1973 to 1983 (IMF 1983).

The main aim of this paper is to examine the validity of the IMF/World Bank policy analysis and programme (see Chapters 6 and 7) to correct this external disequilibrium, particularly in relation to the centrally planned African economies. More specifically, the question of devaluation which is central to this programme and which is invariably a bone of contention between the IMF and the developing countries, will be examined here in some detail.

The analytics of devaluation in centrally planned economies in Africa: some general considerations

One obvious method of adjustment of the external disequilibrium is by means of a devaluation of the country's currency, which is supposed to stimulate exports by reducing their price in terms of foreign currency, and to reduce imports by increasing import prices in local currency. Although devaluation involves only changing a single price – that of domestic currency versus the foreign currency – it is an extremely important policy issue since it has far-reaching implications for the whole economy in the spheres of production, inflation, as well as income distribution.[2]

In textbook economics, the advisability of the devaluation of a country's currency depends on the values of the relevant elasticities for imports and exports – how much exports are encouraged and imports discouraged by a given percentage change in price. However, modern economic analysis recognises that a devaluation is a much more complex undertaking as it has profound repercussions throughout the economy. A proper analysis of devaluation must rest on a careful *empirical* examination of the following kinds of questions:

1. the size of the net effect on the balance of payments;
2. the time period over which the effects on exports and imports occur: is it six months, one year or 5 years? Are imports affected earlier than exports?

104

3. the certainty of the effects; and
4. the impact on the rate of inflation and income distribution. Again what are the short-term dynamics of these effects? Will inflation be affected sooner than foreign balance and what will be the implications? Will that set off a chain reaction of wage changes, further inflation, financial instability, etc?

Outside the sphere of orthodox equilibrium economics, in the real world of dynamic interactions, every one of these questions is vitally important in a decision about devaluation. This is not just a matter of academic refinement but of lessons which economists have learnt from the actual experiences of devaluation in several countries. As a consequence, the economics profession is today much more sceptical about the efficacy of devaluation as an instrument of structural change than it used to be.[3]

In a typical African commodity-exporting country, the general view would be that at least in the short term, say over a one-year period, exports are unlikely to be encouraged by a devaluation since a small country can sell whatever quantity of a commodity it wishes at internationally determined prices. The short-term elasticity of commodity *production* is also usually relatively small. Other things being equal, imports could be discouraged by their higher prices. However, in a centrally planned economy with a serious balance of payments constraint, all 'inessential' imports are likely to have already been restricted by direct central bank controls. To the extent that even essential imports may need to be restricted further for balance of payments reasons, from a social point of view, this is best achieved on the basis of social priorities determined by the government rather than the private profitability criterion of the market.

In view of this low short time price-elasticity of foreign balance in a commodity exporting country, there is a presumption against devaluation which would need to be outweighed by other factors to make it a useful policy instrument. The IMF, therefore, normally advances one or more of the following arguments in favour of large devaluations in African economies.

1. Devaluation, it is suggested, will have a positive effect on the balance of payments even in the short term because (i) it will reduce leakages through smuggling; (ii) discourage the parallel market in foreign exchange and thus diminish the loss of foreign exchange to the government through that channel; and (iii) even though commodity exports may not be increased in the short-term, there will be a favourable impact on the *manufacturing* balance.
2. Devaluation, it is believed, will have a *long-term* favourable effect on the foreign balance.
3. Both in the short or the long term it is argued that a devaluation will help to restore the government's budgetary balance.
4. Devaluation, it is argued, is essential since the rate of inflation in the African countries has been much greater than the world rate of inflation, and there has therefore been an appreciation of the real exchange rate.

These arguments will be taken up below in turn.

Devaluation and foreign balance

As far as the impact of a devaluation on the foreign balance in the *short term* is concerned, the IMF's case for expecting a favourable effect in commodity-exporting countries usually rests heavily on considerations concerning smuggling and the parallel market in foreign exchange. The Fund does not normally provide any empirical estimates of by how *much* the foreign balance will be improved as a consequence. They invariably argue on broad, general grounds that devaluations of the kind they recommend will reduce the scope of the parallel and illegal markets and hence increase the official foreign exchange resources.

On closer inspection, these general arguments do not appear to me to be universally valid. The economic situation, the institutional framework, the social priorities and the effectiveness of the government machinery of course differ between countries. I have examined the Fund's arguments on this point specifically in relation to the Tanzanian economy. I have found them deficient for a number of reasons.

First, the main reason why a profit-maximising Tanzanian coffee producer may sell his produce illegally in a foreign country is not so much because the Tanzanian shilling is overvalued, but that from abroad, he can import luxury goods (hi-fi equipment, white goods, etc.) whose import is prohibited on social grounds in Tanzania. Unless, therefore, Tanzania changes its social priorities, and allows importation of such luxury items by those who directly earn foreign exchange, this kind of producer will continue to export his coffee illegally even if the Tanzanian shilling were devalued to 20 or 40 shillings to a dollar. It is, therefore, unlikely that a devaluation alone will make a significant difference to the level of smuggling activity.

Similarly with respect to the parallel market for the foreign exchange, the primary determinant of demand in this market is the desire of a section of the business community and other rich Tanzanians to repatriate some of their wealth abroad. The exchange rate on this market is not therefore determined by the underlying health of the economy or current account considerations, but by reasons of capital flight. Experience from other countries suggests that a small devaluation in such circumstances is ineffective in this respect. On the other hand, a large devaluation is likely to make matters worse rather than better. This is because such devaluations normally bring in their train an increase in the rate of inflation, wage demands, etc. (see below) and greater uncertainty, thus intensifying the pressures for capital flight through illegal channels. Thus if the shilling is devalued from 10 to 30 shillings to a US dollar, the illegal market rate, instead of being lowered, may go up from 50 to 100 shillings.[4]

Therefore, in the case of Tanzania, I remain extremely sceptical that the short-term foreign balance will be improved by a devaluation because of its effect either on smuggling or on the parallel market in foreign exchange. The situation in other countries may well be different and the Fund's arguments may have greater validity; nevertheless even in such countries the above considerations should be kept in view.

The third argument, under this heading – the short-term effect on foreign balance in manufacturing – has *prima facie* more substance to it. Again the situation differs between countries, but in a detailed analysis in relation to Tanzanian manufacturing industry, I reached a rather different conclusion (Singh 1982). I came to the view that despite the depressed level of world economic activity, there was still some scope for increasing Tanzania's manufacturing exports. But my analysis indicated that this objective would be best achieved not by a general devaluation, but instead by (i) concentration on a small number of large exporting items (e.g. textiles, cement); and (ii) by offering at the point of export differing amounts of subsidies on these products. In conceptual economic terms, policy (ii) amounts to a system of multiple exchange rates, but it is administratively simpler to operate it in the form of export subsidies. With respect to manufactured imports, as argued earlier, they are not competing with domestic production but at their current level are an absolutely essential complement to it. If anything, this consideration makes even stronger the economic argument for *selectivity* and hence multiple exchange rates, to be administered in the form of export subsidies and, if necessary, import duties.

There is a much better case for expecting a favourable effect of a devaluation on foreign balance in the *long term*, whether in agriculture or in manufacturing. However, in relation to the long term, the following points should be kept in mind.

First, with respect to agriculture, although a devaluation may provide an *incentive* to increase production of export crops at the expense of, say, food crops, such production possibilities may only be realised if there is increased availability of infrastructural (e.g. transport) and other vital agricultural inputs (e.g. fertiliser, water). In many African countries today, the provision of these inputs is likely to have a far greater quantitative effect on export crop production than any price incentive resulting from a devaluation. Nevertheless, this is an empirical question, and the relative effects of prices and *other factors* needs to be carefully assessed in relation to each export crop separately and to agriculture as a whole. I have not seen a satisfactory analysis in these terms from the IMF.

Second, even in the long run, in the circumstances of commodity-exporting countries, particularly the centrally planned economies, a system of multiple exchange rates, operated through export subsidies and import duties, is economically more efficient than a single depreciated rate for the currency (Kaldor 1982).

Thirdly, it is extremely important to note that in this context, the 'long run' is crucially dependent on what happens in the short term. This is for the simple reason that the supposed favourable long-run effects of a devaluation on foreign balance can work only to the extent that there is an 'effective devaluation' – i.e. the devaluation is not nullified by an increase in the domestic rate of inflation. Thus the 'long run', as is sometimes blithely believed, does not provide any escape from the short-term dynamics of devaluation in terms of its interacting effects on prices and wages and on the rest of the economy.

Devaluation, inflation and the budget: the politics of devaluation

It is essential to the logic of an 'effective devaluation' that there should be a cut in real wages, by making all imported goods (and their substitutes) more expensive in relation to workers' incomes. An IMF programme of devaluation, credit restraint, tight budget, 'liberalisation' of domestic and foreign trade regimes, if successfully implemented, has two extremely important short-term effects on the economy: (i) it leads to a cut in overall consumption and real wages; and (ii) it leads to a redistribution of income away from those who produce for the domestic market to those who are involved in production for exports or import substitutes.

The seeds of inflation and political destabilisation lie precisely in these two intended effects of a devaluation. As Kaldor points out:

The main objection to this approach is that it assumes that devaluation is capable of changing the critical price and wage relationships within a country in an effective manner, even when domestic fiscal and monetary policies are incapable of bringing about these results. But it cannot be taken for granted that the internal distribution of income, which is the outcome of complex political forces, can be effectively changed by devaluation. It is more likely that a large-scale devaluation will cause an internal price upheaval (at the cost of a great deal of additional inflation) which will end up by reproducing much the same price relationships – between prices and wages and between internal and external prices – as prevailed before the devaluation. (Kaldor 1982)

Inflation is not just a simple monetary phenomenon: otherwise the world would have got rid of it a long time ago by merely reducing the 'money supply'. It is embedded in the struggle over distribution of income or, as we argue in Cambridge, it arises from inconsistent claims over the national income. Let us illustrate in simple terms how this process would work in a country such as Tanzania. With fixed total production in the short term, a devaluation would mean that the real wages of workers and government employees, say, in Dar es Salaam would have to be reduced further in order to benefit, say, the coffee growers in Kilimanjaro: in this way to transfer income from the non-exporters to the exporters. In view of the fact that there has already been a large fall (perhaps of the order of as much as 50 per cent) in the urban standards of living in Tanzania during the last three years, a further fall resulting from a large effective devaluation would inevitably lead to compensating wage demands. Such demands, if they are not met, would produce political conflicts; on the other hand, if they are met, this would fuel inflation and thus require even more nominal devaluation and the process would then repeat itself.[5]

This analysis of the political economy of devaluation is essential to an examination of the IMF's argument concerning devaluation and fiscal balance. It is suggested that whether or not a devaluation improves foreign balance, it is desirable for the very important reason that it will improve the government's budgetary balance. A devaluation will apparently achieve the latter objective by helping to reduce or eliminate export crop subsidies and the deficits of the marketing authorities.

In relation to this argument, it seems to me that there are certain elementary questions which need to be asked first. Why is one interested in improving the budgetary balance? Is it because this will aid the *real* economy – production, employment, etc., or reduce the rate of inflation, or is it an end in itself? As was seen in section 8.2, in a balance of payments-constrained economy, if a devaluation does not help relax this constraint, a devaluation-induced budgetary improvement by itself will not achieve any of these desirable objectives with respect to the real economy. The rate of inflation actually *increases* rather than being decreased as a consequence of devaluation.

It may be argued that the rate of inflation will be reduced in the long run. This argument, however, completely abstracts from the crucial political economy and short-term dynamic considerations outlined earlier. With fixed total production in the short term, a devaluation cannot improve the fiscal balance simply by fiat; somebody has to pay for it in real terms by a reduction in his or her current social benefits or an increase in his or her taxes. What is being implied is that the people will accept this cut in their real income brought about by a devaluation which they will not if implemented directly through domestic fiscal and monetary policy. This seems to me to underestimate people's wisdom in such matters.

As to whether or not the budgetary balance will actually improve as a consequence of devaluation and associated measures is itself problematical. It will depend in a very important way on the rate of inflation. This in turn is a function of the degree of political consensus in the society about the proposed redistribution of income. Thus the estimates of the rates of inflation usually put forward in the IMF exercises on this question are not simply some technical data, but can only be regarded as representing the Fund's *political* assessment of the redistributive conflict.

Devaluation, inflation, and 'real effective' exchange rates

With respect to the economics of devaluation, the IMF increasingly puts forward what it believes to be yet another powerful argument in favour of devaluation in a country such as Tanzania. Essentially, it is argued that since the Tanzanian rate of inflation has been greater than the rate of inflation among Tanzania's trading partners, shillings should be devalued to compensate for the differences in the inflation rates. This line of reasoning has a certain surface plausibility; it therefore deserves systematic examination.

It may be useful to start by considering certain historical experience which is relevant to this issue and with which I am personally familiar. This is the recent case of Mexico where I had been an economic adviser. A very similar argument had been advanced by the IMF and the Mexican Central Bank in support of a Mexican devaluation in 1981, i.e. that since the Mexican rate of inflation was greater than the US rate (the US being Mexico's main trading partner), Mexico should devalue to compensate for this. For all the reasons outlined above, my colleagues and I at the Ministry of Industry had argued that a devaluation would lead to a further divergence in the Mexican and US rates of inflation, hence require a further devaluation and this in turn lead to a wage-price spiral, financial instability, etc. In 1981, the Mexican rate of inflation was 28 per cent and the US rate was about 10 per cent, i.e. a difference of 18 percentage points. A devaluation of the Mexican peso in February 1982 set in train a sequence of events much as had been predicted: inflation, wage demands, further devaluation. As a consequence, the Mexican rate of inflation by the end of 1982 was about 100 per cent per annum, and the divergence from the US rate of inflation (5 per cent in 1982) had widened to 95 percentage points.

However, the IMF's argument on this issue is not based on empirical evidence, or actual experience, but on a very old economic theory called the purchasing-power parity doctrine. There has been a vast literature on this subject since Gustav Cassells first propounded it earlier this century. The subsequent work shows that the theory is valid only under extremely restrictive assumptions; its application to commodity exporting countries like Tanzania requires major modifications, none of which the IMF cares to make.

Very briefly,[6] first, under conditions of competition, the theory makes sense only if it is interpreted in terms of costs rather than prices. Secondly, with respect to 'costs', the only relevant element relates to the value added by domestic operations, excluding the element of imports in total costs. Thirdly, there is a major problem of measuring parity in terms of costs if the *relative* costs of different commodities and services greatly differ as between one country and another. If, say, the ratio of the cost of a unit of A (a manufactured commodity) to the cost of a unit of B (a raw material) is five times higher in country X than the corresponding ratio in country Y, and the weight of the two commodities in the total output of each country is also very different, there is no unique way of deciding how the level of costs *in general* in the two countries are related to each other in terms of a common currency. There is no particular virtue in comparing averages of the two countries; nor is there any reason to suppose that such a 'parity' rate is one at which the balance of payments on current account will also be in equilibrium.

These considerations suggest that the application of the purchasing-power parity doctrine to a country like Tanzania is essentially valid only in relation to the 'domestic' element of the costs of primary products. But as in the earlier case of manufactures where it was argued that a multiple exchange rate, administered in the form of tariffs and subsidies, was preferable to a single exchange rate, here again there may be a whole zone of rates rather than a single exchange rate which is equally desirable from the point of view of the balance of payments. It is only when the exchange rate becomes so over valued that the customary standard of living of workers in the primary sectors is unduly depressed in relation to that of the other sectors of the population, or in relation to their own previous living standards, with unfavourable effects on the production of export crops, that an adjustment is called for.

In the case of Tanzania, there has clearly been a fall in the standard of living of the producers of primary products during the last three years, as indeed there has been of all sections of the population. It is, however, difficult to believe that the *relative* standard of living of primary producers of the rural population has declined more than of, say, urban wage-earners. The evidence I have seen points to the contrary, but this matter clearly needs to be kept under close review. And of course the position in other countries may well be rather different than in Tanzania.

Concluding remarks on devaluation and the global dimension

To sum up, the foregoing discussion suggests that there are powerful arguments against a devaluation – and even more so against large devaluations of the kind being proposed by the IMF in Africa – in a commodity-exporting country, and particularly in a centrally planned economy where the foreign exchange allocation is essentially carried out by the Central Bank on the basis of social priorities. This does not, however, in any way mean that a commodity-exporting centrally planned economy should never devalue. Rather, such a country should carefully examine the extent and the consequences of any proposed devaluation by asking and answering all the questions listed in section 8.1; for, otherwise, there is a serious possibility that the devaluation may make the economic situation worse rather than better. In addition, the country should also examine the relative merits of a general devaluation with those of more selective and targeted action by means of multiple exchange rates which may be administered in the form of subsidies and tariffs.

Finally, there is another general argument against devaluation for commodity-exporting countries which is applicable at a global level – rather than with respect to any particular country. During the last few years, despite stagnant or falling world demand, the IMF has been prescribing large or small devaluations to commodity-exporting countries. Suppose they all follow the IMF advice, manage to achieve effective devaluations of their currencies, and further obtain the hypothesised results with respect to production and exports. What would be the effects of all this at the global level? There will be a fall in commodity prices and the terms of trade will move further against the commodity exporters.

Contrast the IMF's prescription for poor countries with that of another international organisation serving the interests of rich countries, namely the EEC. Faced with falling demand for steel, the EEC's Industries Commission helped set up a steel cartel of European producers to *cut* production and capacity on a co-operative basis and to help stabilise steel prices. It is instructive to note that despite a larger excess capacity in steel, perhaps of the order of 40 per cent, the steel prices since say, 1979, have not collapsed; they have been relatively stable. On the other hand, coffee prices have collapsed – less than halved since 1977 despite a relatively much smaller margin of excess capacity. The sensible answer to these difficulties of the commodity producers surely lies not in prescribing devaluations to each of them individually, but in commodity agreements which will eliminate over production and restore remunerative prices.

The fundamental structural disequilibrium of the African economies: the long-term policy issues

Section 8.3 considered the short to medium-term macroeconomics and the political economy of the IMF approach to economic adjustment. Although it was argued that a large-scale devaluation and associated policy measures are not in general the most appropriate, let alone the only means of achieving such an objective in commodity-producing centrally planned African economies, it is important to emphasise that adjustment will still need to be carried out. This is because, as noted above, many of the African economies are today characterised by a fundamental structural disequilibrium. The correction of this disequilibrium requires major changes in the structure and development of the real economy, of both agricultural and industrial production. The optimal alternative methods of adjustment will depend on the specific economic and political circumstances of each country and on its history and the particular institutional framework. Furthermore, such changes will need to be carried out over a number of years. It is, therefore, important to examine at least briefly the long-term policy issues involved in the correction of the structural disequilibrium.

Perhaps I may illustrate this by taking the Tanzanian example with which I am personally familiar. In the Tanzanian case in the short term, in view of the acute foreign exchange crisis, there may be no alternative but to attempt to increase marketed output of export crops. Of course Tanzania may wish to pursue this goal by means other than a large devaluation recommended by the IMF, for example through a combination of some producer price incentives, changes in agricultural organisation, political and party mobilisation, etc. However, the question is that even if these measures succeed, will they correct the *long-term* structural disequilibrium of the Tanzanian economy?

The central strategic weakness of most third world economies, including the African countries, is that they are still basically producers and exporters of commodities and raw materials. The export demand for these commodities is entirely determined by the economic interactions and the economic policies of the rich countries. At the same time, being industrially underdeveloped, most poor countries are totally dependent on the industrial countries for imports of capital goods, and in many cases for consumer goods as well. This is the main reason for the chronic external disequilibria of the poor countries (Taylor 1982).

The poor countries can only escape from this trap by industrialisation. It is also only through appropriate industrialisation that they can achieve high rates of economic growth and thereby help meet the basic needs of their people (Singh 1982; JASPA 1982). At a time of acute economic crisis for most third world economies outlined in section 8, it is useful to note in this regard the successful performance of two of the world's leading poor economies: India and China.

These two countries, since their independence, have deliberately followed policies of 'self-reliance', based on import-substitution, and 'inward looking' industrial strategies. Over the last thirty years, they have managed to train their people, build their own technical and scientific infrastructures, and develop a range of capital goods and defence industries. The result is that today the rate of economic growth of either India or China is more or less independent of world economic growth. The indigenous factors – e.g. the weather and the growth of agriculture – are far more important in determining the expansion of these economies than the world economic situation. It is an irony of the structure of the world economy today that in this particular respect, these two poor countries are far better placed than a rich industrial country like France. France has had among the highest long-term rates of industrial growth in Europe during the last two decades; it also has huge gold reserves; it has a socialist President committed to expansion of employment and production. Yet France's economic growth is almost entirely determined by the economic policies of Chancellor Kohl and President Reagan (Singh 1983).

It may be argued that India and China have been successful in creating self-reliant economies because of their large size. There is some truth in that, but not the whole truth. France is also a large country. So are Brazil and Mexico, each of whom is also much richer than either India or China. However Brazil and Mexico are today in deep economic crisis, and if they do not default or radically renegotiate their enormous debts, they are likely to be condemned to negative or very low economic growth for the rest of this decade. The essential reason for these economic differences between Brazil and Mexico on the one hand, and India and China on the other is, that during the last 15 years the former chose to follow export-oriented, outward-looking industrial strategies based on multinational investment and foreign debt. As a consequence Mexico and Brazil developed highly import-dependent industrial structures which left them vulnerable to prolonged economic disruption when the world economy ceased to expand.

Although African economies are at a much lower level of industrial development, their extant industrial structures suffer from similar weaknesses. The diversification of these economies from producing simple agricultural products and minerals to the production of some manufactures did not, as envisaged, reduce their degree of dependence on the world economy; instead the latter appreciably increased (Wangwe 1983). As far as economic policy is concerned, the only way African countries can today hope to salvage and make their industrial structures viable is by attempting to reduce the propensity to import and by enhancing import capacity to the extent it is possible. In view of the low level of industrial development in African countries and the present circumstances of the world economy, both objectives are clearly extremely difficult and require exceptional measures suited to the particular conditions of each country. Singh (1982) discusses such measures in relation to the Tanzanian economy.

In conclusion, the lesson to be drawn from the present crisis is not that the pursuit of industrialisation by African countries during the last two decades was mistaken, but that the industrial structures which they developed were invariably unviable and inappropriate. In a slow growing world economy viable industrial development in these countries in the future will require a thorough reconsideration of their industrial policies. In particular, these policies will need to pay special attention to issues such as (i) income distribution and sustainable patterns of consumer demand; (ii) the proper short and long-term relationship between agricultural and industrial development; and (iii) where the country is small, appropriate forms of economic co-operation with other countries.

Conclusion

It has been argued in this paper that the present world economic crisis has extremely important short and long-term policy implications for national and rural development in Africa. The policies being recommended by the IMF/World Bank[7] to deal with the crisis are not the only ones which are feasible. They are also not the most appropriate ones for correcting the fundamental structural disequilibrium of the commodity-exporting, centrally planned, African economies. In many cases such policies are likely to worsen the economic and social situation rather than improve it. Further, even to the extent that these policies succeed, the price of adjustment will tend to be paid disproportionately by wage-earners and other lower income groups.

More generally, it is not difficult to see that although the arguments are couched in technical terms, the IMF and the World Bank are using the present economic crisis to push the centrally planned or socialist countries in Africa towards market-oriented, non-socialist development, in return for which these organisations provide some economic assistance. The alternative path before these countries is to attempt to solve their grave economic crisis within the framework of their existing economic and political institutions but without Fund/Bank assistance. In view of the seriousness of the economic situation, the latter path is extremely difficult, particularly in the short run, but more often than not it is not in principle an unviable one (Singh 1984b). This is the serious choice confronting the African countries today.

NOTES

1. This chapter has been abstracted from a longer paper which was originally presented at the ILO/FAO Workshop on the Transformation of Agrarian Systems in the Centrally Planned Economies of Africa, held at Arusha, Tanzania, in October 1983. The reader is referred to this longer paper for a more complete analysis of the issues presented here.
2. In Singh (1983), I have systematically examined the problem of devaluation in relation to the Tanzanian economy. As I believe this analysis to be of more general relevance, particularly in relation to centrally planned economies in Africa, I have drawn extensively on this paper in the discussion of this section.
3. The Chicago and Cambridge schools of economics, which normally have very different views about the functioning of the economic system, do agree on one point: that exchange rate adjustment is in *general* not a suitable method for structural change and that its major consequence is to generate inflation. The reasoning in each case is, of course, different: the Chicago economists base their case on the 'law of one price' and the Cambridge economists on the concept of real wage resistance. See for example, McCallum and Vines (1981).
4. In the economist's language, not only the demand for foreign exchange may increase for reasons given in the text, the 'supply price' of illegal foreign exchange may also rise for similar reasons.
5. Thus it is no accident that the IMF programmes of devaluation in many developing countries have led to the worsening of inflationary conditions and serious political conflict. 'Several hundred people died during food riots in Morocco (which signed an SDR 819m agreement in March 1981) last June, while protestors took to the streets in Sudan in January after price rises for basic commodities followed agreement on an SDR 198m programme in October. Both governments were attempting to meet targets agreed with the fund.' *Financial Times*, April 1982. See also Helleiner (1983).
6. This statement of some of the required modifications to the theory is based on Kaldor (1982).
7. I have not analysed separately in this paper the World Bank approach to economic policy in Africa. However I note Helleiner's (1983) observation:

The World Bank has also been taking a keen interest in the structural adjustment needs of countries experiencing medium-term balance of payments difficulties. For this purpose, it has developed a new 'structural adjustment loan' that involves IMF-style macroeconomic conditionality. *In fact these World Bank loans have involved more conditions than most IMF loans, because countries typically do not qualify for them until they have first come to an accommodation with the IMF.* In Africa, the bank has so far made such loans to Kenya, Malawi, Ivory Coast, and Senegal. It has also embarked upon far closer co-operation and co-ordination with the IMF, in its approaches to member countries than was usual in earlier times. (Emphasis added.)

9

What's right with the Berg Report and what's left of its criticisms?[1]

John Sender and Sheila Smith

Introduction

The starting point for this paper is that the Berg Report highlights certain problems which are important, and for which solutions have to be found. In particular, many sub-Saharan African (SSA) countries have been experiencing severe balance-of-trade deficits, falling volumes of exports, and hence a diminishing capacity to import the consumer, intermediate and capital goods needed for economic growth. Part of this is attributed by Berg to overvalued exchange rates, which is very difficult to deny. Berg also discusses the difficulties associated with, and the negative effects resulting from, the use of administrative controls on imports: corruption, delays, underutilisation of capacity, etc. Import-intensive industry has been encouraged, while industrialisation based on the use of local raw materials and labour has been discouraged. In the context of severe shortages of foreign exchange, efficiency in its use is particularly vital. Furthermore, the Berg Report indicates that limited benefits have stemmed from public sector activities in many African countries; the large shares of public expenditure allocated to administration and defence; the huge expansion of unproductive employment, are all common characteristics of the public sector in African countries. Furthermore, Marketing Boards and parastatals remove large proportions of potential producer incomes. Trends in world market prices cannot explain the degree to which African agricultural producers have been forced to accept low returns for their crops.

We start by criticising the response of some of Berg's critics (Allison and Green 1983a; Sau 1983; Clough and Williams 1984; Loxley 1984). The first section of this paper is entitled: What's Left of Criticisms of Berg? and is divided into eight sub-sections. The second section is entitled: What is Wrong with Berg? and outlines a somewhat different critique from those discussed in the first section. Finally we have a section called: What's Left of the Alternatives to Berg? in which we criticise the alternative economic strategies put forward by the left as substitutes for the Berg strategy. We will make a virtue of our deficiencies in not detailing our own alternatives. This can be justified on the grounds that the contents of any alternative should vary as between different SSA countries, for example, the degree of priority which should be accorded to the establishment of a capital goods economy in Nigeria is very different from that accorded in Burkina Faso or Mali. We will, however, discuss some of the criteria which any credible alternative must fulfil.

What's left of criticisms of Berg?

1. A common strand in most critiques of the Berg Report is a 'defence of the state'. A defining characteristic of these critiques is a naive and utopian view of the actual or potential role of the state. Some quotations will demonstrate this: Colclough states that, 'In the case of poor rural and urban populations ... government expenditures simultaneously promote both growth *and* distributional goals' (Colclough 1983: 28); Philip Daniel argues that, 'In marked contrast to the thrust of World Bank policies in the recent past, the Report makes very little mention of the redistributive role of the public sector' (Daniel 1983: 12); finally, Sau, on explanations for slow growth rates of food output, states that, 'the post-independence governments wanted to respond to the needs and aspirations of people in remote and disfavoured regions of their countries. They hoped to achieve greater *regional balance* in development, since in the previous decade resources had been concentrated on export-oriented sectors and regions' (Sau 1983: 1900, emphasis in original).

This approach involves a major contradiction; it implicitly or explicitly rejects the notion of 'trickle-down' concerning private economic activity, but asserts a powerful 'trickle-down' process concerning state activity. Perhaps this is based on the hope that a huge increase in the already phenomenal level of public sector employment will eventually ensure that all the rural population has a bureaucratic job. Some proponents of this view, for example Colclough, recognise the contradiction to a certain extent. He reproduces Berg Report figures (see Table 9.1) and then states that what governments ought to do, instead of cutting public expenditure, is, first, reduce expenditure on administration and defence, and increase expenditure on education, health and public services; secondly, they should reduce public sector wages. No explanation is given of the political processes whereby this dramatic change might occur.

TABLE 9:1 Percentage distribution of government expenditure 1978

| | African countries | | All countries | | |
	low income	middle income	low income	middle income	industrial
General public service	22.9	20.5	18.4	14.2	8.2
Defence	11.2	6.5	11.3	11.5	6.9
	34.1	27.0	29.7	25.7	15.1

Evidence on the distribution of public expenditure *within* categories of health, education and housing does not support the equity arguments. Even an 'acceptable' state, such as that alleged to exist in Tanzania, has a less egalitarian record than is usually assumed: the overwhelming majority of state expenditure on health favours urban and relatively high income sections of the population.[2] Mbilinyi's work on education (1973) and Coulson's data on the distribution of the benefits of public sector activities also call the 'equity' argument into question (Coulson 1982). The argument that public expenditure is a 'good thing', or at least that exhortation can lead to it becoming a 'good thing' in terms of its impact on equity and the welfare of the poor, is an utterly apolitical one. It does not attempt to address the question of why public expenditure is what it is, has the effects it has – and implicitly assumes that the politics of public expenditure can be transformed with ease.

The Berg Report's political analysis is said by all critics to be inadequate, yet these critics defend the public sector on the grounds that it is already, or can with ease become, a caring and sharing distributor of Basic Needs. The political analysis of Berg's critics leaves everything to be desired.

2. One critique (Daniel 1983) is devoted entirely to demonstrating that the structural adjustment loans and other strategies advocated by the Berg Report are very much consistent with, in fact suspiciously similar to, the IMF's approach to adjustment and conditionality. No critique of IMF practice is offered – it is, apparently, enough to indicate similarity to anything done by the IMF to prove that it should be rejected. One problem with these arguments is that Berg is recommending a massive increase in aid, and a switch from project to programme aid. In the past, criticisms of aid have stressed the niggardly level and rigidly project-tied nature of aid. Furthermore, there have always been substantial elements of effective conditionality attached to even low levels of project aid disbursed by the IBRD. What new factors have caused the critics to see these positive changes in such a negative light?

For those who regard the IMF as a bogey there are certain additional points which it might be useful to stress: as has recently been pointed out by Killick (1982) and Griffith-Jones (1981), criticisms of the IMF have frequently diverted attention from domestic policy failures, involving gross neglect of the productive capacity of the economy, absurdly ambitious and long-gestating infrastructure projects, and welfare expenditures that subsidise middle-class consumption behind egalitarian rhetoric. Moreover, the IMF has not systematically discriminated against socialist states. The fact that some attempts at 'transition to socialism' have generated financial chaos is not primarily attributable to the IMF. This tells us that such transitions are difficult for poor economies attempting to establish or sustain a manufacturing base, and that the capacity of the economy to earn the foreign exchange required for accumulation has to be assured. In fact, a far more substantial and immediate enemy of transitions to socialism than the IMF, apart from domestic class forces opposed to such transitions, is the Reagan regime. The Reagan administration's attempts to restrict IMF resources and IDA ought to tell us something important about the demands that the left should be making with regard to the future role of the IMF.

Daniel's substitute for a critique of the new World Bank-IMF double act is to pose a number of questions (Daniel 1983: 16), three of which we will quote, briefly answer and/or dismiss as irrelevant.

'Is a largely uniform approach to domestic policy appropriate across the whole range of countries in SSA?'

The IMF does not take a uniform approach to domestic policy, nor have the terms of its intervention been uniform across countries (see, for example, Killick 1982).

'Is a sharp move to export orientation justifiable or even practicable in current and expected international conditions?'

We argue below that it is not only justifiable and practicable, but also essential.

'Why have questions of income distribution suddenly become unimportant?'

This question assumes that these issues have been important in the recent past. To whom were they important and what difference did it make? In what ways, apart from naive presumptions about the state, can it be demonstrated that Berg's recommendations will lead to particular patterns of income distribution?

3. The third issue is income distribution. Nearly all critics are united in asserting that Berg's recommendations will inevitably and obviously lead to a worsening income distribution. Aside from those that rely on the very dubious assumption that the public sector invariably has a positive distributional effect and that, therefore, a smaller public sector will worsen distribution, the basis of the 'distributional' criticisms of Berg is not made clear.[3]

What are the distribution critics arguing? To what aspects of distribution are they referring: between men and women, poor, middle and rich peasants, farm owners and capitalists, recipients of wages, profits, rents and dividends? Without any clarity about the categories of income recipient being referred to, the argument that Berg's proposals will 'worsen' things is no more than empty rhetoric. If the group whose fate is being lamented is 'the poor', it might be instructive to consider whether 'the poor' are worse off, in terms of nutritional status, life expectancy, etc., in areas of growing export crop output, or in areas of stagnant, falling or no export crop output. We are unlikely to find that it is the former.[4]

4. The fourth set of criticisms of Berg concerns the terms of trade and elasticities of demand for primary commodities; it is, apparently, still received wisdom that the terms of trade for ldcs and for primary commodities are inevitably subject to a secular decline, despite the well-trodden ground indicating that empirical evidence does not support such clear and simple conclusions (Spraos 1982). Sau (1983) and Loxley (1984a), for example, assert the secular decline without discussion. Godfrey (1983), more sophisticated than the latter two, uses a different argument: that the elasticities of demand and large share of world markets for many of SSA's primary commodities are such that increasing the volume of primary exports will be a recipe for reduced, rather than increased, foreign exchange income. This is unconvincing: first, there are also 'many' primary commodities for which SSAs share in world markets is very small indeed (see Table 9.2).

TABLE 9:2 World market share of sub-Saharan Africa in selected export commodities, 1976–8 (%)

Beef	1.6	Cotton	11.3
Palm Oil	5.7	Tobacco	8.9
Bananas	4.6	Rubber	4.8
Maize	0.4	Hides	4.4
Timber	5.1		

Source: World Bank (1981b: Table 3.5)

There are, in addition, other primary commodities produced on a large scale in Africa that hardly figure as exports at all, whose share in world markets is therefore miniscule. The exports of these could certainly be increased without any impact on world prices. Secondly, in the case of a long list of agricultural commodities, non-African countries have been increasing exports whilst Africa's share has been falling (cocoa, groundnuts, groundnut oil, palm oil, bananas, maize, timber, tobacco, rubber, hides and skins, sisal). Table 9.3 shows the sustained rapidity with which Africa has lost its share of the world market for some of these commodities. It should be noted that even if Africa's share was 50 per cent, one would have to assume a price elasticity of demand with respect to exports of less than 0.5, if one wishes to argue that an increase in the volume of Africa's exports would lead to a reduction in Africa's export earnings.[5]

TABLE 9:3 Africa's share in world exports of selected commodities (%)

	1970–2	*1976–8*	*1982*
Cocoa	80.1	69.3	65.0
Groundnuts	53.5	35.5	26.8
Groundnut oil	55.7	43.2	42.2
Palm oil	20.8	5.7	2.5

Source: 1970–72 and 1976–8: World Bank (1981b) 1982: FAO, *Production Yearbook* (1983)

Thirdly, price movements for several primary commodities have been favourable during 1970–80: of those commodities which experienced positive rates of growth of price during the 1970s, *only* coffee increased in export volume from SSA (out of coffee, cocoa, timber, rubber, sisal). Fourth, if we consider export unit values and volumes for African agricultural exports as a whole, we find that in the aggregate, price trends cannot be regarded as the source of falling export earnings, with export volume in 1982 more than 10 per cent less than in 1971 (see Table 9.4).

TABLE 9:4 African agricultural exports

	Export unit value	*Export value*	*Export volume*
1971	53	52	99
1974–6	100	100	100
1982	132	119	89

Source: FAO Production Yearbook (1983)

Finally, of those countries which experienced a reduction in their income terms of trade during the 1970s (14 countries), only one (Liberia) had a positive rate of growth of export volume. For the Godfrey hypothesis to be convincing, we would expect that more than one country would have shown a negative association between export volume and export income. In some cases, the decline in export volume has been, and continues to be, dramatic (see Table 9.5). Note that, in addition, between 1979 and 1982, in Tanzania, the volume of cotton and sisal exports has halved; the volume of cashew exports fell to a quarter of 1979 levels, and the volume of tea exports fell to less than three-quarters of 1979 levels (IMF 1983: 17). How can the left deny the significance of these declines and fail to consider their policy implications?

TABLE 9:5 Selected SSA economies: average annual export growth rate (volume, percentage)

	1970–79
Benin	−11.4
Sierra Leone	−6.5
Tanzania	−6.6
Sudan	−4.4

Source: World Bank (1981b Table 7)

It is possible, then, to agree with Godfrey, that 'The consequences of increasing export incentives on a continent-wide basis have to be looked at extremely carefully, commodity by commodity' (Godfrey 1983: 40), but it is not clear that the results of such careful scrutiny would support Godfrey's arguments. It is not, however, possible to agree with Griffith-Jones' pessimistic critique of Berg's 'unrealistic' projections of growth in the volume of world trade in primary commodities of interest to African exporters. Griffith-Jones argues that the volume of world trade in these commodities is unlikely to grow as rapidly as Berg suggests, and is generally pessimistic about export growth in the context of slow growth of world trade in the 1980s. This point is irrelevant: the rate of growth of exports of a range of African primary commodities in the 1970s was substantially below the growth of world trade of those commodities (copper, iron ore, zinc, tin, lead, sugar, groundnuts, groundnut oil, beef, palm oil, bananas, timber, cotton, rubber, and hides and skins).

5. This leads logically to the next problem: of food imports, food self-sufficiency, food self-insufficiency, self-sufficiency and insufficiency in general. Food imports seem to be regarded very widely as a Bad Thing, which ought to be stopped or at last, made unnecessary, yet it is not clear why this has become a tenet of left thinking. In fact it is amazing that it should have become so. What matters is how much people have to eat, which is not determined by whether countries import food or not. In fact, countries that can afford food imports are more likely to be characterised by sufficient food availability than those which cannot.

The world's largest food importers are Japan and the USSR; the SSA countries which increased food imports most rapidly in the 1970s were among the fastest growing (see Table 9.6), Kenya, Ivory Coast and Nigeria. On the other hand in Ghana, where

TABLE 9.6: Total growth of cereal imports (volume, percentage)

	1974–81
Kenya	3,460
Ivory Coast	260
Nigeria	527
Ghana	45

Source: World Bank (1983a: Table 6)

GDP 1970–81 fell by an average of 0.2 per cent per annum, and where the recorded fall in domestic food output per capita was among the largest, the growth of food imports was relatively tiny. This should not be surprising, since historically, rapid economic development has often been associated with rising food imports – Holland in the seventeenth century, Japan in the twentieth (see Wagstaff 1981).

There is no discernible relationship between changes in food output per head and trends in food imports. there is, instead, a relationship between trends in export earnings and in food imports: of total food imports by sub-Saharan Africa, 50 per cent of all animal and vegetable oils and cereals, and more than 50 per cent of sugar, meat and wheat imports are accounted for, not by the poorest countries facing the most disastrous trade experience, but by oil-exporting countries. In fact, it was only in the category of Middle Income Oil Exporting SSA countries that the share of food imports in total imports failed to fall between 1960 and 1978 – it remained constant at 14 per cent. Wagstaff has shown, for the world as a whole, a significant positive relationship between changes in food imports per head and changes in GDP per head. Furthermore, despite the rapid growth of food imports in Ivory Coast and Kenya, the share of food in total imports fell during 1960–80, from 12 to 8 per cent in Kenya, and from 18 to 15 per cent in Ivory Coast. Only in five SSA countries did food imports rise as a percentage of total imports: Central African Republic, Uganda, Sudan, Liberia, Congo. To the extent that there is a relationship between food imports and food availability, it is more likely to be positive than negative, in contrast to the presumptions of many critics of Berg.

6. Another feature unifying Berg's critics is their attitude to devaluation. Their approach excludes posing the most important question, which is: under what circumstances would devaluation increase foreign exchange earnings? This question involves others, concerning the elasticity of demand for imports and of supply of exports. Furthermore, the domestic inflationary consequences need to be analysed, as well as contractionary implications. In addition, there are important questions about the forms that currency depreciations should take, i.e. the costs of large infrequent devaluations as compared with small frequent depreciations. Bird's survey of devaluation indicates a dearth of empirical studies of either the short-run or long-run effects of devaluation on SSA countries (Bird 1983). This is, unfortunately, not surprising given the approach of perhaps the majority of development economists. Aside from precluding the asking of crucial questions, their approach involves problems concerning alternatives: Bird argues that alternatives to devaluation have proved to be far more administratively cumbersome, and that most foreign exchange controls in practice involve considerable delays in the acquisition of imports, generating underutilisation of domestic industrial capacity; that foreign exchange controls in practice frustrate, rather than reduce, the demand for imports. The administrative difficulties of implementing a Kaldorian export-subsidy-cum-multiple-exchange rate system in the SSA context also have to be faced and discussed by the left.[6]

7. Before concluding our discussion of Berg's critics, it is by no means a waste of time to note some criticisms which are so obviously flawed that they merely discredit the left, allowing the dominant neoclassical 'get the factor prices right' strategies to present themselves as the only viable basis for economic policy in ldcs.

Sau (1983), for example, presents a three-sector model (export crops, superior food and inferior food), in which a decline in the terms of trade will lead inexorably to a reduction in the output of inferior food, and an increase in the output of superior food.

This remarkable conclusion is arrived at by a tautological analysis in which resources are perfectly mobile between export crops and superior food, so the terms-of-trade-induced decline in export output leads to an increase in superior food output and, since the reduction in export output is assumed to generate fewer domestic resources for total food production, output of inferior food must fall.

Sau states, in addition, that since the deterioration in ldcs' terms of trade for primary exports is largely attributable to the price manipulation of transnational corporations (TNCs), Berg's arguments concerning domestic taxation and price policies are, therefore, irrelevant. Presumably the conclusion is that it is easier to abolish TNCs, and thereby increase export producer prices than it is to change bureaucratic or parastatal price policies.

Further, Sau advocates both an indiscriminate (or undiscriminating) reduction in export output and an equally indiscriminate increase in exports of 'resource-based industrial exports'. Aside from the inconsistency, no attempt is made to discuss the feasibility or consequences of these policies for foreign-exchange availability in particular countries, or even particular commodities.

Finally, Sau resorts to the utopian advocacy of industrialisation based on regional economic integration, without any reference to the fact that ldc experience with economic co-operation, let alone integration, allows very little ground for optimism.

A further criticism in this category is by Allison and Green, who substitute nationalism for class analysis: they state than 'only Africans are primarily concerned with the well-being of Africa' (Allison and Green 1983b: 9). To whom are they referring? The dominated classes, or members of Haile Selassie's family, or ex-Emperor Jean Bedel Bokassa?

Secondly, Green states that real producer prices for agricultural producers in general 'paralleled the evolution of prices at the global level' (Green 1983a: 32). This is incorrect: real producer prices fell faster than world market prices in a number of well-documented cases (Ellis 1983; Muhtar 1983). Further, Allison and Green state that the export targets set by the Berg Report 'are not feasible' (1983b: 6). No arguments or data are adduced to show this; 1983 data indicate that world market prices of non-oil primary commodities exported by African ldcs rose by 8.4 per cent over 1982, and that, for all low-income ldcs the 1983 increase in export volume was 6.1 per cent (IMF 1983: 183).

The final criticism to be noted in this section is by Griffith-Jones, who argues that the Berg Report is recommending a programme of ultra-orthodoxy similar to that adopted in Chile, involving the rapid elimination of all tariffs and other import restrictions. This is not the case, nor has this ever been a condition of IMF loans (see Killick 1981). Indeed, in another context Griffith-Jones herself has argued that the ultra-orthodox policies adopted in Chile had less to do with the requirements of the IMF than with the strength of right-wing domestic political forces (Griffith-Jones 1981).

8. Specificity deserves a brief mention. All critics agree that Berg suffers from not enough of it, but demonstrate very little of it themselves. We have given some indication already of the kinds of specific questions which urgently require answers – such as the conditions for a successful devaluation, the type of distributional questions which need to be addressed, which crops can be exported in increasing quantities with positive effects on income, etc. The problem which arises is that traditional left ways of approaching these issues often lead to the wrong questions being asked. Because of the baggage that many of the left carry around with them, e.g. the public sector is a good thing; devaluation is a bad thing; TNCs and the World Bank and the IMF are very very

bad things; primary products are a bad thing; prices of primary products decline secularly; external factors are more important in the explanation of ldc economic misfortune than internal factors; regional co-operation among ldcs is a serious possibility; etc., it is not surprising that persons such as Deepak Lal write what they write (e.g. Lal 1983). This is not to say that all of the people believe in silly things all of the time, but that enough continue to carry around so much of this baggage for it to be a problem.

What is wrong with the Berg Report?

In this section some of the more important objections to the analysis and, particularly, to the policy prescriptions of the Report will be discussed: these concern the nature of the state, the Report's exaggerated pessimism, the analysis of import-substituting industrialisation, and the central role of 'getting prices right' in Berg's policy recommendations.

Politics and the nature of the state

According to Berg there are several 'mistakes' that most African states have made during the 1970s. The origins, or the historical and political context in which these mistakes arose, are only very briefly and crudely discussed, suggesting that, although Berg's political analysis has some interesting points of similarity with some mechanical marxological simplicities (e.g. the desire to identify and heap opprobrium upon a bureaucratic bourgeoisie), the most obvious defect of Berg's approach is how very little it has to say about political forces, wars and class realities in Africa. Consequently, the impression conveyed by the Report is that merely reading the lessons of ten years' experience, plus the careful perusal of certain econometric studies helpfully provided by the Bank, (plus, of course, a little bit of Bank co-ordinated donor leverage), will – like a sudden flash of pure light – illuminate areas of policy choice that were previously murky, allow those silly 'mistaken' policies to be jettisoned immediately and the 'correct', cost-effective paths for state activity automatically to be chosen.

In sum, Berg relies on the notion that ignorance and mistakes (or, at best, the shortsighted selfishness of bureaucrats) can account for the pattern of state intervention in SSA. The Report offers no analysis of how the balance of political and economic forces has changed historically and how these changes have affected different regimes in Africa in the 1970s. This approach leads to naive exhortations and policy prescriptions that are rather confusingly contradictory. For example, we are told that it is the finance ministries in Africa that represent the general interest in the struggle for resources (p. 83) – as if there were such an animal as the 'general interest', and that a package of technocratic reforms would improve the quality (and reduce the quantity) of state intervention: so, improved collection of statistics, the establishment of Project Preparation Units (armed with the most up-to-date Little and Mirrlees Manuals to screen out the line-ministries' non-viable investment proposals), and a reform in the terms of reference of the Planning Ministry – constitute the kernel of the magic institutional reforms that would give the technocrats the upper hand in the allocation of resources and the design of policy. These types of technocratic solution, together with some ritual genuflections in the direction of co-operatives and the beauties of small-scale organisations, would suffice, according to Berg, to override such 'mistakes' as the allocation of excessive investment to those projects that provide substantial benefits to the political/ethnic supporters, or the home village, of the Ministers of Health, Agriculture, Transport, etc. This is naive.

The contradictions arise because, while the general ideological tenor and thrust of the Report is anti-planning, denying that the state can do anything other than have a retrogressive effect on economic development (as a result of crowding out, for example), the Report at the same time attempts to provide a series of apolitical prescriptions for improved planning and benevolent state interventions in the interests of society as a whole.

Exaggerated pessimism

One of the most progressive aspects of the Report is that it makes a serious attempt to argue for the necessity of substantial additional flows of concessional finance. However, these arguments are weakened and the analysis is flawed in more general ways, by Berg's assumption that the more you exaggerate the disastrous performance of capitalism in SSA, the stronger will be the case for accepting the pro-aid argument, and all other arguments in the Report.

Take the case of agricultural production – central to almost all of Berg's conclusions. The Report states that 'Low agricultural growth rates typify all but a few African countries in recent years' (p. 49), and claims that there has been a continued, systematic decline in agricultural production over the last two decades (p. 45). We would argue that this, and similar statements in the Report, are exaggerated and misleading:

1. Using the Report's own data, several (seven) African economies had growth rates of agricultural output well over 2.5 per cent per annum, 1969/71 to 1977/9. We would also question what Berg means by 'low' agricultural growth rates. Low relative to what? If one takes a sensible criterion of comparison, such as the rates of growth of agricultural output achieved by France or the UK during their experience of industrialisation in the nineteenth century – when growth rates very rarely rose above 1 per cent per annum and at their very fastest were of the order of 1.5 per cent – then it should be stressed that over half the population of SSA lived in economies that achieved a faster rate of growth of agricultural production than this (i.e. a general average rate of growth of agricultural output of more than 1.6 per cent over the decade) (see Heywood 1981).

2. There are even more serious problems with the Report's treatment of agricultural and food production data. First, all of Berg's stories about declining rates of growth of food production ignore data on the production of fruit, vegetables, fish and meat.[7] Clearly there are problems in collecting consistent time-series data for these commodities, although it is hard to believe that the available data covering these items are systematically *less* reliable than the data on cassava, maize and other cereals that the Report does attempt to provide. Jane Guyer has pointed out that roots and tubers are very much more important in accounting for calorie consumption in Africa than are all the cereals taken together, and that the production figures for roots are nothing like so gloomy as those presented by Berg for cereals: the rate of growth of production of roots and tubers has been more stable than that of any other major food crop, varying between 1.8 and 2.0 per cent per annum, and the growth rate of per acre yields has been higher than that of almost all other food crops. Furthermore, Guyer presents good micro-based and historical evidence which strongly suggests that the Berg Report has underestimated actual levels of yield for these crops in the 1970s (Guyer 1984: 188).

The failure to provide a satisfactory discussion of roots and tubers and, more generally, the pessimism regarding non-export crop performance can probably be traced to the ludicrous equation in the Report of all non-export agricultural production with 'subsistence'/'traditional' production (p. 12), and to the implicit notion that anything which is not collected in the official export statistics is not marketed and probably is not produced. Given the prevalence of smuggling, the limited, and in many countries, decreasing coverage by official marketing agencies of the domestic food sector, are there any adequate grounds for making unqualified statements about production levels and trends – let alone dogmatic pessimistic assertions?

There are similar tendencies toward exaggerated pessimism in Berg's statements concerning current account deficits and debt crises. Here, one of the methods employed (e.g. p. 3) is to provide data in terms of billions of current dollars on current account deficits and external indebtedness – while neglecting to note that between the beginning and end of the 1970s, inflation was by no means an insignificant phenomenon. Another method employed is to measure current account deficits as a percentage of GDP by a procedure that excludes the contribution to the current account of foreign aid grants. Note that even with the use of this procedure current account deficits in Africa only averaged about nine per cent of GNP in 1980. Debt service as a percentage of GNP or as a percentage of exports of goods and services amounted to about 2 and 7 per cent respectively for SSA in 1979 – figures which were dramatically lower than those for other developing countries. For example in the late 1970s newly industrialising countries' debt service amounted for 21 per cent of export earnings. Unfortunately, most of SSA was unable to finance the enlarged real current account deficits that would have been required if imports were to grow at a satisfactory rate.[8] Exaggeration of the size of Africa's current account deficits and its debt burden is misleading, because it is clearly desirable, and part of Berg's own project, to argue for the necessity of financing much larger import levels than those achieved by SSA over the last decade.

The final comment that we wish to make concerning Berg's exaggerated pessimism relates to certain of his remarks on import substituting industrialisation (ISI). In common with a major strand of left-dependency theorising, Berg argues that ISI behind protective walls is 'quite effective in encouraging simple IS industries, but, once these have been established, industrial development faces an impasse' (p. 27). Does the evidence from SSA provide unambiguous support to this prognostication? We think not: there are about ten African economies that have experienced average annual rates of growth of industrial production of over 6 per cent for well over a decade. We are still waiting for the apocalyptic moment when the 'easy' stage of ISI will peter out and industrial stagnation becomes the order of the day in these SSA countries. These countries, as well as many other ldcs (such as Brazil), have sustained historically unprecedented rates of growth of industrial output over remarkably long periods, on a basis that was precisely ISI behind protective walls.

'Getting prices right'

These comments on industrialisation serve as a convenient starting point for a far more fundamental set of critical points regarding Berg's proposed policy strategy.

Berg's whole emphasis, what he calls 'the centre of his analysis' (p. 55), is on the positive effect of a change in farm gate prices on agricultural output. The fact that an increase in domestic industrial production, via its effects on the availability of incentive goods and producer inputs, might have an equal or even larger effect on real incentives and the ability to increase agricultural output, is systematically underemphasised. The accumulation of extra kwacha, cedis or shillings is presumably of much less immediate interest to producers than the possibility of exchanging their output with such manufactured goods as soap, kerosene, cooking oil, sugar, batteries, pots and pans, corrugated iron roofing material, radios, bicycles, cloth, etc. Similarly, the decision and ability to invest in increasing yields in the short run will be determined, to an important extent, by the assured availability of pesticides, fertilisers, storage construction materials, agricultural implements, transport equipment, etc. In many African countries the supply of these manufactures can be readily increased by improved capacity utilisation, or an expanded domestic import substituting industrial sector. The acute difficulties faced by domestic infant industries resulting from the reduced protection and other policies stemming from Berg's critique of IS will have a serious negative impact on agricultural output.[9] Besides, Berg chooses to ignore the fact that those SSA countries that achieved high rates of growth of agricultural exports (Ivory Coast, Kenya) can hardly be characterised as having spurned the import substituting road.

At a broader level the incentive issue must be viewed as a complex and many-sided one (Sen 1983), and Berg's simplistic analysis of the effects of price manipulation requires considerable qualification. Labour shortages or bottlenecks at peak periods are often the critical constraint on raising the marketed output of particular crops (Richards 1983); it is, therefore, vital to appreciate the determinants of labour supply, which will include the relative returns to labour in a range of non-agricultural activities as well as in those agricultural activities (including processing) that are competing for labour in the same season.[10] These features of the production process have been important in accounting for the failure of simple price elasticity of supply models to explain marketed groundnut output in Nigeria (Muhtar 1983), and marketed cassava flour output (Guyer 1984). Access to education and health facilities in particular rural areas is also likely to influence labour availability (and productivity), and thus the degree to which output can respond to price changes.[11]

Neither Berg, nor IMF research by Bond (1983) on the empirical response of agricultural output to prices in SSA, show that short-run increases in agricultural export volume will be achieved by devaluation or increases in nominal producer prices. Berg, however, often appears to be suggesting that devaluation would be both a necessary and a sufficient condition for achieving increased export volumes. Econometric work suggests that, although short-run own-price elasticities may be positive for some export crops, these are very small. This undermines one major thrust of Berg's prescriptions: the immediate problem addressed by Berg, i.e. the recent falls in export volume of many SSAs, will *not* be alleviated rapidly by price changes.

What is left of the alternatives to Berg?

It is, first, necessary to remind ourselves of the central issue addressed by Berg, namely the persistence of structural balance of payments disequilibria: the inability of most African countries to generate enough foreign exchange to cover their import requirements. Berg advocated two sets of measures: a massive increase in aid and a change in the nature of aid; and certain domestic policy changes to increase export earnings. The alternatives to Berg must be judged, at least in part, in terms of their effectiveness in relation to this objective.

Three critics of Berg – Bienefeld (1983), Loxley (1984a) and Sau (1983) – provide general alternatives, while Godfrey provides some suggestions on alternatives for Kenya. The latter are unobjectionable, in proposing specific primary processing activities as a basis for increased export earnings, plus an argument for gradual, as opposed to sudden, changes in trade policy. Neither of these are inconsistent with Berg, in fact Berg explicitly recommends the former.

Sau's recommendations are the most easily dismissed, so we will start with these. They are as follows:

1. reduce output of export crops;
2. increase output of food crops;
3. promote regional economic integration as a basis for further import-substituting industrialisation; and
4. increase resource-based exports.

The third has been mentioned already in terms of its (in)feasibility; the first and second are presumed to go hand-in-hand on the grounds that export crops and food crops are substitutes in production, a presumption which is at variance with experience. Those countries which have had relatively successful trends in export output are also those with relatively successful trends in food output. The second, taken alone, is based on the implicit assumption that domestic food supply is the single most important determinant of whether people have enough to eat, and of whether their food intake is secure or insecure. This assumption is also at variance with both historical and cross-country experience. So nothing is left of Sau that is of any use for serious thought on African economic problems and policy.

Bienefeld and Loxley both present similar alternatives, so they will be discussed together. Bienefeld's alternative is as follows: 'some states – under present or new management – may cut back on and change consumption patterns for elites drastically, and place primary emphasis on securing the population's basic necessities on the basis of a less volatile and more controllable domestic production structure which operates with a lower import to output ratio. That would certainly require extensive state intervention, usually by governments which are differently constituted politically than those presently in power' (Bienefeld 1983: 22).

Loxley's alternative is based on the autocentric model of C.Y. Thomas (1974), in which production is geared 'to utilising local resources to meet democratically defined needs and foreign trade is simply an extension of domestic production, not its determinant. ... This model presupposes collective ownership of the means of production, economic planning in physical terms, and the desire to build a socialist society. The political prerequisites for implementing this model are obviously very demanding' (Loxley 1984a: 203).

There are several difficulties with both of these, of which three are outstanding:

1. It is, politically, a game of Alice-in-Wonderland to presume that Africa's urgent and immediate problems can be wished away by the invocation of a socialist government. Aside from the far from admirable record of socialist governments in the spheres of democracy, economic success and the ability to control the economy, it is as much use as the joke about assuming a can-opener[12] to think that a socialist revolution is on the cards in most African countries in the short term. What do these alternatives have to offer to persons living in places where no such revolutionary options are actually on the agenda? This is particularly serious in the light of the criticisms that these same people make of Berg in terms of its inadequate political analysis. Is 'taking politics seriously' just another way of saying 'socialism now'?

2. There is the usual recourse to the 'golden egg' approach to poverty, i.e. that if imports of luxury goods can be cut, and the excessive consumption of the elite reduced,

then problems of poverty can be solved. Cutting the consumption of the rich may be important for political reasons, but it will certainly not yield the resources on the scale necessary to significantly affect the lot of the poor. Only a strategy which secures growth of output can make any inroads into the problem of poverty.

3. The advocacy of autarkic – or more autarkic – strategies is fundamentally flawed. There are complex interrelationships between imports and domestic markets, and between exports and domestic markets. Imports have connections with domestic markets through the availability of inputs and incentive goods, exports through the expansion of demand for domestically produced output resulting from increased incomes. The 'enclave' story about exports is the opposite of the truth – as Hirschman (1977) has shown for Latin America – increased exports in Africa have been associated with generalised linkages, with an increased, rather than a diminished, domestic market for domestically produced output. The importance of imported inputs (both capital and intermediate) and imported incentive goods in production for both domestic and export markets, is so marked that the alternatives which stress reduced involvement in trade, far from reducing the vulnerability of African economies, will increase it. The idea that involvement in trade has at worst impoverished African economies and at best increased their vulnerability, is utterly at variance with historical experience over the last decade, and indeed over a much longer perspective. By increasing incomes, state revenues, and by increasing the demand for domestically produced consumer goods and inputs, increased export production has developed both the home market and the market for imports. It is a major distortion of African economic history to emphasise the latter to the exclusion of the former, aside from the spurious credence which the enclave story gives to disastrous economic policy recommendations. Those economies in Africa with better performance in export production are also those with larger domestic capitals, and more advanced industrialisation, and this is no coincidence. Where is the evidence that compares, in any detail, the full array of forward and backward linkage effects associated with the expansion of different crops, minerals or industries in Africa?

It should not be necessary to add, finally, that we are wholeheartedly in favour of policies – such as increased flow of concessional finance – that have the effect of increasing the rate of growth of imports into SSA. A concentration on the remediable defects in the composition of imports should not continue to allow the left to ignore the fact that a very substantial and sustained growth in the total volume of imports is a precondition for the transformation of the productive structure in SSA – and for the alleviation of the brutality of life for most of SSA's inhabitants.

NOTES

1. An earlier version of this chapter has appeared in *Capital and Class 24* (Winter 1985).
2. For example, in the early 1970s, 87 per cent of state expenditures on health were concentrated on preventative facilities (Coulson 1982). See also Mukandala 1983.
3. There are major contradictions in the literature: for example, Williams (in Clough and Williams 1984) argues that World Bank *projects* have had unfavourable distributional consequences, while Loxley and Daniel criticise the Berg Report's recommended 'programme' aid approach on distributional grounds.

4. Some evidence relating to these questions is available in Anker and Knowles 1983. This regionally disaggregated study provides no support whatsoever for those distributional critics who assert the negative consequences of export crop production.
5. Take the case of groundnuts: Africa's share of world exports was 26.8 per cent in 1982. If Africa's exports rose significantly, say by 10 per cent, world exports would rise by 2.68 per cent. In order for Africa's export earnings to fall, world prices would have to fall by at least 10 per cent, i.e. the price elasticity of demand would need to be -0.26. Berg's critics provide no evidence that the relevant elasticities facing Africa are of this order of magnitude.
6. Of the critics of Berg and the IMF in Africa that we have been able to read, only A. Singh's work on Tanzania (1983) makes a serious attempt to assess the circumstances in which, in specific countries, the exchange rate should be changed. But does the left really want to argue that, for example, it was an integral part of socialist strategy that in Tanzania between March 1979 and December 1982 the real effective exchange rate should appreciate by 92 per cent, or that in Nigeria the real effective exchange rate should appreciate by 28 per cent between January 1979 and December 1981?
7. For example, small domestic livestock are very important indeed in farming systems and nutritional provision throughout SSA. See, for example, Richards (1983).
8. During the 1970s, middle income developing countries achieved an annual average rate of growth of import volumes of 5 per cent, compared with only 3.3 per cent for SSA (World Bank 1981b: 149). It should also be noted that current account deficits as a percentage of GDP during 1973–81 were systematically lower in low-income ldcs than in other categories of ldc (IMF 1981: 126).
9. This is especially so if imports of interest to the mass of rural consumers are the first categories to be cut in the face of periodic balance of payment difficulties.
10. Richards (1983) provides the following data on the share of processing in total labour requirements: groundnuts 35 per cent, cassava 50 per cent, palm oil 50 per cent (p. 36).
11. For example, labour mobility in SSA has often been a response to rural/urban differences in social infrastructure.
12. A physicist, an engineer and an economist are stranded on a desert island, with only tins of corned beef to eat. None of them has a can-opener. The physicist and the engineer put their heads together to work out what to do. The economist says: 'There is no problem: let us assume a can-opener.'

10

The IMF and World Bank conditionality: the Tanzanian case

Kighoma A. Malima

In a rigorous examination of Tanzania's economic plight, one finds a chain of external factors which account for most of the present difficulties. The first is the inescapable fact that Tanzania, like all other primary product-exporting countries, is forced to sell cheap and buy dear. In other words, while the prices of her exports have either been stagnant or falling, those of her imports have been rising. Thus, more and more of our products are needed in order to purchase less and less of what we require from outside. If such an arrangement cannot possibly be viable for an individual businessman, it can hardly be otherwise for a country. In 1973, for instance, we needed no more than 5.4 tons of tea in order to purchase one tractor, while in 1983 the same tractor required us to export 10.1 tons of tea. Consequently, such an international environment, aggravated in practice by drought, has given rise to a very acute foreign exchange crisis with ramifications in practically every economic sector.

The lack of foreign exchange, for instance, has meant an inability to import essential spare parts, replacement equipment, and industrial raw materials, all of which are needed for domestic production, as well as transport and other services; it also means an inability to buy from abroad the consumer goods that still cannot be produced locally. The productive capacity of our domestic industry is thus grossly underutilised because of the lack of imported spare parts and raw materials, creating a grave shortage of essential industrial commodities. This situation has further fuelled domestic inflation, the current rate of which is estimated to be 38/40 per cent per annum – much higher than we were used to until the end of the 1970s. Inevitably therefore, as the utilisation of domestic productive capacity has been reduced, on the average, to about 25–40 per cent, the revenue base for the government has also been eroded. Unprecedented budgetary deficits have resulted. For since very little is being produced or imported, government revenues in the form of sales, import, as well as Corporation taxes, have been drastically reduced. These external and budgetary imbalances have also starved the domestic transportation services, the educational system, and the health services, as well as rural water supply services, of critical spare parts, replacement equipment and other essential materials, hence adversely affecting our most cherished basic needs programme.

The devastating effect of the foreign exchange crisis extends to agriculture as well. In Tanzania, agriculture accounts for over 75 per cent of the output of the productive sector, 80 per cent of the export earnings, and provides 85 per cent of all employment. Thus, agriculture has truly been described as the backbone of the Tanzanian economy. However, as in most developing countries, Tanzania's agriculture is extremely dependent on imported farm implements, fertilisers, insecticides, seeds and even various packing materials. Where the basic farm implements and fertilisers, for instance, can be, and are, produced locally, the requisite raw materials have still to be imported from outside. Consequently, with the dearth of foreign exchange, agricultural production in Tanzania has not only been adversely affected by weather but also by the lack of various and critical agricultural production inputs.

It is, of course, true that some of the problems afflicting agricultural production in Tanzania are internal, and the government's effort and attention are presently directed at dealing with these as effectively as possible. Thus, for a long time, the proportion of public investment allocated to agriculture was not commensurate with the importance and dominant role which the sector plays in our economy. During the 10-year period of 1972–82, the share of public investment going into agriculture was 10–13 per cent. At the Party Congress in October 1982, it was therefore decided that the government should re-examine the national development plans in order to accord to agriculture the importance it deserves. Since then the share of public investment going into agriculture has been raised from 13 per cent in financial year 1982/83, to 28 per cent in 1984/85. Secondly, while government now accords great importance to the setting of remunerative agricultural producer prices, an exercise which is undertaken annually, it has also been vividly recognised that the whole question of *incentives* to the farmers encompasses not just producer prices but also timely provision of agricultural production inputs as well as cheap technology, on the one hand, and availability of incentive consumer goods on the other. Thirdly, the question of efficient and responsive institutions, in order to serve agriculture and the farmers, is equally being tackled with the carefully planned reintroduction of co-operatives, which were abolished in 1976, as well as by redefining the role and structures of the various crop authorities.

In general, however, the severity of the economic difficulties which Tanzania, like most developing countries, currently faces underlines the inherent weakness and vulnerability of her economic structures to external shocks and disturbances. Indeed, the inescapable conclusion remains that, while the internal factors like declining agricultural production may have made an extremely grave situation worse, they were not decisive. Indeed, even if Tanzania is slighted by her detractors for her failure to adopt what they call 'appropriate' economic policy reforms, there are surely other

TABLE 10.1 Socio-economic performances of selected sub-Saharan countries

	Adult Literacy rate, 1980 (%)	GDP per capita growth, 1960–81 (%)
Tanzania	79	1.9
Kenya	47	2.9
Ivory Coast	35	2.3
Malawi	25	2.7
Nigeria	34	3.5
Senegal	10	−0.3
Zaire	55	−0.1

Source: World Bank, *World Development Report* (1983)

developing countries which have adopted those so-called 'correct' policies and are today still facing as severe, if not more severe, economic problems as Tanzania. Table 10.1 shows the socio-economic performance of Tanzania, compared with other countries in sub-Saharan Africa with differing socio-political strategies. Thus, the indicators of adult literacy rates as well as GDP per capita annual growth rates in the table clearly demonstrate that, if anything, it is 'socialist' Tanzania which has performed best with the limited resources at the disposal of the developing countries in question. For, not only was Tanzania able to attain a modest, but comparatively above average, income per capita growth rate during her first 20 years of independence, but what was even more spectacular, she achieved one of the most impressive rates of adult literacy in Africa. The long-term importance of general education in any economic transformation effort cannot be overemphasised.

A critique of IMF/World Bank conditionality in the light of Tanzanian experience

The foregoing provides the necessary background for appraising the standard IMF prescriptions offered to all developing countries as a panacea for their economic ills.

The present negotiations between Tanzania and the IMF date as far back as mid-1977. At that time, as a result of the temporary coffee boom, Tanzania found itself with foreign exchange reserves larger than usual. Consequently, the IMF, through its routine Article IV consultations, advised the Tanzanian government to liberalise its import control system, because it was claimed that such large foreign exchange reserves were 'embarrassing' for a poor country. The government did accept the IMF prescription in a moderated form, but it did so rather grudgingly and reluctantly, because it felt that what a country such as Tanzania could least afford was general import liberalisation. Indeed, it took less than 12 months of even the 'liberal' importing to which Tanzania had agreed to exhaust whatever foreign exchange reserves the country had. Very soon after that, the IMF and the Tanzanian government were therefore negotiating an extended fund facility. Those negotiations collapsed in October 1979, leading to the resignation of the then Minister for Finance, because the conditions which the IMF was trying to impose were unacceptable to the Tanzanian government. However, in August/September 1980 the negotiations for an IMF stand-by credit were resumed and concluded. The total amount involved was SDR 166.5 million, or US$235 million, which was to cover a period of two years, ending in June 1982.

The first drawing of SDR25 million, or US$35 million, was made as soon as the agreement became effective. This was the only drawing made by Tanzania under the IMF stand-by agreement of 1980 because, it was claimed, Tanzania was not fulfilling the conditions. In further efforts to reactivate the programme, a number of IMF missions have visited Tanzania since that time, but to no avail. Instead more and more stringent conditions were required of Tanzania; conditions which could not be fulfilled without avoidable, destructive – and to us unacceptable – social upheavals.

In fact, as one examines the political implications of one IMF condition after another, the argument that the IMF's main preoccupation is with technical recommendations becomes less and less plausible. In discussing the IMF conditionality, however, a clear distinction has to be made between two issues. First, the condition that resources (including 'aid' resources) should be used efficiently and also, as far as possible, for the purpose for which they were intended, is not really at issue.

Unfortunately, this condition has not received as much attention or emphasis as the others, even from the aid agencies themselves.

What has become controversial, as well as unacceptable, especially to those developing countries with clearly defined socio-economic strategies, is the prescription of policies laid down for the recipient as a condition for receiving assistance. It is, therefore, most illuminating to assess briefly the major policy prescriptions and their relevance to the economic conditions existing in Tanzania.

Exchange rate policy

In a country such as Tanzania, which is an exporter of primary commodities, devaluation makes no difference to the overseas currency selling price of their export commodities, because these prices are determined in the international commodity markets. What devaluation does mean is that the country buys its essential and irreducible imports at an even higher domestic price than before. And although the devaluation will mean that the country can pay more Tanzania shillings to the farmers, the effect on production of such action is not altogether certain. For it takes a year to increase the production of commodities like cotton and tobacco, and from five to six years to increase appreciably the output of crops such as cashew nuts, coffee, tea, and sisal. And in the meantime the farmers' costs will have gone up considerably.

Further, as a result of the austerity programme, arising from both the difficult foreign exchange position and deliberate social policies, Tanzania no longer imports inessential commodities. In fact, practically all serious observers have described Tanzania's imports as having been reduced below the socially acceptable and economically efficient minimum. Thus, since all of Tanzania's present imports consist of only essential commodities which cannot be reduced further without serious and unwarranted socio-economic consequences, devaluation inevitably imposes additional hardships, without an immediate compensating effect through the expansion of exports or domestic production.

Thus, while it is true that there is a need to pay farmers higher producer prices, from not only an economic but also an equity point of view, devaluation does much more than enable the payment of higher producer prices. For by raising import and domestic production costs, its effects on real producer prices cannot be predicted with any certainty. It will certainly be no incentive to the farmer if the money prices paid for his crops increase, while at the same time the prices of essential imported agricultural inputs as well as basic non-agricultural goods, which he must purchase, also increase to a compensating degree as a result of devaluation.

Thus the use of devaluation as an instrument for correcting the budgetary imbalance of the government or export organisations should be resorted to only after examining all the available and feasible options for tackling such an admittedly genuine problem. In fact, devaluation cannot be a lasting and dependable tool for shielding exporting organisations from financial losses, because of the frequent fluctuations in the world market prices of primary commodities. This means that when such sound socio-economic arguments against indiscriminate use of devaluation are not even taken into serious consideration, the case for devaluation undoubtedly becomes political and no longer economic.

In Tanzania, for instance, while we have not yet found a convincing case for massive devaluation of 60–70 per cent, we are not anti-devaluation, *per se*. Thus, in March 1982, June 1983 and again in June 1984, the Tanzanian shilling was devalued by 12, 20 and 26 per cent, respectively, in terms of local currency, even when it was absolutely unnecessary and unjustified, mainly as a result of concerted pressure from our major donors. Thus, we do make a clear distinction between exchange rate adjustments which have some element, however far-fetched, of economic as well as empirical justification, on the one hand, and the massive devaluation proposals made to us by IMF and which purport to rectify balance of payments deficits, government budgetary imbalance or even facilitate the payment of higher agricultural produce prices, on the other. For these would, it seems to us, create more problems than they solve.

Interest rate policy

In a developed market economy, the rate of interest is supposed to work as an instrument for achieving both internal and external balance. Thus, a higher rate of interest is intended internally to reduce the level of investment expenditures, by increasing the cost of capital funds in the market, and by so doing eventually reduce domestic inflation. Similarly, higher interest rates are also supposed to increase the return on savings and thus encourage the population to save a larger proportion of their incomes. However, in recent years there has been increased scepticism about these theories, especially in those advanced industrial economies that suffer not only from inflation but also from unemployment and/or social unrest. Similarly, in the external sphere, an increase in the interest rate is intended to discourage capital outflow and encourage capital inflow into the country concerned, and ultimately help to reduce or even eliminate the balance of payments deficit.

Whatever the validity of these arguments elsewhere, the fact is that in a developing economy such as Tanzania, the main internal effect of a large increase in interest rates would be to increase domestic costs of production and other services because of the increased financial costs of operations. The bulk of investment allocation is determined by the Plan, which is drawn up in the light of the need to promote accelerated, balanced, and self-reliant development. A very large increase in interest rates has, therefore, been resisted for fear that its real effect will be merely to inflate the cost of investment and domestic production generally. As the prime causes of domestic inflation in Tanzania have been the rising prices of oil and other imports, with the consequence of low levels of productive capacity utilisation and investment, substantially increasing interest rates would make desperately needed investment unnecessarily costly, and thus make an already bad situation very much worse. Indeed, the rational course in such a situation would not be to discourage investment through punitive interest rates, but to direct investment into breaking bottlenecks which exist in the productive sectors and in strategic social and economic infrastructures. Only by this means can the economy be rehabilitated and the level of production and productivity substantially and rapidly raised. In the *external context*, the use, in a developing country like Tanzania, of higher interest rates as a mechanism to attract short-term capital flows is obviously a figment of the imagination! The necessary and tight exchange control system and general poverty of even the most capitalist inclined developing country means that people are more inclined to take their capital out than to bring it in, however high the interest rate.

Finally, there remains the argument for the interest rate as means of mobilising domestic resources, primarily from the small savers. In the first place, in Tanzania about 85 per cent of the population live in rural areas, with the vast majority of the people earning incomes which are barely adequate to keep body and soul together. Secondly, the main constraint to savings mobilisation has been found to be the proximity and availability of banking services. It is extremely implausible that people would travel long distances, sometimes between 80 and 160 kilometres, in order to deposit their modest funds, merely because the rate of interest has been raised to a theoretical 'optimum'. The decisive factor in such a situation has been the spread of banking services to the rural areas. In Tanzania that means, ideally, to cover each of the over 8,000 villages – an objective which at the moment appears attainable only in the far distant future.

In short, the proposals that interest rates in Tanzania should be increased to 40/45 per cent, has been resisted because it is irrelevant to the real problems and could cause seriously adverse socio-economic consequences. As in the case of exchange rate policy, the critical question for Tanzania is the level of interest rates which would on balance bring the best macroeconomic result in light of objective reality. Thus in August 1983 the levels of Tanzanian interest rates, for both deposit and lending, were increased, on the average, respectively, from 6.15 and 9.75 per cent to 7.25 and 10.5 per cent. Those rates are kept under constant review by the Central Bank in order to determine if any further revision is necessary or appropriate.

Removal of price control

It is claimed that dismantling the price control system would eliminate the need for government subsidies to parastatals and the incidence of black marketing. The case for agricultural subsidies in developing countries is clearly very similar to that for agricultural support prices as practised by the governments of Europe and North America; that is, the imperative of paying the farmer (producer) remunerative and equitable prices and of ensuring reasonable food prices to the urban and non-agricultural population.

Further, the objective of general price controls is normally to achieve a certain amount of equity, so that no one should be denied the basic essentials of decent living because the pricing system has made such commodities inaccessible. In that sense, price control is essentially an integral part of an incomes policy. The claim that price control brings about black marketing, is not substantiated by the 12-year practical experience of price control in Tanzania. When there are reasonably adequate supplies of a commodity the black market problem is non-existent. Thus, it is very much preferable to cure the illness (shortages as a result of a drastic decline in import capacity and therefore domestic production), rather than deal with the symptoms (black marketing).

In Tanzania, in June 1984, again as a result of external donor pressure, the subsidies on maize flour and fertilisers were removed, and wages and agricultural producer prices, respectively, were enhanced as compensation for the removal of those subsidies. Similarly the number of commodities subject to price control has been substantially reduced and the system of supervision has been simplified. Time will tell if we made a correct judgement about the greater efficiency, from the point of view of economic production and social equity, of these steps. But the indications are already that the higher food and fertiliser prices have adversely affected the already flagging nutrition standards of the population as well as agricultural production itself.

Reduction of government expenditure and freezing of wages

When considered alongside proposals for massive devaluation, substantial increases in interest rates, and the de-control of all prices, the proposal that government recurrent expenditures must also decrease – or at the very least should not increase – is bound to have very grave socio-political consequences. In the case of Tanzania, among the first casualties of such a cut-back in government spending would certainly be essential social services, such as education, health services, and rural water supply, since these together take the lion's share of the country's government recurrent budget. But how can developing countries, like Tanzania, be advised to direct their socio-economic programme to the poor, and then be asked to cut back on precisely those very programmes that meet the basic needs of the people? To answer such a question by saying that the people should pay for such services is, at best, begging the issue. For how in turn can people who are least able be asked to pay for services which everyone agrees are absolutely essential?

In addition to all those very harsh measures normally included in the IMF conditionality list, there is usually also a requirement that there should not be a general increase in wages, or at best there should be a nominal one. The real question then, is, how can a rational government, especially in a poor country such as Tanzania, increase the price of a staple food, like maize flour, at once by 200 per cent, without at the same time offering any increase in wages, which are in the first place at a subsistence level? What incentive would there be for the workers to increase production, without resorting to repression? Some observers have aptly described such measures as a prescription for social disorder. That is why in Tanzania we could not, in conscience, remove food and fertiliser subsidies, as we did in June 1984, without at the same time making compensating increases in both wages and agricultural producer prices.

In Tanzania, the government is of course, more than acutely aware of the need to bring the annual rate of increase of government recurrent expenditure into line with government revenues, as well as the monetary gross domestic product (GDP). The problem, however, has been that the government revenue base, as explained previously, is very much tied to the availability of foreign exchange, necessary for making possible efficient domestic production and the purchase of essential goods not domestically manufactured. Under such circumstances one cannot trim government recurrent expenditure simply because government revenues are falling as a result of declining imports and domestic production, without weighing the ensuing socio-political consequences. Adjustments have to be made. But if the burden of such adjustment is not to be born solely by the most vulnerable segments of the population, a three to five-year perspective is definitely needed in order for such adjustment to be achieved relatively smoothly.

Privatisation of the economy

Another aspect of IMF conditionality which has received great prominence recently, is an emphasis on the magic of the private sector in solving the problems confronting poor countries. In the first place, a realistic assessment of the situation obtaining in all developing countries would reveal that in none of them are the activities of the private sector non-existent; it is merely the relative size of the public and private sectors which differs – and even this partly for historical and nationalist reasons rather than because of ideology. Thus, even in Tanzania, whose stated socio-political objective is to build a socialist economy, the private sector still plays a very important role in almost all activities including agriculture, industry, transport and commerce.

Secondly, even conventional development theory accepts the fact that private sector cannot be expected, at least in the currently underdeveloped countries, to build the required economic infrastructures, like roads, railways, harbours and power stations. These have to be provided by the state if any development is to take place at all. But in the industrial market economies which are most active in preaching the gospel of private enterprise as the panacea to all the third world's economic problems, the public sector is not absent!

No one in Tanzania disputes the fact that public corporations have to be run efficiently. But we do not accept that the solution to loss-making public enterprises, is to hand them over to the private sector or even to shut them down. The latter could mean that an essential service may not be provided at all (and both USA and Britain have sometimes found it necessary to subsidise key private enterprises – or to nationalise them). And looking at contemporary Africa, as I have already pointed out, the difference between 'socialist' Tanzania, on the one hand, and the 'non-socialist' Kenya, Ivory Coast, Malawi, Senegal and Zaire, on the other, in terms of their respective socio-economic indicators during the last 20 years, does not do much, if anything, to strengthen the case for relying entirely on unfettered private enterprise in our economies.

Liberalisation of imports

The other major IMF condition is usually a demand for the removal of all forms of import and exchange control in a developing economy. In the case of Tanzania, import and exchange controls were instituted for the sole purpose of husbanding scarce foreign exchange resources, in order that they may be utilised for the benefit of all the people, instead of a select and privileged few. Thus, if at the moment, despite such controls, we are unable to import even the minimum industrial raw materials, etc., which we require, it is difficult to see how import liberalisation will help. What is obvious is that such import liberalisation can only be at the expense of highly essential imports, as the little foreign exchange would be offered to the highest bidder, who may well import luxury goods. Indeed, our experience of liberalisation of 1977/8 is still a sombre reminder to every serious Tanzanian of how things can go. We felt the effects of that debacle for many years.

Furthermore, as if the experience of 1977/78 was not enough of a lesson, in 1984/85 there was further liberalisation, in the sense that people with their 'own' foreign exchange outside the country, could use it to import a certain number of essential commodities which were in short supply domestically. The results were more or less predictable. Not only did the list of commodities imported go far beyond the prescribed items, and include lipsticks and imported beer and spirits, but the goods in question were selling at prices very much above what the ordinary working population could afford. Thus, the price of imported khanga, an important dress for ordinary Tanzanian women, sells at between 600 and 800 shillings a pair! Indeed, any attempt to control the prices of such imported goods has been resisted not only by the domestic business interests concerned but also by their spokesmen in the party and government. Thus, the city of Dar es Salaam, for instance, today is full of imported commodities not because of genuine abundance, but because their prices are so high as to exclude practically everyone except a handful of speculators and corrupt bureaucrats. Similarly, the 1984 liberalisation has stimulated black marketeering of currency, as hawkers of all descriptions struggle to get dollars for the importation of goods which they can sell at whatever price the market can bear. In addition, the 1984 liberalisation and devaluation has also led to a further decline of exports and an increase in imports, thus intensifying the balance of payments crisis. There is also some indication that liberalisation has led to an increase in the smuggling of our commodities, outside the country, as the scramble for dollars to import commodities which no-one can afford mounts. Yet despite all this glaring evidence, the IMF and World Bank and their domestic supporters are counselling more and not less liberalisation. The erosion of the moral and social fabric, as people try to obtain those commodities by whatever means, has somehow been relegated to the wayside or is being conveniently ignored. Once again developing countries are used as guinea pigs for discredited and obsolete economic theories.

Conclusion: conditionality and adjustment

The gravity of the economic situation, throughout the third world, is increasing. I have already pointed out that it is no longer rational to ascribe the economic plight facing a developing country like Tanzania to particular socio-economic policies; the difficulties do indeed cut across countries with differing socio-political perspectives. Those who continue to pursue that line of reasoning are, indeed, doing so primarily for self-serving political purposes, or looking for an alibi for the failures of the international economic systems. For certainly such political posturing cannot be the result of an objective assessment of the actual situation obtaining in the developing countries.

Thus, what we are witnessing in Tanzania and other developing countries today is a new and even more pernicious form of colonialism. The carrot of very limited financial support is being dangled before countries in a desperate economic situation. But concealed in that carrot is a denial of sovereignty. Thus, one developing country after another is put under immense pressure to abandon any kind of enlightened and equitable socio-economic policies based on social justice, in favour of the privatisation of their economies. Unless they are able to muster enormous reserves of political strength so that they can resist this pressure, and either hold out until they can get tolerable IMF Agreement or rehabilitate their economy by some other means, the result of getting IMF aid is all too often 'IMF riots' or other forms of political instability – to say nothing of the suffering of the weakest people in the population.

Thus, in a conspiracy of silence or indifference on the part of the developed countries, the independence and political integrity of Tanzania and other economically weak third world countries is being undermined. What is worse, the medicine offered is often worse than the disease, hence bringing not only a short-term nightmare, but also a bleak future, without any ray of hope for a better tomorrow, especially for the poor and vulnerable groups. How much more suffering, one may ask, should befall those innocent and helpless victims, before an enlightened and concerned public opinion in the advanced capitalist countries comes to their long-overdue rescue?

In belabouring the question of conditionality it is not my intention to underplay the need and importance of adjustment in the developing countries. The present unfavourable economic conditions, by all indications, are going to be with us for quite some time, and they present a challenge to both the developing countries and the developed countries to implement some adjustment policies in an orderly manner. such adjustments would undoubtedly involve difficult choices for both types of economies, but the longer such adjustment measures are delayed, the tougher will be the measures required at a future date.

In Tanzania, for instance, we have come to associate the process of adjustment necessary to cope with a changing and hostile external environment as consisting essentially of three elements. The first involves adjustment in favour of production in contrast to services. Given the fact that resources are extremely limited, it is not possible to increase appreciably the share of investment going into productive activities and at the same time also expand considerably the social services. In the case of the latter, we have therefore decided to place emphasis on the consolidation of the social services that we have already established. In the case of productive sectors, the priority will be agricultural production in order to meet the growing requirements for food, raw materials for the domestic industries, as well as export earnings.

The second element of adjustment concerns production techniques that predominantly favour or rely on locally available raw materials and spare parts, instead of imported ones. Thus, on the one hand, adjustment requires expansion of the export base, to include not just primary products but also semi-finished manufactured products. On the other hand, the drive for *export promotion*, in order to relieve the foreign exchange bottleneck, has to go together with an aggressive programme of *import-saving*. To mention only a few, as an illustration, the increased use of hydro-power, coal, solar and wind energy, etc. instead of imported fuel is a clear example of such an effort, although even these require foreign exchange in the first instance.

The third element involves adjustment in consumption habits and patterns, in order that they be sustainable by domestic production and incomes. This last element essentially has three interrelated implications. First, the need for the government itself to live within its means so that, as far as politically possible, government expenditures should be brought into line with government revenues – or vice versa. Secondly, in the external accounts also, exports of goods and services should at least finance recurrent import requirements. Thirdly, the consumption habits of the general population as a whole have also to be consistent with domestic production of both food and other commodities. This may sometimes mean using locally available but somewhat lower quality products, instead of the usually preferred and 'superior-quality' imports. Thus, the importance of adjustment in all these three aspects, especially for a country like Tanzania which has embarked on an independent, socialist and self-reliant strategy, cannot be overstated.

Nevertheless, two paramount questions have still to be faced. The first concerns the speed of such adjustment. In other words, what is the appropriate dose which cures the illness without killing the patient? Indeed, the issue of speed can make all the difference between adjustment taking place at all in an orderly fashion, on the one hand, and social disintegration and disorder, on the other. The wrongs of decades, or even centuries, cannot be corrected in a year.

Secondly, who bears the burden of such adjustment is another crucial socio-political question. Tanzania regards it as essential that the burden of adjustment be equitably shared among the various social groups of the population. The adjustment measures usually recommended by the international financial institutions, which attack the poor instead of attacking mass poverty, inevitably create enormous social tension and unrest, because they invariably impose a disproportionate burden on the poor and the dispossessed. Thus, as already stated, there is a definite and glaring inconsistency between the economic conditions offered as the price of aid to the developing countries by the international financial institutions, and the lip-service references to the provision of basic needs and the eradication of mass poverty which they claim to promote.

Lastly, some observations about the Tanzania Structural Adjustment Programme (SAP) (1982/83–1984/85) are in order. This programme was drawn up with the assistance of experts provided by the World Bank. While it took account of both the various forms of adjustments necessary, as well as the need for an adequate time-span and a just and equitable sharing of the burden of adjustment, it had one inherent weakness. That is, it put excessive reliance on IMF/World Bank assistance, rather than on the people's own efforts and capacity for self-reliance. Consequently, the programme floundered as IMF/World Bank funds became a hope which could not be realised. Initially, the World Bank experts drew up a programme which contained two possible scenarios, one with IMF/World Bank funds and another without. In the first place, the experts themselves deliberately and, perhaps, understandably, downplayed the self-reliance scenario. Secondly, and perhaps as a result, the government in turn opted for the first (IMF/World Bank) scenario, believing, maybe with the benefit of hindsight, but wrongly, that the self-reliance scenario was more austere and difficult. In reality, however, we have had to live with a no – IMF/World Bank scenario which was unplanned and therefore, *ad hoc* and disorderly. The price has been incalculable, not only in terms of crops uncollected and resources squandered but also missed opportunities to save imports by substituting locally available materials and resources. Indeed, for Tanzania as well as for developing countries in general, it is not yet too late. I am convinced that the self-reliance scenario is the scenario for liberation. This is not a scenario for autarky, as it welcomes genuine assistance from friends who respect self-determination for small and developing nations, instead of forcing them to take the route which brings more disorder, misery and suffering for the people.

11

The IMF and Tanzania – a solution to the crisis?

Werner Biermann and Jumanne Wagao

Tanzania never succeeded in establishing an autonomous economic cycle (Coulson 1982). The economy is still dependent and open for two main reasons. First, her commercial agriculture is wholly dependent on the world market, which absorbs more than 80 per cent of the entire crop production (Biermann 1985). Secondly, there is the pattern of Tanzanian industrialisation: its reproduction and enlargement rely on imports via the world market. Despite socialist proclamations, the economic structures and processes are determined by capitalist regulations. It is here where the basic factor of crisis is rooted. In the face of dependency and capitalist orientation the Tanzanian government is pursuing an articulated nationalist economic policy whose targets are twofold: first, to increase the bargaining power of national capital in the world market, and secondly, to establish a solid political platform of legitimation. The latter aspect is of primary significance given the recent political tactics directed towards economic reforms. A nationalist economic policy reunifies under the national banner antagonistic social forces in favour of a populist approach. In order to recognise the current state of the economy and what the implications with the IMF are, we shall analyse the economic structures.

Tanzania's crisis is represented by the gap between stagnating productive labour (agriculture and industry) and the ever increasing amounts absorbed by unproductive labour, as shown in Table 11.1.

From the table three central implications can be drawn:

1. the growth figures indicate a low rate of economic expansion;
2. growth does not lead to development as the central pillars on which industrialisation is based, commercial agriculture and the manufacturing sector, declined and/or stagnated; the performance of subsistence oriented agriculture indicates a failure really to subsume this sector under capitalist regulations; and
3. the public sector expanded steadily: it is here that the results of economic growth were absorbed.

The implications lead us to the conclusion that one has to look at the roots of this failure in the political sphere, i.e. the unchecked growth of bureaucracy. A study of the story of the negotiations between Tanzania and the IMF gives insights into the effects of bureaucracy.

TABLE 11.1 Economic performance, main indicators

Year	GDP (monetary)		Commercial agriculture		Manufacturing		Public sector		Subsistence agriculture	
	(1)	*(2)*	*(1)*	*(3)*	*(1)*	*(3)*	*(1)*	*(3)*	*(1)*	*(3)*
1970	5501	5.0	1589	29	716	13.0	866	16	1661	30
1971	5778	6.2	1522	29	784	13.0	952	16	1644	28
1972	6138	3.4	1620	26	850	13.5	1071	17	1805	29
1973	6355	3.7	1625	25	888	13.8	1157	18	1833	29
1974	6590	4.3	1516	23	903	13.9	1562	24	1799	27
1975	6876	3.0	1567	23	903	13.7	1481	23	2029	30
1976	7081	5.6	1614	23	1013	13.1	1634	23	2246	32
1977	7480	5.3	1656	22	1152	14.3	1804	24	2420	32
1978	7879	4.8	1694	21	1104	15.4	2013	26	2632	33
1979	8259	9.2	1713	21	1244	15.1	2107	26	2644	32
1980	9019	1.9	2314	26	1048	11.6	2313	26	2246	25
1981	9194	−1.6	1337	14	761	8.3	2673	29	2847	31
1982	9047		2227	24	568	6.3	2907	32	1592	18

Notes: (1) in absolute terms, and at 1966 prices in Tsh m;
(2) rate of growth per annum; and
(3) share to GDP
Source: own computation on basis of *Economic Survey 1977/78* (p. 11) and ibid., 1982
(p. 18)

The history of the IMF negotiations

Like all ordinary members of the IMF Tanzania is entitled, at any time, to draw so-called tranches limited by the quota-share she holds.

The discussion, therefore, is oriented towards the hard credits which necessitate bilateral negotiations between the Fund and the prospective debtor. Applications for these credits occur once other alternatives have not materialised, indicating either the depth of the economic crisis or the risk which the international banking system might stand in any further investment in that country. Applications for these credits normally imply interference with the economic model.

Back in 1974 Tanzania applied for a second credit within the Fund's tranche-scheme. The IMF tied the loan to a demand to reduce domestic credit drawings by the Tanzanian state. The Tanzanian government refused to accept this condition recognising it as endangering the implementation of her Basic Industry Strategy just outlined in the Development Plan (Coulson 1982: 310). Despite the stalemate this did not bring about economic calamities as Tanzania received sufficient financial relief from the Oil Recovery Fund in 1975. In early 1976, the unexpected coffee boom on the world market which had been caused by the near destruction of the Brazilian crop set in. The income from coffee exports led to a restimulation of domestic growth. Although during 1976 the Tanzanian state maintained a strict policy on imports, at the beginning of 1977 the restrictions were loosened (Payer 1983: 798). Therefore, instead of securing industrial capital reproduction through importation of the means of production, the foreign exchange reserve was almost completely spent on commodities of final demand. Already in mid-1978 the reserves were evaporated down to an amount equalling an important requirement of one week whereas at the beginning of the same year they had covered more than four months' equivalent (ibid.).

Despite its dilapidated financial position the Tanzanian government became fully committed to the war against the Amin regime in Uganda at the end of 1978. The reasons leading to the military engagement, necessitating mobilisation of all available resources, were political. This illustrates the tendency to create domestic political platforms on the basis of populism and nationalism which overlook the economic repercussions. Having overthrown Amin and with disillusionment from the international community's lack of appreciation for defeating a notorious tyrant, Tanzania had finally to approach the IMF. The intention was to achieve an agreement on an extraordinary credit allowing for financing basic industrial imports (Green et al. 1980: 107 *passim*). At the same time, the Tanzanian government had to and could immediately draw Tsh360 million from the Fund's tranche scheme and its compensatory financing facility (World Bank 1981c: iii). Despite the short-term relief, foreign exchange reserves equalled less than one month's import requirements in June 1979 (ibid.: ii). Having largely overdrawn the short-term facilities which the Fund was entitled to grant, Tanzania could now no longer expect any exception to the Fund's regulations she, as an ordinary member, had accepted when joining the Fund; any new credit had to be combined with structural adjustments and/or changes. Tanzania at that time had been treated by the IMF as another case in point to show that the African country had not been exposed to a strategy of covert intervention, i.e. reversal of the social model implemented, and this is evidenced by (i) the main donors maintaining their level of funds and grants; and (ii) the IMF demanding the implementation of its classical tools – devaluation, budget cuts, reduction of state domestic borrowing, reduction of price controls and liberalisation of exports and imports (Green et al. 1980: 136). In addition the Fund intended to see the producer price on cash crops drastically increased (Greenberg and Wagao 1983). Within a short time the Tanzanian government seemed to have accepted the proposals which were designed to be combined a credit amounting to US$235 million.

In 1981, however, a complete reversal of events was witnessed with the Minister of Finance outlining in his budget speech that the Tanzanians were not prepared to implement all conditions imposed by the IMF. The IMF regarded the unexpected change as obvious provocation and immediately cancelled its commitment. The reasons for the Tanzanian government's sudden change of mind remain obscure. But some of the elements, which are believed to have contributed to a factional feud within Central Committee and NEC (National Executive Council), can be traced: divisions between government and party, tactics simply to gain time, speculation to reach a favourable bilateral agreement with Sweden (whose anti-IMF position is well known), or even a brilliant political move *gradually* to prepare the Tanzanian public for drastic cuts and to appeal to the nationalist sentiments in support of the government in its firm stand against the IMF.

Nevertheless, the Tanzanian economy was by now fully exposed to a crisis. When in mid-1982 the Tanzanian government presented its Structural Adjustment Programme (SAP), it relied on new and unnegotiated IMF and World Bank loans. In actual fact, SAP did not succeed and it was clandestinely buried in the Minister of Planning's speech to Parliament in June 1984 (*Daily News* 15 June 1984).

Tanzanian optimism is well illustrated by the fact that the SAP was based on an IMF loan amounting to US$440 million – an amount significantly larger than the first loan to which the Fund had agreed.

Since late 1983 Tanzania has been fully exposed to a pincer movement, namely, the deepening of the domestic crisis and the reluctance of donors to contribute to financial relief. On the one side the IMF has stiffened its position and on the other the main donors now relate their prospective aid schemes to Tanzania's willingness to settle with the IMF (ibid.: 3). Even the Nordic countries have joined this band-wagon, as they now insist on a final arrangement with the IMF (*Daily News* 6 December 1984).

The economic crisis is very severe; Tanzania's economic survival depends on foreign resources, the present inflow of which is obviously limited. Nevertheless, Tanzania is bargaining hard; she was able to survive another two years and has presented a new austerity budget (June 1984) which, according to the Minister of Finance's parliamentary speech, is designed to steer the economy autonomously through the crisis (*Daily News* 15 June 1984).

The Tanzanian government's firmness has to be looked at from the social and political spheres. There is social solidity and political stability. Both are great assets which reflect achievements of the past, the mass commitment to participate in building a new society – ujamaa and nationalisation were targets of high identification. As long as the government and party maintain a course of authentic nationalism, articulated as populism, mass support will prevail. In this context, it has to be acknowledged that social achievements make Tanzania unique in comparison with other African societies.

Nationalism is ambivalent. On the one hand, it constitutes a massive bulwark against articulation of external threats; on the other it allows for uncontrollable internal moves. Finally, nationalism has to be reproduced in economic terms, and there a great trap is formed: autonomous economic recovery under conditions of dependence requires measures that attack the material life of the mass of the population.

The structural adjustment programme: the conflicting role of the state

Undoubtedly, the basis for IMF's criticism and rejection of the proposals is its primordial focus on economic policy issues. However, if the fund were interested in the substantial contributions towards economic recovery as such, then the focus should have been on short-term and microeconomic aspects such as the rehabilitation of industrial output and utilisation of the idle industrial capacity. Instead the Fund neglected this level completely and concentrated on long-range macroeconomic conditions and structures of the economic model; in short, the role of the state.

The strategy adopted by the Fund seems to be completely misleading in political terms: to demand a reduction of the role of the state from a nationalist and populist-oriented government comes next to demanding a cut in its central pillar of power and rule. Ostensibly, the Tanzanian government recognised the IMF approach as an act of confrontation, against which the government could easily mobilise mass support.

The IMF proposals included a package deal centred on:

1. devaluation;
2. increase of producer prices;
3. lifting of price controls;
4. import liberalisation; and
5. balancing the budget deficits (IMF 1981: 12 *passim*).

According to the IMF the Tanzanian currency was highly overvalued; the high domestic inflationary rate of approximately 40 per cent (in absolute terms) and in relation to the rates of inflation the core economies experienced (below 5 per cent per annum; cf. IMF 1984) detracted potential investors and creditors and caused the emergence of a significant parallel market in foreign exchange. A drastic devaluation was required to reattract foreign capital, to stimulate Tanzanian exports and to dry out the parallel market. Although the precise ideas are not known, a devaluation by 150 per cent was the most probable. In 1980 the IMF demanded a devaluation of 300 per cent (Singh 1984a: 4). Between 1982 and June 1984 Tanzania devalued the shilling by a cumulated 100 per cent. The present rumours say that in 1985 another devaluation in the range of 25 to 50 per cent is to be expected. Thus, the IMF position will be approached half-way.

The relief effects of devaluation on exports are well-known as well as its stabilising impact on the balance of payments. The negative social implications are severe. With the present rural relations of production the smallholders would have positive reactions to price incentives, especially if they are already market oriented. Augmentation of production, expanded acreage under cultivation and demand for labour are to be expected when devaluation coincides with a revision of the producer price scheme. Notably subsistence oriented producers will see a real alternative to their present living and will abandon their land to enter into wage labour relations. Further stratification of rural societal relations and proletarianisation of subsistence producers are the implication. Thus, Tanzania becomes very attractive for foreign capital investment by agro-business (Joinet 1981: 165 *passim*).

The price increases cum inflation will highly affect urban labour whose present level of reproduction has already deteriorated. Since there is an intention to rehabilitate the industrial sector, it would defeat this aim if wage increases combined with rising costs of imported machinery. Even worse, the pledge for liberalisation of imports would drive the private sector into economic ruin as it could not stand international competition. And the private sector is still the major employer.

These implications of the IMF proposals were well-known to the Tanzanian government. To what extent they were accepted as inevitable is illustrated by the SAP. By now it seems evident that the Tanzanian government intended to maintain full political control over the processes of implementation. SAP reads as a compromise with the IMF and as a platform of mutual understanding between the two components constituting government: the higher echelons of bureaucracy and political cadres. This claim is supported by the fact that SAP was preceeded by a National Economic Survival Programme, the party strategy to overcome the economic crisis (Hanak 1982: 65). The latter focused on a revival of nationalism which culminated in the appeal by the President to the Tanzanians to wage 'economic warfare' (*Daily News* 24 June 1981).

SAP was designed as a short-term initiative on budget strategy covering fiscal years 1982–85 and as an avoidance to admit openly the existence of a crisis. It therefore substitutes for various imbalances in the spheres of external trade, productive and unproductive activities and the budget (SAP 1981: 3).

The main recommendations by which existing imbalances are to be rectified are stimulation of export activities, rationalisation of producer and retail prices, and budget cuts (ibid.: 4). At first glance, these recommendations have similarities with the IMF proposals, and this therefore helps to explain why the Tanzanian government could base SAP on large IMF loans which she had not yet negotiated. This intention is explicitly stated: 'government will now proceed to negotiate with the IMF and the IBRD to seek the required programme funding' (ibid.: 11). Let us consider the underlying strategies in SAP in more detail.

First, in order to stimulate exports the Tanzanian government devalued the currency twice – by 12 per cent in March 1982 and 20 per cent in July 1983. Also the new policy to revise producer prices by introducing a sliding price system (ibid.: 19) was intended to link producer prices with the overall economic trend. In addition, the present national price scheme was to be abandoned. The proposed regional price scheme was regarded as an effort to adjust prices to reflect the regional condition of production. Underlying these revisions was the belief that rural producers withholding their production from marketing, and therefore price incentives would restimulate marketing of crops on the official channels.

The producers responded very reluctantly as their experience of the past with the state marketing monopolies had been extremely bad. The theoretical assumptions underlying agricultural policy reveal the processes of alienation between bureaucracy and the rural realities: price increases were too little to attract the producers as their money income no longer bought them the basic items of physical reproduction. Barter trade and smuggling to Kenya, Malawi, Rwanda and Zambia prevailed.

The next strategy was budget reduction. It was envisaged that a balanced budget could be achieved by 1985. However, with a projected increase of 12 per cent per annum (nominal) a real reduction of expenditures was visible once rates of inflation were considered. Although cuts were planned to cover current and investment expenditures alike (ibid.: 9), in reality it was mainly investment projects which were affected. They were reduced by two-thirds in comparison with the 1981/2 level. Whereas the budget of fiscal year 1979/80 showed a ratio of 64:36 (current: investment expenditures), the budget for fiscal year 1984/5 was projected at a 77:23 ratio. This implied that the government did not intend to curtail its level of immediate reproduction.

This is where the double role of the state is in conflict: the state as an agent of social egalitarian reproduction and as an economic prime agent. The state cannot – for political reasons – withdraw from the first function, although it contributes to deepen the crisis. In order to escape from this structural trap the Tanzanian government opted for an offensive position to relieve the financial constraint, and this is outlined below.

First, by urging producers to increase food production the government hoped to reduce the balance of trade deficit. This, according to the assumptions, would allow for new industrial imports to rescue the ailing industry and ultimately increase state revenues.

Secondly, contrary to the IMF's insistence the Tanzanian government intends to save the central role the state plays. In order to save that centrality the government was – according to SAP – even willing to cut down on the economic prime function of the state.

The compromise offered implied a retreat from classical Tanzanian positions on self-reliance. The government was willing to augment and foster the place the economy played within the network of the international division of labour. A review of the political course which Tanzania has pursued since the Arusha Declaration in 1967 is obviously the utmost the Tanzanian side can offer.

SAP formed the last but one compromise Tanzania offered. With the financial planning implanted it became evident from the start that the programme was bound to fail if IMF and IBRD withheld their credits. And this actually happened. In 1984, the Minister of Planning publicly admitted it (*Daily News* 15 June 1984).

With the hard line pursued by the IMF and the pressure various donors exercised on Tanzania the government was driven yet another step further into making new concessions. It finally gave in to a central IMF demand – abolishing subsidies, marking the beginning of a change from a once state-planned economy into a liberal one.

The new concession also indicates the silent move of bureaucracy and influential circles within the party from their mass basis towards leaning on metropolitan bourgeoisies.

The budget of 1984: concession and liberalisation

Under the overall political circumstances it was a hidden truth that the new budget would include more measures of austerity and redirection than the preceding ones. It was obvious that it would also contain some elements on which the IMF and the various Western 'free traders' were insistent. That in fact the Tanzanian government did even go a step further, was more than surprising. The most important elements of the new budget were:

1. abolition of subsidies in various economic areas;
2. foreign exchange allowances; and
3. devaluation (*Daily News* 15 June 1984).

Before commenting on these, the minor issues should be dealt with. The obvious drive towards austerity was reflected in the job freeze within the public sector. Moreover, given the chronic budget deficits it is appropriate to increase taxes on those commodities that are in high demand – beer, tobacco and petrol – in spite of the fierce resistance by the political left inside the party.

Despite the latter's opposition, subsidies on commodities of immediate reproduction were abolished. The already ailing material reproduction received an additional push: with real wage reductions of over 80 per cent since 1980 the situation of the wage-earners was precarious (Biermann 1985). Abolition of subsidies worked for the advantage of commercial farmers as did devaluation: the devaluation of 36 per cent against the dollar had an immediate pull-effect on export-oriented agriculture. In order to stimulate exports the domestic producer prices have to – and will – be increased.

Lastly, and politically striking, the government offered 'absolution' to the racketeers who hoarded foreign currency. These citizens were invited to invest their money-capital and to import duty-free those commodities that are not locally available. This forms a gesture of reconciliation towards the ethnic minorities controlling the retail trade.

The intended actions and incentives incorporated in the budget allow for the following interpretation.

Firstly, the Tanzanian economy is pushed further into the status of a periphery. Commercial agriculture, the key sector, is even more exposed to the world market than before. For the individual farmer this might constitute an asset – for the national economy, however, raw material exports do not contain badly needed components of development. By devaluation the state supports the outward orientation of its farmers and smallholders as the demand for Tanzanian exports automatically increases. An increase of exports leads to an increase of foreign exchange reserves. On the other side, Tanzania will consequently have to pay more for imports.

As industry depends on imports its rehabilitation will be hampered unless the export earnings exceed imports. This assumption is highly speculative since the growth of the world market is not steady and to revitalise industrialisation there must be massive imports. Given the structures of balance of trade, imports traditionally exceed export earnings.

In addition, the government intends to liberalise imports. This forms a further setback for domestic industries which cannot withstand competition from multinational corporations. Deindustrialisation of private enterprise can therefore be expected.

This change is evidently taken into account for the benefit of commercial agriculture designed to become, again, the focus of growth. To interpret it in political terms, the new budget is 'midwife' of a new social alliance: with the bureaucracy having secured its place as a dominant social class it has fostered its links with commercial agriculture of which more than 70 per cent is still under private ownership. The common platform is easily discernible: liberalisation articulated as extended sphere of realisation (domestic market and world market) for the latter helps to consolidate the revenue income of the bureaucracy. The budget also foresaw a massive redistribution away from wage earners, the political stronghold of the party's left-wing. Their socialist conception was thwarted as nowhere in the budget was the left able to impose its positions, let alone to protect wage earners and peasantry from further economic sufferings. The former strong alliance between party, workers and rural producers is definitely lifted to the extent that subsistence producers as economically active subjects are not at all mentioned in the budget.

It is obvious that the 1984 budget was a new demonstration of Tanzania's willingness to concede to the IMF. With a state now openly favouring a liberal economic outlook; with the disposition to play the desired role of a raw material producing economy fully integrated into the world market; with streamlining the working class and the reduction of the state from strategic economic and social functions, the politically dominating segments of society now regard the IMF as a partner and no longer as a threat.

The reluctance on the side of the IMF is more of a political character of cautiousness as the implementation of the new budget bore social and political conflicts. After more than six months the political climate in Tanzania remained stable and social unrest did not occur. The entry of the IMF is therefore a matter of appropriate political timing but no longer a structural concern inside the commanding heights of the Tanzanian society.

12

The 'success' of IMF/World Bank policies in Sudan[1]

Dirk Hansohm

The Sudan is well suited as a case study for the effects of IMF/World Bank policies on African economies. The six-year long history of an economic stabilisation policy pursued by the government on the advice of the IMF/IBRD allows an evaluation of its 'appropriateness' to the problems of a low income third world country in economic crisis. To make this evaluation possible I summarise in section 12.1 Sudan's economic policy from the beginning of the 1970s up to 1978 in order to point out the main causes for the deep economic crisis which led to the involvement of the IMF/IBRD. The next part is devoted to a diagnosis of the IMF and IBRD and their proposed strategies. Section 12.3 analyses the government policies and its outcomes. The final section tries to outline the necessary elements of an alternative strategy.

Emergence of the economic crisis in the 1970s

Like most former colonies, Sudan is characterised by a structurally heterogeneous, non-integrated economy. Its modern sectors are linked with the world market via (i) export of agricultural raw materials; and (ii) import of consumer goods and capital goods. While this structure was a colonial heritage, none of the national governments aimed at or succeeded in changing the structure fundamentally after independence. There was no consistent policy towards the development of the 'traditional' agricultural sector (which gives a living to 80 per cent of the population) and the development of an economy based on the use of domestic resources.

In the beginning of the 1970s the Sudanese government initiated an ambitious development programme called the 'Breadbasket Strategy'. This strategy involved a massive restructuring of production and trade in order to take advantage of a regional Arabic division of labour. It was based on large-scale investments by the oil-rich Arab states. The plan was to overcome the unilateral dependence on the world market based on the export of a few agricultural raw products (cotton, groundnuts, sesame, gum arabic) by exporting foodstuffs (grains, meat, sugar, oilseeds, fruits and vegetables) to the Arab region.

The objectives of the relevant development plan – the Six-Year Plan 1977/8–1982/3 – seem to reflect the need to overcome this deformed economic structure. The objectives included balanced growth (regionally and socially), development of the 'traditional' sector and self-sufficiency in food. However, these objectives were not reflected in the actual allocation of resources. The emphasis on agricultural export production and on the modern sectors of the economy was maintained. While the government concentrated on investments in irrigated agriculture, the Arab investments were directed to the sub-sectors of mechanised cereals production, large-scale cattle husbandry and various agro-industrial branches. The concentration on the east-central region was maintained as well.

The implementation of the Breadbasket Strategy depended on foreign capital to a large extent: this was planned to cover 52 per cent of total investment. Even 38 per cent of the domestic share of public sector investment – which made up 59 per cent of total investment – was planned to be financed by borrowing (Ministry of National Planning 1977 Vol.1: 55/6).

In the second half of the 1970s the over-ambitious and inappropriate character of the Breadbasket Strategy became obvious. The huge investments necessary had effected new distortions of the Sudanese economy and strengthened old ones:

- the imbalance of public revenues and expenditures;
- the imbalance of investments and savings; and
- the imbalance of exports and imports.

From 1970/1 to 1978/9 the import value rose by 318.6 per cent compared with a 65.9 per cent increase of export value. In the same period the government deficit increased by 1,003.6 per cent. From 1973 to 1978, Sudan's indebtedness increased by 386.7 per cent (World Bank 1984c: 98). At the same time, the debt structure worsened. It had become obvious that the main assumption on which the Breadbasket Strategy was based did not hold: the concept of pan-Arabism, of Arab integration containing a regional food sufficiency. In reality, the Arab states were willing to invest in projects but not to support Sudan sufficiently with the necessary balance of payments aid for the time up to the completion of the projects. Instead, they started to make disbursements conditional on IMF agreements. As a result of shortage of foreign exchange and declining international assistance Sudan had to rely on commercial credits with higher rates of interest to a rising extent. At the same time there was a shift from long-term to short-term loans and from project loans to balance of payment loans. This was a vicious cycle reducing the government's options more and more.

As a result of rising import costs and rising deficit financing made possible by increasing the money supply, the inflation rate was standing officially at 17.6 per cent per annum from 1974 to 1978 (Fadlalla 1983), which is believed to be highly underestimated. The inflation effected an overall decline of standards of living, especially hitting low-income groups and the rural population. While the terms of trade were calculated to move against Sudan at an annual rate of 12–15 per cent, the main cause for Sudan's unsatisfactory export performance was falling quantities of exports. In real terms, exports registered a decline of 13 per cent between 1970 and 1977 (Umbadda and Shaaeldin 1983: 8). The export of the main commodity, cotton, declined continuously. This was a consequence both of falling yields and of a reduction in area in order to make room for groundnuts, wheat, sorghum and rice. The decreasing productivity was a result of shortages in imported inputs, agricultural machinery and equipment, ageing irrigation systems and, most importantly, the decreasing profitability of cotton for the tenants in the state schemes. This resulted from the system of sharing of costs and profits which charged all production costs on the cotton crop which was marketed by the state corporations, while the other crops were sold by the tenants themselves giving much higher returns for them.

The second very disappointing production performance – gum arabic – was attributable to the very low producer price level and to the beginning of its displacement by an intensification of agriculture (especially through mechanised farming).

An important factor for the weak production performance was the high import dependence of irrigated and mechanised rain-fed agriculture as well as industry (cotton has an import content of 43 per cent; (see UNDP/IBRD 1982: 32). In fact, the quantity of most imported commodities was falling considerably during this period in relation to its value.

The import dependence of the modern projects resulted in a cost explosion. The costs for Kenana, planned to become the world's largest sugar factory, were calculated at $150 million in 1973. By 1976 the figure had risen to $475 million and unofficial sources estimated the costs as high as $1 billion (African Contemporary Record 1977–8, B: 134; Wohlmuth 1983: 198).

A second important bottleneck is the shortage of both skilled and unskilled labour. Acute shortage of labour is recorded in most of the modern schemes both in agriculture and industry as a severe restriction to production. While this is believed to be a major reason for the high degree of mechanisation practised in some agricultural schemes and industrial plants, it can be argued that the apparent present shortage of labour neither is an absolute one nor is it likely to rise in the future.

Instead, it is caused by the insufficient level of wages. In fact, wages have been declining from the 1950s onwards. For skilled labour there is a strong labour drain to Arab oil-producing countries; for unskilled labour many people revert to subsistence agriculture and to other sources of income, which is more advantageous for them (Hansohm-Woltersdorff 1984). However, the decomposition of subsistence agriculture and a high population growth rate enforce the pressure to migrate and will do so to a rising extent in future.

Lack of infrastructure is a constraint for most projects which has been extremely underestimated. It resulted in an even enforced dependence on foreign inputs for some of the new projects. Other bottlenecks were shortage of raw materials and of power supply. All of these causes together led to low capacity utilisation and to production losses. Under the condition of shortage of foreign exchange, new projects had been implemented at the expense of existing ones. The result was decapitalisation of the traditional industries in different branches (Oesterdiekhoff 1982: 61).

Besides the financial problems, the ambitious development plan had gone beyond the government's planning and implementation capacity. The overall plan objectives were not reflected in an integrated and consistent approach at project conception and implementation level. The lack of project co-ordination prevented a creation of intra and intersectoral linkages which would help to overcome the economy's structural heterogeneity.

Analysis and proposed strategies of IMF/IBRD

At the beginning of an evaluation of the crisis diagnosis and stabilisation programmes of the IMF and the IBRD one has to bear in mind that the same institutions had encouraged the Sudan actively in pursuing the described capital-intensive and import-intensive development path. Also they were not much faster than the national government in recognising or in admitting the extent of the adverse effects.

The diagnosis and the policy recommendations of the IMF and the IBRD do not differ basically but only in the degree of precision, the policy emphasis and the time horizon. The IMF tries to give the impression of not interfering in internal affairs and therefore concentrates on a monetary analysis and fixes quantitative macroeconomic performance criteria, mostly on the demand side, as conditions for stand-by credits. Its financial programmes are characterised by a short time horizon (from one to three years). Compared with this, the IBRD concepts are real economy programmes, giving more precise advice, including both supply and demand aspects and having a longer time horizon (from five to seven years). In the case of Sudan, the policies of the two institutions have become more integrated and co-ordinated among others in the frame of the Consultative Group of Sudan's creditors.

The starting point of their analysis is the reflection of the distorted structure of the Sudanese economy as evidenced in the fundamental disequilibrium of the balance of payments. The diagnosed imbalances include those between consumption and savings, investment and savings, exports and imports, public revenues and expenditures and physical and management capacity of the economy.

It is striking that the balance of payments crisis is described as a consequence of 'inadequate economic management' in most IMF/IBRD documents. This 'technical' point of view has important consequences for the policy recommendations. Internal factors are regarded as the primary causes:

- distortions in the allocation of resources resulting from an overvalued currency (a disincentive for exports and a benefit for imports), restricted trade and payments regimes and inadequate government price policy;
- expansionary public sector financial operations;
- overinvolvement of the government and suppression of private sector activities;
- inefficiency of parastatals;
- inflated money supply;
- inability to mobilise domestic resources;
- lack of skilled and unskilled labour; and
- lack of infrastructure.

Very recent studies also mention the excessive rates of profit in trade which have negative effects both in draining investments from productive sectors and in furthering luxury imports.

In the second instance, external factors are claimed to aggravate the situation:

- worldwide inflation;
- weak international demand for Sudan's export commodities; and
- falling terms of trade.

From this analysis the recommended strategy is deduced. The IMF criteria being the conditions for stand-by credits include:

- exchange rate adjustments (devaluation);
- an overall ceiling of domestic credit;
- reduction of the deficit in the government's budget by holding down both current expenditures and development expenditures and by increasing the ratio of tax revenues to GDP;
- restraint of consumption; and
- removal of state subsidies.

Besides these exchange rate and demand-oriented targets the IBRD provides some supply-oriented policy suggestions:

- deferment of all new state projects and rehabilitation of the existing ones to raise the degree of utilisation of their production potential;

- removal of price and cost distortions;
- price incentives for export production;
- removal of price controls to allow prices to rise with the result of a shift of income from those who save less (consumers, traders) to those who save more (producers);
- shifting emphasis from large public projects to support the small-scale entrepreneur;
- liberalisation of production relations in the state schemes: displacement of the Joint Account System by individual account systems and land and water charges;
- reallocation of land from food crops to cotton and groundnuts.

Furthermore, it is suggested that foreign advisors be employed in order to improve state management.

However, their concept is characterised by some misconceptions and inconsistencies. Some of these can be deducted from the ideological model of the Sudanese economy and society underlying the analysis. Its basic assumptions are:

- the free play of market forces will produce an acceptable pattern of investment, production and trade;
- internal and external imbalances (inflation and balance of payments deficits) are caused by excessive internal demand; and
- market forces will be able to produce a sustained growth in production and employment, if not disturbed by government intervention or inflation (cf. Tetzlaff 1980: 249).

These conditions are perhaps fulfilled to a high degree in integrated Western industrial countries. However, this model does not account for the structural deformities of peripheral economies such as the Sudan. Therefore, some of the measures proposed will have different or even contrary effects. Most important, the IMF/IBRD analysis confining itself to the economic sphere fails to appreciate the reasons for the apparent 'mismanagement' of the Sudanese economy. It does not take account of the different meanings of the term 'state' in Sudanese reality. Firstly, the state policies do not represent the general interest of the Sudan but the interests of a few social groups: the military, the 'national capitalists', the state employees and intellectuals and, in the second instance, workers and Gezira tenants. Secondly, the state's dwindling economic and social basis restricts its real options severely. The overall policy aim of 'development' has been replaced by the fight for survival of the government.

The approach to raise industrial and agricultural output by giving incentives to primary producers is to be welcomed. However, it does not account for the marketing structure which prevents producers receiving a reasonable part of consumer/export prices for most commodities (Oesterdiekhoff 1979). Instead, the profits accruing to the big traders far exceed the returns to the farmers. The traders' position is enforced by lack of alternatives to the traditional credit system which is based on crop sales in advance and secures excessive trade profits.

The proposed change in production relations in the state schemes from crop sharing systems to cost recovery systems will favour large farm units because it results in high fixed costs and a larger share of marginal production increase for the tenants. Furthermore, this approach does not account for another level of production relation between the *de jure* tenants and the *de facto* tenancy operators. In the main agricultural scheme – the Gezira – the tenant's family is assumed to contribute only 20 per cent of the total tenancy labour requirements.

The term 'private sector' is misleading because it covers two groups very different in regard to social background and economic interest: the 'traditional' agricultural producers and international and domestic investors (mainly from the trade sector). In fact, the implemented as well as the proposed policy measures aim at the second sub-sector almost exclusively to the detriment of the first sub-sector.

The great hope set in private investment both overestimates the capability and willingness of private capital owners to invest in productive enterprises and underestimates the adverse effects of private investments. The development of mechanised farming – supported by the IBRD – is an impressive example of 'negative development'. The government subsidises a type of production which is hardly economically feasible, is directed to short-term profits accepting high ecological costs and leads to income inequality and displaces the original producers.

The proposition to hand over economic activities to the private sector is substantiated by the inefficiency of the parastatals. At the same time there is a series of private failures in the same branches. Other factors than inherent inefficiency of state enterprises – such as lack of spare parts, maintenance, infrastructure, etc. – may be more important for an explanation of the poor performance of industrial enterprises (Umbadda and Shaaeldin 1983: 17).

Because of a lack of domestic facilities the alternative to government action has often been the engagement of foreign capital. However, the history of this engagement has shown that its terms have been disadvantageous for the Sudanese economy in several respects. It enforced the processes of adjustment of the local production systems to the international demand conditions and of adaption of the domestic demand structure to the production profile of the foreign firms (luxury goods production) which was accompanied by an income redistribution favouring the rich segments of the population (Oesterdiekhoff 1983). Furthermore, foreign capital succeeded in getting special advantages such as exemption from taxes, import duties and restrictions, shifting of capital and market risks to the government (Wohlmuth 1983).

As the IMF/IBRD reports themselves recognise, two main objectives of stabilisation programmes are contradictory: first, the drive to rapid export production to relieve the economy from the immense debt burden and second, the reduction of imports and current and development expenditures. As the irrigation sub-sector which is supposed to yield the highest output growth in the short term and the industrial sector are highly import dependent, their performance had to suffer from import restraints, effected by foreign exchange shortages and devaluations. Furthermore, credit became less available due to credit ceilings. Thus, a devaluation without the backing of considerable foreign exchange for inputs resulted in shortages throughout the production structure and led to a contraction of the economy.

The main conflict between programme goals occurs between the short-term objective to restore financial equilibrium in the shortest possible time and the long-term objective of a sustained economic development. This includes the adverse social impact of lifting food subsidies with the result of reinforcing income inequalities. The requirements of short-term financial stabilisation policies definitely threaten to destroy the long-term perspectives of the Sudanese economy.

The programme enforces the regional concentration on east-central Sudan, the sectoral concentration on modern sectors and the commodity concentration (cotton, groundnuts). This means a continued high dependence on the world market, and an unpredictability of economic development even in the short term (one season). Infrastructural projects, which are considered to be of central relevance – the neglect of these was identified as a major cause for low economic performance are neglected again because of low rates of return and long gestation periods.

Government policies and outcomes

Since mid-1978 the Sudanese government pursued an economic stabilisation policy consisting of an exchange and trade reform programme, a financial stabilisation programme and a restructuring in the agricultural sector to promote export cultivation. In 1978 the government was refusing to accept IMF conditions because of the negative social impact (especially of cutting the food subsidies) and in the following years there was social unrest threatening the government when austerity measures were imposed.

From 1979 onwards, however, the government fell closer in line with the IMF conditions. Sudan witnessed a six-year long history of austerity policy consisting of:

- five devaluations;
- restraints of expenditures, especially development expenditures;
- a moratorium on most of the new schemes and rehabilitation of existing projects;
- cutting of subsidies on imported food, medicines, petrol and other commodities; and
- credit ceilings.

Additionally, agricultural land was reallocated to the traditional export crops of cotton and groundnuts, the above-mentioned changes in production relations in the state schemes were implemented, privatisation was promoted and the foreign exchange market was liberalised.

These six years have been a chain of economic recovery, stabilisation and rehabilitation programmes which could not achieve the desired aim of reversing the trend of economic crisis. On the contrary, the economic indicators showed that the situation has become worse. Nevertheless, none of the programmes constituted a substantial change in priorities and measures of stabilisation policy as well as any change in the expectations on its outcomes.

From 1978 to 1982 Sudan's indebtedness increased by 109 per cent to $6.5 billion. Foreign observers put the total debt figure at more than $10 billion in 1984. Foreign exchange shortages were chronic and insolvency could be avoided only with the help of five rescheduling agreements. Inflation increased to an average of 25.7 per cent annually (official figures) from 1978 to 1982 (Ahmed and Fadlalla 1983: App. X). The GDP growth rate was -3.9 per cent per annum (deflated) and the real interest rates are estimated to be -10 per cent or more. At the same time, the shift to rather unproductive branches of the services sector was enforced. The efforts to restrain government expenditures implied a bias against development expenditures: its share in total budgeted expenditures declined from 38.5 per cent in 1977/8 to 24.8 per cent in 1983/4.

The heavily import-dependent industrial sector had to suffer very much from devaluation. Prices for industrial commodities rose considerably, production declined for most commodities and the capacity utilisation rate for most factories was between 20 and 40 per cent (Umbadda and Shaaeldin 1983). Under conditions of liberalised foreign trade regulations the economic stabilisation programmes implied a bias against industrialisation and a commitment of Sudan to a role of a supplier of raw materials to the world market. In spite of these disastrous figures about Sudan's economic development the government and the IMF/IBRD maintain their judgement that the economic performance is encouraging. This surprising evaluation is substantiated by the rise of export production, which is interpreted as a result of the incentives reform and the technical rehabilitation. While cotton yields could be increased, an overall view on agricultural production gives a less positive result. From the main crops only cotton and wheat realised significant increases of productivity, the rest (especially rainfed crops) stagnated or declined. Furthermore, the rise in absolute agricultural production was not reflected in a parallel rise in export earnings: for the whole stabilisation period export earnings decreased by 15 per cent.

The failure to reach export earnings targets even with rising production was due to weak international demand. This shows drastically the risks of unpredictable future developments of an economy based on the export of a few products whose price is a fixed external datum.

Conclusion: Lessons and Alternatives

The analysis of the stabilisation policy since 1978 gives evidence to the fact that this policy failed to attain its own targets and, more importantly, to achieve any significant improvements in the direction of structural changes necessary for any long-term sustained development of the Sudanese economy. Basically, the structural malformation of the economy was reinforced instead of being surmounted both during the Breadbasket period and during the stabilisation period. Both planning concepts did not only represent particular interests, but they are also characterised by lack of realism and consistency.

During the second period Sudan has lost its capability to pursue alternative options to a rising extent because of the pressure to earn foreign exchange in order to continue the interest payments on foreign debt. At the same time, the Sudanese government lost essential elements of national sovereignty. Its economic policy is conditioned by external advisers: the Consultative Group of Sudan's creditors, the Joint Monitoring Committee and the External Finance Co-ordinator. While national sovereignty is a condition for any real development which is to the benefit of the broad population, this condition is not sufficient. Instead, as the history of the Breadbasket Strategy showed, the basic reason for inappropriate development was the power concentration in small social groups within the country. This allowed for a capital-intensive, import-intensive and export-oriented development policy concentrating on modern sectors, neglecting the 'traditional' sector.

Thus, the question 'What tactics and strategies are open to those countries that wish to resist World Bank and IMF advice?' gives a false alternative for countries with extreme forms of class domination such as Sudan and most of the African states. Instead the decisive question is which strategies aiming at strengthening the position of the producers themselves are realistic under the conditions of international dependence?

The role of the IMF/IBRD is ambivalent. They represent the interests of Western capital. However, this does not necessarily imply a contradiction with the population's interests in every case. Their policies should be evaluated with the criterion 'To what extent can they further political emancipation of the population or do they strengthen traditional class domination?', as Tetzlaff (1980) suggested.

For the Sudan, the conventional stabilisation policy of the IMF/IBRD has reinforced the country's unilateral dependence on the world market, aims at denationalisation/internationalisation of the economy and did not – not yet? – succeed in improving the material situation of the producers significantly.

Anyway, for Sudan there seems to be no alternative way without the IMF/IBRD, neither for the present government nor for a new government formed by the present opposition groups, because the economy is too small and the international dependence relations are too unilateral. However, with a background of the series of failures of stabilisation policy the international organisations and foreign creditors might be willing to accept an alternative strategy. This would include:

1. More reliance on their own resources and production for the domestic market, with the most pressing aim being to attain food self-sufficiency;
2. Reduction of the dependence on foreign co-operation (trade and capital), with the Western countries as well as with the rich Arab countries (the present Arab co-operation is an example of unequal South-South co-operation;);
3. Development of a South-South co-operation on a more equal basis, i.e. with neighbouring African countries and Arab ldcs;
4. Promotion of small-scale agriculture;
5. Restructuring of the industrial sector to 'basic needs' commodities production, to integration with agricultural development, to decentralisation and to more appropriate technologies;
6. Reduction of the tertiary sector;
7. Political decentralisation; and
8. Political participation.

As was noted above, presently Sudan's political system is characterised by a minimal degree of broad participation. While the process of capitalisation – which is promoted by the IMF and the IBRD – might tend to change this situation, any impetus from outside cannot substitute for the domestic articulation of popular interests.

NOTE

1. This paper is based on studies for an unpublished report for the World Bank at the University of Bremen: Karl Wohlmuth and Dirk Hansohm, *Economic Policy Changes in the Sudan*.

PART THREE
The food crisis and famine in Africa

The chapters in this part of the book deal variously with aspects of the crisis as it related to agricultural production, food availability and famine. Philip Raikes and David Seddon (Chapters 13, and 14) address themselves to different aspects of the relationship between international economic institutions, IMF, World Bank and the EEC, and agriculture and food policy in Africa. O'Brien and Schoepf (Chapters 15 and 16) look at the consequences of a policy of promotion of capitalist farming in Zaire and Sudan respectively, while Andrae and Beckman (Chapter 17) and Toyo (Chapter 18) deal with aspects of the same process of capitalist agricultural development in Nigeria. Finally a cluster of papers on southern Africa looks at different features of the drought which has afflicted the region in recent times.

Raikes sees the causes of Africa's food crisis as many-sided and does not regard as useful attempts to apportion responsibility between internal and external factors. He is especially concerned to look at the role of the EEC in relation to food and agricultural production in Africa. He argues that Europe (and the US) have promoted food consumption patterns in Africa's urban areas which are not consistent with Africa's capacity to grow the food required, and therefore there is a reduction in food availability to the poor. The EEC has previously seen the solution as one of throwing money at projects and these have failed because of hasty construction on the basis of inadequate research. The more recent 'food strategy' policy of using aid to subsidise producer prices and thus enable the government to pay producers more simply leads to greater food aid dependency in order to maintain food output at higher levels. Raikes sees agricultural modernisation attempts as likely to generate further crisis and dependency rather than as a way of resolving the food crisis.

Seddon documents an increasingly widespread and predicted consequence of swallowing IMF-World Bank medicine: bread riots, and in this case the riots in early 1984 in Tunisia and Morocco. As Seddon notes here, the causes of the bread riots lie neither in minority agitation orchestrated from the outside, as the governments would have it, or from the increases themselves, but rather in the widespread poverty and deprivation manifested in high levels of unemployment, especially in the urban areas. Adoption of the IMF package sparked off the riots, but withdrawal of the offensive parts of the package will not remove the underlying causes of the discontent.

O'Brien and Schoepf both trace the food crises of sudan and Zaire to the expansion of capitalist agriculture in these two countries. In the case of Sudan, now threatened with serious famine, the successful development of large-scale capitalist agriculture in the 1960s, combined with an influx of Arab capital has led to Sudan being placed in the role of food supplier (breadbasket) to the Arab world. Solutions to its growing foreign exchange problem are seen by such institutions as the World Bank as lying in export expansion of agricultural products produced on a large scale. Clearly switching output of food for domestic markets to foreign markets will lead to a decline in food supply. The peasant sector is increasingly marginalised and therefore less able to cope with failures in its own food supply in the event of drought. The case of Zaire exhibits similar encouragement of capitalist agricultural development at the expense of the marginalisation of the peasantry, its consignment as surplus labour to 'zones of non-existence'.

The papers on Nigeria address themselves to different aspects of that country's food crisis. Andrae and Beckman see Nigeria as falling into the 'wheat trap', a trap engendered by the policy of allowing unfettered growth of wheat milling plants which can only be supplied by wheat imports, which imports cannot be substituted by domestic production on a large scale for social and technical reasons. Nevertheless the fiction that an import substitution policy for wheat is possible results in a distorted investment policy in agriculture, favouring expensive wheat schemes, which can however never be successful. This fruitless investment strategy clearly neglects other aspects of potentially successful agricultural development and is a point amplified by the analysis of Nigerian agricultural policy by Toyo. His argument is not that insufficient resources have been devoted to investment in Nigerian agriculture, but that the investment has been misplaced and operated ultimately in the interests of the growing Nigerian bourgeoisie. In the event we have one more example of a quasi-capitalist development process in agriculture leading to the further impoverishment of large sections of the peasantry.

The papers on southern Africa in this volume are concerned with drought and the food crisis as it has affected Zimbabwe, the Ciskei region of South Africa and the potential for reproducing the cheap labour supplied by the marginalised areas of southern Africa to the South African economy. Gaidzanwa in Chapter 19 on Zimbabwe gives a descriptive account of the food supply situation, noting that Zimbabwe's rate of growth of food output is falling well below that of its population growth rate and that failure to develop irrigation, especially in the so-called communal areas of small-scale peasant production will, along with other policies that have not encouraged cereals production, including pricing policies, lead to Zimbabwe not only losing its export revenue from grain, but also not being able to feed its own population. She also emphasises the importance of switching out of maize and into millet and sorghum in those areas less favoured by the rains. Roger Leys, in a complementary paper, Chapter 20, is concerned to analyse the socio-economic effects of drought, and does so by looking at four villages in an area affected by drought in the south of the country. He identifies clusters of households based on different sources of income and shows how drought relief was distributed on the basis of such social and economic differentiation. He tentatively suggests that the rural salariat, as he terms the richest cluster, while not receiving, even corruptly, drought relief, have succeeded in consolidating their position in the power hierarchy.

In Chapter 21 on the Ciskei, Meredeth Turshen analyses the drought there and argues that the growth of hunger and malnutrition in this area cannot be adduced to the drought but rather to the policy of the South African government in dumping people into the marginalised 'homelands' where those not in positions of power granted them by the South African government are increasingly impoverished and starved, and incapable of reproducing their means of subsistence. In Chapter 22 Bush, Cliffe and Jansen note a similar process elsewhere in the region. The breakdown of the rural economy, with increasing numbers of unemployed migrant workers unable to send back remittances to their families, has forced women to go out to gain cash income. They are therefore unable to continue their role of reproducing the means of subsistence for the families of migrant labour. Malnutrition and hunger in the labour supply areas increasingly results in deaths from these and related medical conditions. Not only in the bantustans is a policy of genocide being conducted but, as Bush and his co-authors note, the genocidal characteristics of the bantustan strategy are spreading through the region's labour reserves.

13

Flowing with milk and money: food production in Africa and the policies of the EEC

Philip Raikes

Introduction

The primary focus of this paper is the food situation in Africa and the factors which have led up to it. A secondary focus is the role of the EEC in this process. The paper is, however, *not* about 'the impact of the EEC on the food situation in Africa'. Whatever effect EEC policies may have, they cannot be distinguished from others. EEC policies result in part from balances of interest within and between the member states, and in part from external factors, like the policies of the USA. Nor do they affect the food situation in Africa directly, but only as fed through the international system and the local states of Africa. The purpose of the paper is thus not to take the EEC out of context for a closer look, but rather to consider it in the broader context.

After a brief look at general factors affecting food production and security, the chapter looks at trends within tropical Africa and then at relevant international processes. After considering the EEC, and CAP protection, in this context, there follows a section on aid, both EEC and other, focusing on its interplay with local state policy. After a section on food aid, and another, now out of date, on the Commissioner, M. Pisani, a final section draws conclusions.

Food production and security

It is commonly assumed that the major focus of a food policy, and especially in Africa, should be to increase food production. However, it is also increasingly widely recognised that 'malnutrition is almost universally a consequence of people's inability to afford food which is available' (Tarrant 1980: 4). Thus if one is concerned primarily with the availability of food to those in real need and their security of access to it, it is at least as important to study forms of 'entitlement to food' (Sen 1981), as to consider overall production. Sen's purpose in introducing the notion of entitlement is to consider people's access to food on a broader basis than purchasing power, allowing, that is, for distribution other than via the market. One example would be redistribution within extended families and small-scale pre-capitalist societies, not to mention ties of family and friendship, even under capitalism. Another would be the special shops and ration-systems in certain African states, which allow controlled access at subsidised prices to goods in short supply, often with a preference to political party members, the military or state bureaucracy. Among Sen's purposes is to show that those most severely affected by food-shortage or famine are those whose entitlements are weakest and particularly vulnerable in situations of food shortage.

160

This is not to imply that food production should be ignored. Rather it is to introduce an aspect often ignored, that is, the effect of different ways of producing food upon the pattern of entitlements. For example, a policy aimed at the development of large highly capitalised farms may lead to an increase in food production (though there are plenty of examples where it has failed to do so). *If* it does so at competitive prices and *if* such advantages are passed on to consumers (a relatively unlikely combination), then one would expect one effect to be improved food supply to urban consumers. But another predictable effect would be loss of land and/or opportunities for wage-labour in the producing areas.

But there is another quite different aspect to this question, which relates to important policy differences between major aid donors. This is the question whether the best way to improve national food supply and security is to increase local food production (as implied by the recent EEC emphasis on 'food strategies'). Or is it rather to follow policies which aim to improve the balance of payments and in so doing improve national capacity to purchase food (as is implicit in the export-crop emphasis of recent World Bank thinking)? Or is it perhaps neither of these?

There are unsatisfactory elements with both of the positions outlined. The notion of national self-sufficiency, which refers to the ability of a nation to produce enough food for its inhabitants without importing, can be criticised from both 'market' and 'basic needs' viewpoints. On the one hand it ignores all discussion over potential advantages from specialisation and trade. On the other, it has no necessary relation to the availability of food to those who need it. One way to 'improve' self-sufficiency at the national level is to increase the consumer price of food sufficiently to lower aggregate demand enough to achieve a significant reduction in import requirements. At least in many cases, this might be expected to worsen the food supply situation for poorer strata in the country in question.[1] As Tarrant (1980: 153–4) points out, India has achieved self-sufficiency in basic foodstuffs over the past decade, in part through productivity increases related to the Green Revolution. Over the same period, however, all indicators are that the level of malnutrition and outright starvation have remained at their previous appalling level, if not increased further.

But the issue of food production is not irrelevant to food availability and security. One implicit but highly relevant basis for concern with national self-sufficiency in foodstuffs is that the worst possible situation for a country to get into is increased dependence upon imports of food *without* developing the capacity to pay for those imports.[2] Another is variation in international food prices which, following market principles, hit their peaks precisely when food shortage is conceived to be most serious.[3] The third point is that no more than food sufficiency does 'balance of payments self-sufficiency' imply any guarantees for the food supplies of those most in need. Indeed, where the rural population is concerned, there is some reason to believe that their food security is best served by a production pattern emphasising small and medium peasants producing both for the market and for their own subsistence needs. Certainly there is every reason to believe that this is how peasants themselves think and act and, given the failures of official distribution systems in so many African countries in recent years, it is hard to fault their logic. Available evidence indicates that a very high proportion of imported food stays in the major ports and capital cities, especially when they are one and the same. Not only is purchasing power concentrated here, but political pressure is far more easily brought to bear.

There are a large number of other aspects of this question which cannot be considered here, but all of them seem to have similar implications. Increasing food production in a given country does not, *per se* guarantee an improvement in the food supply and its security to those most in need. It is not hard to think of situations where it could have a negative effect by destroying or reducing the food entitlements of those already most vulnerable. On the other hand, as against those who propose that food supply can be as or more easily improved through increased production of export crops, I would propose that there *is* an advantage to domestic food production and specifically to dispersed domestic food production on peasant farms where it produces both food and entitlements thereto.

Trends in food supplies in tropical Africa

As is well known, there has been a widespread and significant deterioration in the food-supply situation of the majority of tropical African countries during the past decade. According to FAO, food supply grew by about 1.6 per cent per annum during the period 1970–79, while population grew by between 2 and 3.5 per cent. More recent FAO figures indicate that the situation has deteriorated further since then (but see below). With relatively few exceptions, domestic capacity to supply the urban areas with food has declined while food imports have increased markedly, both in absolute terms and as a proportion of total urban food-supply. Thus FAO (1983) shows that net imports of cereals into Africa (excluding South Africa and Egypt) rose from about 10 per cent of production in 1972 to over 30 per cent in 1982 while increasing by three and a half times. Imports of dairy products increased by almost 12 per cent per annum between 1970 and 1980. In a number of countries, the urban population is primarily dependent on imported food, including products such as wheat, which can only be grown in a few parts of the continent, and milk, whose production for commercial sale on a year-round basis is highly import-sensitive. Moreover, this trend has occurred while exports have stagnated and indebtedness increased. In short, many of these countries seem to be heading towards the worst possible situation mentioned above – increasing food imports and decreasing ability to pay for them.

It is worthwhile to distinguish clearly between food production and food supply on official markets. There can be no doubt that the latter has deteriorated, but it is not at all clear what the trends in food production have. That is, all that can be measured or estimated with any accuracy is supplies to official markets. Given that peasants produce by far the largest proportion of total food in almost all sub-Saharan Africa, this can only be linked to production by taking into account unofficial market sales and subsistence production. Since it is generally thought that low prices on official markets (further reduced in real terms by the high price and/or unavailability of goods to purchase) are among the major reasons for stagnating deliveries, there is even reason to expect some degree of producer substitution *into* food production, though not for official delivery. One reason to suppose this is that export-production has fared no better and sometimes even worse than official food deliveries. Low prices from monopoly marketing agencies are often blamed for this and the response is said to be substitution by producers into products less easily controlled by such agencies; that is, to a large extent, food. At the same time, with goods for purchase in short supply and subject to rationing and/or unofficial market prices, production of food for unofficial sale or barter at high prices is one means to offset part of this real income decline. To conclude, it is simply not clear what has happened to food production in much of tropical Africa. Correspondingly, it is far from clear that efforts to improve local food supplies to the towns are best concentrated on increasing productivity through technical change – at least until other problems have been solved.

But while the trends in Africa have been particularly serious, they are neither unlike nor unlinked to a more general worldwide trends.

Major trends in the world economy

Overshadowing all other trends of the past 10 or 15 years has been the gathering international crisis of lowered growth in industrial production and trade, increasing unemployment and indebtedness. But while the first signs of downturn were observable as early as the end of the 1960s, it is convenient to consider here processes which date from the early 1970s. More precisely, the oil and food crises of 1973/4 will be taken as the starting point.

While the oil price rises of 1973 and 1979 had as one major effect to shift the terms of trade against non-oil producers, and especially non-oil producing developing countries, the aspect to be considered here is its impact upon international financial flows.

That is, these price rises led to a rapid and massive accumulation of funds in the OPEC countries, their investment with Western banks and the need for the latter to recycle them profitably. One of the initial effects of this was to stimulate a burst of lending to certain developing countries, specifically those where prospects for investment in industrial production for export (and subsequently domestic) markets were bright. This process concentrated upon a number of 'middle-income' and 'new-industrialising' countries in Asia and Latin America, where they did indeed set off a process of industrial investment – and along with it, a considerable expansion both of overall urban population and most specifically of urban and upper income strata.

It is worth underlining that by far the major portion of this flow of funds took the form of commercial non-concessional loans. For a period during the late 1970s, rates of inflation rose more rapidly than interest rates, leaving the real rate of interest negative, but this did not last long. Since 1980, this has been reversed with a vengeance and real interest rates have reached their highest level since at least 1945. Since a large number of developing countries had been beguiled into thinking that they could borrow at will since inflation would take care of the repayment, this left a number of large borrowers over-extended, contributing to the current international debt crisis. That is, a number of large (mainly Latin American) debtor countries now have debts so large in relation to current interest rates and capacity to pay, that it is hard to see how they can ever repay. Certain observers have gone so far as to claim that they simply cannot, at least without major and currently unlikely reductions in the interest rate (Sjaastad 1983).

SSA followed a variant of this pattern though with significant differences. There was a similar upsurge in international commercial lending and this had led to similar problems of indebtedness, though at much lower absolute levels. But for SSA, unlike other parts of the developing world, there was also a major upsurge in concessional flows (grants and subsidised loans) as part of the aid programmes of the major donors. In 1969–71, SSA received about 18 per cent of world 'official development assistance' (ODA); by 1979–81, this had increased to 29 per cent, involving a rate of growth of ODA double that for the third world as a whole. One reason for this, though by no means the only one, was the increase in the proportion of total world ODA deriving from the EEC and its member countries, combined with a general trend in these countries to increase the proportion going to SSA. The EEC itself, as an aid donor, has always concentrated heavily upon Africa, which receives rather over 65 per cent of its total ODA in most years (Raikes 1984).

If one looks at the effects of this combined flow of commercial and concessional funds, it appears to have had effects rather similar to those elsewhere. A considerable proportion were used in large-scale industrial ventures of various sorts, another large proportion for infrastructural investment. One major *difference* has been that, with relatively few exceptions, the industries so generated have been high-cost and heavily dependent upon subsidies of various sorts. In very few cases have they shown any tendency to be effective earners or savers of foreign exchange. Often quite the reverse, they have shown themselves to be voracious users of foreign exchange in the form of fuel, spare parts and services, thus contributing directly to worsening in the balance of payments and increasing debt.

But the subsidies involved have also had important effects upon food production and security. In the first place subsidies require revenue and this has normally come from the largest productive sector, agriculture. Whether in the form of monopoly marketing charges or taxes on basic consumer goods, these have a depressing effect upon agricultural production. But they also affect the demand side, since a common form of subsidy to industry (via wage levels) and to the urban population is via controlled food prices. Since these subsidies are often accompanied by politically-controlled rationing, and are often highest for relatively expensive foodstuffs (wheat products, dairy products, meat), it is far from clear that they do much to benefit the poorer urban strata. But there is no doubt that they increase the aggregate demand for food and especially demand for the high and middle-income products mentioned. Since a large proportion of such foodstuffs have to be imported in any case, and since price controls further limit the ability of state marketing agencies to get hold of local products, the net effect is clearly to increase food imports.

To summarise briefly, recycling of petro-dollars much accelerated a process of commercial lending to (parts of) the third world aimed at industrialisation. Much of this was initially aimed at export-processing, as firms in industrialised countries sought shelter from the first chill winds of depression in the lower labour costs of Latin America and South-east Asia. In most cases, this led to increased urbanisation and the development of urban middle-income strata. This in turn had the general effect of increasing demand for food and food imports, hastened by changes in forms of food consumption. In a few countries, the industrialisation process was well enough embedded before the rise in interest rates for them not to experience major indebtedness. Others were less fortunate (or had invested less well) and found it hard to meet foreign exchange requirements together with interest and repayment, when export prices were falling and protection becoming ever more severe. The African variant of this included more concessional finance and greater state participation in both investment and provision of the conditions for it. In this case trade deficits were increased by policies to protect industry, which also helped to increase food imports.

Major trends in world food production and trade

One very important determinant of the pattern of world food production and trade has been the widespread tendency for advanced capitalist countries to subsidise agricultural production, generating export surpluses, while developing countries almost invariably tax agriculture to subsidise other sectors, thus tending to generate deficits and imports.

Another related tendency, and one of the greatest importance, has been the steady increase in the proportion of animal products and animal feedstuffs in international trade in agricultural products. This phenomenon is very clearly related to those aspects of development which involve urban expansion and specifically the emergence of middle-income strata. This is a dietary evolution which has occurred in all of the currently developed countries, with the added major dimension that in almost all such countries, overall income levels have increased to the extent that the working class also consumes large quantities of meat and dairy products, together with other 'quality foods', starting with wheat bread and proceeding to fresh vegetables and fruit. Only in relatively few developing countries have the mass of the population even taken the first steps on this ladder, though in some cases, sections of the urban working class have somewhat improved their diet.[4] Such strata, where they exist, are most decidedly not the poorest sections of the population. All evidence indicates that the vast mass of the population of the third world exists on a diet as poor as, if not even worse than, in the past.

But when considered in terms of world trade in foodstuffs, this development has had very significant consequences, especially in the period after 1974 when food imports into South-east Asia and the OPEC countries increased rapidly. But to appreciate this trend, it is necessary to consider some of the longer-term processes lying behind it.

Cereals

Since the early years of the present century, world trade in cereals has been dominated by the 'prairie' countries, the great plains of the world, whose previous inhabitants were pushed out or wiped out by white colonists. Of these, by far the most important is the USA, with over 50 per cent of the total, the others being Canada, Argentina, Australia and more recently as a result of CAP protection, the EEC. Together with South Africa, these countries account for some 85–90 per cent of total world exports, the only other significant exporter being Thailand (rice). US dominance is most pronounced for coarse grains (mostly maize), for which its share of world exports is about 60 per cent and least for rice, though even here it is, with Thailand, the major world exporter.

The major change of the past decade has been in the whole balance of supply and demand. Before and after the Second World War, the USA and other major producers had 'chronic' surpluses, which could only be exported on concessional terms. This was the genesis of PL480, the US law allowing use of food surpluses for concessional sales and gifts to selected developing countries, and thus of food aid. PL480 was passed in the mid-1950s and between 1959 and 1964, food aid accounted for no less than 34 per cent of total US grain exports (40 per cent for wheat). On the other side, it accounted for fully 57 per cent of developing countries' imports of grain from the USA over the same period (Tarrant 1980: 232–5).

Development of commercial demand, especially in the third world, led to a proportionate decline in the importance of food aid (still almost solely a US phenomenon) during the 1960s, but the really dramatic change came in 1972–6. Changes in US trade and agricultural policy from 1971 onwards, generated increased commercial exports and reduced the area planted to cereals, thus reducing stocks. This occurred just in time to coincide with a drought which reduced world cereal production by 2.2 per cent (the first reduction since 1965 and a much larger one) and that of the USSR by almost 13 per cent. The massive Soviet grain imports of 1972/3 set off an ugly rush to secure supplies and/or speculate, which drove prices rapidly skywards, enormously increasing the problems of drought-stricken countries in Africa (Tarrant 1980; Garcia and Escudeno 1981). Together with a subsequent fall in world cereal production in 1974, this radically changed the balance between production and needs. Since then, surpluses have re-emerged in some years, but no longer in their previous chronic form. Nor, come to that, is there evidence of a persistent tendency to deficit, though such is invariably predicted after every crisis.

This period of food crisis had an especially significant impact upon sub-Saharan Africa. Overall cereal imports into Africa increased, though not dramatically, between 1973 and 1974, and the rate of growth continued higher thereafter. But food aid to sub-Saharan Africa increased by almost three times between 1972/3 and 1973/4 and from 4 to 19 per cent of the world total. While the level fell again thereafter, it remained at over double the pre-1972/3 level and since 1978/9 has again risen rapidly. As of 1981/2, sub-Saharan Africa took 26 per cent of total world cereal food aid and, by volume, five and a half times as much as in the period 1970/73 (FAO 1984a: 23). There is a good reason to expect this to have had significant effects on the policies of recipient countries. Food imports at well below the cost of either local produce or commercial imports are evidently an attractive proposition and significantly reduce the budgetary cost of consumer-price controls. They can, for similar reasons, reduce the urgency of dealing with stagnating local deliveries, while at the same time accelerating the increase in demand for 'food aid products' like wheat and milk.

Dairy products

While the USA is heavily dominant in cereal trade, world trade in dairy products is dominated by the EEC. Put very simply, the major emphasis of European agriculture changed from grains to dairy production in the latter years of the last century under pressure of competition from the 'prairie lands', was subsidised sufficiently to maintain roughly self-sufficiency until the formation of the EEC, since when protection under the Common Agricultural Policy (CAP) had produced persistent and substantial surpluses. *All* exports of diary produce (and grain) from the EEC are subsidised, since internal prices are roughly double the world level. The EEC accounts for over 50 per cent of world exports for most dairy product categories, this rising to as much as almost 70 per cent for Skim Milk Powder (SMP).

Once again, the events of the early 1970s have set off a rising trend in world dairy trade. Part of this is due to increasing third world urban demand. Another part is due to a change in the form of EEC price support for milk in 1973, which much increased the levels of surpluses generated, and led to redoubled efforts to find export markets. While food aid from the EEC had not been a major proportion of total exports, it has been strategic in certain cases in opening up third world markets for European dairy products. This occurs especially in cases where an agreement to supply SMP and Butter Oil (BO), the constituents of recombined milk, are used to improve the terms upon which factories to produce recombined milk are supplied. In absolute terms, the major third world markets for imported dairy products have been the Arab OPEC countries, together with the Asian and Latin American NICs and MICs, where industrialisation and urbanisation were proceeding most rapidly. However, the rate of growth has been as rapid in Africa, though from a much lower base. As in other respects, the importance of subsidies and concessional terms has been significantly greater than elsewhere.

Oilseeds

The third major group of products traded on world markets are oilseeds and their products. Twenty years ago, the term 'oilseed' was appropriate in that the edible or industrial oils produced were by far the most important final products. Since then, with the increase in animal production and trade, the value of the 'residual' cake, which is used in animal feeding, has steadily increased and with it the relative value of oilseeds with a high quality protein-rich cake. This means pre-eminently soyabeans, which have a relatively low oil content, and which have come largely to dominate world trade with about 75 per cent of world oilseed exports and some 77 per cent of world exports of cake and meal. This has further presaged a major geographical shift in production and trade since the 'traditional' oilseeds dominating international trade were primarily tropical products (with Africa a prominent producer). The USA is the world's major producer of soyabeans, but Brazil and Argentina are also of great importance.

The above points towards a process in which a 'north American' pattern of consumption is being internationalised among the urban middle classes of the third world, involving the increasing importance of wheat products, dairy products and meat. Nor does this apply only to final products. Regular supplies of raw milk for a dairy plant almost inevitably require supplementary feeding, exotic cattle, more stringent (and expensive) veterinary and hygiene controls, not to mention equipment for milking and for the cooling, storage and transport of this highly perishable product. Much the same is true of meat, especially since the increase in consumption usually goes with increased tenderness and decreased taste which, together with the need to cover increased fixed costs requires more rapid turnover (earlier slaughter) and thus more intensive rearing. In short, such consumption patterns require either increased imports or local production with a substantially increased import content.

Since there are a number of observers who see nothing wrong with this 'specialisation', it is worth stressing the crucial importance of subsidies and other price inducements at various stages in the process. Apart from the obvious use of food aid as 'loss-leader' in export promotion campaigns, a large proportion of developed country commercial food exports are either subsidised (all food exports from the EEC) or 'blended' with food aid to improve the terms (as in a recent agreement between the USA and Egypt). One particularly effective means of export promotion has been to combine concessionary finance for the construction of modern food-processing factories (wheat mills, dairies, abattoirs, etc.) with food aid 'to get the factory going' and grant aid for projects ostensibly aimed at developing local (large-scale, modern) production of inputs to the factory. In a number of well-known cases (dairy farms in Tanzania and Mozambique, wheat farms in northern Nigeria) the latter fail to produce the goods, leaving the factory dependent on imports. In others, production is achieved at foreign exchange costs in excess of the costs of direct imports or by the dissipation of minimally replaceable resources (irrigation projects in Libya).

The other side of the coin is that SSA and other third world states also subsidise this process heavily. Food processing factories tend to be considered uncritically as 'industrialisation' and thus 'developmental' and to receive substantial government support and/or investment. The latter makes more likely that if and when the factory runs into problems, it will be further bailed out by the government through further subsidies. This shades into subsidies on consumer prices for food and on 'modern' inputs for local production. Meanwhile the widespread overvaluation of exchange rates subsidises all imports at the expense of all local products.

It thus makes little sense to refer to such developments as the result of either 'efficient specialisation' or 'rational consumer choice'. Certainly there are good reasons for the increasing preference of African urban consumers for wheat products – for one thing, they can more easily be processed into forms which can be purchased 'ready-to-eat' which is a boon to single male migrant workers and others too. But it seems unlikely that their spread would have been so rapid if consumers had had to pay their real social costs.

While it is easy enough to make general statements of this sort, it is much harder to make any quantitative assessment of their effect, let alone to attribute it to the EEC or any other particular actor. There are a number of studies of the effects of EEC and/or 'high income country' (HIC) protection in the agricultural sphere, arriving at widely divergent answers. Apart from the disagreement over the effects, these studies are almost without exception concerned with another aspect of agricultural protection, that of limiting agricultural exports from the third world. Relevant and important as that may be, it is not the concern of the current paper. However, it may be worthwhile briefly to indicate the extent of disagreement from two studies cited in a survey paper by Matthews (1984). Valdes and Zietz (1980) estimated that a 50 per cent reduction in agricultural protection by all HICs would increase the export earnings of the 56 largest LDCs by over $3 billion, of which $200 million would be accounted for by beef. Another study by Tangermann and Krostitz (1982) estimated that a 50 per cent reduction in protection on beef would increase third world export earnings from that commodity alone by $2.2 billion (possibly in part because some important beef exporters, such as Botswana, are not among the 56 most populous LDCs). One study which claims to be broader-based than the others, since based on a general (economic) equilibrium model, claims that the result of a total cessation of EEC protection (without anything else changing) would lead to a 16.5 per cent reduction in EEC agricultural production, with that of dairy products, fruit and vegetables decreasing faster. World prices for agricultural products would rise by just over 15 per cent, the increase being rather higher for dairy products and meat products, a few per cent lower for cereals. The general effect of this would be to re-establish the 'traditional' pattern of specialisation, with the third world increasing production of agricultural goods and Europe re-establishing some of its former dominance in industrial production. It would force third world governments to pay more attention to factors such as agricultural prices. The losers would be European agricultural producers and third world city dwellers.

It should be made quite clear that the authors (Burniaux and Waelbroeck 1984) do not expect any such thing to happen. They are well aware of the political power of the European farm and agribusiness lobby. The model is hypothetical in another way, in that it is quite inconceivable that European protection should disappear without any corresponding change in levels of protection elsewhere (the USA or Japan for example). More generally, whatever the usefulness of general equilibrium models (and many would not rate it very high), they can only be considered relevant in relation to events and changes sufficiently limited in extent not to induce political responses (which could hardly be said of this case).

But when all is said and done, even if one does accept their general conclusions (and it seems reasonable to suppose that eliminating European agricultural protection would have effects something like those proposed), it is much harder to see what the effects on food availability or security would be (even within the model) and much harder to assess the effects of any realistic scenario (if indeed it is at all realistic to predict a reduction in agricultural protection). For one thing, one has to consider the effects of protection in one industrialised country or group upon that of the others. Garcia et al. (1981) cite a number of US sources to the effect that the more aggressively commercial and export-oriented agricultural policy of the USA from 1970 onwards, was partially a response to EEC (and Japanese) protection and more recent events indicate no slackening in this trade war. As just one recent example, the USA in 1982 concluded an agreement with Egypt (a traditional market for French wheat) which in return for the sale of 1 million tons of wheat at markedly concessional prices bound Egypt to give preference to the USA in any further purchases of wheat during the following 14 months. During the previous season, the EEC had sold some 1 million tons of wheat to Egypt (of which 0.2 million tons was food aid) compared with a total of 0.63 million tons from the USA (of which 0.56 were 'concessional').

For the future a broader-based 'war' seems in the offing, over animal (and especially dairy) products. The EEC, the dominant world exporter of dairy products threatens to impose protection on imports of oilseed cakes, of which the USA is the major world exporter. Meanwhile the USA is aggressively pushing the development of domestic dairy production in certain third world countries (especially in South-east Asia). It seems highly likely that this is seen as a safer alternative to depending on exports to Europe at the existing level and, if further broadened, would clearly threaten European dairy exports. It is not quite clear what the implications of this are for Africa except that, to paraphrase Nyerere, it seems likely to be the grass which is flattened when the elephants fight.

The main purpose of this section of the chapter has been to show that aggressive export promotion by Europe and the USA, making use of both food and other forms of aid, has combined with policies in most of the states of sub-Saharan Africa, to generate patterns of urban food consumption and of food-processing and even production which are grossly out of line with the capacities of the countries in question to support and with negative effects upon the food availability and security of poorer sections of their populations. While it is not possible to put numbers to this, there seems little doubt of its significance.

But while this section has been largely devoted to aspects of trade policy and protection, it cannot be separated from aid and it is to this that I now turn.

Aid from the EEC and other donors

The EEC is generally regarded as having a rather poor aid programme – slow, cumbersome and bureaucratic. The time taken for disbursement seems generally longer than for other programmes, most especially for food aid, which takes up to 18 months to arrive. It has been responsible for some more than usually awful projects. It is hard, for example, to see what is developmental about the several allocations which have been made for the building and improvement of a secondary school for the daughters of the rich in Abidjan. A transport infrastructure project in Zaire has taken enormous amounts of time and money for almost nothing achieved. Agro-industrial complexes also in Zaire have cost a lot and achieved very little (see Hewitt 1982 and articles in Stevens, ed. for more details). Stabex, the EEC's much vaunted export stabilisation scheme has largely failed to stabilise export earnings, is grossly maldistributed, omits important crops which are produced within the EEC, but makes up for this by including items such as ylang-ylang and squid, and finally has in certain cases been used for purposes not easily defined as development. In one case this was to fund a civil war, in another to purchase a fleet of limousines (Hewitt 1983; Raikes 1984). But there is no reason to believe that other agencies are markedly superior. Even to the extent that they can be shown to be more efficient than the EEC, this does not mean that they are achieving development; only that they are wasting less time and money in failing to do so.

But when one turns to the more general results of aid activity their failure strikes one forcibly. Over the period 1970–82 flows of 'official development assistance' (ODA), the grant of concessional funds from official development agencies, increased (from all sources to all recipients) by just under 4 per cent per annum in real terms. For sub-Saharan Africa, the rate was over twice as high. During the same period, the flow of ODA to SSA increased from about 40 per cent to about 80 per cent of the amount going to Asia, or in per capita terms, from three to six times as much (Raikes 1984b). Over this period all growth indicators have been significantly poorer for SSA than for other parts of the third world. Clearly such figures are indicative rather than in any sense conclusive. One can question the relevance of many 'growth indicators', while it is obvious that factors other than aid are important.

I would also reject the common defence put up by representatives of development agencies (for example the Berg Report) that their best efforts have unfortunately not prevailed because of policy failures among the states of SSA. It is not that I am concerned to defend such state policies – far from it. My disagreement with this analysis stems from two related reasons. Firstly it seems to me that a large proportion of donor aid has contributed to, rather than countered, the sorts of policy criticised. Secondly, it is not hard to think of projects whose net effect has been fairly unambiguously negative. I am pressed to think of aid projects, especially within the agricultural field which can be claimed to have had unambiguously positive effects, though this may reflect insufficient experience. Given the normal practices of aid agencies, however, one might expect to hear about unambiguous successes in load and clear terms from their ever-active public relations departments.

To take the first point above it seems quite incorrect to distinguish between the 'positive' effects of development aid and the 'negative' ones of SSA state policy. In reality the two are inextricably entwined, and most especially in recent years when, for many tropical African countries, foreign aid has composed a very significant proportion of total 'development spending'. Is it correct to distinguish the 'positive' effect of foreign-aided investment in industry or agricultural modernisation from the 'negative' effects of the subsidies which keep it going? Should one consider subsidised delivery of, say, fertiliser to (selected) farmers as being positive, when the subsidies are finally paid out of the price paid to peasants for their agricultural produce? Can one realistically talk of the inadequacy of transport infrastructure, supply, delivery and service systems, without considering the extra burden placed upon them by development projects and programmes?

This latter is perhaps the most harmful effect of much donor aid. Where systems are already scarcely capable of performing their normal functions, it does not seem helpful to impose upon them further projects and programmes, each with its own requirement for transport, skilled personnel and management (and with the foreign exchange to bid them away from their former tasks). This in turn relates to the common form taken by donor-funded programmes in the agricultural sector, and most especially the larger ones.

Much of the agricultural modernisation policy of African governments and aid agencies alike consists in large part of transferring 'modern' technologies from Europe and the USA, sometimes with adaptation, sometimes without. Since these technologies have been developed in response to conditions of both *subsidies* to agriculture and relatively *high wages* in relation to capital costs, it is scarcely surprising that they do not always work in situations where agriculture is *taxed* to the benefit of other sectors and where *labour-costs* are much *lower* in relation to those of capital. When one adds that the conditions for the operation of modern technologies – systems for the delivery of fuel, other materials, spares and services and marketing systems for produce – often function poorly in Africa, it becomes even less surprising that their positive impact upon production is usually minimal. Nor, given that these requirements are often quite considerable, is it surprising that they should so often overstrain existing systems and contribute to their further deterioration.

Where the second point is concerned, space permits mention of only two of the projects whose effects have been fairly unambiguously negative. The Kenya/World Bank IADP, had as one of its objectives to galvanise both peasant production and 'weak' (read inefficient and corrupt) co-operative unions, largely in western Kenya. One of the major aspects of this was a small-farmer credit programme in which large amounts of money were disbursed very rapidly (under World Bank pressure to get moving) and with entirely inadequate control, to co-operative unions and peasants (some of the latter being given the impression that they were receiving grants since they were unwilling to accept loans).

This (admittedly together with other factors, like coffee-smuggling during the boom of 1977–8) has led to the almost total collapse of some of the concerned unions, one of which had by 1982 debts equivalent to some twenty years' gross income from crop sale and processing). In general repayment rates were about 30 per cent, which is low even by the standards of small-farmer credit schemes, and the government was left wondering what to do about it. To write off the debts of one union, would have every other in the country clamouring for similar treatment. Not to do so, leaves the affected unions largely immobilised.

Tanzania's National Maize Programme (also World Bank) has also been heavily criticised. This involved credit to villages for the adoption of a standard country-wide 'package' of fertiliser, insecticide and hybrid maize seed. It may seem scarcely credible that the same package (with two different levels of application for the same fertilizers) should be expected to cover a country of such widely varying climate, soils and topography as Tanzania, but it was the case. Not surprisingly, it was inappropriate and rejected in many parts. Others have called into question the whole idea of monocrop plus fertiliser as a long-term strategy in conditions where deterioration of soil structure is often a major problem. Among the relatively few successful areas of operation of the scheme were Kigoma, Ruvuma and Rukwa Regions in the far west and south of the country. This results more from the policy of 'pan-territorial pricing' for agricultural products and a transport subsidy on fertiliser, than from the NMP as such. While this has been claimed as a partial success for NMP, other departments of the World Bank have been among the most vocal critics of pan-territorial pricing as having distorted production patterns and lumped the country with the necessity to purchase maize which costs almost as much to transport to Dar es Salaam in foreign exchange terms as would direct imports. The list could be extended to book length and certainly does not concern only the World Bank. The choice of two of its projects relates partly to their size and partly to the tendency of that organisation to consider itself superior to others.

Under such circumstances, it seems to me largely irrelevant to single out the EEC for special criticism. Moreover, some of the criticisms made of the EEC seem to me misplaced. One of these is that EEC aid takes a long time to disburse. This is certainly true of EEC food aid, which takes several months longer than that of most other donors (and over a year more than commercial shipments). Where project aid is concerned, it is also probably true, though part of the reason is probably that, in much of Africa, the EEC aid programme is relatively new and therefore contains a higher than usual proportion of new projects (which take longer than continuations).

But it is highly questionable whether this is a very relevant criticism. At least as strong a case could be made that both the EEC and other agencies are *far too quick* to throw away money on projects and programmes which have been disastrously underresearched. For while the bureaucratic procedures in both the EEC and other agencies commonly take months, if not years, it is far from uncommon for millions of dollars to be allocated on the basis of 'field study' consisting of little more than a short trip by consultants with at most a few days in the rural area affected. Examples abound where projects have been initiated without any consultation at all of the local 'leaders' let alone a representative section of the population to be affected. One thoroughly justified criticism of the EEC project-funding system is that the EDF committee allocates money on the basis of inadequate discussion of even such 'field-study' as has been done, which would argue strongly for an even 'slower' disbursement procedure.

The EDF committee makes decisions on up to 40 different projects in one day and friends working for a European bilateral agency claim that the opportunity for discussion is so minimal that it is hardly worthwhile attending.

Food aid

In one obvious sense, food aid lies between project aid and agricultural protection. That is, it is one means of disposing of the surpluses generated by agricultural protection – and one which can be used to quiet some of the dissatisfaction of those who pay for protection (consumers and taxpayers in the developed countries), since it is a 'good cause'. Historically, it has been very closely linked to the emergence of large unsaleable surpluses; for the USA in the 1950s and for the EEC from the early 1970s. In both cases, there is clear evidence that agricultural policy-makers (and firms in the food industry) have seen it it as a useful means of state-supported export promotion. In some cases, commercial firms have developed new products especially for food aid. Thus 'bulgur wheat', in its modern factory-produced form, was a result of efforts by US grain firms to find a wheat product with cooking qualities similar to those of rice, during a period when US wheat food aid to the Indian sub-continent was running into problems of consumer resistance. More recently, Danish meat-packing firms have (with state assistance) developed a product called 'meatloaf' which is doubly satisfactory to them as a food aid product. Being more highly spiced than 'luncheon meat', it is more acceptable to food aid recipients. But at the same time, this allows the use of offals which would not be acceptable to the Danish public or importers in the developed countries. Its commercial prospects in the third world do not appear to have been tested yet (Sano 1984).

Food aid is a subject upon which opinions differ widely. At one end of the scale are those who note the food shortages in the third world and the surpluses piling up in the developed countries and urge an increase in its use to mitigate hunger. Few serious analysts accept this simplified view, noting that while the surpluses are large in relation to developed country production and trade, they could cover but a small fraction of the world's hunger. They further note that only a very small proportion of food aid actually gets to those in dire need. Those who argue in favour of food aid tend to make use of a different argument – that it is additional to other aid (which may or may not be true) and that, as a form of foreign exchange, it can lead to development (which is clearly true in the abstract but highly questionable in reality). Few question the small proportion of total food aid which is given as disaster aid (about 10 per cent, though many question whether the forms in which it is given are normally helpful; that is, given the long delays common in delivery, it has a tendency to arrive just in time to depress producer prices for the following harvest.

There is, however, a mass of evidence that the 20 per cent or so of food aid, which is used in food-for-work and nutritional rehabilitation programmes, rather seldom achieves its aims (see Jackson 1983). However, the most serious criticism can be levelled at the approximately 70 per cent of the total which is transferred to third world governments for them to distribute. For many years, an argument has raged between supporters and detractors, largely focused around the issue of whether food aid constitutes a disincentive to local producers. In fact, no clear answer can be given to this question since it depends upon the way in which and the price at which the recipient government disposes of the food. However, there is little doubt that food aid has in many cases been associated with increased food imports and there are a number of reasons for this. Firstly, food aid enables governments to keep food prices to the urban population low, without improving the efficiency of the local food purchasing network.

This increases urban food demand (and notably for 'food-aid-products' like wheat products and milk) while doing nothing to increase local supply. Another is that food aid for sale by the recipient government can become an important source of state revenue, to the extent that it cannot afford to achieve self-sufficiency for fear of losing the revenue. Thirdly, when used in conjunction with investment in processing facilities for (imported or import-intensive) foodstuffs, it further expands urban and institutional demand for the products in question and generates pressures for product subsidies, especially when the factories are state owned. Further, it seems naive when hard-headed business interests in the exporting countries have been using food aid for years as part of a strategy for export market development, to suppose that it has had no such effect. It is also important to note what dependency can imply. Any country which has the money can purchase grain on the commercial market – as witness the failure of the Carter restrictions against the USSR in the aftermath of Afghanistan. But once a country depends upon grant aid because of inability to pay, then its government can come under very severe pressure indeed, squeezed between donor conditionality on the one side and the prospect of food riots on the other.

Nonetheless, the argument that food aid leads to dependency upon food imports has for some years been considered radical and not quite respectable. Recently however, it has gained in respectability from the accession of a new adherent, M. Pisani, the EEC Commissioner for development. M. Pisani has been outspokenly critical of the dependency-inducing effects of food aid on a number of occasions and, at the same time, has been responsible for introducing changes in the direction of EEC aid, designed to increase the degree of food self-sufficiency in tropical African countries.

New directions in EEC aid

Until quite recently, the charge could justifiably be aimed at the EEC Commission that it had no clearly articulated aid strategy. But, at least in terms of formal statements, this has changed with the accession of a new Aid Commissioner, M. Edgar Pisani.

Highly critical of the past effects of aid, and most particularly food aid, M. Pisani has switched the focus of EEC aid to a direct confrontation of the food problem in Africa. In a series of cogently argued policy reviews, he has stressed the need to focus upon peasants (as have other donors), to avoid large capital-intensive projects where possible and to use the utmost caution in the distribution of food aid. Noting that aid projects unconnected to other aspects of recipient policy are likely to have negligible effects, he has argued strongly for 'policy dialogues' to ensure consistency where possible. While one can certainly take issue with some aspects of the new policy, it is refreshing, in a sphere so dominated by inflated and meaningless rhetoric, to come across a senior official who gives the impression of having thought carefully about the issues.

One of the major foci of the new policy is 'food strategies'. At the conceptual level, one can certainly argue with the identification of food security with national self-sufficiency in food. My own doubts would centre rather on two different issues.

Firstly, whatever the qualities of M. Pisani, it is hard to see how they will penetrate through the Council of Ministers, the EEC Commission bureaucracy and the commercial consultancy companies who implement almost all EEC projects, to make significant differences in implementation. Secondly, there are so many inherent contradictions in the whole state-to-state aid relationship that again, it is hard to see major positive results emerging. Some of this can be illustrated by reference to activities to date in this area.

The new policy is being embodied in a series of country 'food strategies' which are being tested on a pilot basis in four countries – Mali, Kenya, Zambia and Rwanda – with plans under way to include Tanzania. Of these only that in Mali has passed the planning stage. The Malian example shows some of the problems encountered in turning such strategies into reality.

For some years, Mali has been dependent upon food imports, a problem seen to derive in large measure from low prices paid by its monopoly grain purchasing agency (OPAM). This in turn derives in large part from inefficiency and overstaffing. EEC policy has started out by using food aid as a means to subsidise improved prices to local farmers. That is, food aid substitutes for a proportion of previous commercial imports, and being free, allows OPAM to earn a profit from its sale. This profit is then used to subsidise its local purchasing activities and thus to improve producer prices to farmers. While it is hard to estimate the impact to date, because of variations in weather and harvest, there are some signs of success. Producer prices have increased significantly and this seems to have had some effect upon deliveries to the agency. But the purpose of this is primarily to provide a breathing-space, during which OPAM can set its house in order, increase efficiency and pay better prices *without* food aid. So far, the signs of this happening are limited.

There do seem to have been some improvements in organisation, achieved with a relatively large input of technical assistance, but many of the major problems still remain to be overcome. Nor is there anything in the history of monopoly marketing agencies to lead one to expect a trouble-free development towards efficient operation. But unless this happens, there is a severe risk that Mali will become heavily dependent upon food aid, to the extent that it cannot afford to achieve self-sufficiency. For if it did, there would be no food aid to subsidise prices to local farmers and either they would have to fall again, or urban food prices would have to rise. This latter is not something which the Malian government wishes to risk. Like most other African governments, it is only too well aware that, while the rural population is far larger, the urban population is far more concentrated and organised and thus more capable of political action (not to mention that a very large majority of decision-makers are urban based).

There thus seems a considerable chance that the policy will replace one form of dependency on food imports with another.

Summary

What I have tried to do in this chapter is to trace some of the more important processes which have affected food production and imports into sub-Saharan Africa and to indicate the importance of various EEC policies within them.

The most general conclusion is that Africa's current food problems derive from a wide variety of different sources, ranging from the world economic crisis in its different manifestations, through the agricultural protection of the USA and EEC to policies specifically concerned with 'development' from both donor and local government sides. It is not possible (or even very useful) to allocate weights between these – between internal versus external factors, EEC versus USA, etc. The reason for this is not merely problems of measurement and computation, major as they are. The effort to allocate responsibility or blame rests on two notions, both of which I would reject. The first is that each separate 'cause' works independently which, as I hope to have shown, is clearly not the case. The second is that there are basic policy differences between the states of SSA and donors or, come to that, between the EEC and other donors.

In both cases there are, of course, differences. Between donors or creditors and recipients or debtors, there are rather obvious conflicts which hardly need explaining. While the EEC is not significantly different from other donors as an aid organisation, there can be little doubt that the level of agricultural protection under CAP is higher in aggregate than would emerge from separate national policies.

But when one turns to policies aimed at development – and especially as one moves from rhetoric to practical implementation – the differences diminish markedly. Ill-advised investments and poorly-conceived development projects have been mentioned as among the significant problems and these clearly depend on a degree of agreement from both sides. Donors currently bemoan the high cost and inefficiency of monopoly marketing agencies, but many of them (Tanzania's crop authorities, for example) were given their current form on the specific advice of 'development consultants' in good standing with donors, and for the specific purpose of increasing the funding available for 'development activities' by taxing peasants' crop sales. On the other hand, tropical African states have been no more critical of food aid than the officials of donor agencies – except that there is not enough of it.

At the basis of this lies a common conception of development as being 'modernisation', the introduction of methods, equipment and organisation from the 'advanced' countries. An overwhelming concentration on the technical characteristics of the various innovations pushed, tends to mask their inappropriateness to the conditions into which they are to be introduced – combined with the notion that since these conditions are characteristic of underdevelopment and backwardness, they are to be done away with in any case. The economic/accounting analogue to this is that subsidies and state accounting procedures combine to mask the fact that such techniques are often unviable and wasteful of foreign exchange. The question to be asked about agricultural development projects is not simply whether they 'succeeded' in setting-up the system of production proposed (though it is seldom enough that even this is achieved), but whether that system is viable without aid projects, experts and subsidies.

From the modernisation viewpoint, the 'blending' process described above can be seen as co-ordination for development. A modern dairy factory is investment in industry and supposedly import-substituting. It improves the hygiene of the milk supplied to urban dwellers, even if at costs which either put it beyond the reach of all but the rich or require heavy subsidies, or require reductions in producer prices sufficient to reduce local production. Once the decision to build such plant has been taken, it is 'only natural' to help it on its way with food aid, SMP and butter oil and, since the idea is to develop local production, to set up large-scale modern dairy farms. Then, since much of the above is operated by a combination of the local state and aid donors, further funds will easily be forthcoming to maintain the system in existence in the face of rising costs, shortages of spare parts, failure of raw milk to arrive etc etc. Andrae and Beckman (in Chapter 17 in this volume) have described a rather similar process with wheat mills in Nigeria (1983) and the list could be extended.

But while the above may go some way to improving understanding of the processes whereby local food supplies through official channels to the urban areas, have declined in many African countries, with a corresponding increase in imports, it does not say much about the problem of food security to those in real need. Nor, I must admit, have I yet reached anything which could be presented as even an interim conclusion. It is clear that 'entitlement' is one of the crucial concepts here, but it is not sufficient on its own.

It is, for example, not sufficient to cite a putative more secure entitlement for urban workers over peasants, as an argument in favour of industrialisation, if this is the result of economic subsidy and political pressure which reduces food availability to the much larger rural poor. One man or woman's entitlement may well be another man or woman's starvation in such a case. The links to production are extremely important but very difficult to set in focus. Some are relatively simple to trace, as in the examples given early in this paper. But these are by no means sufficient for an analysis, and still less for drawing policy/political conclusions. Since this is a contribution intended to raise discussion, I feel entitled to end by asking if anyone has ideas which could contribute to this analysis.

NOTES

1. This is not to claim that this will always be the case. The prices open to state manipulation are, by definition, those on controlled official markets. In situations where food subsidies lead to (or increase) a gap between demand and supply, where rationing is used to apportion the inadequate supplies, and where political considerations importantly affect the allocation of rations (not an uncommon situation in SSA – see Bates 1981), raising prices on these markets can actually reduce prices to those excluded from the rationing system (who have to buy on residual black-markets).
2. This, in turn, can mean increased dependency upon food aid whose disadvantage (in this context) is that its supply is controlled by the donors and may be reduced at periods of serious shortage because of (say) their dissatisfaction with recipient policy. Tanzania is said to be facing this problem at present.
3. As Sen (1981, *passim*), Tarrant (1980, Chapter 8) and a number of other authors have shown, it is not necessarily the largest food production shortfalls that produce the worst famines. More devastating is a combination of *expectations* of shortfall (leading to pre-emptive hoarding), delayed and/or counter-productive state policies and the existence of vulnerable social strata, whose food entitlements are reduced (or disappear) when food prices are rising. In the latter respect, Sen cites landless agricultural labourers as a particularly vulnerable group, since reduced harvests mean lay-offs just when food prices are rising.
4. In Zimbabwe, for example, during the first two years after independence, food price controls, combined with rapidly rising money wages, allowed sections of the Harare working class to consume increased amounts of milk and meat. These, however, were definitely not the poorer sections of the working class. Similar patterns can doubtless be found elsewhere.

14

Bread riots in north Africa: economic policy and social unrest in Tunisia and Morocco

David Seddon

The year 1984 began in bloody fashion in the Maghreb. Violent demonstrations, originating in the impoverished southwest and south of Tunisia at the very end of December and spreading throughout the country during the first week of January, followed the introduction of measures by the Tunisian government to remove food subsidies as part of their 'economic stabilisation' programme approved by the IMF and the World Bank. The sudden doubling of bread prices was a crucial factor in the outbreak of mass unrest, although official explanations identified a threat from 'hostile elements' concerned to overthrow the government. Whatever the reality of this supposed threat to the regime of octogenarian President Habib Bourghiba, the state's response to the demonstrations was itself extremely violent. As the unrest spread, security forces opened fire on crowds in several towns, including the capital, Tunis; at least 60 people were killed – as many as 120 according to some reports – and many more injured. A state of emergency and a curfew were declared on 3 January, public gatherings of more than three persons were forbidden, the Prime Minister, Mohammed Mzali, appeared on television to appeal for calm, and the state security forces – police, national guard, *gendarmerie* and the army – were visibly and massively poised for further developments. But the demonstrations and street violence continued; on 4 January there were numerous clashes, and on 5 January the army and police fired on 'rioters' in Tunis, moving into the old *medina* to dislodge snipers. In the morning of 6 January, President Bourghiba appeared on television to rescind the price increases and promise the restoration of food subsidies – an announcement evidently received with pleasure and relief by the crowds in the streets. Three weeks later, after a period of relative calm, the curfew was lifted; by February it appeared that the immediate crisis was over.

As Tunisia returned, warily, to relative normality during the second half of January, Morocco was experiencing its own wave of mass demonstrations and street violence. Starting with strikes by students over fee increases during the first week of January, social unrest increased rapidly as students were joined by large numbers of unemployed workers in the towns of the south (Marrakesh) and northeast (Al Hoceima, Nador, Oujda). On 21 January, *Le Monde* reported violent demonstrations and clashed with the police in the region of Nador, resulting in several deaths and many injuries. It would seem that the disturbances had actually begun as early as 12 and 13 January and that the army as well as civilian security forces had been involved, but heavy news censorship prevented earlier publication of details. Later press reports revealed that demonstrations had broken out as early as the beginning of the second week of

January in the south, where drought conditions were particularly severe. (Over the weekend of 22–23 January, the newspaper of the Istiqlal party, *l'Opinion*, reported that the wave of demonstrations had in fact begun two weeks earlier in Marrakesh, and that troops from the western Sahara and Sidi Ifni had been brought in to quell the disturbances.) In Morocco, as in Tunisia, the demonstrations, although in this case developing out of earlier protests at school and university fee increases, were closely connected to official proposals made at the end of December to raise the price of basic commodities, including food, only four months after major increases in August 1983. The proposals for further increases in prices followed the recommendations of the IMF, which in September had given its approval to a major programme of 'economic stabilisation' involving, among other measures, the withdrawal of subsidies on basic goods. As in Tunisia, however, official explanations for the troubles emphasised the role of 'agitators' of various kinds and, again as in Tunisia, the demonstrators were met with massive state violence. As social unrest spread through the towns of the barren and relatively impoverished north of the country, and broke out even in some of the larger cities of the Moroccan 'heartlands' (with the major exception of Casablanca, scene of violent 'bread riots' in June 1981, which remained virtually unaffected), it was countered by heavy concentration of state security forces. On 25 January, after relative calm had been restored, it was officially announced that 29 people had been killed and 114 injured during the previous weeks; but press reports suggest that at least 100 were killed (as many as 400 according to some sources) and many more injured and arrested. King Hassan moved quickly in response to the crisis and appeared on television in the evening of 22 January to announce that there would be no further increases in the price of basic goods after all. This public statement by the monarch, together with the repressive measures taken against the demonstrators, ensured that 'law and order' were restored within a few days; and by the end of the month it could be said that Morocco, like Tunisia, had returned to 'normal'.

But if the immediate crisis for the Tunisian and Moroccan governments was over when the streets emptied of demonstrators and filled instead with crowds openly rejoicing over the decision – announced by their 'supreme leader' – to halt food (and other) price increases, the underlying economic and political conditions which had given rise both to the upsurge of mass social unrest and to the brutal state repression of January 1984 had not changed. The explanations for 'the January bread riots' and for the state's violent reaction lie deeper than in the immediate causes – those factors which could be said to have triggered off the violence – although these too require analysis; they lie in a detailed assessment of the distinctive economic policies and political structures of contemporary Tunisia and Morocco which have created such a potential for large-scale mass unrest and have failed to create suitable channels or mechanisms for the effective, but peaceful, expression of opposition to those policies and structures.

This chapter considers, in a preliminary fashion, both the immediate causes and the underlying determinants of social unrest in Tunisia and Morocco at the beginning of the year, and also examines briefly the economic and political implications of the events of January.

Organised opposition . . . or 'spontaneous' protest?

It is common for governments to identify mass demonstrations of widespread popular anger and resentment as essentially the work of highly organised small groups of agitators – preferably foreigners or at least foreign-inspired and supported; to accept that large numbers of ordinary citizens may be so moved, and so desperate, as to act openly and violently together would be to admit that deep-seated and intractable problems exist.

There is little doubt that, despite the flimsy evidence, in both Tunisia and Morocco, the regime perceived a dangerous threat from small groups of organised militants. During and immediately after the street violence a systematic programme of arrest and interrogation of known activists was initiated in both countries. In Morocco, not only the left-wing revolutionary groups such as Ilal Alam were targets but even the Union Socialiste des Forces Populaires (USFP) was suspect – and 21 of its members arrested – despite the fact that the party adhered officially to 'the sacred unity' established in the context of the war in the Sahara and that its leader, Abderrahim Bouabid, was a member of the King's cabinet. The Communist Party in particular was harassed, and its newspaper *Al Bayane* seized on several days running. In Tunisia, known activists from both Muslim fundamentalist and left-wing groups were taken in for questioning; 30 or so militants of the Mouvement de Tendance Islamique – which prior to the troubles was seeking to obtain recognition as a political party – were interrogated, as were numerous Communist Party activists. Nevertheless, despite the fear of a threat from organised political groups, and the undoubted involvement of political activists in the demonstrations, there is little concrete support for the notion that these played a key role in orchestrating the social unrest and the mass demonstrations; it would seem, rather, that they – like so many others – were taken by surprise by what was essentially a popular uprising, and sought simply to join in.

Even the trade unions – which in Tunisia had organised numerous strikes in 1977–8, culminating in the violence following the general strike of January 1978, when the army intervened and large numbers (estimates vary between 46 and 200) (Ruf 1984: 109) were killed, and in Morocco in 1981 had certainly orchestrated the strikes and public rallies which preceded the bloody riots in Casablanca – were not evidently involved this time. Certainly, in Tunisia, the Union Général des Travailleurs Tunisient (UGTT) foresaw the economic and social problems that might arise as a result of a dramatic and rapid price increase, and had sought to negotiate concessions for the poor, and a wage review, before prices were put up[1] – but their discussions were with the government at top level and did not involve the union rank and file, let alone the organisation of rallies and strikes to back up their position. A meeting was in fact held on 5 January, after the mass demonstrations had taken place throughout the country, between the president and secretary-general of the UGTT and government ministers, which produced what the president of the UGTT described as 'good and positive results' (*Financial Times* 6 January 1984). The next day, President Bourghiba announced that the price increases would be rescinded; but it is not al all clear what influence, if any, the discussions with the union leadership had on the decision to reverse the removal of food subsidies. Mention of a possible general strike was made, but events had gone beyond this threat and it was not taken (possibly not even made) seriously. In Morocco, it is not clear whether the trade unions played any part, even at the level of discussions with government ministers as in Tunisia, in increasing the pressure on the government to reverse the decision to raise prices again; certainly, there is no good evidence that they did. On the other hand, it was remarkable that in Casablanca and Mohammedia – industrial centres with the greatest concentration of organised labour in the country – there was little sign of disturbances, despite the fact that unemployment runs particularly high among the skilled and semi-skilled manual workers (47 per cent of all unemployed but only a quarter of the labour force) who tend to be concentrated in such centres; had the unions already worked out a compromise with the government? (Findlay 1978: 60).

One social category that was clearly and importantly involved in the demonstrations in both Tunisia and Morocco – as it had been in the past during similar outbreaks of social unrest – was that of the students, from high schools and from universities. In Morocco, it was the school strikes which helped generate the open protest which gradually transformed the generally growing social unrest into overt opposition to the government's economic and social policies, and in particular against further price increases. In Tunisia, particularly in the north of the country, students were actively involved in large numbers in the demonstrations. By 3 January, students in Tunis were throwing stones at buses, shouting anti-government slogans and marching in the streets in solidarity with the demonstrators in the south (*Le Monde* 4 January 1984); during the next few days, as the students took to the streets, the authorities closed down the schools and university. It is interesting to note that those most vocal in their criticisms of the regime, in both countries, during the demonstrations were these children of the middle classes whose standard of living has generally improved substantially as a result of the economic policies of the past decade or so. But graduate unemployment, combined with the effective suppression of political opposition to the regime in both Tunisia and Morocco, ensure that significant numbers of the young, even from the relatively privileged social strata upon whom the regime so crucially depends, are disaffected and highly critical (see Zghal 1984).

Clearly, then, the social elements involved in the demonstrations of January 1984 were various and diverse; equally clearly, no mass protest or social revolt that continues over a period of even a week can be sustained entirely through totally 'spontaneous' action. It must be recognised, furthermore, that in all such essentially popular movements there is a 'band-wagon effect'. In the case of Tunisia, as Godfrey Morrison argued in *The Times*:

as the unrest continued, other organised or semi-organised political forces, ranging from the far left, through Muslim fundamentalists to the well-organised trade unions, all tried to leap on the band-wagon. . . . the interesting thing about last week's disturbances, however, is that they were caused mainly by the young unemployed, a section of society who until now have been largely ignored by both President Bourghiba's government and political analysts. . . . Right until the moment when President Bourghiba made his *volte-face*, cancelling the increases, it was the rage of the unemployed which dominated the protest, and it was they who alarmed the government. (*The Times* 7 January 1984)

In Tunisia, it may be suggested that the social unrest evolved in two relatively distinct phases. First, it broke out in the impoverished areas of the south and southwest, where the population depends heavily on food subsidies and consumes far more than the national average of around 200 kilos of cereal product per person per year; it started as a series of small local uprisings and gradually spread throughout the southern interior. In the second phase, when unrest developed in the north and coastal areas, political orchestration appears somewhat more credible as a factor; and certainly, new social elements were involved. Even there, however, the majority of those involved in the demonstrations were young unemployed people from the 'popular' quarters and the shanty-towns. In Morocco also, it is possible to identify two stages. In the first, students were predominant, and the demonstrations had a limited focus; in the second, students were joined by large numbers of the unemployed and seasonal workers in provincial towns in some of the most disadvantaged regions of the country, notably in the south and in the northeast.

In both countries, the specific immediate causes of the demonstrations – increased school fees, dramatic price rises in basic commodities, particularly foodstuffs, and perhaps a degree of political agitation – served to open up deep feelings of resentment and anger which stemmed from the underlying problems which are characteristic of contemporary Tunisia and Morocco: inequality, unemployment and poverty, and a sense of political and social marginalisation and impotence. The social unrest which broke out in January 1984 had its roots in disadvantage and deprivation and – as far as any such process can be so identified – was essentially 'spontaneous'; as such, it appears significantly different from the organised rallies and strikes of 1977–8 in Tunisia and 1979 and 1981 in Morocco, and indicates how widespread and deep-seated are the fundamental contradictions of Tunisian and Moroccan economy and society today.

In Tunisia, the social unrest began in the Nefzaoua, a semi-arid region southeast of the Chott el Djerid – the salt depression which separates the Saharan south from the industrial north and northeast. The southwest is historically the poorest region in Tunisia; it has the highest unemployment rate, and many workers leave in search of jobs in the more prosperous towns of coastal Tunisia, and Libya where some 60,000 are employed. It suffered severely from drought during the winter of 1983–4, and in the area south of the Chott el Djerid the date harvest, on which many rely, was disastrous. Poor households in the small towns of Douz, Kebili, el Hamma and Souk el Ahad, who live close to the bread line at the best of times, were particularly badly affected. Neglect of agriculture in the south, combined with the relatively rapid development of industry and tourism in the north and northeast over the past decade, has accentuated the historical regional division between north and south, coast and interior. The districts of the interior, such as Sidi Bou Zid, Kairouan, Gafsa and Kasserine, which have always been economically disadvantaged, received only 3.6 per cent of the new factories established during the 1970s. And of the 86,000 or so jobs created between 1973 and 1978 in Tunisia as a whole, around 46,000 were in Tunis and the northeast; only just over 4,000 in the south (Findlay 1984: 225). The connection between economic disadvantage, large-scale unemployment and social unrest in the south of Tunisia was intimate; as one local member of the Communist Party remarked: 'in Gafsa, out of 70,000 inhabitants, 12,000 are unemployed. Their role was crucial' (*Le Monde* 31 January 1984). Even the Minister of the Interior, Driss Guiga, declared that the demonstrations in the south had been the work of 'out-of-work, unemployed and hostile elements' (*Le Monde* 4 January 1984).

In Morocco, the earliest demonstrations appear to have been in the south, and particularly in Marrakesh. Here, as in the south of Tunisia, the drought of 1983–4 had seriously affected the availability of food and the cost of living; the condition of the poor and unemployed in Marrakesh had deteriorated markedly over the winter. This was not helped by a 20 per cent increase in the price of electricity. Small wonder then, under these circumstances, that the students were soon joined by others from the poorer quarters, protesting the prospect of further increases. But the region in which mass demonstrations developed on the most significant scale, and generated the greatest violence, was the northeast. This region, and particularly that part of it that had experienced Spanish colonial occupation between 1912 and 1956, has suffered considerable economic and social disadvantage in comparison with the rest of the country ever since independence. The integration of the old Spanish zone into the former French protectorate between 1956 and 1958 immediately caused great hardship and substantial increases in the cost of living for the population of the north. In 1958, and again in 1959, the region experienced massive social unrest as the people of the northeast expressed their resentment and anger at what they saw as discrimination, maladministration and neglect. A commission of inquiry into the disturbances of 1958 in the central and eastern Rif mountains (the provinces of Al Hoceima and Nador) revealed exceptionally high levels of unemployment, lack of credit for agricultural development, inadequate economic and social infrastructure and poor and corrupt administration (Seddon 1981). The revolt of 1959 was put down brutally by the army under the direction of Crown Prince Hassan, with the support of the airforce, but the underlying causes of social unrest remained essentially unchanged.

During the 1960s and 1970s, as in the case of southern Tunisia, and indeed as in the case of the Moroccan south, many sought employment outside the region; historically, emigration had been eastwards into Algeria, but after independence that route was closed and men from the Rif mountains either went west to the large cities of the Atlantic coastal areas, such as Casablanca, or abroad, to western Europe (Seddon 1981: 179). For the last two decades, remittances from abroad have been the mainstay of the local economy, while agriculture and industry remained almost entirely underdeveloped; levels of employment remained high within the region – in 1971, when some 35 per cent of the Moroccan population was recorded as without employment, the proportion in the northeast was far higher: the province of Al Hoceima, for example, recorded 65 per cent unemployed (Findlay 1984: 120). Investment under the national plan for 1973–7 continued to favour the already prosperous regions of the west, despite its stated objective to ensure a more equitable geographical distribution of economic growth; an evaluation of the plan shows that the north – notably the northeast provinces of Al Hoceima and Nador – was particularly disfavoured (de Mas 1978). The development of irrigated agriculture on the left bank of the Moulouya river (which marks the southern boundary of Nador province) in the second half of the 1970s provided a boost to incomes among the minority of those owning land in the new irrigated perimeters and a small increase in the local demand for labour; but the northeast as a whole, and particularly the mountain areas, remained relatively disadvantaged and underdeveloped, with little improvement in the employment situation for those unable to emigrate. The national plan for 1978–80 again stressed the need for a reduction in spatial and social inequalities, but again also concentrated investment in the most developed industrial and agricultural areas of the Atlantic littoral and neglected the remoter, poorer regions – again particularly the south and the northeast.

But, if the problems of inequality, unemployment and poverty appear to affect certain geographical areas more intensely than others, it must be recognised that these are fundamentally social and not simply spatial problems; the 'poor' regions themselves exhibit major social inequalities and the general lack of investment and economic development in these regions affects certain social classes more than others. In the northeast of Morocco, for example, it was clear even at the beginning of the 1970s that:

while foreign labour migration had increased the number of households with substantial incomes and had raised the average level of incomes within the region, it had also served generally to intensify economic and social inequalities. . . . Those unable to obtain employment abroad were now, more generally than before, from the working classes and small peasantry, and the difficulty of finding reasonably paid jobs within the region ensured that their incomes were depressed both relatively and absolutely as the general cost of living rose. (Seddon 1981: 247–8)

In the south of Tunisia, after the demonstration of January 1984, one local observer in Kebili remarked that if the price of bread was the spark that lit the fire and affected young and old alike, 'it was not for bread that the young demonstrated, but because they were the victims of unemployment' (*Le Monde* 31 January 1984). In the impoverished regions of Tunisia and Morocco, the lack of investment in the rural areas has stimulated a massive rural exodus; unemployment in the countryside has contributed to the drift to the towns, even within the poorer regions, but in the absence of any real growth in employment possibilities within the urban areas, unemployment has grown there almost as rapidly as the population has grown. In the rural and urban areas alike, unemployment and underemployment are the causes of low incomes and poverty; they are also the root cause of the frustration and resentment among the growing number of young people unable to find the means to help support their families and themselves.

Statistics on unemployment are notoriously unreliable, but a figure for the total unemployed in Tunisia often cited is 300,000 (roughly 5 per cent of the total population and about 20 per cent of the active labour force); this is almost certainly an underestimate. With a rate of population increase well over 2 per cent a year, some 60 per cent of Tunisia's 6.5 million inhabitants are under 20; a high proportion of the unemployed and underemployed are therefore young. And with rapid urbanisation a large percentage of the young unemployed are located in the rural areas, largely in the popular quarters and shanty-towns which have mushroomed in the last ten years. Roughly 21 per cent of the population of greater Tunis now lives in shanty-town areas; and 12 per cent inhabit rehousing settlements. The 'city' of Ettathamen, for example, which had a population of 7,000 in 1975, had grown by 1979 to 28,000 and by 1983 had reached 65,000 (Zghal 1984: 35). Morocco has also experienced very rapid urbanisation, largely as a result of the massive rural exodus, particularly from the poorer underdeveloped regions; with a demographic growth rate of some 2.5 per cent a year, a large majority of the population under 20, a massive expansion of the size and population of the popular quarters and shanty-towns, and very considerable youth unemployment, the general features of the problem are similar to those of Tunisia, although arguably more serious. Even in 1971, the rate of unemployment and underemployment was estimated at around 35 per cent of the labour force and half of those recorded as unemployed were aged less than 24 years; and the situation has worsened, if anything, since that time (Findlay 1984: 210). Even within the remoter and relatively impoverished regions there has been a substantial rural exodus and urban growth; and rates of unemployment remain significantly higher even than in the shanty-town areas of the big coastal cities.

With such high levels of unemployment and underemployment, very large numbers of households rely on low incomes; among the mass of workers and small producers, even multiple activities (several household members in different occupations) often fail to maintain subsistence levels of income.

In Morocco, where income distribution is very unequal, the past two decades have witnessed a steady decline in the purchasing power of the poor. In 1960, the poorest 10 per cent accounted for only 3.3 per cent of the total value of consumption, but by 1971 this had declined to a mere 1.2 per cent. The introduction to the 1973–7 national plan recognised that 'the overall improvement in living standards far from diminishing differentials in standards of living has to a certain extent accentuated the differentials' (Morocco 1973: 14). Between 1973 and 1977, food prices rose by an average of 11.1 per cent a year (Findlay 1984: 123), substantially faster than wage increases, which in any case benefited the lower-paid and irregularly employed only marginally. The rate of increase in the cost of living and in food prices slowed down somewhat in the period from 1977 to 1980 (with average annual increases in the cost of living between 8.3 and 9.8 per cent), but then accelerated dramatically again in the early 1980s (with annual increases of 12.5 per cent between 1980 and 1981, 10.5 per cent between 1981 and

1982, and 8.1 per cent in the first nine months of 1983). By the end of 1983, the cost of food index for Morocco, based on 1972–3 prices, had more than tripled; and in the five months between July and October 1983, largely as a consequence of the August prices increases introduced as part of the IMF approved 'economic stabilisation' programme, the food index rose 10.6 per cent and the general cost of living index 8 per cent (BMCE 1983). For those able during the past twenty years to improve their incomes – certain sectors of organised labour, the better situated of the small businessmen and the middle classes as a whole – the rising cost of living has been associated with improved standards of living; for those unable to keep pace with the rising prices – the 'unorganised' workers who account for the vast majority of the unemployed and underemployed, and some sections of the traditional petty bourgeoisie – the rise in the cost of living has meant declining living standards and growing poverty.

In Tunisia, despite a relatively high average per capita income, of about $1,500, the vast majority of households rely on substantially less than this; income distribution is not as unequal as in Morocco, but there are, nevertheless, substantial inequalities. The recent downturn in the Tunisian economy has seriously affected the situation of the lower paid and the unemployed, who now amount to between 20 and 25 per cent of the labour force. Wage rises of around 30 per cent to basic wage earners in industry in 1981 and 1982 had little impact on those with only seasonal jobs or without employment, or on those working in the now extensive 'informal sector'. Indeed, it could be argued that there is a significant divide between the organised workers in industry, who benefit from wage increases and from the protection of trade unions and legislation (health, safety, minimum wage, pensions, etc.), and the mass of casually and seasonally employed, and unemployed. As one local UGTT official in Douz pointed out, with regard to the government proposal to compensate for the price increases by a raise of 1.9 *dinars* on the monthly wage of the most disadvantaged, 'but what can Mabrouk, with his eight children, do when a kilo of meat costs 4 *dinars* and the price of flour is doubled? . . . For the poor, it means despair' (*Le Monde*, 31 January 1984).

For the lower paid, who constitute the majority of workers in Tunisia and Morocco, and for the unemployed, the rising cost of living has had a devastating effect on their capacity to fulfil even their most basic needs. In a report completed only two and a half years ago, the World Bank suggested that well over 40 per cent of the Moroccan population was living below the absolute poverty level (*Financial Times* 24 January 1984); in Tunisia, a very large proportion of households in the southern interior live at or below the level of basic subsistence, while in some of the shanty-towns conditions are at least as bad. Infant mortality in the shanty-town areas of Tunis, for example, ranges from 112 per thousand to as high as 169 per thousand, while in the middle class residential area of El Menzah, for instance, it is only 8 per thousand (Zghal 1984: 35).

When President Bourghiba appeared on television to cancel the price increases he nevertheless made some attempt to justify the original decision, remarking that he had been concerned that bread was so cheap that some were feeding their cats on it. Such profligacy would be unthinkable for the majority of the population and reveals the yawning gap between the lived experience of rich and poor in Tunisia. According to *The Economist*, 'the head of a household of five, earning the minimum legal monthly wage of £90 devotes 5 per cent of his earnings to bread and other cereal products . . . this figure would have risen to 8 per cent if the Prime Minister Mr Mohammed Mzali had had his way. The difference is not huge' (*The Economist* 14 January 1984). One can only speculate on the reliability of this 'data' and stand amazed at the ignorance of the real situation displayed; the vast majority of households in Tunisia rely on incomes well below this 'legal minimum wage', and for them, as Engel's law suggests, basic foodstuffs account for a very substantial proportion of total expenditure: furthermore, even a marginal increase in the cost of any one essential consumption item has an appreciable 'knock-on' effect on the household's capacity to purchase its other basic requirements for minimum subsistence.

When the price increase came in Tunisia at the end of December 1983, it was dramatic, and hit the poorest hardest. The price of the 700 gram flat loaf that is the basic staple for most poor people was raised from 80 millimes to 170 millimes; cheap bread by western standards, but when the average real income of the majority of urban households is low, it represents a significant item of expenditure. In the far south of Tunisia, it was the increase in the price of semolina (used for couscous) which created the main impact; as one local explained, 'the basic food is couscous. We also eat pasta and generally cook our own bread. But a sack of 50 kilos of semolina went from 7.2 dinars to 13.5, and a kilo of flour from 120 millimes to 295. Here, it was revolt of couscous, not of bread, until Bourghiba stopped these intolerable increases' (*Le Monde* 1 January 1984). In Morocco, the major increases came in August 1983, when the 20 per cent reduction in subsidies on basic commodities had its first impact: tea (the national drink and much consumed by the poor) increased by 77 per cent and sugar by 14 per cent, butter went up by nearly half and cooking oil by 18 per cent; on top of these came increases in the price of soap and candles. On 27 December the King announced further increases, and at the beginning of January virtually all basic foodstuffs (flour, bread, tea, sugar and cooking oil) went up by at least 20 per cent, while cooking gas (much depended upon by poorer households) increased in price by 5 dirhams a bottle. And the budget for 1984 proposed further increases still. The effect of these increases was not translated into open social unrest until January; it was reported at the beginning of December that 'so far, the population has accepted the austerity measures and appears resigned to the lean years that lie ahead' (*Financial Times* 1 December 1983), but the second round of price rises, with the prospect of more to come, created an enormous sense of despair and anger which required only the trigger of the school strikes and demonstrations to burst out in open, violent protest.

Despite the emphasis in public announcements by the officials in Tunisia and Morocco on the role of politically motivated agitators, it is undoubtedly the case that the government and heads of state in both countries recognised the massive threat, represented by the upsurge of social protest, to the stability of their regimes. In both countries, after a week or so of widespread violence and an attempt simply to suppress the unrest by the use of state security forces, both heads of state were obliged to recognise their inability to contain the problem in this way and to announce publicly the restoration of the status quo as far as basic commodity prices were concerned. When President Bourghiba cancelled the increases he stressed that he was concerned at the effects on the poor: 'I do not want the poor to pay', he declared (*Financial Times* 7 January 1984). And even before this public statement of 'concern', the government had asked the governors of some of the poorer provinces in the south to open public works sites for the unemployed; it was also reported that cash was sent to these provinces 'to help the poor members of the community and the unemployed' (*Financial Times* 6 January 1984). King Hassan simply stated that after having received the results of the social investigation he had ordered carried on 1 January throughout the country, he had decided that there would be no further increase in the price of basic necessities (*Le Monde* 24 January 1984).

If the governments in Tunisia and Morocco recognised implicitly the crucial role of price increases in triggering widespread popular protest, the various opposition parties and movements were more explicit. In Morocco, the opposition largely echoed the observation of the French Partie Socialiste that 'the serious troubles which have affected several cities . . . reveal the frustrations of a section of the Moroccan people in the face of a deterioration in their living conditions' (*Le Monde* 28 January 1984). In Tunisia, the Mouvement d'Opposition Nationale Tunisien denounced the repression of the 'hunger rioters' by the security forces and argued that the laissez faire economic policies of Mzali had impoverished the deprived and enriched the privileged (*Le Monde* 27 January 1984).

Determinants of economic policy

If we accept that the demonstrations and violence in both Tunisia and Morocco were largely triggered off by the increase (or prospect of further increases) in the price of basic commodities, while the underlying factors were those of inequality, unemployment and poverty, it must be asked why the price of basic goods was to be raised, and why so dramatically. After all, the 1970s provide numerous examples of violent mass protest in response to such measures within the Middle East and North Africa, not to speak of elsewhere (e.g. Brazil). In Egypt in 1977, the Sudan in 1979 and in Morocco itself in 1981, 'bread riots' were a reaction to major increases in food prices (Weinbaum 1980: 3–26). In January 1977, on the advice of the International Monetary Fund and other financial backers to reduce a massive budget deficit, President Sadat cut or eliminated subsidies equivalent to $700 million annually on a wide range of consumer items; as a consequence, there were significant price rises in many basic goods, notably cooking gas. Street demonstrations, some spontaneous, some well organised, quickly assumed a violent, strongly anti-regime character; when police were unable to halt the rioting of tens of thousands of young workers and students in Cairo, Alexandria and other cities, the army was brought in to contain the trouble. Over a two-day period, some 80 people were killed, hundreds injured and 900 arrested. Only Sadat's early decision to rescind entirely the price increases averted a more serious test of his regime. In the summer of 1979, pressed by international creditors to cut a massive budget deficit, President Numeiry ordered increases in the price of several basic commodities; a rise in the cost of food, fuel and transport brought mass demonstrations in the streets of Khartoum and other towns. The police finally gained control after ten days of disturbances, but not without the cancellation of the price increases by the government and direct state intervention to ensure adequate supplies of bread and meat. In Morocco, price increases in June 1981 for a range of basic commodities (notably sugar, flour, butter and cooking oil) provoked a warning strike by the Democratic Labour Federation (founded in 1978 to protest against price increases in staple goods) which in Casablanca turned into violent street demonstrations as workers in both the private and public sectors were joined first by small shopkeepers and then by students and the unemployed from the shanty-towns. The social unrest brought special police units, the national guard and finally the army into action; in two days of clashes throughout the city between 637 and 1,000 demonstrators were killed, depending upon the sources (*The Guardian Weekly* 12 July 1984).

In all three of the instances cited, it is fair to talk of mass movements of social protest. These are importantly different from the organised and carefully orchestrated strikes that were experienced in both Tunisia and Morocco during 1978–9, but those also received very substantial popular support and were also subject to severe state repression; they obtained significant concessions in terms of wage increases for those who came within the protection of the law and the trade unions. In Tunisia, growing social discontent with economic conditions during the mid 1970s was expressed in a series of strikes; eventually, by autumn 1977 the strikes had reached such proportions that whole sectors of the national economy were effectively brought to a standstill, and the army was called in to deal with the striking workers. In response to this move by the government, the UGTT called a national strike for 26 January 1978, which was observed throughout the country; the hardliners in the cabinet voted for a massive repression of the strike movement with a view to destroying the power of the trade union movement, and when there were disturbances in Tunis during the general strike, the army was given *carte blanche*. Estimates of the number killed in clashes vary between 46 and 200; some 800 people were arrested at the time, and shortly afterwards thousands of trade unionists were sentenced by summary courts, while the leadership was arrested and jailed. In Morocco, in 1978, a significant increase in the country's trade deficit led the government to introduce austerity measures, which produced a wave of strikes in April and May. The cost of living continued to rise, as did inflation. Throughout the winter of 1978–9 and into the spring there were numerous strikes; these involved largely organised workers – in textile manufacturing, banking, transport, the docks, the mines and the railways – and teachers. Their rallies were dispersed, often with considerable brutality, but the actions gained increases in the industrial and agricultural minimum wage of 30 and 40 per cent respectively.

Despite the knowledge that raising the cost of living, and particularly the price of basic commodities as a specific policy measure, has in the recent past given rise to widespread and relatively effective action in protest, both organised and 'spontaneous', the governments of both Tunisia and Morocco decided towards the end of 1983 to adopt such measures. Why, given the evident risks?

There can be little doubt that pressure from international creditors, and in particular from the powerful IMF, to reduce large balance-of-payments deficits through specific 'economic stabilisation' programmes, encouraging the 'liberalisation' of the economy and the removal of subsidies, has been important in the case of Tunisia and Morocco, as it was in Egypt and the Sudan. In Morocco, the king himself referred to pressure from the IMF and other creditors to implement austerity measures and further open the economy to the workings of 'the free market'. Liberalisation and the promotion of the 'free market' are part of a package which the IMF has increasingly been making a condition of loans to third world countries over the past few years. In the case of many countries, such as Tunisia and Morocco, which have adopted broadly 'liberal' economic policies over the past decade (and longer in the case of Morocco), these supposedly 'new' measures designed to solve critical economic difficulties in fact represent simply 'more of the same'. But the situation of both the Tunisian and Moroccan economies at the beginning of the 1980s looked grim, and it was clearly believed not only by external agencies but by the national governments also that even more stringent measures were required to improve the balance-of-payments situation and the medium-term economic prospect.

In a period of increasing economic difficulties, given a commitment to the 'liberal' approach to the national economy, the economic cost of maintaining subsidies on certain items of consumption may appear to governments too high to be borne, and the social costs of removing these subsidies simply the price to be paid for improved performance. If those upon whose support the government directly depends can be convinced of this need for austerity, and if the most obvious sources of organised opposition to such policies can be either muzzled or co-opted by preferential treatment, it may well appear that the social and political repercussions of adopting a 'hard line' on subsidies can be managed and controlled successfully.

The annual report of Tunisia's central bank warned last autumn of difficult years ahead. Clearly they believed that an economic crisis was a possibility. In the last few years, lower output and prices for oil and phosphate (the two major foreign exchange earners), a decline in the number of foreign tourists (put off in particular by the relatively high level of the dinar and more generally affected by the recession in Europe), and a slowing down of industrial growth, have all affected the balance of trade and balance of payments. Last year, the trade deficit grew by 24 per cent to 738 million dinars during the first 10 months, which led to the restriction of imports of certain raw materials and semi-finished goods to 80 per cent of 1982 volumes. Agriculture, which has remained a low priority in Tunisia's development strategy, has remained virtually stagnant in terms of output since 1976; and grain imports have become increasingly necessary. Inflation has also risen significantly in the last five years, to reach double figures in 1982. Under these circumstances, the burden of subsidies undoubtedly looked heavy to a regime strongly committed since 1970 to a 'liberal' economic policy. In 1983, the bread subsidy alone cost around £112 million – about 2 per cent of GDP; in 1984 it could climb to £140 million. Subsidies on all cereal-based products (bread, couscous, pasta) account for 60 per cent of the total food subsidy of £255 million (259 million dinars) (*The Economist* 14 January 1984).

But, if the deterioration in the state of the Tunisian economy as a whole in the last five years is marked, it cannot be said to have reached a crisis yet. And, in the view of some commentators at least, 'the financial need to remove subsidies was not so pressing. Food subsidies amount to 2 per cent of GDP and the proportion of food imports is growing all the time. But Tunisia has not needed loans from the IMF to bail it out, like so many third world countries. A foreign debt burden of $3.4 billion and a debt service ratio of 16 per cent, are modest' (*Financial Times* 9 January 1984). *The Financial Times*, which adheres in general to an economic philosophy close to that of the IMF, observed that 'the manner in which the Tunisian authorities set about reducing the growing budgetary burden of subsidies on basic foodstuffs provides an object lesson in how not to do the right thing' (*Financial Times* 9 January 1984). In its view, it was not the removal of subsidies that was at fault, but the suddenness and the size of the increase in the price of basic goods and the failure to consider seriously the social and political implications. it argued that 'neither the IMF nor the World Bank advocated, or would have advocated the approach to subsidies adopted by the Tunisian government at the turn of the year' (*Financial Times* 9 January 1984). While this is clearly not the case – given the evidence of IMF and World Bank pressure on numerous third world countries, including Morocco, to adopt austerity measures without delay and with little heed for the social, and even political implications – it is significant that this view – that the measures adopted by the Tunisian government represented a tactical, but not a strategic error – was held by some within Tunisia itself. Thus, the former minister of economic affairs, Azouz Lasram, who had overseen the gradual and relatively trouble-free removal of subsidies on energy prices since 1980, resigned in October 1983 precisely because he was aware of the implications of a sudden dramatic increase in basic commodity prices; he recognised that the sudden withdrawal of the subsidy on cereal-based products would lead to unacceptably high price increases, which in turn might stimulate social unrest. Lasram argued that the poorer Tunisians should be protected; yet even the price of the *baguette* (mainly consumed by the middle classes) increased by less than that of the popular flat loaf which is the staple for the urban poor or of the couscous made from semolina which is central in the diet of most in the far south. Also, it appears that the UGTT, although representing organised workers for the most part, also foresaw the economic and social problems which might arise as a result of rapid and inequitable price increases, and had sought to negotiate concessions for the poor and a wage review before prices were increased; and certainly, they pressed for compensatory measures at their meeting with government ministers on 5 January in the aftermath of the violent demonstrations of protest. And, in fact, the government did announce on television, on 2 January, that measures would be taken to provide assistance through wage increases and benefit payments of 1.5 dinars a month per person (up to a maximum of six persons in a family – that is, 9 dinars) for hardship cases. but, as was heatedly pointed out by one Tunisian from the south, 'this compensation was to be directed only towards those in regular employment. It would not affect peasants, shopkeepers, seasonal and casual workers, or the unemployed – that is to say, the majority of the people who live in the south. Nor would they affect old people, widows and orphans' (*Le Monde* 3 January 1984).

When on 6 January, President Bourghiba cancelled the price increases, he also stated that he had 'asked the government to present in three months time a new budget which takes account of the poor and which reduces the effects for them' (*Le Monde* 7 January 1984). The new draft budget presented to the national assembly in Tunis in March 1984 included proposals to raise revenues by increasing taxes on a variety of goods (such as cigarettes and petrol) and also to cut back on investment; together, these measures would generate approximately 40 million dinars. Between March and July 1984 several small price increases were introduced for specific foodstuffs and public services; and gave rise to no obvious social unrest. Equally, a slight increase – up to 10 millimes – in the price of bread, semolina and other cereal-based products on 10 July 1984 occurred without any particular reaction from the mass of the Tunisian population. Why, then, had the earlier decision to put up prices suddenly and dramatically been taken? One of the reasons was provided by Mzali, who is reported as stating, in the course of an interview, that the savings that would have been made through the removal of subsidies and doubling of the price of cereal-based products was around 140 million dinars, and he pointed out that 'if the government had relied on taxes, all prices would have increased as in 1982 and the government would not have raised a fifth of that amount' (*Le Monde* 7 January 1984); he also observed that increased taxes would boost inflation – which had been kept at 4.5 per cent in 1983 compared with 14 per cent in 1982. Another is the confidence of the government, in general, that they had the strong support of the middle classes and the tacit acceptance of the unions and organised labour – to whom they appealed through the promise of improved economic performance, wage increases and some concessions for the disadvantaged – for such 'tough' measures. Finally, there was clearly a belief that the security forces could, if necessary, maintain control and prevent social unrest.

In the event, it was not from organised labour that the protest came, but from the mass of the poor and disinherited; and it was not from the middle classes, if one excepts the students. Also, in the event, the security forces were not able to control the demonstrations peacefully and effectively; instead the violence escalated and spread. The government had seriously miscalculated both the response of the Tunisian people and the capacity of the state to implement its 'new' economic policies without repression.

If the Tunisian economy was in serious difficulties at the beginning of the 1980s, the Moroccan economy was already in crisis. One of the most striking characteristics of the Moroccan economy in the early 1980s has been the level of its foreign debt. This is now over $11 billion, and debt servicing alone rose from 70 million dirhams in 1976, to 2,500 million in 1980 and reached an estimated 5,000 million dirhams in 1983. The critical balance-of-payments situation results from internal problems, world price changes and the cost of the war in the Sahara. Industrial output has not increased significantly and agriculture has remained generally stagnant in terms of output over the past decade, while the international price of phosphate (Morocco's major source of foreign exchange together with remittances from migrant workers abroad) fluctuated and declined in the second half of the 1970s. The overall value of exports has grown slowly – from 6,200 million dirhams in 1975 to 7,300 million in 1979 – but in the second half of the 1970s the cost of imports rose steeply (from 10,440 million dirhams in 1975 to 14,300 million in 1979) and the balance-of-trade deficit has steadily worsened (Sluglett and Sluglett 1984: 88). In the 1950s, Morocco was a net exporter of cereals, but by the late 1970s between 40 and 50 per cent of the country's cereal requirements were imported; by 1978, wheat imports alone accounted for nearly 9 per cent of the total import bill, as compared with under 4 per cent at the beginning of the decade. Earnings from remittances and from tourism have failed increasingly to cover the yawning balance-of-trade deficit, and Morocco has become ever more dependent on aid and loans.

Efforts during the latter part of 1983 to reschedule about $530 million of its debts owed to commercial banks (which fell due between September 1983 and the end of 1984) ran into considerable difficulties; but in September, the IMF formally approved the programme of 'economic stabilisation', which it had earlier recommended and made a condition for further loans, and which had been initiated by the Moroccan government in August. The programme included a creeping devaluation of the dirham, the rescheduling of part of the foreign debt, severe cuts in public expenditure (including investment), and the removal of subsidies on basic goods. In August, a 10 per cent devaluation was initiated and a first round of price rises introduced. At the beginning of December 1983 it was reported that the rescheduling of part of the country's foreign debt was nearly complete, having proceeded quite smoothly since the IMF approval of the economic policies being pursued; and it seemed that 'so far, the population has accepted the austerity measures and appears resigned to the lean years that lie ahead' (*Financial Times* 1 December 1983).

But the prospects for the next year or so looked grim even at that time. Just servicing the foreign debt would absorb at least 40 per cent of Morocco's hard currency income, while the visible trade deficit – which was reduced by around 27 per cent during 1983 largely restricting imports and reducing domestic demand – would remain uncomfortably high. The investment budget for 1984 was expected to decline by roughly a third compared with the 1981–5 Economic Development plan projections, while the figure for 1985 was thought likely to drop to 40 per cent below initial projections. Given this bleak outlook, and the pressure from the IMF to maintain tight control over expenditure, the Moroccan government was inclined to seek to reduce even further the burden of subsidies, and the draft budget for 1984 contained proposals to raise prices again. In the case of Morocco, unlike that of Tunisia, the pressure from the IMF to adopt extremely stringent austerity measures was great and immediate. With the recent experience of 1978–9 and 1981 clearly in mind and even further back the memory of the crisis of 1965–5 which involved a general strike and mass demonstrations on at least as great a scale as the January 1984 disturbances (Seddon 1981: 191–2), the Moroccan government must have approached the price increases of August 1983 with very considerable trepidation, despite their relative confidence that they had the backing of the 'big bourgeoise' and the reluctant acceptance of the middle classes generally. In the event, there was no dramatic response at the time, and there are grounds for suggesting that the initial increases created less of a shock than they did in Tunisia. Firstly, they came after two years of rapidly rising food prices, whereas in Tunisia the price of basic foodstuffs had been kept level for a long period of time;

secondly, the price increases in August were between 20 and 35 per cent for the most part, compared with the 100 per cent or more increase in Tunisia; and thirdly, wage increases among certain sectors of organised labour had helped reduce the threat of union organised strikes. But if the price increases did not immediately bring the Moroccan people onto the streets in open protest, there can be no doubt that they added considerably to the sense of desperation and frustration of the large majority whose living conditions have not visibly improved over the past decade and particularly of those who have seen their standard of living deteriorate. When a second round of price increases took place at the end of December, the stage was set for the January 'bread riots'. When these did break out, the immediate response was to send in the security forces, including the army, to suppress the demonstrations; only when this reaction was clearly shown to increase the dangers of political instability did the head of state intervene to assure the Moroccan people that there would be no further increases.

In both Tunisia and Morocco, the logic of the economic policies pursued over the previous decade – economic 'liberalism' – led directly to the growth of inequality, unemployment and social deprivation which themselves underlay the discontent and social unrest which erupted at the beginning of the year. Particularly in a period of world economic recession the 'open door' strategy for economic development has proved a snare and a delusion. It has been observed, of Morocco, that it 'seems to have become imprisoned within the logic of the economic policies pursued by the monarchy, which have resulted in increased food imports, a substantial and expanding trade deficit, and rising dependence on foreign capital and international financial institutions' (Sluglett and Sluglett 1984: 89); while it has been remarked, of Tunisia, recently that 'the government's decision to encourage the extroversion of the Tunisian economy has in many respects forfeited Tunisia's ability to determine its own economic future and many potential pitfalls lie ahead' (Findlay 1984: 236). The pressures from the international agencies (particularly the IMF) and from the greater integration with the world economy that comes from the increased 'outward orientation' of both national economies, certainly provide their own constraints and impetus; but it must be said that the forces that determine economic and social policy are not only those that derive from 'outside'; nor is it adequate to see economic policies as simply 'pursued by the monarchy' or as a function of 'the government's decision'. Ultimately, both the economic policies pursued and the social consequences of these policies derive from the distinctive class structure and dynamic of contemporary Tunisia and Morocco and from the dominance of certain economic interests within the political sphere.

There is insufficient space here to attempt to develop a detailed analysis of the contemporary class structure and dynamic of Tunisia and Morocco, together with an assessment of the balance of forces which has enabled certain sections of the bourgeoisie to maintain their predominance in the political as well as the economic sphere, and thus generally to ensure that the government pursue 'liberal', export-oriented economic policies – over the past decade in Tunisia and for roughly twenty years in the case of Morocco – to their very considerable advantage (but also undoubtedly to the general benefit of the middle classes as a whole) at the expense of the majority of workers and peasants. But if the struggle between the various sections of capital, and that between capital as a whole and organised labour, have resulted in the marginalisation of a significant proportion of the population, and in the perpetuation of economic policies favouring big capital in general, it is also the case that these policies have created their own social and political contradictions, as well as deepening the crisis of the national economy. These contradictions are likely to increase rather than decrease in the coming years, particularly if, as seems likely, the world economy does not substantially recover from the recession until the late 1980s or the 1990s and the economic problems associated with the pursuit of 'liberal' policies in Tunisia and Morocco persist and grow.

For the time being, however, it would seem likely that the governments of Tunisia and Morocco will attempt to pursue broadly similar economic policies, but in a more 'moderate' fashion given the social unrest created by the attempt to remove basic subsidies; at this time there are many indications of an initial reaction to the troubles which stresses the need to strengthen the forces of 'law and order'. On 7 January, Prime Minister Mzali replaced former Minister of the Interior, Driss Guiga, whose failure to cope with the early stages of social unrest in Tunisia led first to his dismissal and then to his indictment for treason; on taking up this additional office Mzali declared: 'the first lesson to be drawn from the events of January is that it is necessary to reorganise the forces of "order" so that they can respond adequately to all situations' (*Jeune Afrique* 8 February 1984). It remains to be seen how long such a policy – which amounts to 'turning the heat down slightly and tightening the lid on the pressure cooker' – will appear viable.

But even if the social unrest of January 1984 does not necessarily oblige an immediate reassessment of the entire economic strategy (rather than a slight revision of the tactics adopted) on the part of government in Tunisia and Morocco, it may stimulate more serious consideration of an alternative economic strategy, particularly among those whose interests are not best served by the 'liberal', 'open-door' policies which have predominated in these two countries for so long, and with such disastrous results for the vast majority of the population. It should also require the opposition parties and trade unions to reconsider their own political strategies and to recognise the potential for a broad based working class movement to include the unorganised and unemployed as well as the 'organised' workers and disaffected members of the middle classes.

NOTE

1. The UGTT issued a statement as soon as the increases were announced calling on the government for an increase in wages to compensate, and warning against 'the negative and dangerous effects on the purchasing power and living standards of the people of the measures adopted, which cannot but involve increasing tension in the social climate' (*Le Monde* 4 January 1984).

15

Sowing the seeds of famine: the political economy of food deficits in Sudan[1]

Jay O'Brien

The drought and famine which devastated the Sahelian countries and Ethiopia in the 1960s and 1970s left Sudan relatively untouched. This good luck did not result from favourable rains in Sudan. In fact, as Nicholson (1976: 186) has shown, much or all of Sudan had low precipitation figures for most of the years from 1965 to 1973. Sudan's central zones – apart from the areas immediately bordering the Nile – showed mean precipitation departures of between 0.25 and 0.85 below normal for 1968, 1970, 1971, 1972 and 173, comparable to the deficits experienced in most of the drought-stricken areas of the Sahel. In addition, the effects of unfavourable timing and pattern of rainfall in relation to plant growth were reported by cultivators to have further damaged yields in some areas. Observers in Khartoum saw transport planes taking off from the capital to deliver relief food supplies to Darfur toward the end of this period and noted increases in the numbers of beggars from that area on the streets of Khartoum. Some rural enterprises, such as the Habila Scheme in southern Kordofan, enjoyed large supplies of seasonal labour from drought-stricken areas of western Sudan in the late 1960s and early 1970s. Yet, starvation does not appear to have been a major problem in Sudan in those years.

This chapter argues that the conditions which were responsible for Sudan's good fortune derived from a pattern of agricultural development during the 1960s which was rare in Africa and indeed in the entire third world, based as it was on the expansion of capitalist food production supplying internal markets rather than on expansion of export production. Since the early 1970s, however, a two-pronged attack has been transforming the earlier pattern and setting the stage for possible future famine. The World Bank, IMF and other external agencies have placed renewed emphasis on policies favouring expansion of export production, a peculiar brand of 'smallholder' projects and, under the rubric of 'stabilisation' plans have carried out a frontal assault on the purchasing power of the Sudanese population. At the same time, Arab capital has promoted Sudan as the potential 'breadbasket' of the Arab world and begun to intervene in various ways which have the effect of reorienting agricultural production in Sudan from local to foreign Arab markets. This paper argues that these changes have been creating conditions in Sudan which leave its rural population, especially in the northern savanna zones, increasingly vulnerable to the drought-induced famine which had by 1983 begun to affect many Sudanese.

The expansion of capitalist food production

The large-scale expansion of domestic food production in Sudan got its start with the

193

political ascendancy of the agrarian bourgeoisie following independence and the concurrent decline in profitability of the cotton-producing, pump-irrigated agriculture which had served as the basis of the initial accumulation of capital in Sudanese agriculture in the colonial period. The recession in world cotton prices which set in during the late 1950s threw into sharp relief the disadvantages of having large amounts of capital tied up in the infrastructure of irrigated agriculture. In this context agrarian capitalists began to search for more favourable investment opportunities.

Partially mechanised sorghum production in the central rainlands provided an equal opportunity. As a last colonial act, the British had established a highly profitable, state-supported pattern of mechanised production of sorghum in government-leased tracts of the fertile central clay plain. This pattern involved low levels of fixed investment and ecologically damaging cultivation practices which produced high rates of profit.

Rapid post-independence expansion of capitalist agriculture boosted internal demand for commercial food crops to feed the large seasonal wage labour force, which was paid partly in kind. Such payments played a key role in keeping cash wage rates from rising as demand for seasonal labour soared. The absolute size of Sudan's potential internal market was already relatively large by African standards due to the great size of the country. An extensive railway system built by the British originally for strategic and administrative reasons provided relatively efficient means of transporting workers to the primary labour markets and moving grain to those same centres for use in wage payments. Thus capitalist production of sorghum enjoyed a buoyant internal market for its product which in turn provided a key to controlling wage rates and the labour force as a whole.

To support the pattern of investment dominated by rainfed mechanised agriculture which began to emerge in the late 1950s, the agrarian bourgeoisie in power used the facilities of the state to aid this sector, often at the expense of the mostly government-operated export (cotton) sector (Ali 1982). This class used its increasing control of the government to channel imports of machinery and spare parts, priority provision of fuel, etc., to private capitalist agriculture, often at the expense of the government-operated irrigated cotton schemes such as the Gezira. The result was that by the mid-1960s private rain-fed farming dominated capitalist growth in Sudan. This growth received a further boost in 1968 with the 'Agrarian Reform Movement', which nationalised the private cotton pump schemes on generous terms, thus freeing agrarian capital to invest in sorghum production just at the time that the World Bank initiated its first project for assisting mechanised farming in Sudan.

The effects of these and related policies of the period on the export sector were severe. As noted by the ILO's 1976 Mission report (p. 467), there was a significant reallocation of government expenditure away from economic services to defence, security and general administration, with economic services declining from 30.4 per cent of total current expenditure in 1961/2 to 14.3 per cent in 1972/3. During the same period development expenditure fell from a ratio of 35 per cent to current expenditure in 1955/6, and the special level of 95 per cent in 1963/4 (when several large new projects reached completion), to a ratio of only 18 per cent in 1972/3 (ILO: 26). In the 1960s and early 1970s, according to the ILO (p. 467), 'development finance has been treated more as a £residual£ after growing current expenditure needs were met . . ..
The level and pattern of the government's development expenditure has in fact been influenced more by the availability of external project assistance than by the availability of domestic resources'. Starved of resources, the export sector declined. Between 1960 and 1970 Sudan's export revenues increased by only 0.8 per cent per year, and from

1970 to 1976 they *decreased* by 9 per cent per year (World Bank 1978b: 86). Neglect of the irrigation infrastructure in Gezira and other cotton schemes led to massive deterioration and to declines in yields (see World Bank 1978a: Annex 9, 24).

Lack of resources and insufficient maintenance were not the only problems faced by the cotton schemes and the export sector in general. As export revenues declined the central government sought to make up the declining revenues by increased taxation of foreign trade. By the mid-1960s taxes on imports and exports accounted for 45 per cent of all central government revenues (ILO 1976: 468). Tax revenues grew in relation to non-tax revenues (e.g. government shares of cotton receipts), reaching 81.4 per cent in 1975/6, and were weighted heavily towards indirect taxes, which comprised 71.1 per cent of tax revenues in 1975/6 (World Bank 1978a: Annex 8, 3). A development tax of 10 per cent was levied on cotton in 1967. As a result, the total implicit rate of taxation of cotton, the principal export, rose to 26 per cent in 1972/3 as compared with an implicit tax rate on sorghum, the principal crop produced by private capital and marketed internally, of 12 per cent in 1972/3 and 10 per cent in 1974/5 (World Bank 1978a: Annex 7, Table 1).[2] Clearly, the export sector was being made, by indirect as well as direct means, to bear the burden of sustaining the state in an era of private capital accumulation in rain-fed agriculture.

However, the hegemonic agrarian bourgeoisie took no significant steps to resolve the contradiction of the switch to a pattern of internally oriented growth from a structure of acute export dependency. Growth continued to depend on export revenues to finance imports of agricultural machinery, fuel and luxury consumption goods, and Sudan's import bill soared at an annual rate of 7.8 per cent between 1970 and 1976 – as export revenues *declined* by 9 per cent (World Bank 1978b: 86). The balance of trade and payments deteriorated rapidly, financed primarily by foreign borrowing. The external public debt rose from US$408 million (15.3 per cent of GNP) in 1970 to $3,097 million (37.2 per cent of GNP) by 1980 (World Bank 1982: 138), and amounted to $5,300 million in December 1982 (Sudanese Economist 1983: 66). Foreign reserves were insufficient to pay for even half a month's imports. By 1979 debt service had risen from 10.7 per cent of export revenues in 1970 to 33 per cent (World Bank 1981: 158), a figure expected to reach 51 per cent in 1984 (Sudanese Economist 1983: 69).

Pursuit of capitalist growth led by expansion of food production for the internal market without any solution to the problem of export dependency to finance the imports involved thus paved the way for a crisis of massive proportions, which is discussed below. For a period of about 15 years, however, this strategy adopted by the Sudanese agrarian bourgeoisie resulted in a pattern of growth which differed sharply from the export-led growth pattern which has dominated in African and other third world economies since colonial times. In a recent study of the agricultural production performance in 35 sub-Saharan African countries between 1961–5 and 1976–80, Hinderink and Sterkenburg (1983: 2) found only two countries which showed a substantial growth in per capita food production at the expense of export crop production. These were Sudan and Botswana, in both of which per capita food production rose from an index of 100 to 112 while overall per capita agricultural output was virtually stagnant. Only five other countries in the study showed significant growth in per capita food production, and among them only Ivory Coast showed a greater increase in food production than in export production. Four other countries showed stagnation in food production as well as in overall agricultural output per capita while output in the remaining 23 countries failed dismally to keep pace with population growth.

Impact on rural populations

The overall structure of Sudan's rural economy led peasants to become oriented toward the production of food crops on their own plots, supplemented by seasonal wage labour, rather than toward the production of export crops as happened in the savanna zones of West Africa. Peasants did produce export crops, especially sesame, but generally within the framework which did not involve large-scale dependency on high-risk hybrids but was dominated by the criterion of self-sufficiency in grain. This situation protected Sudanese peasants and pastoralists from famine in several ways, despite unfavourable rainfall and poor or failed crops during the period of the Sahelian famine. Many were able to maintain food reserves from their direct production. Slow development of rural market-orientation inhibited capitalist social differentiation from developing to the extent of undermining the ability of most people to produce substantial proportions of their subsistence requirements directly. This went significantly beyond simple food production to include – through maintenance of bush and forest fallow and other resources – the ability to provide other consumption needs, such as animal protein, vegetables, fuel and building materials, directly rather than through the market. When all else failed, there were plenty of opportunities to find wage labour, which usually included as a conventional component payment in the form of food – thus insulating seasonal labourers from some of the impact of price inflation. In addition, many cultivators produced sufficient grain surpluses in good years to maintain reserves, in the form of livestock as well as grain stores. Such reserves were a regular aim of production in many communities and helped to enable peasants to survive frequent low yields due to fluctuations in rainfall.

These conditions can be attributed to the orientation of the most dynamic sector of the economy to the internal mass market and the overall dominance of agricultural development by large-scale projects employing seasonal wage labour, rather than by peasant cash crop producers, as in most of the areas in West Africa hit hard by the famine. It was also important that there was considerable room for expansion before the point was reached that capitalist agriculture and peasant agriculture came into significant direct competition over land. Many pastoralists were displaced from their pastures by the rapid expansion of the 1960s and 1970s, but either found land to cultivate instead or maintained sub-optimal herding units through heavy reliance on seasonal wage labour to supplement herding incomes.

Crisis and struggle

The effects of incorporation of rural populations into the wage labour force and the growing encroachment of their lands by spreading capitalist agriculture began, by the mid-1970s, seriously to inhibit the ability of the rural masses to meet their subsistence needs, especially for food, through their own direct production. Forest and scrub rapidly began to disappear as new schemes were cleared, commercial charcoal-making expanded to meet growing urban demand for fuel, and people, especially pastoralists, displaced by the schemes sought new land on which to settle. Capitalist agriculture expanded by at least five million acres in the 1960s and 1970s, and most of the land taken had previously been prime seasonal pasture of nomadic herds. The pattern of capitalist farming in the rainlands itself deepened the predatory nature of its expansion. Tracts of hundreds of thousands of acres were clear-cut with World Bank assistance, reducing humidity and cloud formation and increasing soil salinity, and the farms were 'mined' for quick profits before the soil gave out due to erosion and nutrient depletion.

With the help of World Bank loans to the investors and technical facilities provided by the state, capitalists whose farms were exhausted in an average of five to seven years moved on to new fields.

The displaced pastoralists fought unsuccessfully, if sometimes bloodily, to retain access to their grazing lands. Ultimately defeated, they sought new pastures, moving into areas already used by other pastoralists or small-scale cultivators, or else shifting to increasingly marginal ecological zones. Bloody conflicts over land ensued, particularly in Blue Nile, White Nile, Upper Nile and Southern Kordofan Provinces (see el Medani 1978; O'Brien 1980). Pastoralists are thus often the direct agents of the depletion of fallow and scrub and generally receive the lion's share of official blame for Sudan's current rate of desertification, estimated at about 10 km per year. As conflict rather than co-operation has come to dominate most relations between settled and nomadic, herds have come to be barred from agricultural fields, which thereby lose the fertilising benefits of their manure (cf. Franke and Chasin 1980: 46).

Cash needs began to increase rapidly as more and more people came to depend on markets to supply their needs for building materials, cooking fuel and other important items of consumption. As cash needs rose and rural producers felt increasing pressures to maximise cash returns to their labour time, ecologically important fallow and crop rotation practices came to be abandoned or attenuated – even where fallow land continued to be available. Again here, pastoralists tend to be most vulnerable and first blamed. As the economic viability of herding units has been undermined and urban markets for meat have expanded, herding practices have changed in ecologically damaging ways. Where most herds were previously composed of at least two or three different species of livestock which make complementary and undamaging demands on grazing lands, single-species herds – especially of sheep, which yield the greatest cash returns, or goats, which are easiest to maintain – have recently come to predominate. Where integrated herds had to be moved frequently in order that each species could find its preferred food, these herds tended to be kept in a pasture until there was nothing left for them to eat, resulting in the disappearance of the best grasses (see Sørbø 1977). Pastoralists whose herds decline below ecologically determined minimum sizes necessary for subsistence no longer find alternatives to the herding way of life, and instead maintain small herds while supplementing their incomes through wage labour – thereby further contributing to the overstocking of pastures.

Cultivators also become participants in the process of destroying delicate ecological balances. A vivid example was provided by a village in Blue Nile Province where I conducted research in the late 1970s. Located in woodland savanna, this village had depended on surrounding forest and scrub for convenient sources of firewood and building materials. In 1975, urban merchants had begun to truck wage labour into the area to make charcoal, setting up operations less than 200 metres from the houses of the village. As the villagers saw the forest visibly retreat from their homes and began to have to walk farther afield for their daily wood supplies, they decided that they might as well get some of the profit from the decimation of the forest and began to make charcoal for sale on their own account. Elsewhere in Sudan I have been told of similar processes of deforestation of whole regions already accomplished.

Expansion of cash needs has also led to basic changes in crop selection and rotation practices, some of which have been damaging. In Blue Nile Province, as an example, long-standing cropping patterns involved a primary alternation of sorghum and sesame, supplemented by small amounts of millet which was cultivated primarily because of the protection it afforded to sorghum against the parasitic weed strega. As a crop it was too labour-demanding and vulnerable to birds to cultivate extensively under conditions of market integration. But in the 1970s, both the most prosperous and the poorest farmers were dropping millet cultivation altogether and suffering declining yields in their other crops as a result. For the rich, a crop from which they derived no profit was of no interest, and they could always clear new lands when yields fell. For the poor, all labour had to be devoted to producing food for their families to eat immediately, and the returns from sorghum cultivation were much better than from millet. Yields have consequently declined drastically in many areas, forcing even greater dependence on markets, both for income and for consumption, and resulting in still further disregard for any concerns other than the short-term need to feed a hungry family (or, for the rich to turn a profit). At the same time, the expansion of capitalist agriculture into new rural areas has provided new opportunities for wage employment that have made it increasingly difficult for kin-based production units to retain the labour of junior members.

In response to these conditions, seasonal wage labourers became increasingly aggressive in pursuit of higher cash wage rates. Increasingly workers came to refuse payments in kind and to seek the highest available cash piece rates. By the mid-1970s, this pressure on wage rates, combined with growing problems of externally induced price inflation, deteriorating export performance and general fiscal and balance-of-payments problems, brought on a crisis of the agricultural labour force as a whole.

Heavy external pressure was also brought to bear on Sudan. Beginning about 1972, the World Bank became more insistent in pressing its arguments about Sudan's 'comparative advantage' lying in cotton production for export and against the policies which the government had pursued toward diversifying production in the irrigated schemes – including growing more import-substitution elite food crops such as wheat and rice. The World Bank's Third Mechanised Farming Project of 1978 halted Bank support for further expansion of this type of agriculture. At the same time, the Bank offered Sudan a massive 'rehabilitation' programme – currently its largest undertaking in Africa – to rebuild and reorganise Gezira and other cotton-exporting irrigation schemes.

The IMF imposed an austere 'stabilisation plan' on Sudan in 1978, involving drastic currency devaluations, removal of government subsidies on food and other consumption items, a moratorium on new development projects and other draconian measures. By 1984, the value of the Sudanese pound had declined from US$2.87 in 1978 to less than half a dollar, and living standards of urban workers as well as rural producers had sharply declined.

Foreign Arab capital began, following the October War of 1973, to promote Sudan as the potential 'breadbasket' of the Arab world. Arab oil exporters agreed to guarantee Sudan's mounting debts, provide short-term balance-of-payments support and development aid in return for Sudan's acceptance of the stringent terms of the IMF stabilisation plan and Arab access to Sudan's agricultural resources for direct private investment. Saudi and other Arab capital, mainly private, took over further expansion of rain-fed mechanised farming with the aim of using the sorghum and other products to feed livestock and poultry for export to oil-producer markets. Saudi Prince Mohamed el Faisal has a 99-year lease on 1.2 million acres in Blue Nile Province, and other concessions to foreign investors have reached several million additional acres. Mohamed el Faisal's Faisal Islamic Bank has also become one of the most profitable in Sudan.

These foreign influences played an important role, but the reorientation of Sudanese agriculture during the 1970s and 1980s was not simply imposed on the Sudanese. The combined crises resulting in the early 1970s from the policies pursued by the hegemonic agrarian bourgeoisie brought about intense internal struggle among the fractions of the Sudanese bourgeoisie and their allied power blocs. Foreign intervention gave a decisive advantage in these struggles to the import-export oriented commercial bourgeoisie, which captured control of the state by 1972 and has been gradually – and not without spirited opposition – consolidating his hegemonic position since, through altering government policy (e.g. the landmark 1972 Investment Act liberalising conditions for foreign investment) and establishing itself as the commercial agents in Sudan of big foreign Arab capital. The fact that Nimeiri has been President continuously since 1969 seems to have obscured the nature of this power shift for many analysts, despite the fact that the nationalist policies adopted early in his regime have been systematically dismantled since 1972.

Retrospect and prospect

The two contrasting patterns of peripheral capital accumulation referred to correspond to what de Janvry (1981) has termed 'articulated accumulation' and 'disarticulated accumulation'. Capitalist expansion in Sudan during the 1960s occurred on the basis of a pattern of articulated accumulation in the sense that the leading sectors of the economy, under the control of the hegemonic agrarian fraction of the bourgeoisie, produced for and therefore made their profits from the internal mass market. Under such conditions famine represents the collapse of purchasing power and is thus very bad for business.

Patterns of disarticulated accumulation stand in stark contrast, because the welfare, or lack of it, of the producing population has little direct impact on the profitability of export production. The logic of capital accumulation within such a dominant pattern thus leads to the marginalisation of producers as consumers; profitability within the system does not depend in a significant way on the purchasing power of the domestic workforce. Wages figure only as a cost of production which can be kept as low as prevailing social and political conditions allow without damaging profitability in marketing the products.

As I have argued elsewhere policies adopted by the Sudanese government since the mid-1970s, such as mechanisation of cotton picking, which are nonsensical from a strict cost-benefit standpoint, do make sense in terms of the logic of disarticulated accumulation. Such measures represent components of a new programme aimed also at halting the rising tide of agricultural wage rates that characterised the mid-1970s and aimed at resisting the efforts of rural workers to integrate themselves into consumer markets to make up for their losses in subsistence production.

Faced with rising prices for a widening array of necessary consumption items for which they must pay cash, but unable to increase their wage incomes sufficiently to meet these needs, rural producers have been making adjustments which threaten to exacerbate their difficulties in the long term. Increasingly in direct competition with capital for land, peasants and pastoralists adopt equally ecologically damaging practices which further reduce their abilities to provide for their own needs directly. As their crop yields decline and they come to buy a growing proportion of the food they eat, they lose the ability to maintain food reserves – whether in the form of grain or livestock. As they alter their crop selection to maximise cash returns rather than direct consumption requirements, they incur greater risks of crop failure in times of unfavourable rains and, in the long run, further impoverish their soil (cf. Franke and Chasin 1980). As the surrounding forest and scrub recede, they also lose natural sources of food they used to fall back on in times of shortage. As more operations in the capitalist farms are mechanised, the main demand for seasonal labour is increasingly concentrated in a short peak season, increasing wage-competition among workers and reducing their ability to compensate for village crop failure through agricultural wage incomes. In short, agricultural growth on the basis of a pattern of disarticulated accumulation in the conditions of the 1980s makes rural producers in Sudan dangerously vulnerable to starvation as the result of drought. Indeed, the prospect becomes more likely with each passing year that cultivators in some of the more northerly parts of Sudan's savanna zone may face starvation as the result of even relatively minor drought. In fact, by 1983 back-to-back poor harvests due to poor rainfall had depleted the grain reserves of even the more prosperous peasants in at least Kassala, Northern and Southern Darful and Northern Kordofan Provinces, thus driving up grain prices to the extent that a bowlful of unprocessed sorghum was going for as much as Sudanese £6 in the markets near Gedarif at the end of the 1983/4 harvest season. Unreplenished for several seasons, the formerly vast grain stores of the big crop merchants were reduced to badly deteriorated sorghum, which they could nevertheless sell at fantastic prices to hungry peasants. People began to starve. (In January 1984 one bag of sorghum was selling for S£140!)

For months the Nimeiri regime successfully covered up the presence of these appalling conditions in the Sudanese countryside, and Sudan failed to appear on the lists of countries affected by the current African famine. In the meantime, there were incidents of hungry peasants attacking the granaries of merchants in El Obeid and Gedarif – who responded by hiring armed guards to protect their granaries – and unrest mounted, most notably in the south where guerrilla attacks became frequent. In response, Nimeiri played his tried and true Libyan and Ethiopian menace cards and the Reagan administration responded appropriately with US$166.5 million in US military aid in fiscal 1984 and a request for $190.7 million in 1985, and by sending American AWACs to Sudan three times in 13 months (*Africa Report* March 1984: 39). Finally, Nimeiri requested emergency food assistance on his visit to Washington in early 1984. The Reagan administration submitted a request for 70,000 tons of grain for Sudan in a supplementary Appropriation Bill, but approval was delayed by the debate over aid to the contras in Nicaragua. By late 1984, the FAO listed Sudan as one of the twelve countries hardest hit by the famine and conservatively estimated that over a million of its people were at risk of starvation. It remains to be seen how many Sudanese farmers will be wiped out or how many will die – by mid-1985 UN estimates put 12 million Sudanese at risk of starvation. What is already clear, though, is the devastating consequences for rural communities of supply side, export-oriented solutions to Sudan's capitalist crisis.

NOTES

1. This chapter has also been published in *Review of African Political Economy* 33.
2. Implicit taxation of cotton in 1973/4 fell to 19 per cent, reflecting higher producer prices occasioned by a drastic reduction in cotton acreage that season as part of an abortive diversification plan. Cotton was restored to its normal dominance in the following season. The heavy burden borne by cotton was not reduced until the elimination of some of the taxes under World Bank insistence in 1978 (see World Bank 1978a).

16

Food crisis and class formation in Zaire: political ecology in Shaba[1]

Brooke Grundfest Schoepf

Introduction

A prominent concern of the past decade has been to analyse food crises in Africa as a product, not merely of ecological change but of political, economic and social forces originating in colonial and post-colonial domination by the capitalist mode of production. Ecological change has been shaped by the same forces, as increasing commoditisation altered land-use patterns and impeded natural regenerative cycles. Although less devastated than the drought-stricken areas to the north and south, Central Africa also is experiencing food crisis. Caloric shortfalls, endemic to many areas during the colonial period, have reached crisis proportions so that even areas with rich resources, such as Zaire, today import increasing amounts of foodstuffs. Some aspects of Zaire's food crisis are explored here, using an example based upon field research in a copperbelt village in 1975–8, and subsequent shorter visits.[2]

Although Zaire imported an estimated 323,000 tonnes of cereals in 1982, development of the country's vast resources to provide food self-sufficiency could be a realistic goal. Zaire's agriculture – including food production – has been in crisis for at least two decades, since the peasantries of several regions, finding themselves poorer than before the 1960s, embarked upon armed struggle for a 'second independence'. The peasant uprisings, merged in what one sympathetic historian has called a 'great inchoate upheaval', were interpreted in Western circles as a class struggle inimical to capitalist interests. They were suppressed by armed force supported by international intervention.

The Mobutu regime attracted new foreign investments which led to economic growth averaging 6.8 per cent annually between 1968 and 1972. Nevertheless, the generally favourable statistics masked continuing agricultural crisis. Peasants, hard pressed to reproduce their conditions of existence, sought to avoid state controls, similar to those imposed during colonial rule. Furthermore, the distorted colonial industrial pattern dominated by the mining sector continued. Relatively few new production jobs were created in import substitution industries. A period of contracting economic activity followed the 1973 rise in petroleum prices and decline in the price of copper from 1974. This resulted in a cumulative negative growth rate of 18 per cent over the past decade. Despite the crisis, uneconomic prestige projects continued to receive foreign financing. The national debt rose to $5.1 billion in 1983 and repayment has been rescheduled repeatedly.

Meanwhile a new class developed as a result of the crucial role played by the state in the economy and particularly in the process of capital accumulation and redistribution following independence. The politico-commercial class enlarged its economic base by pillaging public resources and acting as 'gatekeepers' for both international business and local clients. Zairianisation measures, *de facto* suspension of the remarkably favourable foreign investment code and widespread bureaucratic corruption rendered conditions difficult for the foreign firms which dominate the economy. They also contributed to galloping inflation as prices rose 6,580 per cent over the decade and made possible rapid advancement of the state bourgeoisie. This locally dominant class is made up of interlocking networks of senior state officials, political office holders, owners of industrial and commercial firms, executives in parastatal and multinational firms, banks and so forth. Individuals often hold several positions or circulate between them. Under cover of nationalist rhetoric, the wealthier among them have now become partners of international capital. They serve not only as agents and facilitators but also as suppliers of capital to multi-national production and commercial ventures. Their comprador role is tempered by accumulation on their own behalf in competition with foreign interests.[3]

During this period the state strengthened administrative control over the peasantry in many areas. Rural taxation provided virtually no return in public services beyond the poorly staffed and ill-equipped primary schools. The mammoth state apparatus has served mainly to facilitate extraction of wealth and to repress all forms of political opposition. The main function of agricultural agents continued to be enforcement of obligatory crop cultivation regulations dating from the colonial period. These agents were members of the *police judiciaire* with power to impose fines and jail sentences. Peasants demonstrated their reluctance to collaborate in the spectacular enrichment of the new class by furnishing food, export and industrial produce at government-fixed low prices. Only areas where crops could be sold at prices higher than official rates showed production increases. The general effect was failure to produce sufficient surplus to feed the rapidly growing urban population. This urban growth is itself an indication of rural despair, as young peasants continue their exodus despite the rarity of employment opportunities in capital intensive industries. Within the next decade one half of Zaire's population – the second largest in black Africa – will be urbanised, and if present trends continue, poverty stricken and undernourished. The mass of Zaire's peasantry and sub-proletariat are considered by some observers to be among the most miserable in Africa (Jewsiewicki 1979; Young 1978, 1983).

This failure of food production to keep pace with population is a structurally determined outcome and not merely conjunctural, since the state bourgeoisie's 'position depends upon enlarged reproduction of dependency, accentuated by the progressive decline in food self-sufficiency...' (Jewsiewicki 1979: 7–8). Tactics employed by the local accumulating class to capture for itself a share of the extracted surplus led to repeated subversion of the interests of foreign capital and conflict with its representatives. Mounting debts as well as the regime's demonstrated political and military weakness gave the institutions of finance capital enormous policy-making leverage which they employed to improve both reimbursement performance and the operating environment for foreign investors. While IMF-designed austerity measures fell immediately upon the working class, salaried employees and professionals, they also affected the majority of peasant cultivators.[4]

The past several years have brought several important changes in the pattern of agricultural neglect. Foreign advisers have promoted an end to government price controls, as part of the renewed emphasis on market forces. The national currency now floats on the international market and foreign exchange controls have ended as part of the IMF reforms. New sources of agricultural credit are available to investors with collateral. There is pressure to free agricultural inputs and machinery from import duties (the latter only sporadically enforced). Some public agricultural resources, including research stations and former demonstration projects have been 'privatised'. Private ownership of land, termed 'land reform', is growing. Policy makers affirm that these initiatives will lead to increased output, capital formation and productive reinvestment in agriculture, thus resolving Zaire's food crisis.

In theory rising prices should benefit peasants as well as local capitalists and multinational agro-industrial firms. While peasants are still bound by obligatory crop and acreage decrees, price decontrol became national policy in May 1982. By 1983 producer prices had risen and peasants were selling more food. In Shaba, however, pressure from employers and fear of urban unrest in the Copperbelt spurred re-imposition of an official maximum producer price for maize in 1985. Two years after decontrol peasants and observers report that rising costs of agricultural inputs and consumer goods have outpaced receipts from increased production in all areas of Zaire except the Kasai diamond fields. In the rest of the country monopsonist trading firms, collaborating with local officials, keep terms of trade unfavourable for peasant producers.

In communities located along the roads, physicians report that younger children continue to be undernourished. The crisis deepened as declining terms of trade led to increased food sales out of the family supply. Apparently many parents skimp on consumption in order to obtain cash to maintain an older child in secondary school in hopes of entering him in the elite patronage circuit. Although the entry gates to the state bourgeoisie have narrowed considerably over the past decade and low-level government posts were trimmed in 1985, a child with a steady income still represents the family's only hope of escape from poverty. The vast majority face a grim future.

Political ecology

In most areas food production increases have been made by extending the area under cultivation, leading to decreased fallow periods without the introduction of practices maintaining new soil fertility. This is a 'rational' practice if one considers that the only new input available to most peasants is increased application of labour. In these areas, as in areas occupied by extensive export crop plantations and ranches and in the equatorial forests now being stripped of hardwoods, serious degradation of natural resources is taking place. The state bourgeoisie is deeply involved, both on its own and in partnership with expatriates, in expanding the latter type of activities. Land acquisition – which generally entails expropriation of food-producing peasant communities – is a consuming interest of members of the new class. It is they, rather than the peasants, who have benefited form new credit sources and other policy measures in favour of agricultural growth. To date, although some are active in transport and wholesale trading, few have shown much interest in establishing new large-scale farms producing food staples with modern means of production. Thus while food production remains largely in the hands of peasants, resources continue to be withdrawn from peasant production. Moreover, the destructive pattern of resource use is one which will have serious consequences for the future.

The conditions adumbrated here indicate that the crisis of peasant reproduction is deepening as a result of expanding capitalist penetration of agriculture. In view of this situation there is little likelihood that Zaire's food crisis will be met simply by freeing prices paid to peasant cultivators from government control, improving the transport infrastructure and providing support for capitalist production. Nor is Zaire's crisis atypical of that of other African nations, although it is particularly poignant in a country so well endowed with resources.

The remainder of this chapter will focus on the situation at the local level in southeastern Shaba during the past decade. It indicates some of the interconnections between peasants, the state and capitalist class interests, showing how measures taken in favour of capitalist enterprise contribute to deepening impoverishment of many peasants.

Local peasant perspectives

In the southeastern Shaba copperbelt rural villages continue to be dominated by the great mining complex. The crops that must be grown are foodstuffs – particularly maize and cassava – imposed in an effort to provide cheaply for urban consumption needs. The road network and a heavy military presence facilitate government control and coercion.

Extracts from field diaries indicate the climate in which food production takes place.

An elderly peasant complained that he had been fined by the agricultural monitor for refusing to sell maize at the decreed minimum price. Friends urged his silence: you never know who can be listening (1975).

The local government Secretary warned peasants at a public meeting that fines and jail sentences awaited those who sold at prices above the minimum. He also warned that barter is illegal (1976).

A regional official reiterated the proscription of barter, preferred by many peasants to sales, even following price 'liberalisation' (1983).

A student reported that peasants mistrust the agricultural agent. Peasants often flee when he appears in the village (1974).

Chiefs continue to function as intermediaries in the system, profiting from the labour of prisoners put to work on their fields. They sometimes direct their policemen to use corporal punishment and the practice is considered normal by officials (1976).

The JMPR (party youth wing) has been out on the paths collecting fines from people not carrying their party cards to work in the fields (1976).

The JMPR is fining people whose tax stamps are not in order. Since insufficient stamps were issued to the *collectivité* the result is a Catch 22 situation (1977).

Minor chiefs report that they are victimised along with the peasants by officials, the military and traders – particularly those with political protection (1975).

Visits of officials require gifts of goats and beer which the chief has the village notables collect from families in their *quartiers*. The *collectivité* treasury is reported to be emptied of funds repeatedly by the zone commissioner (1977).

A chief reports the proceeds of his vegetable crop confiscated by soldiers at a roadblock upon his return from the railhead (1976).

A former co-op director reports failure of his church-sponsored organisation as a result of military harassment at roadblocks. Soldiers frequently took produce and cash, and once sent him to jail (1975).

Buses carrying women on their way to Lubumbashi with huge headloads of vegetables are regularly stopped and passengers turned out by soldiers levying an unofficial tax. Now the bus drivers have systematised the collection in order to speed passage through the roadblocks. They pass the hat before reaching the barricade and all passengers contribute. The driver takes his cut and hands the money out to the soldiers (1977).

The wife of a chief discovered that her vegetables (produced with prison labour) were selling at 1,000 per cent mark-up in Lubumbashi's Kenia market (1977).

Traders in the area complain of high overhead costs incurred at military checkpoints. They stress the need to form partnerships with officials in order to circulate in the interior. One trader reported a standing arrangement with the military commander (1977).

Such incidents are reportedly typical of the area.

Not only poor peasants but small entrepreneurs and even chiefs feel powerless to reverse the situation which they consider typical of 'le mal zairois', a term applied to official corruption and private theft. While some analysts have noted the ineffectiveness of the Zairian state (cf. Callaghy 1984b; Schatzberg 1980), evidence of its coercive power is ever present in the villages of southeastern Shaba.

Despite the unfavourable political, economic and natural environment, peasants in many small Lufira Valley communities have attempted to increase household production in order to pay taxes and purchase tools, consumer goods, health care and education. When they have had a choice in terms of available markets they have not opted out; they are firmly committed to market production within the prevailing constraints because markets have become crucial to subsistence at the minimal level now considered socially necessary. Although they cannot withdraw to an 'economy of affection' (Hyden 1980), where even they can peasants attempt self-reliance.

Co-operatives have been initiated in the area with seed-money loaned by the Catholic Church. The one we studied, in a consolidated village of 2,500 inhabitants, is comprised of 40 men and women members. In addition to purchasing inputs and marketing crops, it operates a tractor-plowing service (members first), a truck and a grain mill – the latter instituted at the behest of the women. The machines, for the most part, are locally maintained although the machine shop at the parastatal farm will occasionally fashion spare parts otherwise unobtainable. It also sells the co-ops imported fertiliser and SR52 hybrid maize seeds now that the Maize Programme's outreach project has ended (see below). Collective fields have expanded as the members' understanding of their common interest has increased. When young people asked to join, the elders helped them to form their own co-ops instead, so that there are now three small groups in the village, each with about forty men and women members. One of the juniors' groups runs a poultry project and all three are involved in crop diversification and capital construction: clearing, stumping, draining and irrigating collective fields.

These groups are of a size which permits face-to-face interaction between all members. They also are the size of many villages prior to their consolidation in the large community. Church ties are reinforced by the multi-stranded web of kinship. The co-operatives have introduced agricultural change by gradually modifying the local farming system – including technology and social relations of production. Their own accomplishments and the church loans have made it possible for them to survive. The members' solidarity and the leaders' commitment have kept the co-ops from becoming a vehicle for enrichment of the wealthier among them. Neither of these offers automatic assurance of success and in fact these peasant groups have worked very hard at consciousness-raising. They are helped by traditions which value adult autonomy and consensus decision-making, and which support the participation of women in public life.

Women in this part of the valley are said to be 'owners of the land' and once had important religious roles now eroded by Christian teachings. Most remain in their own villages following marriage and older women with married daughters can expect help from them and from sons-in-law in field labour and house repairs. However, as there is no way for them to circumvent the constraints of the wider environment, they, like other villagers, remain prey to traders, officials and the military for whom they serve as a means of primary capital accumulation.

Shaba price policy in practice

Confiscatory crop prices used by colonial and neo-colonial states in Africa as a means of extracting surplus from the peasantry are an acknowledged disincentive to increasing production for sale. While government officials continued to repeat the colonial view that peasants are target-earners and only produce for the market if coerced, it is clear that they had other reasons to hold the line on peasant prices. Many officials trade in food. Their first objective is to maintain profit margins. Should the peasants obtain significantly increased returns, there is reason to doubt that a market equilibrium, bringing reasonable consumer prices, could be achieved unless traders' margins were to be reduced. At the same time, the larger copperbelt employers exert pressure to hold down food prices. Officials are aware that rioting has occurred in several countries acquiescing to IMF – imposed austerity measures. Conflicting pressures have resulted in vacillation.

In 1981 the US Consul General in Lubumbashi described his efforts to have maize prices decontrolled by the Governor of Shaba Region. The latter, however, expressed his support for no more than 'limited price increases', citing the heightened danger of urban unrest resulting from vertiginously mounting food costs. Under pressure from both employers and the IMF to hold the line on wages, he found himself operating 'between the hammer and the anvil' (BGS interviews, 7 August 1981).

Actually, Zaire's price policy is based on political expediency. With rampant inflation exceeding 100 per cent in some years, real incomes of workers and peasants have declined drastically. Thus in 1983 living levels had declined to below those of 1960 for the majority of workers and peasants. When maize prices rose in 1983 following the Governor's announcement of decontrol, peasants had to sell two bags of maize to obtain six yards of printed cotton cloth, as in 1975. Salt, palm oil and fertiliser purchases required about 25 per cent more maize. By 1985 the price of fertiliser had more than doubled over that of 1983 while the new regional Governor had reimposed maize price controls at the 1983 level – 4 Zaires per kilogram.

Urban consumers in Lubumbashi were no better off. In 1974 when the minimum monthly wage was 18 Zaires, a 50 kilogram bag of maize cost Z13.50. In 1983 consumers were lucky to obtain it at Z350 per bag – nearly twice the minimum wage of Z180. Most could only afford to purchase small amounts, at much higher cost. Government officials and the military were served at the mining company mills where they were charged Z182 per bag. By early 1985 milled maize cost Z850 per bag in commercial channels; the urban minimum wage was Z350; the rate for casual labour was Z10 per day.[5]

In 1983, Z4 per kilogram had sounded like a good price to village cultivators, at least until they began to evaluate their crop results. Maize yields were relatively low due to the bizarre rainfall pattern of the 1982/3 growing season (details in Schoepf 1985). Most families had no surplus above their own food requirements, particularly since the cassava plantings which in 1981 had fallen prey to insects and disease gave diminishing harvests and could not be used as a reserve. Only the largest producers – polygynists with more labour than the average household, the chief with prisoners to work his fields, an entrepreneur using hired labour – had much maize surplus. Even the co-operative members using their tractor to plant larger plots could not pay back their planting credit and had to call upon the Catholic diocese to make good the deficit.

Nevertheless, maize was sold in order to reimburse fertiliser and seed loaned by a neighbouring parastatal firm. Traders purchased grain at Z4 per kilogram in the village or Z4.5 in Lubumbashi, 95 kilometres distant. Theoretically, the co-operative could rent a truck and sell directly to the mill which in 1983 offered Z6 per kilogramme for large quantities. However, the ever-present threat of harassment by the military on the road encouraged peasants to deal with intermediary traders (see Lemarchand 1979 and Newbury 1984a for similar situations in other areas of Zaire), who in 1983 reported profits of about 25 to 30 per cent on capital engaged for very short periods.

In the interior, trader-transporters operate in an environment of scarcity which they manipulate in collaboration with officials – who also trade themselves – to establish exclusive trading zones. Some of the traders operate as part of a network supplied with trucks, cash and goods by a major firm with headquarters in the regional capital. Supplying consumer goods through their stores at harvest time, they maintain clientelist relations with influential local leaders. These, rather than the peasants, are the groups which have gained most from decontrol. The poorest families, including the elderly and households headed by single women faced both food shortages and indebtedness. Due to general economic crisis, inflation and unemployment, most families have little hope that urban migrants can help them to the extent necessary. Village leaders reported that few received remittances in the 1983–5 period.

The conjunction of unfavourable ecological factors, including climate and disease, in 1983, is admittedly unusual. Nevertheless rainfall patterns in the area are locally erratic and poorly distributed at least one year in five. Moreover, cassava harvests have been seriously affected by disease and pests throughout Zaire. The 1983 experience indicates that low crop prices are but one constraint to peasant agricultural development. Peasant strategies must assure family survival in years of poor harvest when neither remittances nor labour migration are possible alternatives. Cultivators in the Lufira Valley are correct when they opt for farming systems incorporating crop diversification rather than monocropping, even of a major food staple. They are also correct in insisting that they must have labour-saving technology if they are to benefit from higher produce prices by cultivating larger areas. Meanwhile, in 1984 the co-operative members began cultivating a maize field to provide food for the poor. Emblematic of the 'mal zairois', peasant leaders in 1985 identified post-harvest grain theft by outsiders as their greatest problem.

State-sponsored technology transfer

All government-sponsored agricultural projects in the area have involved food production. These included a World Bank-funded cattle ranching project, an FAO chick hatchery, an urban vegetable farm run by the Chinese and a CIMMYT-assisted National Maize Programme.[6] This last was a project designed to bring green revolution technology to Zaire. Explicitly aimed toward raising peasant maize production and incomes, it was selected for intensive study.

The first two projects provided animals and advice for those members of the bourgeoisie who have acquired large ranches and/or begun poultry raising in Lubumbashi. The Chinese project grows European vegetables used by the bourgeoisie employing unskilled labour. The Maize Programme is no longer active in extension and subsidised input supply among peasants in the Lufira Valley. Now that its international support has ended, the Zairian research staff is minimally active, while the large INERA research station has been converted to a Presidential Domaine.[7] Run by Israeli technicians, the farm sells poultry products to the Lubumbashi bourgeoisie.

The PNM devised a locally adapted package of high-yielding maize seeds bred on their station, high density planting, and imported fertilisers supplied on credit to be repaid at harvest. The technology package was aimed at 'small farmers' using hoe cultivation. By 1975 PNM extension agents had achieved outstanding yields of up to seven tons per hectare on fields lent by peasants for demonstration. The researchers were elated at the results and saw no limits to increasing production. The more fertiliser was added, the higher the yields from their new varieties. With each household planting one hectare, PNM scientists envisioned field upon field of maize planted in orderly rows marching across the red clay soils of Shaba and Kasai (fieldnotes 1975).

Despite favourable results observed with their own eyes, peasants remained sceptical. Throughout the valley they badgered the PNM for tractors, for in their experience, labour resources were stretched to their limit in peak seasons. Women, particularly, feared that increased labour requirements – especially in weeding – would interfere with gardening on which their families depended for a varied diet, and which cash from maize sales could not replace (B. G. Schoepf 1975b). Many feared becoming indebted to the government as a result of input purchases should harvests fail. Village elders expressed their mistrust at a public meeting when one man said, with evident support from the others:

We have been developed and developed so many times that we don't believe any of the promises. We are tired of being developed. Even you [he pointed to the PNM extension head], we don't believe you'll stay. . ... We think it's all a show. (Fieldnotes 1975)

Those accepting the PNM technology were obliged to follow the directions of the extension agent. This sometimes caused problems. For example, a young agent insisted that a peasant chop down a mature mango tree in order to grow maize in continuous rows. Fruit trees, inherited as private property, may belong to persons other than the current user of a field. Nevertheless, the refusal was interpreted by the extension agent as obduracy; he excluded this cultivator from participation in the PNM extension programme (fieldnotes 1977).

Peasants were able to alter the PNM planting methods to follow one aspect of their own system. Supported by a Zairian agronomist in the programme, they insisted on growing maize on 50 centimetre ridges built upon vegetal debris of the previous year rather than cultivating on flat fields. Their ridging technique is well adapted to soil maintenance under local conditions. It also keeps maize roots out of the water left standing in clay fields following torrential rains. The expatriate methods are more appropriate in temperature climates where organic content, soil texture and drainage may not be significant problems.

The peasants proceeded cautiously, planting 0.2 or 0.3 hectare of PNM maize at first, then integrating 0.5 hectare plots into their existing crop cycle. Their cropping strategies spread out labour requirements across the year and provided several different sources of food as well as cash for both women and men. The locally designed solutions are similar to the optimum strategies derived from computer modelling using linear programming techniques on the basis of field data collected by Claude Schoepf. He concludes that technology which increases labour productivity throughout the cycle and still offers subsistence security is necessary for peasant agricultural development (C. Schoepf, forthcoming).

Easing labour requirements – by reducing necessary labour time and the amount of human energy expended in drudge labour – is crucial to expanding peasant production. Zairian peasants (and salaried plantation workers, as well) for the most part use hand-held hoes and cutlasses for working the soil. Transport from fields to village and villages to roadside markets is generally done by women carrying headloads. Malaria, shistosomes and intestinal parasites – all common, particularly from the onset of the rainy season – reduce the vigour of the labour force. Thus, community-based rural public health is an essential element of increased production.

A 'green revolution' project which seeks to provide a limited technological solution to what is essentially a set of interrelated sociopolitical, economic, ecological and technical problems is, as the peasants perceived, an exercise in futility, notwithstanding the fact that maize yields per hectare under favourable conditions can be increased markedly. The obduracy of this interrelated set of 'bottlenecks' in peasant production systems leads many Western planners back to the large farm strategy. Despite its serious limitations, however, the PNM represented a new departure in government agricultural activity in the area for it did not seek to compel peasant compliance. Its technology was available on a trial basis and peasants were able to collaborate voluntarily in field testing. Following the departure of the expatriates, peasants were also able to use their knowledge to modify the recommended planting methods.

A new programme designed for the Lufira Valley will not be voluntary. Zaire's Man and Biosphere (MAB) programme has included 50,000 hectares of peasant lands in its Ecological Reserve. Peasants will be forbidden to hunt, fish, cultivate, fell trees on or burn over the land on 17,000 hectares at the centre of the reserve. When chiefs of affected communities in the valley protested at the MAB plan, they were ignored or dismissed as 'uneducated' and 'obdurate' by officials who refused to recognise the presence of peasants farming in the area (fieldnotes 1981; B. G. Schoepf 1983, 1984).

Class conflict over land

Community leaders are particularly concerned that once evicted, peasants will forfeit claims to these fertile alluvial lands resulting in proletarianisation and misery for those evicted into Zaire's labour surplus economy. Their fears are not unrealistic, for such was the aftermath of the first ecological research programme undertaken in the area. The community most intensively studied in the late 1950s by an interdisciplinary team from the University of Lie was the first to be expropriated in the creation of what is now the parastatal CEPSE farm. Subsequent expropriations have brought the area of monocropped maize fields to 4,000 hectares. While land itself is plentiful in the valley, fertile alluvial lands are scarce. In the large consolidated village land is the subject of bitter conflict on occasion, particularly when outsiders, generally petit bourgeois government employees, seek to obtain fields. Furthermore as villagers are acutely aware, large properties are being carved out in nearby communal domaines by members of the state bourgeoisie and roads are being built to reach them. The Ecological Reserve boundaries were redesigned to avoid encroaching on those lands, and lands belonging to a parastatal farm and commercial foresters. The latter, producing industrial charcoal, destroy more than 10,000 hectares of forest each year.

The bourgeoisie and the parastatals claim that as they rather than the 'backward', 'traditional' peasantry are contributing to national development, their activities must be supported by the state and not hampered by ecological concerns. The MAB proposal, ignoring the limitations of the area's ecology, includes a plan to force peasants living on the reserve's outer 33,000 hectares to cultivate larger fields of designated food crops.

The study village is only relatively homogeneous, for its people are differentiated on the basis of wealth, occupation, education and ethnicity as well as age, sex and rank in what remains of the pre-colonial sociocultural structure. The young chief is now an elected member of the national Legislative Council, a *Commissaire du Peuple*. He, along with the trader-transporters, bar owners and the miller are the community's wealthiest stratum. The government workers also form a stratum distinct from the peasantry. These people have access to steady cash income, are able to hire labour and to register land holdings in Lubumbashi. They are an incipient class with interests that will soon find themselves opposed to the majority of the small peasants. At present, however, the major conflict is between the peasants and outsiders, with the small upper stratum not only supporting but leading the protest against the Man and Biosphere reserve.

By 1983 another project providing solar electricity to the community buildings and the entrepreneurs was evidently aimed at co-opting the latter, once again in the guise of 'development'. Along with the reintroduction of cummunal elections, it signals a return to the colonial strategy of the 1950s based on the creation of a rural petty bourgeoisie (cf. Demunter 1975; B. Schoepf 1975; Schoepf and Schoepf 1981, 1984). The growth of this class is enhanced by policy supporting 'progressive farmers' and thereby promoting ethnic clienteles to serve as a barrier against class conflict. Whether land appropriation and exploitation of wage labour by the local entrepreneurs will result in conflict here as it has in eastern Kivu region remains to be seen.

Villagers in the Lufira Valley are aware to some degree of the basis of their condition. However it was a trader who reported a new wrinkle in the process of *embourgeoisement*. In the view of this informant, land acquisition will not be used productively on a large scale any more than it was by most of the 1974 *acquereurs*; rather, it will be used as a means of primary capital accumulation in the following manner:

The President announced the creation of an agricultural bank, ostensibly for peasants. . .. A big wheel takes an empty farm and corrupts the expert who supplies him with a favourable assessment of the farm's value. . .. He gets three millions at the SOFIDE bank which he gives to his brother-in-law who trades in gold and diamonds to make the money yield the most rapid profit. Even this would be all right if he then invested the profit inside the country. But the big men are not investing. . .. (Interview 1983)

The inventiveness of the state bourgeoisie in turning new policy measures to its own account is amply documented (cf. Gran et al. 1979). Another stratagem reportedly used by a high official in this area was to register and survey a large tract, obtain a development loan and then rent a smaller, maize producing farm in order to demonstrate his good faith. While not everyone exports all profits, the already substantial outflow of capital will be augmented by the recent relaxation of foreign exchange controls.

This chapter presented examples of two types of agricultural development projects of the 1970s. Both aimed to increase peasant food crop production. The international agricultural project proved to be of limited applicability for two reasons: because the PNM professionals neglected the adaptations made by local cultivators to local ecological conditions, and because they ignored the wider political economy. The first problem is designed to be met by a farming system research strategy – which nevertheless cannot isolate the fields from their macro environment (B. G. Schoepf 1980; Schoepf and Schoepf 1980). The locally run participatory project supported but not dominated by an outside non-governmental agency is more directly transformative.

It benefited from the technology developed by the PNM and adapted it to local needs. Nevertheless, the co-operatives' vulnerability to outside forces beyond its control is patent, while its limited success is possible only in relatively homogeneous communities. Neither project could succeed without investment in improved means of production which peasants cannot afford.

Zaire's current policy is not an isolated event. The design for sub-Saharan Africa promoted by the World Bank (1981b) and USAID, proposes 'liberal' macro-economic policies to streamline the state bureaucracies, expand economic infrastructure and rationalise management through a reinvigorated partnership between national and multinational capitals. Promoted in the name of free enterprise, the policies are likely to increase monopoly control of agriculture and industry.

Privatisation draws legitimacy from the view that since capitalist and peasant agriculture are discrete, unrelated 'sectors', policy measures favouring capitalist interests will not affect the peasants – or, alternatively, will provide employment for surplus rural labour. Seldom is it acknowledged that policies favouring large farm interests simultaneously tend to worsen the already miserable condition of the peasantry. When a major share of resources are allocated to capitalist agricultural development, peasants, as a class, are not just neglected. They are harnessed to provide the dominant class with capital, labour and land.

In Zaire this partnership cannot achieve productive efficiency so long as the state continues to depend upon a clientelist redistributive system, for the spoils of office draw upon resources needed for the economic infrastructure. Despite its success in 'performing. . .functions associated with the pre-industrial state: the accumulation of resources and the creation of a dependent workforce' (Newbury 1984: 114), the Mobutist state promoted chaos in the economic domain of modern capitalism. The international financial community, using the national foreign debt as leverage, is attempting to increase its control by means of fiscal reforms.

At present there is optimism among the agents of international finance about Zaire's response to IMF structures. Whether the favourable investment climate soon will attract new industries or even use fully existing plant capacity remains doubtful in view of the global capitalist crisis. Even in the best of times, Zaire's double dilemma of low wages and low peasant incomes will continue to result in food crisis.

In agriculture this scenario calls for export crop production on locally and expatriate-owned large farms and plantations. Input supply and international marketing are to be handled by agribusiness. Export crops generate foreign exchange needed to service the foreign debt and attract new loans for capital construction projects. Expanded production will employ some of the vast pool of labour pauperised by the process described above: ecological disaster, land alienation, demographic accident and unequal exchange. This surplus labour will continue to be remunerated below the cost of its own reproduction. However, since mass deprivation inherently gives rise to unsteady states, Zaire's condition is more than an epiphenomenon, as Ruth First (1970) prophetically proposed. We may go further and suggest that Zaire's tragic condition is a harbinger, a paradigm for African neocolonial development, with the masses condemned to 'zones of non-existence' (Ilunga 1984) as pauperised sub-proletarians.

Neither peasant nor capitalist food crop production will be developed on a large scale in Zaire under the present regime. The production crisis is not merely due to lack of resources, planning and research. It is an aspect of the class system which has emerged since independence. The local level example of food production in the Shaba copperbelt is a manifestation of the national crisis.

NOTES

1. Data were collected while the author, an anthropologist, was employed at the Université Nationale du Zaire in Lubumbashi as a member of the Rockefeller Foundation's field staff (1974–6) and the US Fulbright Program (1976–8). A grant from the Rockefeller Foundation supported field research undertaken jointly with Claude Schoepf. Grateful acknowledgment is made to the above institutions as well as to the US Agency for International Development, the Tuskegee Institute and the US Peace Corps. Together they made possible further research visits in 1978, 1979, 1981, 1983 and 1985. Other papers have been written in collaboration with Claude Schoepf. However, I alone am responsible for errors of facts and interpretation in this chapter. An earlier version of this chapter appeared in *Review of African Political Economy*, no. 33, 1985.
2. Zaire's food problems are not of recent date. Throughout the early colonial era chronic food shortages and periodic famines resulted from withdrawal of labour from food cultivation to serve the colonial project. Food production rose during the Second World War as forced labour was put to planting new lands (by 1954 seven times the amount of land cultivated in 1939). Subsequently, however, production declined as the harsh planting regulations were relaxed. Following Independence violence broke out in several areas and colonial pass laws fell into abeyance. The urban population grew rapidly, transportation became difficult and food production declined still further. The population of Kinshasa trebled, reaching one million in 1963. Food reserves were exhausted and the government urged the umemployed to return to the land (May 1965: 94–6).
3. A parallel to the process of class formation in Zaire occurred in Nigeria (cf. Williams 1977).
4. More than half of the 80,000 government employees sacked in 1984 were teachers; the majority were withdrawn from rural schools, thereby reducing the already slim chances of peasant youth 'making it' into the ranks of salaried employees.
5. As noted above Zaire's currency is no longer artificially maintained. In April 1985 one US dollar was equal to 50 Zaires. The official minimum daily wage for plantation labour in Kivu was 6 Z.
6. CIMMYT is the acronym for the Centro Internacional de Mejorimento de Maíz y Trigo, an international research institute concentrating on maize and wheat improvement. Funded by grants from international donors it operates collaborative research programmes in various countries. Its Zaire programme ran from 1972 to 1977.
7. INERA is the acronym for the Institut National de Recherches Agronomiques.

17

The Nigerian wheat trap[1]
Gunilla Andrae and Bjorn Beckman

Nigeria is trapped between the growing dependence on North American wheat, on the one hand, and the illusory policy of import substitution, on the other. We have sought to establish the anatomy of this dependence and the reasons why the effort to solve the problem by growing wheat in Nigeria is self-defeating. We have been particularly concerned with identifying the factors which have served to entrench such food policies. We have argued that they contribute to the underdevelopment of the Nigerian economy and agriculture in particular. Here, we discuss how the process of entrenchment can be understood in terms of general theories about underdevelopment in the third world, especially theories which suggest that external dependence obstructs the development of domestic production. We summarise the factors which reinforce dependence and make disengagement more difficult.

It is easy to identify policy measures which would bring an end to wheat imports. But what are the political preconditions for such policies? If food imports are so entrenched within the institutions of the ruling class, who is going to take the necessary steps to restrict them? We emphasise here the role of the working class in defending continued food imports. We discuss the preconditions for working class support for a policy of disengagement.

We conclude by discussing alternatives to bread, both in terms of direct substitutes, and, more generally, in terms of the prospects for domestic food production and self-sufficiency. We end on a reminder that the problems of food go beyond the problems of imports and import substitution which have been the focus of this study.

First, however, let us summarise the argument as it has been developed so far, starting where we ended, that is, in the failure of wheat import substitution.

The wheat trap: a summary of the argument

1. Imported wheat cannot be substituted on any significant scale by wheat grown in Nigeria. Domestic wheat faces major natural and social constraints which reinforce each other. For wheat to grow well over wide areas, a number of technical and social preconditions must be met. The problems of establishing and maintaining these are staggering and so are the financial and social costs involved.

2. Even if the technical and social constraints, which are now restricting the area under wheat, could be removed, the cost of wheat import substitution is likely to be excessive. For the foreseeable future the price of Nigerian grown wheat can be expected to be several times that of imported wheat. No foreign exchange savings are likely. The foreign exchange content of domestic wheat exceeds the price of imported wheat.

3. The policy of wheat import substitution provides justification for heavy public investment in irrigation schemes which are basically irrelevant to the problems of food deficits in the Nigerian economy. They constitute a massive misdirection of resources which could be used more productively elsewhere in the economy (including in support of rainfed agriculture).

4. The illusion of wheat import substitution has also provided justification for the continuation of large wheat imports, which have been treated as temporary, waiting to be replaced by domestic wheat. Other strategies to deal with the rising wheat imports have been ignored. Flour millers and bakers have been allowed to establish themselves without restrictions on the fictitious assumption that they will ultimately process domestic wheat. In practice, they entrench the dependence of the economy on imported food.

5. The continued, massive importation of wheat, encouraged by the illusion of wheat import substitution, undercuts the market for domestic food producers. It obstructs domestic solutions to the food deficits which have followed in the wake of the transition to a petroleum economy. The competitive strength of wheat is first of all related to its cheapness. A high rate of domestic, oil-induced inflation has further widened the price differential between local and imported food.

6. Domestic food production is also undercut by the development of new consumption patterns related to the restructuring of the economy: urbanisation, labour migration, changing family structure, etc. Bread is well adapted to the accompanying rise in the demand for fast, pre-cooked portable food. Its availability reinforces the shift in demand and pre-empts the potential markets for local food processing based on domestic staples.

7. The shift of policy in the USA towards encouraging commercial wheat exports has greatly enhanced the push factors behind wheat in the Nigerian market.

8. The importation of wheat is accompanied by the rapid diffusion of advanced processing technology, in milling as well as baking. It greatly enhances the competitive force of wheat in an economy where domestic food processing is highly labour intensive and closely tied to the household economy.

9. Wheat flour milling, by drawing on standardised bulk supplies from the world market, maximises economies of scale. This is in sharp contrast to the fragmented pattern of supplies on which the domestic food market depends. The economies of scale lie in the bulk transport and trading system as well as in the processing technology itself. As a result, the cost of bringing domestic crops to final consumers in a processed form are higher than bringing them all the way from North America.

10. The economies of scale in flour milling, using the most advanced technology available in the world market, feed into a highly flexible, lower-level technology in the bakery industry. A wide range of enterprises, from simple mud-oven bakers to fully automatic, electric bakeries, coexist and compete in the same market.

11. Mud-oven bakers spearhead the bread business in remote rural areas and open up new territories for more advanced producers with their basis in the towns. As electric bakers flood already established markets producers at all levels are pushed out in search for new ones, ensuring that increasingly inaccessible communities are exposed to the new consumption pattern.

12. As they struggle among themselves to protect and expand their markets into the hinterland, the bakers pull the millers along with them. The bakers form strong pressure groups for the establishment of local mills in the hope of improving their access to wheat flour.

13. The 1983–4 economic crisis brought to a halt the rapid diffusion of regionally based flour mills. Some of the already established ones faced difficulties in ensuring adequate supply of imported wheat. The spread of smaller regional mills, however, is evidence of

the consolidation of the nation-wide penetration of the imported wheat economy. Bread is no longer the food of the major cities and the South alone.

14. The establishment of new flour mills and the expansion of old ones have also been legitimised by the policy of industrialisation. Local processing of imported wheat is seen as a progressive step as compared with the continuing importation of already processed flour. The presence of the mills, however, makes it more difficult to scale down imports. Dependency on imported food is built into the industrial structure of the economy.

15. The spread of flour mills into the hinterland draws support from regional planners and industrial lobbies. The need to decentralise industrial development is in line with progressive ideas of national development. The centralisation of economic command brought about by the military regime may possibly constrain the further diffusion of mills.

16. The location of wheat mills close to the irrigation schemes makes it more difficult to shift the production schedules of these schemes away from wheat. The mills serve to legitimise the continued commitment of scarce irrigation resources to the wheat growing schemes. The latter, in their turn, help to justify the diffusion of wheat imports into the populous northeastern and northwestern states. The mills serve as bridgeheads for the international wheat traders with the active support of the state, including finance.

17. At a lower level, state finance is involved in assisting in the diffusion of bakeries, which has become a favoured field for government-sponsored, small-scale industrialisation schemes. It is in line with official ideas about industrial development 'from below', and the need to tap flourishing entrepreneurship and generate employment at this level. State institutions also invest directly in this profitable business, buying technically more advanced units from foreign firms on a turn-key basis.

18. The state bakers are particularly well placed to capture the special markets which have been established in state institutions, schools, universities, and military establishments. Schools are powerful channels for the diffusion of the new consumption pattern. Direct state involvement in these captured markets provides additional support.

Why Nigeria has been trapped

Why is it that a growing proportion of Nigeria's population depends on food which has to be imported from the advanced capitalist countries, and the USA in particular? Why is it that Nigeria's policy of import substitution only serves further to entrench this dependence?

Explanations have been offered at two levels. Firstly, these are the causes of the general food shortage itself, arising from the uneven development of the Nigerian economy, the expansion of the petroleum-based economy, on the one hand, and the constraints facing domestic food production, on the other. Such causes relate also to changes in economic and social structure of the population and to changes in consumption patterns which give rise to specific shortages.

The second set of causes concern the factors which push Nigeria into seeking solutions to problems of food shortages and changing consumption patterns in the world market, and, in particular, serve to entrench the dependence on imported food. Here, we discuss primarily the forces of entrenchment ('the logic of underdevelopment'). Let us first summarise briefly the more obvious cause of food dependence: the food shortage.

The rapid growth of food imports after 1970 may be taken as evidence of food shortage. It is not necessarily that. New patterns of demand, following in the wake of rapid, oil-induced growth of towns and wage employment, favour imported food such as wheat without necessarily being evidence of food shortage. Cheap imports may similarly shift demand away from domestic food without the latter being in short supply. The sharp rise in domestic food prices, over and above prices in general, however, suggests real shortages, rather than a mere shift towards new sources of supply. The manner in which real deficits can be expected to interact with such structural shifts, on the other hand, should caution us against using the figures for food imports as measures for the shortfall in domestic food production.

That real food shortages developed should, of course, surprise nobody. The 1970s witnessed, as we have outlined, a rapid growth in the non-agricultural population, triggered off primarily by the spending of oil money by the state. Labour was pulled out of agriculture and a declining number of producers were left to feed a greatly inflated number of non-producers. They failed to do so. How shall we understand this failure? Is such backwardness the ultimate reason why Nigeria has been caught in the wheat trap?

Not at all. The food shortage cannot be taken as evidence of the failure of a backward, stagnant peasant economy to respond to new markets. On the contrary, as we shall discuss further below, the evidence of response is massive. The gap, as we see it, arises partly from the excessive rate by which the non-agricultural population has been allowed to expand, largely due to the rather reckless manner in which the state has pumped oil money into the economy. But we also stress the changing structure of demand itself, and the openings and competitive advantages which have been created for new types of imported food and bread in particular.

Food imports help to structure demand in the direction of commodities which cannot be supplied by domestic agriculture. They obstruct the development of local products and processing techniques which could be better adapted to the new structure of demand. They slow down the process of commercial transformation and technological change and they deprive domestic food producers of incomes which would not only improve levels of earnings in the rural economy but expand the market for domestic industry in general.

Myths of domestic agrarian stagnation (backward peasantries, the 'lights of the cities', etc.) help to justify the continuation of these massive food imports, presumably as a stop-gap measure, while waiting for the fanciful and expensive development schemes pushed by state and international capital to 'revolutionise' Nigerian agriculture.

The logic of underdevelopment

The case of wheat in Nigeria is a case of underdevelopment. We use the term in the sense of radical underdevelopment theory to mean a process where the development of production in third world countries is obstructed by their mode of integration (in a subordinate position) in the world capitalist system. Underdevelopment in this sense is not an original state of backwardness which all societies have experienced but something which emerged ('the development of underdevelopment') as a result of colonialism and other forms of imperialist domination (Brewer 1980).

This position has in recent years come under attack from some Marxists. The critics claim, and we agree, that the employment school fails to explain the development of production and the advancement of productive forces, which actually takes place. The nature of the relationship between imperialism (foreign economic and political domination) and underdevelopment has been questioned. Is it true that subordinated integration in the world economy holds back the development of production? Or is it more correct to claim the opposite: that imperialism promotes the development of production in the third world, including the expansion of internal markets, and the transformation of social relations of production (Warren 1980)?

We agree with much of the Marxist critique. There is a tendency, however, to throw out the baby with the bathwater. It is a failure to recognise that capitalism, in the course of its expansion into new territories, generates contradictions which obstruct domestic production (Beckman 1980, 1981, 1982, 1983). This is obvious in much of the colonial experience. In the Nigerian case, for example, it has been demonstrated how domestic manufacturing was held back by colonial monopolies, despite the rapid growth of a domestic market (Kilby 1969). But also in the post-colonial situation, externally-oriented solutions hold back national development.

The relation between these two sets of contradictory impulses (expansion – stagnation) is central to the theory of imperialism, of which underdevelopment theory is one contemporary manifestation. The wheat trap highlights some of the issues involved.

At one level, the wheat trap offers evidence of expansion. There is the exceptional growth of the milling and baking industries in the wake of oil exports and wheat imports. The flour mills represent highly standardised and internationally controlled technology. Yet, this growth cannot be reduced to a question of advanced, foreign enclaves. The 'forward linkages' are strong. The mills are linked to a flexible, adaptive, and partly indigenous technology in the bakery sector. It demonstrates how externally induced industrial growth succeeds in mobilising local resources and entre-preneurship. At another and more fundamental level, however, the wheat trap demonstrates the link between such externally induced forces and the obstruction of domestic agriculture. It is thus a contradictory process. Flour mills and bakeries are tied to a commodity which cannot be effectively produced domestically. But the absence of a 'backward linkage' to domestic agriculture is not enough to support the underdevelopment thesis. Historically, food imports can be shown to have played a useful role in the development of countries which are currently industrially advanced. Labour was released from low-productive agriculture and made available for industry. Cheap imports held down the cost of labour and thus promoted the expansion of industry.

Such experiences may still be relevant for some third world countries engaged in successful export-industrialisation. For most, however, they are not. The capacity of modern industry to absorb 'surplus' rural population is very limited. In most countries, including Nigeria, industrial production is primarily for domestic markets and is certainly not able to pay for food imports. The feeding of the domestic working class, including the control of wages, therefore depends primarily on the development of domestic agriculture. The low productivity and limited purchasing power of the mass of rural producers are simultaneously major constraints on the expansion of domestic markets for manufactured goods. It is in that context that the entrenchment of food imports at an increasingly massive level contributes to underdevelopment: a process which makes genuine advances in industry as well as agriculture more difficult.

The entrenchment of food dependence

The critical question to answer is why food imports are entrenched, despite their 'dysfunctional' role in the development of the national economy. Underdevelopment theory suggests that we should look for answers in the manner in which a society is integrated into the world economy at the level of production, class formation, and the state. Explanations can be offered both in terms of the interests of those who make the decisions and in terms of the logic of the system in which they operate. Those who make money from importing, processing, and distributing wheat and wheat products are close to those who control the allocation of public funds, and regulate imports and investments. They are certainly much closer than those who make a living from producing, processing and distributing domestic food crops. But it is also a question of the resources and the technologies, which can be mobilised behind particular 'solutions' to the food problem. The food importers, on their side, can draw on a world market and on transnational business organisations ready to supply large quantities of food at short notice. They co-operate closely with those who, equally swiftly, supply advanced processing technology designed for such imported crops.

Over the past decade, this system has been able to inject millions of tons of wheat into the Nigerian economy through the decisions of a small number of firms and individuals. Many of the decisions have, in fact, as we have shown, been taken by the management of one single firm, the Flour Mills of Nigeria, which dominates the Nigerian wheat market. Its role as a subsidiary of a US-based shipping and wheat trading company underscores the transnational ties which shape such solutions to the food problem.

In contrast, the domestic system for supplying food involves hundreds of thousands of individual producers, traders, and transporters. The flow of produce faces numerous bottlenecks at all levels, including new requirements for storage and processing necessitated by a rapid shift in the structure of demand.

The control over superior technology and organisation at all stages of the process, from farms to final consumers, places wheat traders, millers and bakers in a superior position vis-a-vis the local food trade. Much of it is a question of logistics, the capacity to handle bulk with speed. As a result, those who are in the wheat business are in a position to capture expanding markets long before local producers and traders have had a chance to respond. In the meantime, demand itself is restructured in the direction of the standardised commodities of a vertically integrated, transnational food industry. Market access for genuine domestic substitutes is obstructed.

At the bottom lies the uneven development of productive forces on the world scale. This gives US wheat its original 'comparative advantage'. But the crucial factor is the organisation which makes this wheat available in the Nigerian market place on such superior terms.

This still does not explain why billions of naira are spent on importing foreign grains rather than buying food from local producers. If there were no food imports Nigerians would no doubt feed themselves. Prices would certainly be higher, but high prices can be expected to pull more local produce into the market. Nor do such comparative advantages explain why hundreds of millions are invested in the establishment of a processing capacity exclusively linked to imported grains rather than to local produce, and why so much is poured into large-scale irrigation schemes with only marginal relevance for the mobilisation of Nigeria's food production potential.

The advantages of bread, its convenience, social attraction, relative availability and price can only be understood in the context of a social organisation which gives priority to imported solutions, despite their counterproductive consequences for the national economy. It is not primarily a question of superior systems of production and marketing, but of the social forces controlling them. The nature of that control explains why the resources are mobilised behind wheat rather than behind domestic food crops.

The controlling forces are made up of firms, businessmen, public institutions, bureaucrats and politicians who make money out of wheat, either directly or through the class to which they belong. The Nigerian ruling class is connected to the wheat business in a multitude of roles, as share owners, managers, importers, commission agents, distributors etc. But it is not just a case of direct individual or corporate interests and profits. There is also a ruling class model of development which favours technologically advanced, corporate solutions. Such solutions provide the structures within which the ruling class reproduces itself and expands its own frontiers.

Conversely, the direct gains which may accrue to this class from efforts to raise the productivity of peasant agriculture are not very tangible. Alternative, ruling class models for agricultural advance (large-scale, 'modern' farms) are bound, simultaneously, to have only a marginal impact on overall output in such a peasant dominated environment.

There is nothing surprising about ruling classes promoting their own interests and their own models of development. Nor is it surprising that these pursuits bring them into conflict with subordinate classes. What needs explanation is rather why ruling class interests come to be defined in such a narrow manner as to bring them into conflict with the long-term transformation of production. One expects the Nigerian ruling class to have a self-interest in the accelerated commercial transformation of peasant agriculture for a number of reasons, including the need to hold down wage-costs, expand domestic markets, save foreign exchange, constrain the 'rural-urban drift' etc. Similarly, foreign capital – in a general and abstract sense – should also have an interest in such transformation for much the same reasons. The World Bank strategy of 'integrated rural development', so actively pursued in Nigeria, may in fact be taken to represent such broader, longer-term interests of the Nigerian state as well as of international capital (Beckman 1985).

The wheat trap demonstrates the ambiguous character of the Nigerian state, being simultaneously committed to long-term strategies of capitalist transformation and to short-term solutions to immediate problems which obstruct such strategies. Powerful foreign economic interests push Nigeria deeper into the trap. But they can enlist the full co-operation of the Nigerian state and a wide range of domestic social forces. The dependent, neo-colonial or comprador features of the Nigerian state and ruling class are exposed, to use concepts particularly associated with underdevelopment theory. The wheat trap reveals the extent to which the Nigerian bourgeoisie, inside and outside the state apparatus, continues to serve as an intermediary for foreign interests in ensuring their access to Nigerian markets.

The success of the wheat interests in influencing public policy reflects simultaneously the weakness of the agrarian basis of the Nigerian state. There are no organised agrarian political forces capable of claiming state protection against the advances of the transnational food industry. Although petroleum has greatly enhanced the economic basis of the state, the bourgeoisie continues to expand primarily through a complex pattern of partnership with foreign firms, where the main contribution of the Nigerian, junior partners is to facilitate access to markets and contracts. The wheat business is a case in point.

From this perspective of class and state power, the wheat trap demonstrates not so much the comparative advantage of American wheat, as the extent to which transnational wheat interests with their primary base in the US and their special access to the Nigerian ruling class have succeeded in structuring Nigerian food policy at the expense of national production.

Stopping the wheat imports

The massive importation of wheat contributes actively to the underdevelopment of

Nigerian agriculture. The imports must be stopped if Nigerian farmers, traders, and food-processing industries are to be allowed to respond productively to the changing pattern of demand. This again is one important precondition for an increase in rural incomes, which is an objective in its own right, but also important for the expansion of the domestic market for manufactured goods.

In the Nigerian context, whatever import substitution is achieved by growing wheat locally is likely to be marginal, at least at the present (or higher) levels of consumption. A policy for stopping wheat is therefore first of all a question of tariffs and licensing. At present an import duty is placed on wheat flour in order to protect the local flour mills. A duty on imported unprocessed wheat would protect domestic agriculture. A combination of import duties and licences could remove the competitive advantages of wheat products in the Nigerian food economy. As imports go down and prices go up, bread would be pushed back into its original role as a luxury food, something to be enjoyed on special occasions, but not relied upon as a significant part of the overall diet.

In such a context, some limited domestic wheat production could perhaps be justified, on similar grounds as the local production of raw materials for breweries and tobacco factories. But not necessarily. It would depend on the alternative productive uses to which the present wheat schemes could be put, as well as the foreign exchange costs of domestic wheat. Such factors may suggest that importing wheat, at this greatly reduced level, may make more sense than domestic production, from the point of view of the rational utilisation of national resources.

The Zaria Wheat Committee envisaged a combination of support prices for domestic wheat and import duties to protect local production (AERLS 1979: 88 ff.). The expressed intention was that consumers, ultimately, would be made to pay the full cost of domestic wheat and that the latter would be protected at a price level which would allow for this. Such a policy, if put to actual practice, would effectively price out wheat products from the everyday diet of most of the present consumers. It would thus be less of an import substitution policy than a policy for eliminating wheat as a mass consumers' item.

Was this the intention of the Wheat Committee? We doubt it. Individual members of the Committee may have seen it in this way, but the possibility of a drastic reduction in consumption is not spelt out. There is rather an uncritical acceptance of the government's assumed wheat policy and of the massive investment programme for wheat growing schemes.

Whatever degree of import substitution is eventually considered, the present public commitment would have to be urgently reviewed. It would have to be done within the framework of an overall review of irrigation policy. Present investments in this sector can be seriously questioned on many more grounds than those related to wheat import substitution alone.

An embargo on the establishment of new flour mills would, of course, be an early measure in any policy to constrain or stop wheat. The present spate of contracts and plans for new mills makes the need to consider such an embargo particularly urgent, although the foreign exchange squeeze may block implementation. Installed wheat-milling capacity could be phased out in step with the planned reduction in consumption. For this purpose, the Federal Government may have to ensure full government ownership and control in those mills where this is not the case already. The mills could be assisted in adjusting their capacity to handle domestic crops, especially maize. The recent rapid increase in commercial maize production should allow, for instance, for a shift in industrial milling from wheat-based to maize-based semolina.

The existing milling capacity can in itself not be the yard-stick for the level at which wheat imports should be allowed to continue. This would be to concede victory to the wheat-importing interests, for which the mills have served as bridgeheads. The cost of not fully utilising already installed capacity must, as in the case of the wheat growing schemes, be weighed against the cost of continued imports, including the detrimental impact on domestic agriculture. From the latter point of view, there is a far greater reason to worry about the numerous groundnut, palm produce, and cotton processing mills which have been left idle because of the lack of local raw materials. In comparison to that problem, the underutilisation of processing capacity based almost entirely on imported grain seems to be a minor one.

The further importation of bakery equipment could be stopped. but as restrictions on the import and milling of wheat start to bite, such an embargo would no longer be necessary. Replacements and fresh investments could be allowed at a level commensurate with the reduction in consumption. There might be a strong case, though, for protecting local, labour-intensive bakery technology against further importation of more automated technology, also at such reduced levels of consumption.

Present policies of public financial and technical support for the bakery sector should of course be discontinued, not to speak of further direct state investments of the Kaduna State Investment Company type.

It goes without saying that the public or commercial propagation of bread and other wheat-based products should be discouraged. The present massive advertising campaign pursued by the flour millers ('Join the Energy Feast – Eat Bread!') could perhaps be disarmed and turned into its opposite by pasting fresh texts across the existing posters reading 'STOP FOOD IMPERIALISM' or some similarly stirring slogan, capable of highlighting the issue at stake. Schools and public institutions, instead of offering bread and semovita, should propagate consumption habits which are compatible with national self-sufficiency.

Now, who is going to do all this? How far is such a radical shift of policy compatible with our understanding of the balance of social forces which have brought about the entrenchment of wheat in the first place?

The prospects of disengagement

Underdevelopment theory, of the varieties discussed here, suggests that only a radical disengagement from the world market can remove the factors which cause underdevelopment and create the conditions for self-centred national development. In the case of wheat, the arguments for breaking with the world market seem strong enough.

But who is to bring about the breach? Here we touch on the weak spots of underdevelopment theory, where it has opened itself to justified criticism for 'voluntarism', that is, for not identifying the social forces which can be expected to sustain a radically different policy. From where will the organised challenge come, capable of confronting and overcoming those entrenched domestic and foreign interests which constitute the political basis of the wheat trap?

Much depends on one's understanding of the depth and ramifications of the entrenchment. How central is the wheat syndrome to the present Nigerian state? How critical is the role played by wheat in maintaining and reproducing existing power structures? We have argued elsewhere against attempts to use a simple neo-colonial or comprador model to explain the orientation of the Nigerian state (Beckman 1982,

1983a). In that context, we emphasised the common concern of sections of the Nigerian ruling class and international capital to transform Nigerian society on capitalist lines, including the technical and commercial transformation of peasant agriculture. The present policy of massive food imports is incompatible with such strategies, also from a ruling class perspective.

It does mean that changes will come lightly. There is an obvious conflict between long-term strategies of capitalist development, on the one hand, and short-term, 'comprador' interests, on the other. It may well be true that the wheat interests are by now so effectively entrenched at the level of politics and the state that only major political changes can oust them from that position. But the balance of forces within the ruling class is difficult to assess.

The proclivity of 'comprador' tendencies to play havoc with national production plans in recent years is well illustrated in the case of rice imports, an issue closely related to that of wheat. Here we have witnessed how the Nigerian government has repeatedly undercut its own policy of achieving self-reliance in rice production, by indulging in occasional import sprees, including a scramble for licences and distributorships for the imported, subsidised 'Presidential' rice among various sectional interests.

But the case of rice demonstrates also that the issue of whether or not to import grains in large quantities is not simply a conflict between short-term and long-term ruling class strategies of accumulation. Trade union organisations featured prominently among the rice distributors. At one level, this may be taken as evidence of the manner in which trade union bureaucracies themselves are integrated into the network of clientele resources which provide underpinnings to the Nigerian state. At a more fundamental level, it reflects the dependence of the working class on the importation of food.

Food imports and the workers

Workers' interest in the continued importation of cheap food is as central to the wheat trap as the comprador syndrome within the ruling class. To workers as well as to other sections of the non-agricultural population bread has become a valuable, reasonably cheap and reliable part of the diet. In terms of numbers, the self-employed, the craftsmen, the petty-traders, etc. constitute a larger group than the wage earners. In the present context, we speak of workers and working class partly as a shorthand in order not to have to keep on enumerating these other groups, some of which stand in a floating relationship to the wage earners.

But there are also more substantive reasons for focusing on the wage-earning workers. More than traders and craftsmen, they are vulnerable to price increases. They cannot as easily compensate themselves by raising their own prices. But there is also the workers' higher level of organisation as a result of their place in production. The two factors taken together (vulnerability, level of organisation) enhance the political role of the workers and unions in the context of food policy. Only a minor portion of the workers are organised in trade unions. Yet, the latter also articulate the grievances of non-unionised workers on such issues as food prices. They are about the only non-ruling class organisations which have a significant influence on the affairs of the Nigerian state.

The real income of the wage earners has become dependent on access to imported food. It is therefore natural that they should react strongly against attempts to tamper with the free flow of such imports. If deprived of their daily bread, workers are likely to take to the streets in protest, just as they do elsewhere (see Seddon, Chapter 15). Radical political organisations and unions can be expected to support such efforts to protect real incomes. They are unlikely to be impressed by ruling class appeals to their sense of 'national responsibility' in support of reduced food imports, at least not as long as it is apparent that the ruling class is unrestrained in importing what its own members consider necessities of life, including air conditioners, private cars, videos, and three-piece suits. Working class organisations could be expected to expose the hypocrisy of ruling class 'nationalism' in this respect.

The commercial wheat interests, foreign and domestic, can therefore count on working class support in defending continued wheat imports, as well as protecting the myth of potential Nigerian wheat production that provides national, ideological cover for the imports. The direct involvement of unions in the rice racket indicates the scope for institutionalising popular support for a comprador line. The broadly based bakery industry, with its mass of small entrepreneurs, proprietors and distributors, ensures additional mass political leverage for the wheat interests. We saw how Master Bakers' Associations played an active role in mobilising opinion in support of the establishment of new flour mills, closer to bakers and consumers alike.

Political preconditions for disengagement

Authoritarian governments may be able to ignore popular opposition to a policy of radically cutting wheat imports. They may also be increasingly motivated to do so, as they find their own financial basis threatened by stagnant or declining export earnings, on the one hand, and the rising costs of maintaining an export-financed public sector, on the other. Symbolic cuts in luxury imports (such as the ban on champagne and lace) combined with the propagation of self-reliance might help to defuse, ideologically, workers' resistance to cuts in food imports.

Still, what are the long-term bases for such a change? What could prevent a conjuncturally motivated policy of self-reliance from being abandoned, once oil sales pick up? Does not the experience with the 'Presidential Task Force' for rice suggest that the commitment to self-reliance is unreliable, especially when the temporary easing of financial constraints again gives space for popular solutions to the food problem, that is, for fresh imports?

Questions must be asked about the type of political arrangement which could make a policy of self-reliance more reliable and long-term. We also need to enquire into the prospects and preconditions for such an arrangement of social forces to emerge. Its orientation, we suggest, would have to be national, by grouping together those social and political forces which have a direct stake in an alternative, long-term development of the national food economy; democratic, by being able to draw on popular support, at least so as to neutralise the political consequences of the rise in food prices and the fall of real wages, which are likely to follow in the wake of cuts in food imports in the short term.

The conflict between the policy of wheat and the policy of self-reliance has, as we have seen, national as well as class dimensions. The dimensions cut across each other. On the side of wheat we find an array of ruling class forces, foreign and domestic, but also workers and other popular strata to whom bread is important. On the side of self-reliance, we find domestic food producers of all classes, from the emerging agrarian bourgeoisie – state and private – to small peasants. We find nationally oriented politicians, administrators, and scientists, committed to self-reliance and opposing the compradors and their foreign allies. But we find that foreign interests are engaged also on that side, including firms which make money from financing and supplying strategies of self-reliance. International organisations, such as the World Bank and the FAO, are also likely to be found in support of self-reliance of a sort; that is, strategies aiming at expanded domestic food production, although depending on foreign inputs, seeds, chemicals, machinery and management.

Little will happen, we believe, in terms of a sustained shift towards a policy of food self-reliance as long as it is possible for the wheat interests to mobilise workers and their organisations on their side. The critical point to examine is therefore the conditions under which the working class may be prepared to tolerate a decline in real income in support of a policy of self-reliance. It seems to us, that for this to be achieved, workers must be convinced not only that this – theoretically – is in their own long-term interests, but that the political-institutional arrangements are such as to make such a theoretical possibility also plausible. It has much to do with their overall confidence in the state. Why should workers trust the promises of rulers whose 'development policies' are essentially a question of a reckless scramble for contracts, licences, and commissions among corrupt bureaucrats, politicians and businessmen, who stuff their foreign bank accounts with their illegitimate wealth, and enjoy their exclusive foreign tastes behind the iron gates of their well protected mansions? Why should workers not be expected to protect what they already have?

Major concessions must be made to the workers if they are to be deprived of their daily bread. Wage increases are not good enough. By now, workers know all too well that inflation will eat them all, as long as they are not matched by more commodities. Such concessions are even less plausible when, as in this case, the wage increases would be linked to a reduction in the volume of commodities (the import cuts).

The concessions must therefore be political. Workers must be convinced that those who manage the affairs of the country do so with some amount of consideration for workers' interests. This may relate to concrete issues such as the management of imports and public expenditure and may also concern workers' political rights and representation. There is no point in speculating further what kind of policies may make workers support a strategy of food self-reliance. The important thing to stress, however, is that a policy of stopping wheat imports cannot be pursued in isolation from the wider economic and political aspirations of the classes which now depend for their subsistence on imported food.

The working class must be given a significant role within the alliance of national political forces if the comprador nexus is to be broken; the nexus, which ties Nigeria to US food imperialism, which causes the underdevelopment of Nigerian agriculture, and obstructs the growth of domestic markets for industry.

Alternatives to wheat: in search of bread substitutes

We have discussed the problem of how to stop the wheat imports and the need to discontinue the present illusory policy of import substitution. What is to take the place of wheat? What is the alternative to bread in the Nigerian food economy?

Part of the answer has already been suggested: if domestic food producers are protected against cheap food imports they can be expected to fill the gap because there are vast potentials for the accelerated commercialisation of domestic food production. It is a process already on the way. We shall return to it below. First, however, we wish to discuss the prospects of finding bread substitutes in a more direct sense. This is a problem which has been given much attention by food technologists. It relates to the wider problem of why bread is so attractive and fits so well into ongoing processes of social transformation, the growth of towns and wage employment, changing family structure, and other factors. These are factors which relate to the quality of bread as a processed food and to the technology and social organisation of food processing.

It is not just the superiority of US agriculture and the international trading network at its disposal that gives bread its competitive power vis-avis domestic food. This power is also determined by the superior processing technology linked to wheat and by the social organisation capable of reproducing and expanding such technology throughout the Nigerian society. These are the qualities that make bread a fast, reasonably clean, easily distributed, and easily consumed food.

It is therefore natural to ask how the processing technologies can be developed also for domestically grown crops which can make locally-based food items equally fast, clean, and available. The most organised efforts in Nigeria have been directed at substituting as large a proportion as possible of the wheat in a loaf of bread with local crops, while retaining the shape, texture, taste, and colour as similar to those of a wheat loaf. The greatest problem with local crops from this point of view is their low gluten content, which means that dough made from them will not rise like dough made of wheat. But an in-mix of up to 25–30 per cent has been found to be possible, while allowing the product to behave reasonably like bread. Anything from cassava, maize, sorghum or millet has been found to work as in-mixing flours. Research on these lines was initiated by the FAO in the mid 1960s (Europe Outremer 1983). In Nigeria the Federal Institute for Industrial Research in 1974 issued an information bulletin (FIIRO 1974), recounting such experiments and exhorting the government to propagate particularly the in-mix of cassava flour as being especially successful in resembling the 100 per cent wheat bread. Cassava bread has since been found displayed at the 'made in Nigeria' trade fairs.

A Canadian experimental mill in Maidurguri has also attempted through a demonstration bakery to propagate the in-mix of sorghum. On our visit there in 1981 the project had however been abandoned and the bakery left with minimised production of pure wheat bread. The mixed product was said to be unacceptable to the customers mainly because of the different colour (interview IDRC 1981).

Other West African countries have also tried this way to substitution. In Senegal, there is, since 1979, a law which compels bakers to use 15 per cent flour made of millet. It has been disregarded in practice because of difficulties in getting adequate quantities of ground millet (Doucet 1983; Europe Outremer 1983), which may, however, be a temporary problem.

A cut in the supply of the cheap wheat imports, e.g. by raising the prices, might raise the attractiveness of the mixed varieties which have cheaper inputs compared to pure wheat bread even at the present. A legislation like that in Senegal might also be made to enforce such efforts. But the fact remains that one would be left with the requirement to supply up to 70 per cent of the inputs by wheat all the same. There is also the risk that such policies would serve to provide continued national legitimacy for a product which would remain basically imported.

A more effective approach to import substitution must be the development of local food processing technologies so that they can perform the labour-saving functions which are so essential in making bread attractive. These are located both at the stage of the basic processing of the raw crop and in the final preparation of the food.

If we consider a staple grain processing, we discover that so far it is the first stage which has experienced the highest level of technological development, to facilitate the tedious dehusking and milling of millet and sorghum. A pilot project in Maiduguri, the same as the experimental mix-in bakery referred to above and involving the

International Development Research Centre in Canada, has been followed by a similar one in Kaduna, on the basis of whose experience a larger mill of 3 tonnes/day capacity was started in 1983. This latter mill is part of a major federal grains production and milling programme under the auspices of the National Grains Production Company. It envisages the establishment of mechanised farms of some 4,000 ha in every northern state, with large-scale modern milling facilities attached. Parallel projects for root crops are being established in the southern states (interview NGPC 1983). For some time to come the organisation of raw material supply for such project-based mills is likely to meet with the same problems that are experienced by other agro-industry projects in the country (Andrae 1983). The Kaduna mill is so far the only operating one. It is supplied from several states, mainly Niger (Mokwa), and in 1983 processed mainly maize, and only marginally sorghum and cowpeas.

A few private mills have also been established, e.g. in Kano, and the Danish United Milling Systems is currently negotiating with NGPC to establish one in Sokoto State as well as one in Ondo. The latter rely on co-operative and open-market grain supplies. Their product will be a fermented meal that requires only brief preparation with boiling water, for fast consumption, (interview UMC 1983).

Thus middle-class shops carry industrially processed and packed flour from beans, maize, and some root crops, but these items are rarely seen in this form in the general marketplace. They are considered too expensive. Middle-class consumers are prepared to pay the difference in order to get a presumably more hygienic and standardised product and to avoid the hustle and haggling of the market.

The rate of development in such large-scale milling of the local staple grains for food is so far glaringly slow in comparison with the tremendous expansion seen in the simultaneously developing feed milling industry for animal production, but may with time also gather momentum, including the already expanding rice milling industry.

In the meantime, however, the immediate scope for expansion seems to lie elsewhere, in the development of milling and processing at the lower level of organisation which fits the highly fragmented structure of agricultural production and trade. The small plate and hammer mills which are already found in most villages and towns, usually operating on a customer-service basis, are the main functioning food processing industry in the country apart from the wheat bakeries. Removing any obstacles that stand in the way of their efficient operation, including their need for credit and access to tools, energy and other inputs seems to us a particularly important way of supporting a drive for local food expansion which already possesses great force.

This first stage of processing thus has the potential to develop local staples to a stage where very little labour is required to make foods ready for consumption. Their prospect for competing with wheat-based semovita and macaroni should be there, particularly if relative prices can be made attractive. But this prospect is limited to household-based production, and possibly to some commercial street sales for those who do not cook, like the large groups of male migrants.

To achieve the same convenience of a portable, instant, and long-keeping snack which attaches to bread would, however, still require development of the final processing stages for domestic foods, in order to manage the supply of the quantities now absorbed in bread consumption. No invention comparable to the local dough-brake, so instrumental to the low-level penetration of bread bakery to every nook and corner of Nigeria, has so far come forth to surpass the constraints of household and very small-scale petty production of local snacks. It remains to be seen if prices more favourable to the local snacks and to the disadvantage of the wheat bread would urge local entrepreneurs to come up with some similar way to raise the productivity and distribution potentials of such products to fill the obvious demands for them, demonstrated in the bread market. It is at this level the major break-through must come, we believe.

Prospects for food self-sufficiency

Developments in processing, closely linked as they are to problems of storage and marketing, will no doubt help domestic food producers to reconquer markets lost to wheat. But the significance of 'fast food' in the Nigerian economy should not be exaggerated. The rapid diffusion of bread must primarily be explained by its relative cheapness and availability. If deprived of bread, consumers will have to accept less fast, less convenient, less neat, less 'modern' types of products. There is no point in making the cut in wheat imports dependent on the development of new forms of domestic processing capable of replicating the special qualities of bread. Once competition from imported food has been eliminated the market will tell how much consumers will be prepared to pay extra for such qualities. In this way they will provide domestic investors with the relevant signals as to what emphasis to place on the fast food business.

The question remains: will domestic food producers be able to deliver a sufficient commercial surplus to feed the greatly inflated non-agricultural population which has emerged from the oil economy? It depends on what we mean by feeding. If we mean adequate volumes and types of food to ensure adequate diets at prices which are within the reach of all these people, the answer is no. Just as now, large sections of the population will not have sufficient money to pay for an adequate regular diet. The cut in food imports will increase the pressures on these groups. New openings in commercial food production may absorb some, who may be induced to go back to farm, on their own or for others, rather than to continue to starve in the towns. These are the difficult options faced by large populations all over the third world, not primarily because of major changes in the availability of food, but because of the ups and downs in the availability of work and money in the non-agricultural sectors.

The question of food adequacy is primarily a question of the adequacy of work and income. This point has been made so well by others that there is no need to go further into it here. There should be no illusion that somehow, by banning food imports, mass hunger and starvation in Nigeria can be eliminated. We are not addressing ourselves to the problem of food self-sufficiency in this more fundamental sense. Our argument is more limited: domestic food production has 'failed' to meet existing commercial requirements because of a combination of an excessive, oil-induced growth in demand and the manner in which massive imports have been allowed to absorb much of this new demand, constraining the commercial transformation of domestic agriculture. With a ban on imports, that constraint will be removed. The process of commercialisation will accelerate, pushing commercial food production to a level more in line with commercial demand.

The basic assumption underlying this position is, of course, that there exists a capacity to expand commercial output, and quite fast, for that matter. Food imports constitute one constraint. But what about others, which are internal to the domestic production system itself? What about all those constraints which so frequently are mentioned either to justify or explain the food imports in the first place? Are we not repeatedly told that Africa is unable to feed herself because of a number of weighty reasons: ecological constraints (erosion, soil depletion, insufficient rainfall); inadequate social organisation (fragmented holdings, insecurity of tenure, labour shortage); technological backwardness (primitive tools, low levels of mechanisation, low-yielding planting material, lack of fertilisers; financial problems (lack of credits, insufficient public investment); problems of markets (prices, transport, feeder roads, storage); only to mention some of the more commonly listed obstacles. In addition, the World Bank and other guardians of sound commercial practices have pointed to the negative effect of excessive state intervention in markets: state marketing, price controls, distorted exchange relations between town and country.

This is not the place to go into a discussion of all these problems. They are real, and they may vary in intensity from one country to another they are certainly present in Nigeria as well. Our objection, however, is to the manner in which the presence of such constraints have been combined with observations about food shortages (high prices, high imports) into a false conclusion of agricultural stagnation. It is a dangerous conclusion because it leads to false strategies out of the impasse.

Our own studies of Nigerian agriculture (Beckman 1985) suggest, on the contrary, a highly dynamic situation where food production is commercialised on a wide scale, extended into new areas, diffusing new crops and improved technology, and transforming social relations of production towards forms which are more efficient in extracting commercial surpluses.

The massive exodus from agriculture into other types of employment caused by the circulation of oil money has certainly caused stagnation of a sort in overall food production. Simultaneously, it has provided a strong push to the commercialisation of food production, with far-reaching implications for social organisation and technology. This is not the first time that West African agricultural producers have demonstrated their preparedness to respond to sudden market openings. West African agriculture has undergone a series of commercial revolutions of which the shift to food production for domestic markets is only the latest (Hopkins 1973). The stagnation in overall output has thus gone hand in hand with a dramatic shift towards commercial food production among those who have remained on the land.

High food prices have stimulated private investments at all levels, holdings have been consolidated and expanded, more labour has been hired, on terms which demonstrate how pre-capitalist forms of labour relations are transformed in step with expanded market opportunities. The state (and the World Bank) have had a hand in this by stepping up the diffusion of chemical fertilisers, new seeds, mechanised services, and technical advice. Our studies suggest that these elements of state intervention primarily tend to reinforce ongoing processes and influence their social character, including for example the strengthening of the internal differentiation within the farming communities.

There are numerous agents, as we have seen, outside these communities, who are busy cashing in on this process, including international companies selling inputs, assembly plants, and projects. Food traders expand their enterprises and reinvest in production. A new brand of commercial farmer is entering business with the backing of the state and domestic and international finance capital. But at the base of it all lies the accelerated transformation of the peasant communities themselves, preparing the way for new forms of ownership and control of land and labour which facilitate commercial production.

We have little doubt about the potential of the social forces now at work for taking advantage of any vacuum created by the forced withdrawal from the market of the wheat merchants and their domestic agents. It does not mean to say that we believe that such potential will be automatically realised, once such withdrawal has been secured. But neither does it mean that we believe that it can only be achieved as a result of major 'development efforts' by the state and international agencies such as the World Bank.

On the contrary, the momentum of this commercial expansion lies essentially in the interaction between the internal dynamics of the peasant economy and a growing domestic food market.

In Nigeria and elsewhere, the major threat to the realisation of this potential comes from the failure to make such goods available which the farmers want and on terms which are attractive enough to warrant the increased efforts on their side. The threat of failure in this respect is closely bound up with the vicissitudes of the export economy, where periods of high export earnings lead to the entrenchment of large public service sectors and low-productive manufacturing which tend to absorb much of the import capacity during the lean years, cutting farmers' access to inputs as well as 'incentive goods'. Prosperous Ghana was caught in this terrible trap. Prosperous Nigeria may follow suit.

This is also the context in which we can see the threat of such agricultural strategies as represented by the irrigation schemes (Andrae and Beckman 1986). Here as well the state risks becoming bogged down in large unproductive commitments which restrict its capacity to provide incentives to the mass of commercially oriented private producers. Also the essentially smallholder-oriented support schemes, so energetically pushed by the World Bank, risk becoming costly unproductive bureaucratic structures, once the flow of oil money and international credit is disrupted. These Agricultural Development Projects may become just as many empty shells with little to distribute of value to the producers but drawing heavy costs in feeding and maintaining staff, offices and vehicles.

Potentially, the prospects for food self-sufficiency in Nigeria are bright, but only as long as it is fully realised where the potential lies, and that ambitious and costly public investments in this field are likely to be more part of the problem than part of the solution.

Whose food? whose income? a concluding note

We repeat: what we have said so far has little to do with the more fundamental food problem, that is, the problem of how all Nigerians should be ensured sufficient food. The question of national self-sufficiency, in the restricted sense discussed here, can be solved, we believe, by relying on the vast scope for commercial transformation and surplus production which exists within the parameters of already established social and political structures. The wider food problem, on the other hand, can only be solved as a result of long and intense struggles of social forces at the level of production as well as of the state. In fact, there is reason to believe that the accelerated commercialisation of the peasant economy that is necessary in order to bring about national self-sufficiency will simultaneously act as a powerful force pushing more people into the risk zone of hunger and undernourishment.

Commercialisation increases the competition for resources in the peasant economy. Some are better placed than others in taking advantage of the situation. The expansion by some restricts the resources available to others, or pushes the cost of resources out of their reach. This has happened elsewhere. It can be observed currently in the areas of intensified commercial expansion in Nigeria. Intervention by the state and international capital intensifies the process of differentiation, exploitation and marginalisation which follows in the steps of commercial expansion. Methods vary from the brutal land grabbing of Bakolori to the more subtle interventions of the World Bank schemes. But brutality is not the preserve of the state. It permeates the relations over land and labour within the farming communities themselves.

The future we envisage is one with more rather than fewer people starving or being undernourished. To the non-agricultural groups which will suffer from the cuts in cheap food imports, we would thus have to add a growing number of people who are likely to suffer as a result of the intensified commercialisation of food production.

How can such a gloomy perspective be justified politically? What are the alternatives? It is easy to identify some which are a good deal more unattractive: the prospects of intensified food dependence and rural stagnation; a self-suffocating, import-fed public economy, trapped in its own inability to create an alternative to the shaky productive base provided by dwindling oil resources.

Are there no alternatives which take their points of departure in the rights of all people to secure food and other essentials for themselves and their dependants? Cannot the state be mobilised on the side of the weak and vulnerable, on the side of those who are most likely to suffer from the curtailing of food imports and accelerated commercialisation?

Such a state does not exist in Nigeria and it will only emerge, we believe, as a result of the protracted struggles of social and political forces, representing the interests of the oppressed. Such forces are as yet weak. They cannot be expected to sustain, for example, a policy of rural development which supports the interests of the poor farmers against the big ones. Well-meaning state intervention in this direction is unlikely to achieve much at this stage. In fact, it may well serve to obstruct the development of productive forces, as represented by the commercially oriented farmers, without being able to put anything in their place.

The hope, as we see it, lies in the broadening of the national democratic forces which may emerge as a result of the broadening of the economic basis of the national economy, including the consolidation and expansion of production for domestic markets both in agriculture and industry. The accelerated commercialisation of the peasant economy is not only the most realistic way to feed the mass of non-agricultural producers. It is also the prerequisite for the expansion of domestic mass markets for manufacturers and other local producers of goods and services. The viability of industrial development in a country like Nigeria hinges on the simultaneous development of such mass markets and the ability of domestic food producers to feed an industrial labour force. The present industrial crisis in Nigeria demonstrates the extreme vulnerability of an industry which depends on foreign exchange not only for raw materials, spare parts and other inputs, but for the feeding of its workers (Andrae and Beckman 1984). For industry in Nigeria to survive it must ensure the reproduction of its labour force by supporting the continued commercialisation of the peasant economy.

And this applies to the workers as well. The present crisis demonstrates that their welfare and survival are tied to the expansion of domestic food production. While they may struggle to protect food imports, they must clearly see the limits to such a strategy at a point where the import capacity of the economy collapses, not just because of the shortfall in oil exports but because of the overload of competing claims to which these export earnings are exposed.

NOTE

1. This is Chapter 9 of *The Wheat Trap: Bread and Underdevelopment in Nigeria* by the same authors, London: Zed Press, 1986.

18

Food and hunger in a petroleum neocolony: a study of the food crisis in Nigeria

Eskor Toyo

A food crisis is raging in Nigeria. In Nigeria there prevails a tendency to attribute undesirable developments to the fall in petroleum revenue or to so-called 'mismanagement' of the economy by this or that wrong-headed regime.

In a neo-nationalist mood also, it has become convenient to exude 'patriotism' by attributing untoward developments not to capitalism but to dependency on 'multinationals', 'great powers' or the 'industrial countries of the north'.

In the first spirit, the popular explanation of the food crisis is that agriculture was neglected by government policy, especially since large petroleum earnings started. This sounds plausible, since the food crisis occurs at the same time as a raw material import crisis supposedly caused not by the great capitalist depression but by the fall in petroleum revenue.

However, it is our position that what is involved is not neglect of agriculture but the kind of attention that was paid to it. That attention was neocolonial and designed for comprador capitalist development which is necessarily parasitic. The policy has led to an export-import orientation and the postponement of an agricultural, and an ancillary industrial, revolution.

In the second or neo-nationalist mood, the food crisis is seen as an aspect of dependency which brings about balance-of-payments problems. Again, the country is said to have been too dependent on petroleum exports and raw material and food imports. Our position is that there is a more disturbing aspect of the food crisis. This goes along with a process of impoverishment not brought about simply by the decline in petroleum revenue.

We try to show how the food question itself first arose: it in fact arose at the height of the petroleum boom. Then we show that in the last ten years governments have battled, with much fanfare, with the food crisis, only to produce results which military men could hold as grounds for a coup d'etat.

Crisis symptoms

To the layman, the symptoms of food crisis are the high cost of food in the local market, and the incidence of hoarding. One of the reasons for the 1983 coup d'etat was the inability of the Shagari government to contain food prices. The food situation is also a boon to corrupt bureaucrats and their private sector associates. To cite only one instance from a flood of newspaper stories, the governor of Bauchi State in August 1984 ordered the setting up of open government distribution stalls for government supply of rare commodities in competition with private enterprise when he discovered that some 'unscrupulous' civil servants 'used their positions to procure the commodities (including milk, sugar, semolina and vegetable oil, all as precious as gold – E.T.) and sold to businessmen who, in turn, sold them at exorbitant prices' (*Punch* 10 August 1984).

To the economist, the food crisis appears in certain indices: stagnating production, mounting imports and ascending prices. These indices are presented below.

Stagnating production is illustrated by the index of agricultural production shown in Table 18.1. The table shows a fluctuating but generally declining trend for staple food crop production and a fluctuating but stagnating trend for the aggregate index. The average compound rate of decline of staple food crop production is 5.5 per cent per year.

TABLE 18.1 Index of agricultural production in Nigeria, 1976–83 (1975 = 100)

	1976	*1977*	*1978*	*1979*	*1980*	*1981*	*1982*	*1983*
Crops	88.8	79.7	77.7	71.9	77.7	84.3	85.5	74.3
Staple food crops	88.7	75.7	70.8	64.4	67.6	71.6	73.8	61.5
Other crops	89.1	94.0	99.1	104.0	109.4	124.1	122.2	108.1
Livestock	103.2	106.0	109.3	113.4	117.1	94.2	104.4	99.3
Fish	106.2	108.2	111.4	114.8	102.8	104.3	107.5	109.9
Aggregate index	93.9	88.7	88.5	87.2	89.4	90.1	92.5	83.8

Source: Central Bank of Nigeria, *Annual Report and Statement of Accounts*, 1981 and 1983.

The data on imports of food are presented in Table 18.2. The data show a sharp decline in food imports in the civil war years (1967–9) from the 1966 level. It will be observed that from 1960 to 1966, food imports hovered between 40 and 50 million naira per year. From 1973 when the Organisation of Petroleum Exporting Countries (OPEC) first raised the price of petroleum, imports as a whole as well as food imports surged upward. Whereas before 1976, food imports were generally between 7 and 12 per cent of imports, from 1977, they were generally between 10 and 17 per cent of imports, reaching above 16 per cent in 1981.

In 1979, the military government took steps to restrict imports in general and especially the import of rice which had shot up from 1,100 tonnes in 1973 to 770,000 tonnes in 1978 as can be seen in Table 18.3. However, in 1980, the Shehu Shagari administration which succeeded the military administration in October 1979 proceeded to relax overall as well as food import restrictions. By 1981, therefore, the general and food import situations became alarming. The rulers had to do something, especially as the petroleum revenue showed the first sign of decline in 1978/9 after rising continuously and rapidly from the end of the civil war in 1970, as shown in Table 18.4.

TABLE 18.2 Food imports into Nigeria, 1960–83 (Naira million)

Year	Total imports	Food imports	Share of food (%)	Percentage change of food imports
1960	425.9	47.8	11.2	
1961	439.1	45.5	10.4	−4.8
1962	401.3	47.0	11.7	3.4
1963	410.3	43.8	10.7	−6.8
1964	505.4	41.2	8.2	−5.9
1965	550.1	46.1	8.4	11.9
1966	512.7	51.6	10.1	11.9
1967	447.1	42.6	8.9	17.4
1968	385.4	28.4	7.4	−33.3
1969	497.4	41.8	8.4	47.2
1970	756.4	57.8	7.6	38.3
1971	1,076.4	88.2	8.2	52.6
1972	990.0	95.0	9.6	7.7
1973	1,224.8	126.3	10.3	32.9
1974	1,737.3	154.8	8.9	22.6
1975	3,721.5	298.8	8.0	93.5
1976	5,134.7	441.7	8.6	37.7
1977	7,368.4	780.7	10.6	76.8
1978	8,136.4	1,027.6	12.6	24.0
1979	7,472.5	766.5	10.3	−25.4
1980	9,658.1	1,091.0	11.3	42.3
1981	12,919.6	2,115.1	16.4	93.9
1982	12,565.5	2,048.2	16.3	−3.2
1983	9,723.0	1,477.9	15.2	−27.8

Note: The data up to 1972 were originally in Nigerian pounds and are converted at the rate of one Nigerian pound to two naira.

Source: Central Bank of Nigeria, *Annual Report and Statement of Accounts*, 1981 and 1983.

TABLE 18.3 Rice production and importation in Nigeria, 1970–79 (tonnes)

Year	Domestic production	Importation	Total
1970	345,000	1,700	346,700
1971	383,030	300	383,330
1972	447,000	5,900	452,900
1973	487,000	1,100	488,100
1974	525,000	4,000	529,000
1975	519,000	6,700	525,700
1976	534,000	45,000	579,000
1977	667,000	413,000	1,080,000
1978	695,000	770,000	1,465,000
1979	850,000	700,000	1,550,000

Source: *Business Concord*, 4 March 1983, pp. 8–9.

TABLE 18.4 Major exports, petroleum exports, exports of major agricultural commodities and food imports, Nigeria, 1960–83

Year	Exports of major commodities (Naira million)	Exports of petroleum (Naira million)	Petroleum as % of major exports	Exports of major agricultural commodities (Naira million)	Imports of food (Naira million)
1960	339.4	8.8	2.6	250.5	47.8
1961	347.3	23.1	6.7	252.5	45.5
1962	337.1	34.4	10.2	242.5	47.0
1963	378.7	40.3	10.6	267.9	43.8
1964	429.3	64.1	14.9	283.4	41.2
1965	536.6	136.2	25.4	309.5	46.1
1966	568.2	183.9	32.3	274.2	51.6
1967	483.6	144.8	29.9	247.6	42.6
1968	328.9	74.0	22.5	256.0	28.4
1969	534.8	172.0	32.2	223.3	41.8
1970	781.3	509.8	65.3	230.1	57.8
1971	1,204.5	953.0	79.1	220.9	88.2
1972	1,327.6	1,157.0	87.1	144.1	95.8
1973	2,277.4	1,893.5	83.1	255.0	126.3
1974	5,794.8	5,334.7	92.1	269.1	154.8
1975	4,829.4	4,629.6	95.9	220.5	298.8
1976	6,751.1	6,321.7	93.6	273.2	441.7
1977	7,630.7	7,072.8	92.7	371.1	780.7
1978	6,064.4	5,401.6	89.1	412.3	1,027.6
1979	10,836.8	10,166.8	93.8	468.0	766.5
1980	14,077.0	13,523.0	96.1	340.1	1,091.0
1981	11,023.3	10,680.5	96.9	178.4	2,115.1
1982	8,722.5	8,601.6	98.6	92.0	2,048.2
1983	7,612.3	7,337.4*	96.4	274.9	1,477.1

* estimate

Sources: Central Bank of Nigeria, *Economic and Financial Review* (several issues) and *Annual Report and Statement of Accounts*, (several issues).

To avoid the autarchic implication of the concept of self-reliance in food, we can define a concept, namely, 'agricultural export coverage' (AEC) for food imports. We define this as

$$\frac{\text{value of agricultural exports}}{\text{value of food imports}}$$

We propose to describe the AEC as neutral, favourable or unfavourable according to whether the ratio is 1, greater than 1 or less than 1. Using this concept, we can see from columns (4) and (5) of Table 18.4 that it is between 1974 and 1975 that the country reached approximate 'neutrality'. Thereafter, the AEC became 'unfavourable'. The degree of unfavourableness is presented in Table 18.5.

TABLE 18.5 Agricultural export coverage (AEC) for food imports, 1974–83

1974	1975	1976	1977	1978	1979	1980	1981	1982	1983
1.74	0.74	0.48	0.40	0.61	0.31	0.08	0.08	0.05	0.19

Source: Central Bank of Nigeria, *Annual Report and Statement of Accounts*, 1981 and 1983.

In Table 18.6 we present the principal indicators of ascending prices. In general the composite price index numbers for food rise faster than the index numbers of all items. Whereas the compound growth rate of the composite price index for all items is 15.1 per cent per annum over the period, the corresponding rate of the food index is 16.4 per cent.

TABLE 18.6 Consumer price indices in Nigeria, 1976–83 (1975=100)

	1976	1977	1978	1979	1980	1981	1982	1983
Composite (urban rural)								
All items	123	143	167	186	205	248	267	328
Food	122	146	177	186	200	250	272	336
Urban								
All items	124	142	176	196	218	264	283	340
Food	128	155	196	210	234	303	328	401
Rural								
All items	124	143	165	185	203	245	264	327
Food	121	145	169	182	195	243	265	326

Source: Central Bank of Nigeria, *Annual Report and Statement of Accounts* (several years)

The alleged neglect of agriculture

Was agriculture neglected?

In general agricultural policy in Nigeria since 1960 has been part of a general three-sided neocolonial development strategy. It consisted of export of raw materials, import of foreign capital and encouragement of import-substituting industrialisation.

Let us first deal with the raw material crisis which, taken along with the food crisis, gives the impression that agriculture was neglected. The import-substitution policy was based on the presumption that the industries would use local raw materials. What happened was that the raw materials were imported, because the industries were not redesigned to use local raw materials, and the processing industries which might prepare the local raw materials for use did not exist.

Consequently, Nigerian manufacturing industry has a high raw material import component in its cost structure. In 1979 and 1980, for instance, imported raw materials formed 73.6 and '/ . 3 per cent respectively of total raw material costs in Nigerian manufacturing (Central Bank of Nigeria 1980). If we add to this the importation of plant and equipment, we have a very heavy import bias. As is well-known, not only this import bias but also the repatriation of profits made by the import-substituting industries and debt servicing in respect of portfolio foreign capital imports for infrastructural investment intensify the foreign exchange problem of neo-colonial economies.

All this has been true of Nigeria (Toyo 1983), although the inevitable foreign exchange crisis was staved off by the steady increase in petroleum exports since independence evident in Table 18.4. The petroleum-earning boom resulting from the increase of petroleum prices by the Organisation of Petroleum Exporting Countries (OPEC) enormously expanded both the import of raw materials and food. Hence, as soon as a decline in petroleum income set in in 1978 and further in 1981 the import dependence of the country, not only in food but also in raw materials, was exposed by the foreign exchange crisis that has since occurred and the increased need for foreign borrowing to cover food and raw material imports (Nwanko 1984; Ozoaga 1984).

The explanation then began that the country had all along neglected its agriculture. Actually, however, every Nigerian Plan had paid considerable attention to agriculture. Out of a total capital expenditure programme of the equivalent of ₦135 million in the 1962–8 development plan, ₦183 million or 13.5 per cent was allocated to primary production. In the 1970–74 Plan, a total public sector capital expenditure of 215.4 million naira was allocated to agriculture out of a total public sector capital expenditure of 1,560 million naira, that is, 13.8 per cent. In the 1975–80 Plan, we had the distribution of public capital expenditure within the economic sector plan shown in Table 18.7. Agriculture received 18.5 per cent of the total.

TABLE 18.7 Allocation of public sector capital expenditure in the economic sector in the Third Plan, 1975–80

Subsector	Value (₦ million)	%
Agriculture	2,207.7	18.5
Mining and related activities	2,680.4	22.5
Manufacturing	5,315.9	44.6
Power	1,075.2	9.0
Commerce and finance	539.4	4.5
Transport and communication	93.2	0.9
Total	11,911.8	100.0

Source: *Third National Development Plan, 1975–80*, Federal Ministry of Economic
    Development, several pages

Within the agriculture programme the allocation was as follows:

Crops	₦1,646.0 million
Livestock	344.1 million
Fishery	101.6 million

All in all, this is hardly a picture of neglect.

Thus the claim that agriculture was neglected is not borne out by the facts, but a question remains as to the kind of attention given to agriculture.

The attention that agriculture received contained a number of elements. First, as is consonant with neocolonial strategy, emphasis was on export production not on food production. The situation in this respect began to change only around 1975 for reasons not unconnected, as we shall see, with other aspects of neocolonial policy.

Secondly, the policy after 1960 was a continuation of colonial policy in that it aimed at 'stimulating' the traditional peasant rather than transforming agriculture. The orientation of the policy-makers of the Shagari era (1979–83) continued to be of this kind. Thus the Federal Government's Strategic Food Mission said in 1980:

Two options are available to the government: either to pursue large scale capital-intensive projects, or to stimulate improvements for the traditional smallholder sector. (Ministry of Agriculture 1980)

Along with this false dichotomy which ignores many scale, capital-intensity and ownership-organisational possibilities, the document shows considerable hostility to state direct production and, with its conservative and colonial-cum-capitalist preference, urges 'heavy reliance on the Nigerian smallholder as the centrepiece of incremental food production' (Idachaba 1980).

Thirdly, on the assumption that the peasant had no alternative but to continue to produce, policy aimed at extracting as much of a surplus as possible from peasant agriculture and using this surplus to develop capitalism. This policy was vigorously pursued by governments through the marketing boards from 1954 to 1977 (Onitiri and Olatunbosun 1974).

Fourthly, in so far as the use of modern production methods or agricultural marketing was concerned, policy aimed at encouraging capitalism in agriculture.

All the government efforts to promote 'progressive' individual farmers through loans, input subsidies and large land concessions through the Land Use and Allocation Decree have the effect of trying to evolve capitalist farmers. Moreover, as Titiloye and Ismail note, in the 1960s 'the Nigerian marketing boards took a number of steps to help promote growth of indigenous Licensed Buying Agents' (Titiloye and Ismail 1974), that is, middlemen who actually bought produce from the peasants at negotiated prices and sold to the boards at government prices.

We claim it is impossible satisfactorily to explain the food crisis without analysing these policy orientations. We shall take up these orientations briefly one after the other.

Neocolonial orientation

Policy continued with a colonialist orientation in two major respects. First, attention in the first two plans was concentrated on export crops. Secondly, as mentioned in the previous section, the centrepiece in production continued, as in colonial days, to be the individual peasant or the hardly present 'progressive farmers'.

In speaking about crops, the second National Development Plan (1970–74), like the First Plan (1962–8), gave pride of place to export crops. In the Second Plan, these crops were called the 'major crops' (Ministry of Information 1970: 104–7). Whereas considerable attention was given to them individually, the treatment of the 'food crops' was very generalised. In the Third National Development Plan (1975–80), however, the emphasis was the other way round. Precedence was given to food crops which were treated of in some statistical detail. The other crops received a less meticulous treatment (Ministry of Economic Development 1975: 67–78). In the Fourth National Development Plan (1981–85), the objectives in agriculture are listed in the following order:

1. increased production of food and other raw materials to meet the needs of a growing population; a basic objective in this respect is the attainment of self-sufficiency in food in about five years;
2. increased production of livestock and fish to meet domestic needs and create a surplus for export;
3. increased production and processing of export crops. . . (Ministry of Planning 1981: 19–20)

The shift of emphasis after 1977 is obvious and is reflected in the figures for fertiliser imports shown in Table 18.8.

TABLE 18.8 Consumption of fertilisers, actual and projected, selected years

Year	Consumption in nutrient tonnes (N + P + K)
Actual	
1953	603
1960	3,337
1965	3,900
1970	10,682
1974	26,900
1978–9	53,765
1979–80	117,473
Projected	
1981	624,000
1982	780,000
1983	984,000
1984	1,217,000
1985	1,474,000

Note: *Fertiliser delivered is presumed to be consumed. This is not the case, however, as large quantities of unused fertiliser have been widely reported.
Source: Ministry of Agriculture, May 1980, Vol. 2, pp. 85–112

It is also explained by the launching of spectacular campaigns, namely, the 'Operation Feed the Nation' campaign of the military regime of General Obasanjo (1975–9), and the 'Green Revolution' campaign of the Shagari regime (1979–83).

There are two reasons for the shift in emphasis. The first is that with the enormous rise in easy petroleum earnings, earning of foreign exchange from export agriculture became insignificant, whereas the same petroleum boom both stimulated a spectacular increase in food imports (thus diminishing the foreign exchange gains) and occasioned a steep rise in wage employment and an inflation in food prices leading to a wage restraint policy. A wage restraint policy cannot long succeed without a corresponding cheap food policy achieved either through food imports or through intensified domestic food production.

From 1969 to 1979, the Federal Military Government maintained wage-restraint and wage-freeze policies (Toyo forthcoming). This was, in fact, continued by the

Shagari regime. It is not only because of inflation that wages were restrained; it was in order not to discourage capitalist investments on account of increases in wage costs. With the policy of attracting foreign capital, the wage restraint policy was, in fact, one of the concessions made to imperialist capital in order to increase its role in the economy. Even in 1984 the IMF insisted on a wage-freeze policy as one of its conditions for lending Nigeria between 1 and 2 billion naira.

Thus, at bottom, the concern with food only pays lip service to the standard of living of the population. The concern started only when it became necessary to match a low-wage policy with a policy of availability of food in such a way as to save foreign exchange for the importation of raw materials needed by the largely imperialist-owned import substituting industries whose high profit rates are to be preserved.

Such is the essence of the so-called food crisis. Of course, since 1972, the indigenous capitalists have been fully in partnership with imperialist direct investors as owners of Nigeria's industries through the Nigerian Enterprises Promotion Decrees (1972 and 1977). These Decrees compulsorily transferred all of the small commercial enterprises and 40–60 per cent of the ownership of others into the hands of Nigerians. These decrees enabled Nigerian capitalists, Nigerian governments and expatriate capitalist firms to go into joint ownership and operation of medium and large enterprises. That being so, a policy of wage restraint is a boon to indigenous capitalists as well, since it cheapens labour for those capitalists operating on their own as well as for those who own investments in the transnational enterprises.

Apart from emphasis on export crops up to 1975 and a shift in emphasis to domestic food production after 1975, the other side of neocolonialist policy affecting food production generally was the continuation of the colonial emphasis on individual peasant production with some encouragement offered to 'progressive farmers'. In the colonial period, export production was done predominantly by individual peasants, although expatriate firms owned a few large plantations involving rubber, oil palm and tobacco. Food production was entirely done by traditional peasant methods. The colonial pattern has largely remained.

However, there is a definite limit to the capacity of individual peasant production to cope with increased raw material exports and increased food demand at the same time. Urbanisation means a relative increase in the demand for food from non-food producers, a reduction in the relative population of food producers, and a change in the age structure of food producers in so far as it is the most productive age groups that move from the countryside. A revolution in food production is therefore necessary.

Such a revolution consists of a change from peasant methods and involves a transformation in organisation, inputs, infrastructure, storing and marketing. In none of these has any effective step been taken in Nigeria. As late as 1980, the Food Strategies Mission attributed the 'poor performance of the agricultural sector' to:

- population drift from rural to urban areas, leaving an ageing labour force;
- external trade competition resulting primarily from an overvalued naira;
- inadequate and ineffective extension services, inadequate supply and erratic availability and inputs and other farm support services;
- inappropriate research support for extension;
- inadequate rural physical infrastructures; and
- imbalanced utilisation of available financial and manpower resources. (Ministry of Agriculture)

Our own study does not confirm an overvalued exchange rate as an important factor. The other factors are sufficient to explain the 'poor performance' of agriculture. Of these the first is decisive. No matter how much fertiliser or infrastructural improvement is brought to the countryside the situation cannot be saved if it is the ageing peasants who are to utilise these aids.

TABLE 18.9 Migration of school leavers and its effect on food production, Akpor Clan, 1975–83

Year	Number of graduands (a)	Number that left (b)	Number that remained (c)	(c)/(a) (%)	Yam output
1975	15	5	10	66.7	4,500
1976	19	10	9	47.4	3,750
1977	22	10	12	54.5	3,500
1978	16	11	5	31.3	2,750
1979	20	13	7	35.0	2,000
1980	24	19	5	20.8	1,900
1981	27	22	5	18.5	1,750
1982	31	28	3	9.7	1,000
1983	34	31	3	8.8	900

Note: The figures for output are the numbers of yam stacks in the given years.
Source: N. Olumati (1984)

An indication of the gravity of the drift from the countryside and the changing age structure is given by Table 18.9. The table reveals an intensification of the migration of young people from one area and a subsequent decline decline in the production of yams. Such data can be reproduced from any part of the country.

Bourgeois parasitic accumulation

From 1954, when Nigerian leaders started participating in decisions affecting agriculture, up to 1977 when the marketing boards were reorganised so that they no longer had surpluses in view, the operation of these boards had the effect of all but killing the goose that laid the golden egg.

The marketing boards had a monopoly in the purchase of all crops for export as well as for resale to processing plants or factories in Nigeria. The authorities fixed the 'producer prices' (state purchase prices). These were well below world prices, varying from 22.8 to 79.7 per cent of world prices (Olatunbosun and Olayide 1974).

The exported products paid export taxes. The marketing boards paid excise taxes on local sales, and local processors excise taxes on their products. In addition to these taxes, the state absorbed windfall profits arising from fortuitous increases in world prices. In addition to the state receipts, middlemen employed by the marketing boards to buy produce from the peasants usually paid the peasants much lower than the state prices. Sometimes the underpayment was as much as 40 per cent (Kriesel 1974).

The consequence of all this was that the peasant lacked the funds to effect any improvements in method or even to expand hectarage. Such funds become important the more necessary paid labour becomes and the higher the price of paid labour, which by the 1960s was well over 20 per cent of the farming population in some states (Federal Ministry of Agriculture 1980).

In that situation an alternative source of funds would be credit from the banks. However, although funds are not lacking, the banks cannot lend to peasants because they do not have the sort of security that the banks require. There is also the fact that the peasants often misuse credit in cash. Credits could be given through inputs, but this is more effectively done through co-operatives whose organisation no one takes up vigorously.

The surpluses extracted as taxes and grants from the marketing boards were used in part to aid development in general (Aluko 1974), but this general development meant giving contracts to the indigenous bourgeoisie and foreign firms to provide various facilities. Out of these contracts the bourgeoisie have acquired capital which they have not ploughed back into agriculture.

This brings us to the question of capitalist development in agriculture. Those who complain of agriculture having been neglected ignore the fact that the prevailing outlook gave preference, especially in agriculture, to private initiative. Indeed agriculture has been ignored, but certainly not by the governments. It has been ignored by the private-sector capitalist investors.

A section of the bourgeoisie has made money out of agriculture. Some have done so through contracts from the state for the importation of fertilisers and other inputs. Some have done so as produce buyers who inflate the cost of their services to the marketing boards and underpay peasants, or who hoard scarce produce so as to extract higher producer prices from the marketing boards. Some have also made money as money lenders to peasants enabling them to negotiate very low prices for peasant produce in exchange for loans (Akomeso 1984). Finally, many have made money in organising food distribution between the country and the city. In this role they have taken advantage of transport and other difficulties to profit from high food prices.

Capitalists, however, shy from investing in Nigerian agriculture itself. The reason for this is simple and springs from capitalist logic. The rate of profit in commerce and industry varies from 30 to 60 per cent. Real estate *in urban areas* offers the prospects of immediate and high returns. With drought, the risk of loss *in the savanna areas* where medium farms are easier to create is quite high. In *forest belt* areas it requires a high capital cost to create a medium-sized farm. Even with a lot of inducements – low interest rates, state expenditure on irrigation and the infrastructure, fertiliser and improved seed subsidies, pesticide subsidies and tax holidays – the capitalists remain unattracted towards farming.

The Land Use and Allocation Decree was meant to facilitate the creation by capitalists of large and medium farms out of unused land. However, this decree requires a would-be holder to acquire a certificate of occupancy. The bureaucratic delays in acquiring this certificate and the capital gains tax or stamp duty which the state charges on the bank loan acquired with the backing of the certificate increase for a capitalist the cost and unattractiveness of owning a farm.

The indigenous capitalists prefer real estate, contracts from the Federal, state and local governments in the execution of various projects out of which they make large and easy profits, general commerce, and partnership with expatriate companies in the undertaking or expansion of one or other manufacturing venture.

Pauperisation and hunger

One can, as does the government and many economists, look at the food crisis in terms of rising food imports and the intensification of the 'balance-of-payments' crisis. In that case the fall in petroleum export revenue which reduces food import capacity is the problem.

In fact, food imports, about which much noise has been made, are actually imports of commodities mostly used by the middle class. The food import items are wheat and flour, fruits, sugar, milk, beverages, beef, fish and stockfish. Apart from stockfish which is substantially consumed as a substitute for local meat and fish in Imo and Anambra states and to a lesser extent in other parts of the country, none of these items is an essential food item for the generality of peasants, the working class and the class of artisans and petty-traders. Apart from salt, essential food items for the people are maize, sorghum, millet, groundnut oil, palm oil, yams, cocoyams, plantains, cassava, beans, local meat, and fish, most of which is local.

The phenomenal rise in food imports which corresponds not to any growth in other exports but to growth in mineral oil exports has already been shown in Table 18.4. The food import expansion represents the influence of imported middle class consumption patterns, as recently noted by Ekpo (1984). It is thus an index of embourgeoisement.

TABLE 18.10 Estimated output of major agricultural crops in Nigeria, 1971/2–1978/9 (thousand tonnes)

Crops	1971/2	1972/3	1973/4	1974/5	1975/6	1976/7	1977/8	1978/9
Millet	1,825	2,391	3,794	5,554	2,550	2,893	2,579	2,386
Sorghum	3,794	2,298	3,125	4,738	2,920	2,950	3,950	2,409
Groundnut	1,381	1,380	878	1,946	449	459	567	801
Beans	802	408	530	1,099	858	727	408	498
Yam	9,766	6,900	6,936	7,160	8,621	6,470	6,376	5,866
Maize	1,274	639	808	528	1,332	1,068	651	659
Cassava	4,516	2,573	2,912	3,582	2,324	1,786	1,696	1,621
Rice	279	447	487	525	515	218	411	280
Melon	63	91	182	49	205	167	142	106
Cocoyam	880	1,357	1,106	480	504	532	346	182

Source: *Annual Abstract of Statistics, 1981*, published by the Federal Office of Statistics, Lagos, p. 75

TABLE 18.11 Estimated production growth rates of principal food crops in Nigeria, 1962–75

Crop	Estimated annual growth rate (%)
Maize	0.13
Sorghum	−0.84
Millet	1.20
Rice	4.56
Groundnut	−0.04
Oil palm	1.90
Yam	0.04
Cassava	0.60
Sowpea	1.07

Source: IBRD, Nigeria Agricultural Sector Review, Vol. 1, June 1979

That the decline in food production has been a prolonged affair is obvious from Table 18.10. That table shows that in the most important items, namely, millet, sorghum, yam and cassava, there has been a fluctuating decline since 1971/2, relieved only by a fairly good harvest in 1974/5. Table 18.11 summarises the situation from 1962 to 1975 and shows that up to 1975 only in the production of rice – of which production was not large – did the rate of growth of production exceed the population growth rate of 2.5 per cent. Of course, the heavy importation of rice took over from 1973.

Table 18.12 documents the parallel decline in the consumption of livestock products and fish between 1968 and 1974.

TABLE 18.12 Per capita consumption of livestock products and fish in Nigeria, 1968 and 1974

Products	1968 consumption (kg per capita)	1974 consumption (kg per capita)	Difference
Beef	3.34	2.49	−0.85
Goat	1.84	0.86	−0.98
Sheep	0.42	0.30	−0.12
Poultry	0.84	0.71	−0.13
Pigs	0.48	0.40	−0.08
Other meat	3.54	0.83	−2.71
Offals	6.65	1.03	−5.62
Eggs	0.84	1.40	+0.56
Fish	13.38	7.79	−5.59
Milk	2.76	1.90	−0.86
Cheese	0.03	0.09	+0.06

When we look at several indices, it is difficult to avoid the conclusion that a process of pauperisation had been going on even before the great capitalist depression that began in 1980 and that while it is not wrong to worry about the balance of payments and relate food to it, it is even more important to see the food crisis in relation to pauperisation and hunger. While the middle class feel intensely the restriction on the importation of items such as televisions and motor car tyres and are understandably concerned with balance of payments and so-called leakages in foreign exchange earnings, a process of pauperisation is going on which is reflected by a recent press focus in Nigeria on hunger and the growing incidence of kwashiokor, which is the physical consequence of malnutrition.

For instance, the 'New Nigerian' reports that according to investigations conducted by Ahmadu Bello University, kwashiokor is on the increase and sleeping sickness is resurfacing (*New Nigerian* 11 September 1984).

The economists' typical indicators of pauperisation, hardship and hunger can be summarised. As we know, the population is growing at an annual rate of 2.5 per cent. Urbanisation is also growing. Meanwhile, the food production index, which reflects the availability of the basic food items which the workers and peasants – as distinct from the middle class – do use, has been on the decline as shown by Tables 18.1, 18.11, 18.12 and 18.13.

Side by side with the contrast between the population and food trends, the consumer price indices have been increasing at the rate of at least about 15 per cent per annum.

As far as the incomes of the people are concerned, wage restraint and wage freeze policies were in place from 1969 to 1979, and wage restraint ruled from 1979 to 1983. The Central Bank report for 1981 observed that 'on wages, emphasis [would] be on restraint on growth' during the Fourth Plan period 1981–85. However, come the second military regime in December 1983, a wage freeze was reimposed. Apart from the wage freeze, in many establishments workers do not get paid for several months on end and this is true not only of the private but also of the state sector. As a result of the current great capitalist depression, there has been a massive retrenchment of workers in both the private and the state sectors. It should be understood that in Nigeria with her extended family system the sacking of a worker means misery for his dependent brothers, sisters, nephews and cousins as well. For the very young, school fees – to be paid by their parents or other relatives – have been increased and books are now as dear as gold.

As for the incomes of the peasants, what has happened in recent years can be read from Table 18.13. The table reveals that the producer prices

TABLE 18.13 Percentage changes in producer prices 1976/7–1983/4

	1976/7 – 1977/8	1977/8 – 1978/9	1978/9 – 1979/80	1979/80 – 1980/1	1980/1 – 1981/2	1981/2 – 1982/3	1982/3 – 1983/4
Cocoa	56.1	0.0	6.5	8.3	0.0	0.0	7.6
Cotton	7.1	0.0	0.0	21.2	16.3	0.0	15.7
Groundnuts	−21.4	5.5	20.7	20.0	7.1	0.0	0.0
Kenaf	n.a	7.1	0.0	14.9	0.0	0.0	0.0
Palm kernels	0.0	0.0	20.0	11.1	0.0	15.0	0.0
Palm oil (special)	11.3	20.3	26.8	10.0	0.0	0.0	0.0
Palm oil (technical)	n.a	22.6	0.0	35.4	0.0	0.0	0.0
Rubber (latex)	n.a	0.0	15.1	15.5	23.7		
Rubber (processed)	n.a	0.0	20.4	14.9	25.7		
Rubber (dry lumps)						16.7	0.0
Rubber (top grade)						20.0	0.0
Beans	n.a	0.0	91.6	0.0	4.9	0.0	0.0
Maize	36.8	0.0	53.8	0.0	5.0	0.0	0.0
Millet	37.5	0.0	100.0	0.0	5.0	0.0	0.0
Rice (milled)	n.a	0.0	42.5	0.0	4.6	0.0	0.0
Rice (paddy)	29.7	0.0	37.1	0.0	4.8	0.0	0.0
Sorghum	37.5	0.0	90.9	0.0	9.5	0.0	0.0

Source: Derived from Central Bank of Nigeria, *Annual Reports and Accounts* (several years)

hardly changed at all. Where they did change in a positive direction, only in one, two or three years out of the seven did the change manage to be higher than the general inflation rate in the countryside, which was 14.8 per cent.

Futility and coup d'etat

As harrowing as the foregoing picture is, even more frustrating is the apparent futility of the heated efforts made in recent years by governments to pull the country out from the disaster. As earlier noted, the Obasanjo regime launched and maintained 'Operation Feed the Nation' from 1975 to 1979. The Shagari regime launched a 'Green Revolution' campaign and maintained it from 1979 to 1983.

In keeping with these campaigns, federal capital expenditure on agriculture leapt from ₦8.2 million in 1971 to ₦250 million in 1975 and was maintained at a level over ₦100 million a year in 1981. The approved expenditures in the 1982 and 1983 federal budgets were ₦636.3 million and ₦472.4 million respectively (Central Bank, Annual Reports).

Whereas total federal and state capital expenditure on agriculture in the 1970–74 plan period was ₦173.2 million, the equivalent expenditure in the 1975–80 plan period was ₦944.1 million (Ministry of Economic Development 1975: 25; Ministry of Planning 1981: 29).

The 'Green Revolution' programmers proclaimed in 1980 that 'a basic objective of the Federal Government [was] the attainment of self-sufficiency in food by 1985' (Ministry of Agriculture 1980) – the terminal year of the Fourth National Development Plan. However, as shown in Table 18.14, the rate of growth of the domestic supply of food crops needed to reach 6.6 per cent per annum in order to achieve that goal. From Table 18.1, we find that the overall compound growth rate of staple food production between 1980 and 1983 was -2.6 per cent.

TABLE 18.14 Projected food demand, supply and deficits, Nigeria, 1980–85
(thousand tonnes of grain equivalent)

	1980	1985	Deficit in 1985
Crops and crop products			
Gross demand	18,620	22,125	
Domestic supply			
at 1.0% p. a. current growth rate	16,000	16,835	(5,290)
at 2.0% p. a.		17,600	(4,525)
at 4.0% target growth rate		19,400	(2,725)
at 6.6% deficit closed		22,125	0
Livestock products			
Gross demand	895	1,060	
Domestic supply			
at 1.75% p. a. current growth rate	620	645	(415)
at 2.0% p. a.		695	(375)
at 3.25% p. a. target growth rate		720	(340)
at 6.0% p. a.		830	(230)
at 11.25% p. a. deficit closed		1,060	0

Source: Federal Ministry of Agriculture, May 1980, Vol. 1, p. 2.

One of the responses of the Federal government to the situation was to start large irrigated farm projects of its own, called river basin development projects. It created 11 special river basin authorities to do this. These authorities were to produce especially the imported items: wheat, rice, sugar, fish. In the Fourth Plan period, the Federal government initiated an expansion of the scope of the so-called Integrated Rural Agricultural Development Projects started in 1975 and financed by the World Bank. This is a special extension-service programme. In 1980 an Accelerated Development Programme for food production was launched, an emergency stand-in for the necessarily slow expansion of the Integrated Rural Development Project scheme. For 1982 and 1983, the expenditures on, and output performances of, the river-basin and 'integrated rural development' projects are as shown in Table 18.15.

TABLE 18.15 Capital expenditure and output of river basin and integrated rural development projects, 1982 and 1983

River basin	1982	1983	Integrated rural development	1982	1983
Capital expenditure (₦ million)	487.4	317.6	*Capital expenditure* (₦ million)	604.0	38.0
Production Grains (thousand (tonnes)	346.0	287.7	*Production* (thousand tonnes) (a) Rice	103.7	9.4
Fish (tonnes)	890.2	1,983.1	(b) Beans	61.3	29.2
Poultry			(c) Sorghum	519.2	798.1
Layers	64,684	82,722	(d) Millet	344.0	681.1
Broilers	69,070	70,218	(e) Maize	201.1	270.6
Turkeys	7,140	1,407	(f) Yam	1,327.7	280.0
			(g) Cassava	425.9	55.5

Note: Data for 1983 are provisional
Source: Central Bank of Nigeria, *Annual Report and Accounts*, 1983, pp. 21 and 22

TABLE 18.16 Expenditure and output in the Peremabiri rice project, 1981–3

	1981	1982	1983
Total expenditure (₦ thousand)	5,950	1,190	2,060
Total area cultivated (ha.)	51	81	45
Total output (in bags of 70 kg each)	255	486	360
Production cost per ha. (₦ thousand)	12.9	8.4	16.1
Production cost per bag (70 kg)	2.5	1.4	2.0
Price of (50 kg) rice from Project (₦)	n.a	30.0	40.0

Source: (1) Assistant General Manager (Planning), Niger Delta Basin Development Authority (NDEDA)
(2) Station Manager (Agricultural Officer) of the Peremabiri Rice Project (PRP)

In global terms, such statistics look spectacular. Does the output from these projects justify the heavy capital expenditure on them? A Federal source comments:

There are few facts on the performance of existing large-scale (1,000 hectares and upwards) farming enterprises sponsored by Federal and State Government, but they are widely alleged to be costly failures. (Ministry of Agriculture 1980)

To understand such a remark and why the 'Green Revolution' programmers thought they had grounds for doubting the wisdom of the large-scale' capital intensive' schemes of the 'river-basin' type, let us look at one of the earliest of such projects, the Peremabiri Rice Project. Table 18.16 shows the expenditure on this project and the results in more meaningful terms.

The summary of the information from Table 18.16 is that this project, established in 1972/3, produced rice nearly ten years after its establishment at the cost of between ₦1,400 and ₦2,500 per bag of 70 kilograms (perhaps the weight includes the husk), but sells the rice at less than ₦50 per bag of 50 kilograms.

But will another military regime succeed where the first failed? In spite of the declaration of 'War Against Indiscipline' economic policies are not today fundamentally different from those of previous regimes, and, as this chapter has shown in some detail, it is not the short-lived Shehu Shagari regime that created the food, pauperisation and hunger crises. It only failed to find a solution to them, and this only repeated the failure of the first military regime.

The Buhari military regime believed in solving the problem through 'discipline' and 'austerity'. Both were supposed to justify retrenchment of workers and curtailment of state expenditure on education while the government refused to reduce the subsidy on fuel oil for capitalist firms and middle-class users of vehicles. 'Discipline', 'austerity' and 'national emergency' are supposed to justify government's wage freeze policy, while it has not proved possible to bring down the rate of inflation. Thus all the measures conform with the kind of 'efficiency' which the World Bank and the International Monetary Fund suggest to capitalistic policy makers in the third world as the golden key to salvation from the great capitalist depression.

Students of the history of economic thought will recall that it is precisely the 'parsimony' and 'efficiency' solutions which these two world financial bodies currently advocate (World Bank 1983a) and which various policy-makers in Nigeria have adopted that were recommended as solutions to capitalist depression in the early 1930s. Even John Maynard Keynes rejected this solution which in theory and in practice are actually inimical to recovery.

While the government erroneously hopes for recovery as a result of austerity, there is the fact that the economy is a client one, so that recovery is dependent on recovery by the metropolitan capitalist economies that buy Nigeria's raw material exports.

Meanwhile, there is a complication. 'Efficiency' is being called for and practised in the context of the new phenomenon of stagflation – the simultaneous occurrence of depression and inflation – which afflicts Nigeria even more than it afflicts some other capitalistic economies. Normally, 'austerity' and 'efficiency' (of the World Bank variety) only intensify pauperisation. Stagflation accelerates this process. Meanwhile, wage freeze and inflation increase the wealth of the bourgeoisie.

No matter with what justification a military regime may wage a war for 'discipline' against corrupt politicians and bureaucrats, the great fact to which the present writer has repeatedly called attention remains, namely, that many of the millionaires that existed in the Shagari era (1979–83) were created during the 13 years of the 'discipline', 'austerity', 'wage freeze' and 'patriotism' of the first military regime. The 'discipline' of the Buhari regime has also been designed to help rather than undermine capitalist accumulation in Nigeria.

As far as agriculture itself is concerned, the only new idea which the Shagari and Buhari regimes have come up with is that of modifying the Nigerian Enterprises Promotion Decree in such a way as to permit foreign agricultural firms to undertake farming ventures in Nigeria. Thus we are to believe that the 'patriotic' solution to the food, hunger and raw material crises is to turn Nigeria into something of a 'banana republic'.

Whatever might have been the weaknesses of Nigeria's previous bourgeois regimes, their brand of patriotism rejected encroachment by multinationals in Nigerian agriculture. Now such colonialism is supposed to be the country's salvation.

Needless to say, any regime that can for one moment conceive of the intensification of colonialism as the way to save a third world people from hunger has passed a verdict of damnation on itself. Not without significance, the former President of the Nigerian Labour Congress warned amidst applause that any attempt to move this suggestion from idea into action would meet with resistance (Sunmonu 1984).

Conclusion

Nigeria has a food crisis which is far from having merely a balance-of-payments significance which any revival of the petroleum market can obliterate. The food crisis, much more tragically, is associated with a long festering process of rural decay and general impoverishment. This has not happened because agriculture has been neglected by the state. It has happened because the attention to agriculture has been neocolonial in orientation and bourgeois-parasitic in design and effect. With an eye fixed rather on the balance of payments than on the nutrition of the masses or their income, the government has embarked on some heroic and much orchestrated salvage operations. However, these government efforts have yielded hardly comforting results. Nothing short of an agrarian revolution can save the situation. But the trade unions have become bureaucratised and are prostrate. The peasants are unorganised. Political agitation has been replaced by a military dictatorship. The deep depression in metropolitan capitalist economies, to which this neocolonial economy is linked by a thousand chains, shows no certain sign of coming to an end.

19

Drought and the food crisis in Zimbabwe[1]

Rudo Gaidzanwa

Zimbabwe and other countries in southern Africa are currently suffering from a bad drought. This drought occurs amidst the economic crisis which is being felt in the whole world. On the political front, South Africa has made its power felt through pressure on Mozambique, as evidenced by the Nkomati Accord. The liberation war continues in Namibia and South Africa. This is the scenario within which the food crisis can be examined and analysed in Zimbabwe.

At independence, Zimbabwe was faced with the task of maintaining productivity in agriculture while at the same time improving the lot of agricultural labour which comprises one-third of the entire labour force in wage employment. To this end, a minimum wage policy for different sectors of the economy was instituted with the aim of raising wage incomes and the consumption of necessary commodities and services within the economy. The wage policy was coupled with a food and agricultural price policy as a device to reallocate resources and the purchasing power of the different categories of labour. Initially, the price levels set for maize, the major food crop which will be considered in this chapter, produced a big increase in maize production. The intervention of a crippling drought a year later, changed the expected yields and highlighted a number of problems that not been anticipated when marketing and pricing policies were formulated. This chapter will focus on maize as a cash and food crop in Zimbabwe. However, this is not to deny the close relationship between maize and other food and non-food crops in agriculture. Here the focus on maize will serve to highlight such relationships as for example, that between maize and wheat in Zimbabwe.

The 'breadbasket of southern Africa' contention

Maize is both a cash and food crop in Zimbabwe. As of 1981, Zimbabwe was largely self-sufficient in food. In fact, Zimbabwe has been cited as an example in food production and self-sufficiency. However this view has been questioned by different people for various reasons. It has been pointed out that even before independence, internal distribution of food within the country was inequitable and characterised by pockets of hunger e.g. in the Zambezi Valley. The World Bank has also indicated that Zimbabwe's performance is not particularly impressive. It is also important to recognise that productivity in large-scale commercial farms up to independence was offset by a decline in productivity in most communal areas. In Zimbabwe, there is a heavy reliance on the large-scale commercial farmers as the growers of most food and cash crops. Little is known about yields, investment and productivity in the small-scale commercial areas and communal areas. Most planning is based on the large-scale commercial farms. This is a very narrow base when one considers that in 1981, the gross agricultural production was Z$738 million, $664 million of which was contributed by commercial farmers. In 1981, exported primary and processed agricultural products earned a substantial amount of the country's foreign currency. This amounted to $417 million in 1981 or 47 per cent of total exports (excluding gold). Estimations based on the 1969 Census hold that commercial farmers number 4,700 and employ about 273,000 workers. There is a need to broaden the base from which foreign exchange in agriculture is derived. From this perspective, one can question the wisdom of using the model of 'self-sufficiency' that has such a narrow base. It is therefore necessary to encourage investment in small-scale commercial and communal area farming if the 7.5 million population growing by 3.6 per cent per annum is to be supported.

Pricing policy of maize in Zimbabwe

Pricing policy in Zimbabwe is decided by the government after consultation with the relevant organisations of farmers and the Agricultural Marketing Authority. The Ministry of Agriculture invites the above bodies to present projected costs for production, the profit margins they think necessary to encourage growing of a particular hectarage that would reach the quota necessary for delivery to the Grain Marketing Board. The Ministry of Agriculture also does its own estimates on the above and then recommends to the Cabinet the price structure arrived at after consulting the interested bodies. This process applies to all controlled grains and commodities.

In Zimbabwe, the commercial farmers are required to sell maize only through the Grain Marketing Board. This requirement does not extend to the communal area farmers, hence the difficulty in computing yields and sales to marketing and other outlets that are not formalised. There is a fragmented marketing structure in Zimbabwe and it is exacerbated by the transport and storage problems that are experienced by the communal farmers. How the pricing outside the formal marketing channels relates to that of the Grain Marketing Board, which is formalised, is little known and this information is necessary if real producer prices, especially to communal farmers, are to be computed within an overall plan for food self sufficiency.

Marketing policy for maize in Zimbabwe

In Zimbabwe, the Grain Marketing Board is the official body charged with the marketing of controlled grain such as maize. It exists within the structure of the Agricultural Marketing authority which deals with the marketing of all major crops (other than tea and sugar) and livestock products (other than poultry and pigs). The Grain Marketing Board can also sell any surpluses on the export market. Maize is graded according to quality and the sellers are then paid by cheque after all debts have been deducted. Local buyers who are approved by the Grain Marketing Board operate within the communal areas. They handle the grain brought in by communal farmers and forward it to the grain marketing depot nearest to them. They deduct their handling and transport costs and this is resented by the communal area sellers of grain since they feel they cannot pinpoint the bases for the charges.

Pricing and marketing practices on maize since independence

In 1980, the government raised the producer price for maize from $85 to $120 per tonne. This increase resulted in a big harvest since the rains were good and a lot of maize was marketed through the Grain Marketing Board by both peasant and commercial farmers. The cheap food policy which was being pursued by the government in 1981 was characterised by subsidies on staples such as beef, maize meal, milk and white bread. For peasant producers of maize, it proved more economic to sell their maize to the Grain Marketing Board and buy milled maize through retail and other outlets. This resulted in large amounts of maize being sold by peasants so that they could obtain income to buy other necessary commodities as well as maize meal at subsidised prices. This reaction to a high maize price coupled with subsidised prices for maize meal proved to be a problem when the drought started in the 1982–3 growing season. Peasants were caught by the drought without substantial grain reserves while at the same time, whatever income they had realised was quickly spent on buying maize at scarcity prices when subsidies were being reduced. Transporting maize from retail outlets also cost more than it did in normal seasons and this undercut the value of the income realised in the 1980–81 season. Internally then, the high maize price and maize meal subsidies had the effect of putting peasant farmers at risk when a bad season followed a particularly good one.

The pricing policies on maize also helped to increase the hectarage under maize, as Table 19.1 illustrates. In the 1982–3 season, the static price reduced the hectarage under maize. The 1983–4 price helped to restore the hectarage under maize to 1980–82 levels.

TABLE 19.1 The relationship between price and hectarage under maize

Price/tonne	Year	Hectarage in millions
$ 85	1979–80	1.1
$120	1980–81	1.4
$120	1981–82	1.4
$120	1982–83	1.3
$140	1983–84	1.4
$180	1984–85	n.a

Source: Ministry of Agriculture, Zimbabwe

From 1980, it was clear that the government thought the price paid to producers sufficient since there was a bumper crop. The drought necessitated the rise in the producer price on maize. However, whatever interpretations are made about hectarage, yields per hectare need to be considered. In Zimbabwe, commercial farmers' yields range from 4.5 to 5 tonnes per hectare. Communal area farmers' yields range from 0.3 to 3 tonnes per hectare. The yields per hectare reflect a number of factors in the relationship between state, commercial and communal area farmers. The first factor to consider is the distribution of land between the different categories of farmers. Coupled with that, it is necessary to consider the quality of that land and the infrastructural development that goes with it.

In Zimbabwe, the land is divided into five agro-ecological regions. Region I is suited for specialised and diversified farming. Rainfall is high and permits fruit, livestock production and forestry. Region II is suited for intensive farming of crops and livestock. Region III is a low rainfall area and is marginal for maize, tobacco and cotton. Region IV has a low rainfall and is suitable only for livestock production. Region V is not suitable for grains so ranching is the only possible activity given the lack of rainfall in the region. Given these classifications, it is necessary to examine the distribution of commercial and communal farms by agro-ecological region (see Table 19.2). This will help to highlight the distribution of land by quality and quantity between different farming groups.

TABLE 19.2 Land classification by natural region (hectares)

Natural region	Communal areas	Parks and wildlife areas	Forest areas	Small and large-scale farming areas	Totals
I	135,000	50,000	70,000	450,000	705,000
II	1,200,000	25,000	2,000	560,000	5,857,000
III	2,820,000	545,000	145,000	3,780,000	7,290,000
IV	7,340,000	2,510,000	620,000	4,300,000	14,770,000
V	4,790,000	1,840,000	70,000	3,750,000	10,450,000
Totals	16,355,000	4,970,000	907,000	16,840,000	39,072,000

Source: Natural Resources Board

Given that most communal lands are in regions IV and V, the yields per hectare for them are affected by the agro-ecological conditions which make them unsuitable for the cultivation of maize without irrigation. This implies that more investment is needed in such areas for irrigation or alternatively, that there should be more investment in those communal areas in regions I, II and III for maize growing. There seems to be some basis for that suggestion because investment into communal area farming is very low compared to the commercial areas. In the 1983/4 season, the Agricultural Finance Corporation gave loans valued at around $44 million to small scale farmers and those in communal and resettlement areas while about $58.5 million was loaned to commercial farmers. Table 19.3, which is from Kay (1972), illustrates the landholding by natural regions.

TABLE 19.3 Land tenure by natural regions

Land category	Natural region					
	I (%)	II (%)	III (%)	IV (%)	V (%)	X (%)
National and unreserved lands	16	6	12	18	23	44
Communal areas	13	21	39	50	49	48
Small-scale farming areas	–	4	4	4	2	6
Large-scale farming areas	71	69	45	28	26	2

Source: Kay (1972)

The large-scale commercial farming community was estimated at 4,400 farmers by the President of the Commercial Farming Union in 1984 (*The Herald* 24.8.84).

In terms of yields per hectare and the possibilities for increasing them in the future, the greatest potential lies in the communal areas. Compared with other countries, the commercial farmers in Zimbabwe stand favourably (see Table 19.4).

TABLE 19.4 Maize yields 1978–80 three-year averages in all cases

Country	Tonnes/hectare
USA	6.3
France	5.2
Zimbabwe	4.4
USSR	3.1
Argentina	3.1
Thailand	2.1
Mexico	1.5
Brazil	1.5
India	1.1

Sources: FAO Production Year Book and Central Statistical Office (Zimbabwe) quoted by the Commercial Farmers' Union, Zimbabwe

In order to raise the yields above present levels, it would be necessary to extend hectarage, mechanize or increase efficiency. In the communal areas hectarage has increased consistently except for the drought years. Commercial Farmers' Union data indicate that the hectarage under maize in large-scale commercial farming areas has actually declined consistently. In 1979/80, 218,300 hectares were under maize. These figures apply for labour harvested maize. The yields per hectare have been consistently above 4 tonnes except for the drought season of 1982/83. The 1983/84 yields are not yet known.

In general, the position of Zimbabwe, as of 1980, vis-à-vis other African countries still causes anxiety where overall food production is concerned (see Table 19.5). Zimbabwe's population growth rate is estimated at 3.6 per cent per annum. The increases in agricultural production of 2.6 per cent for food products and 3.8 per cent for non-food products still do not match the population growth. The drought from 1982 has tended to highlight this problem. From this perspective it is necessary to aim for increased hectarage, better yields per hectare in all farming areas as well as to improve the profit margins on all food crops and other agricultural commodities. It is also worth noting that mechanisation as a possible efficiency measure in agriculture in general and maize production in particular, is still not a possibility on a large scale in the short run. Foreign currency constraints still apply. This means that for food self-sufficiency to be assured, drastic changes in investment and improvements in marketing, technology and pricing policy are necessary. A few of these will be considered in the rest of this chapter.

The targeting of pricing incentives needs to be reconsidered. In 1980–81, the high producer price for maize encouraged the growing of maize in marginal areas such as regions IV and V. This blanket effect of maize pricing policy was harmful in the following year when the drought struck. The peasant farmers in marginal, inaccessible

TABLE 19.5 Indices of agricultural production 1980 (1969–71 = 100)

	Total agricultural production	Total food production	Agricultural production per capita	Food production per capita
Angola	55	81	45	66
Kenya	168	164	120	113
Malawi	134	115	98	93
Mozambique	77	79	61	65
South Africa	126	128	97	99
Tanzania	128	141	95	109
Zambia	114	112	82	86
Zimbabwe	122	101	87	72

Source: World Indices of Agricultural and Food Production (1981) USDA – ERS, Statistical (Bulletin)

areas had to be fed by the state and such drought relief was costly. This may happen again in the 1984/85 growing season, especially if there is another drought. It does not augur well for food self-sufficiency in the long run. The drought may actually have nudged Zimbabwe into a food-deficit situation from which it will be difficult to withdraw. This is particularly important where wheat is concerned since it is increasingly important for bread. The Commercial Farmers' Union anticipates that demand for wheat products will outstrip the rate for maize. The reason for declining production of wheat was identified by the Commercial Farmers' Union as the lack of water due to droughts and unsatisfactory prices. Given the security problems in Mozambique and the less than cordial relationship with South Africa, self-sufficiency in wheat is necessary. Transport of imports through Mozambique and South Africa has proved costly in the past so it is imperative that wheat production is stimulated. Bread and food riots have resulted from bread and food shortages in parts of the world and Zimbabwe would do well to avoid this situation.

There is need for more research into maize varieties suitable for marginal areas in region III. The research policy for drought tolerant maize needs to be complemented with a price that is competitive on the market relative to other maize grown in regions I and II. The drought illustrates the need for appropriate maize varieties for particular regions because a lot of grain depots were not utilised. There was no maize coming out of some marginal regions. Such underutilised infrastructure is costly to the government especially in view of the lack of alternative water sources.

Closely linked to the last point is the need to relate maize research policy and pricing to research policy and pricing of other grains that are drought tolerant. These grains are sorghum and millet. Very little is written about millet despite its importance as a food crop for black rural Zimbabweans. Since September 1984 millet has become a controlled crop and it is still not clear how the relationship of millet and sorghum to other crops will develop. However, there is little doubt that the drought helped to precipitate realisation of their importance in the food self-sufficiency programme for Zimbabwe. If pricing and marketing policies for millet and sorghum are made favourable and focused relative to maize, then their production in less favoured rainfall areas may alleviate the food deficit in the country.

In terms of storage, millet stores very well, in comparison with maize. This is particularly important for communal area farmers who do not have enough capital to invest in growing and storage technologies. Millet requires less labour when it has been planted although it is more labour intensive when it comes to harvesting. Should other droughts eventuate, millet may become important given the high cost of importing maize and wheat.

Where exports of grain are concerned, Zimbabwe has featured in maize exports. The export of maize also needs to be discussed within the context of the pricing policy for maize. Before independence, maize was exported to neighbouring countries by road or rail. Zaire and Zambia have bought maize from Zimbabwe for the last few years. However, the export of maize was brought into question in the season of 1982–3 and 1983–4. Maize exports proved to be uneconomic because of high bulk and low prices in world markets. For example, in 1981–2 maize was exported at $90 per tonne when farmers had been paid $120 per tonne. Where maize has been exported under aid agreements or the World Food Programme, Zimbabwe has exported at a loss because it is a high cost producer. Only when bilateral negotiations can assure profitable prices is it useful to export maize.

The export of maize after a bumper harvest needs careful consideration of levels of food security that are viable. The drought followed a good season and caught Zimbabwe unprepared. On the one hand, after a bumper crop, it was quite costly to store the 2.1 million tonnes of maize. Administration of storage absorbed a lot of staff and fumigation services and strained the transport system within Zimbabwe and in neighbouring countries. On the other hand exporting at world prices would not have been profitable. There is also the political dimension to the issue since front-line states would not look very kindly on Zimbabwe's insistence on realistic prices geared to her domestic costs for producing maize. As it turned out, grain was given in aid to key countries such as Tanzania. Thus the calculation of costs and benefits went beyond the purely and obviously 'economic' levels. Zimbabwe gained in that she had replaced South Africa as a source of maize in SADCC. However, South Africa retaliated by offering easier terms of payment for her maize. Food politics thus continues to be of great importance in southern Africa specifically.

During the drought years, the security level was eroded partly because of export obligations that had been incurred through bilateral contracts. Within southern Africa, Zimbabwe felt that she had to maintain her reputation as a reliable and honest supplier of maize. For this reason, Zimbabwe had to export maize and to import more from sources as diverse as Argentina, the USA, Indonesia, Malawi and Taiwan. Some of the maize imported was yellow and unpopular with some sectors of the population. The cost of importing this maize ranged from $250 to $300 per tonne. It was paid for in foreign currency. It presented problems in transportation since both South Africa and Mozambique were also importing food and thus needing their own transport infrastructure. Within Zimbabwe, millers found that the harder imported flint bounced out of the mills and the dent got caught within the mills. Transportation and distribution to all parts of the country was also costly and problematic since it had not been anticipated.

The drought bill was probably upward of $500 million if loss of exports is reckoned. However, there are some areas of planning and decision-making whose importance has been brought to the fore. The level of self-sufficiency and security has to be decided. As has been stated, the higher this level, the costlier it is when it comes to food. Government then has to decide what level of security and self-sufficiency it is willing to pay for.

Planning also took place on the assumption that, climatically, every year is a normal one for food growing. This assumption proved to be erroneous and costly since the Grain Marketing Board was not warned quickly enough and could not take a quick decision on importation of food from the world market at reasonable prices. The important lesson for Zimbabwe is that pricing policy is important so that the desired level of self-sufficiency is reached without having too big a surplus to export or store. It is equally necessary to pitch the price at the right level, so that the volume of grain produced does not necessitate huge storage capacities or export as happened in 1980–81. Too high a producer price can militate against the production of other necessary crops as happened to wheat in 1980–81.

Farmers also get affected by previous negative experiences. After being caught without adequate grain reserves for themselves or their labour during the drought, it is probable that in 1983–4 and 1984–5, farmers retained more grain than they normally would for themselves. This can lead to grain losses, especially of maize, since the storage technology for communal area farmers may not be very advanced. This is a loss to the farmers themselves and to the Grain Marketing Board which may have imported more grain than it needed.

On the investment front, the drought helped to indicate and pinpoint problems in allocating consumption-oriented, as opposed to productive, investment in agriculture and other sectors of the economy. Some economists feel that government policy on development is too service sector and consumption-oriented. They feel that investment in the productive sectors of the economy is too thin to be useful on a long-term basis. The example that is cited often is that of the government's water policy, particularly during the drought. There has been a lot of emphasis on the provision of drinking water without emphasis on water for irrigation and other agricultural purposes. In the commercial farming areas, the Farm Irrigation Fund has not been activated. The Agricultural Finance Corporation has also given seasonal loans but long-term investment is still not considered important enough. Water is a very critical component for agriculture but the level of investment in it remains low compared to short-term investment in drinking water and other consumption oriented services in agriculture. Irrigation and other water related investment could stimulate the growing of crops such as wheat especially when the price is competitive. It is quite possible that the growing of wheat and other winter crops could also institute a new demand structure in the rural areas. Vegetables, wheat and maize could be a basis for a vibrant and constant flow of income for rural people throughout the year if water is available all year round. A service industry could spring up around such agricultural production. Within this kind of situation, it would be necessary for the Ministry of Agriculture to be more involved in the planning of investment in agriculture. This step would go some way towards ensuring that decisions concerning productivity, investment and development in agriculture would be in harmony with the other policies and activities currently administered by the Ministry of Agriculture.

This chapter has briefly outlined the socio-political and economic context within which Zimbabwe's food policy can be viewed. There has been an emphasis on maize as a food and cash crop for different categories of farmers. Marketing and pricing policies for maize have been outlined. The practices in marketing and pricing maize after independence and during the drought that started in 1982 have also been examined. Some effects of these policies such as food deficits that necessitated food imports have been indicated. Zimbabwe is in a precarious position where food self-sufficiency is concerned. Possible areas for examination with respect to pricing, marketing and investment were indicated. It will also be necessary to concentrate on those areas of agricultural production that do not prove too costly in the long term. General food security requires more planning and attention to the relationships of crops, prices and the people in agriculture. If Zimbabwe is to fulfil her role of co-ordinating food security within SADCC, she will have to have managed and co-ordinated her national food security first. Short of this, food security and self-sufficiency for southern Africa in general, and Zimbabwe in particular will by default, become the prerogative of South Africa and her allies on their own terms.

NOTE

1. I am indebted to the following people: Professor Chavunduka, for pointing out sources of data in general and Tables 2, 3 and 5; Mrs Ross in the Agricultural Marketing Authority for general background information on the role of the AMR in maize pricing and marketing; Mr Chinyadza in the Zimbabwe National Chamber of Commerce for his thoughts on maize policy and pricing; Mr Fulks in the Commercial Farmers' Union for his ideas on maize pricing policy in general; and Mr Masanzu in the Ministry of Agriculture for his ideas on maize exports. Other sources for this chapter are: FAO (1984b), Commercial Farmers' Union (1984) and Gaidzanwa (1981).

20

Drought and drought relief in southern Zimbabwe

Roger Leys

Introduction

In Zimbabwe, as throughout southern Africa, the summer rains failed in 1981–2: and failed again in the two subsequent years. One consequence of the drought for some of the rural African population was hunger, and on occasion and specific places, deaths from starvation.

This chapter is about the drought as it affected the rural population. The subject is, I think, of some relevance to many parts of Africa which, too, have suffered prolonged drought. Whether the subject is of more than historical interest to Zimbabwe is more open to question. For, in late April 1984 parts of the country experienced quite heavy rainfall. The harvest of marketed maize – the staple food of Zimbabwe – was considerable (one million tons according to one estimate). The Minister of Agriculture described this harvest as a 'miracle' and particularly praised the African peasant farmers who produced one-third of this marketed crop. Describing this performance as an 'African success story' at least one observer contrasted this performance to the disaster of agricultural production almost everywhere else in Africa (Frankel 1984) and the miracle of 1984 looks like being repeated in 1985.

So perhaps the 1982–4 drought is of only historical interest. But not only do droughts recur, they can also have long-term effects. In particular, they can both be caused by, and result in, increased inequality in the distribution of resources. For not only is it quite possible for certain groups to live in plenty under conditions of drought, it is also possible for people to starve under conditions of plenty. Indeed, the 'miracle' of the performance of African peasant farmers in 1984 – like the 'miracle' of white farmer agricultural output and yields per hectare – might disguise such increased socio-economic differentiation (partly as a result of the drought) that the lot of certain groups of the rural population has deteriorated. And there is ample precedent for this in the colonial history of Zimbabwe.

This chapter seeks to examine some of the effects of the drought by a detailed examination of four villages within the southern province of Masvingo (formerly called Fort Victoria). My intention is to indicate how certain families became increasingly marginalised as a result of the drought, and how other families – and in particular a kind of 'rural salariat' – tended to consolidate their position. I would argue that the drought exacerbated processes of social, economic and political differentiation whose roots lie deep in the colonial past. But these processes are not a once-and-for-all product of the development of capitalism and of migrant-labour-proletarianisation in the colonial economy. New patterns of differentiation are emerging in post-colonial Zimbabwe.

This study cannot prove these contentions since it is extremely limited in empirical and historical scope. It is further limited by the methodology involved in studying rural villages by means of household surveys. But I hope it suggests some paths for further research.

In a subsequent paper I intend to indicate some of the links between the 'rural salariat' and the state by relating these villages to district, provincial and national politics in Zimbabwe. For even the use of the term 'rural salariat' raises the spectre of a kind of class analysis whose contours and trajectory can only be traced by relating the village to the state.

Differentiation

Drought and differentiation

Given the extreme inequalities of Zimbabwean society, that the drought has had differential effects is not surprising. For example, in the areas of commercial farming the failure of the rains had less marked effects than it did in the African Reserves (communal areas) partly because much of the commercial farming areas have access to irrigation. But in the African Reserves where irrigation is almost non-existent and lowland areas with poor fertility and high population density predominate, these effects were very marked.

It would be incorrect to assume that these differential effects were not linked. Indeed a whole body of critical studies has established the primary linkage between capitalist development in the commercial farming areas and the underdevelopment and impoverishment of the African Reserves.[1] In summary outline, this linkage took the form of marketed crop production in the commercial farming areas and the provision of cheap labour for this production by the adult population of the African Reserves. This primary linkage is now so well established – and, since independence, so politically opportune – that it is part of the conventional wisdom of development planning in Zimbabwe.

But what is not so well established is the linkage between the development of capitalist production and the patterns of inequality in the communal areas. Indeed, within 'reformist' historiography, this subject has been comparatively neglected. Those who established the primary linkage tended to assume that, once African peasant producers had been forcibly precluded from competition with European farmers, then the peasant families subsided into the mass of migrant-worker families.

This assumption is misleading – and critically so for the study of the effects of drought on the population of the communal areas. For this study attempts to show that the pattern of access to resources, and in drought conditions specifically to resources that can command food – principally cash income and cattle – is unequal. Furthermore the pattern of differential access is regular and from the study a series of 'clusters' of such access to resources emerges.

The differential access of food-commanding resources must be conceived in a situation of drought combined with food availability. For unlike Mozambique – where the effects of banditry combined with the breakdown of the food distribution system led to the complete absence of foodstuffs in parts of central Mozambique and, in 1983, to widespread starvation – there was no shortage of available food in the villages under study. The distribution system provided relatively well-stocked stores throughout the African reserves. But it is perfectly possible for people to starve while food is available.

Hence the starting point for the conceptualisation of drought is the entitlement to food, not its availability. For 'starvation is the characteristic of some people not *having* enough food to eat. It is not the characteristic of their *being* not enough food to eat' (Sen 1981: 1). In other words, a study of the effects of drought is a study of the entitlement to food. In a wider sense, it is a study of the pattern of socio-economic differentiation in which the local unit must be linked to the wider pattern of differentiation in the political economy of Zimbabwe as a whole.

This starting point inevitably raises a number of further conceptual issues which can only be touched upon here. The absence of rain 'precipitates' a drought. But neither the ecological nor the social, economic and political causes and effects of a drought can be measured by the rate of precipitation. Such analysis requires detailed historical study in which the absence of rainfall is linked to the pattern of resource distribution and to state response to drought. And this shifting pattern of resource distribution must be examined locally, nationally and internationally. In this sense, a drought is a political phenomenon.

Such a detailed historical study cannot be provided here. However, we can illustrate the contours of the problem by reference to certain historical records of the district in which three of the villages surveyed are located.

Cattle and colonial policy in the Chibi District

Phimister has a very illuminating monograph on the underdevelopment of peasant agriculture in the province (Phimister 1977). The primary focus of his study is on the rise and later collapse of peasant commodity production in grain in the early years of this century. As a factor in undermining peasant market production for rapidly expanding urban domestic markets, Phimister emphasises the importance of the opening of the railway linking the town of Gwelo with the capital, Harare (then Salisbury). This railway link had the effect of making it almost impossible for local producers in the Victoria region to compete with the commercial farms in the Salisbury and Charter districts for the expanding market of the Selukwe mines near Gwelo. Phimister notes, however, that cattle sales were not so affected by this development.

In the interwar period, Chibi District was more heavily involved in cattle as a market commodity than in grain. Some evidence, though far from conclusive, indicates that it was deliberate colonial policy to promote cattle sales at the expense of grain production (both as subsistence and as market production). Indeed, a major theme in the correspondence of the Native Commissioner for Chibi in this period is a series of efforts to persuade Africans to sell cattle: efforts were thinly disguised within a general Native Administration Department policy of promoting destocking.

The policy of successive Chibi Commissioners was to encourage Africans to sell their cattle to resident white traders, to visiting traders from Fort Victoria and to white settlers. Legally, all traders had to have the permission of the Commissioner to enter and do business in the Reserve; though there is no documented evidence in this period of a request being refused. But the Commissioners did insist that cattle purchases were paid for on the spot and in cash.

Clearly, an overriding interest of the Commissioner was in cattle sales as a source of taxation revenue. For one of the forms of resistance to colonial policy that van Onselen has so vividly described (1976) was to accumulate tax arrears on the host of tax impositions to which adult Africans were subject. In this correspondence, the connection between tax revenue and cattle sales is a recurring theme:

[Since] I anticipate difficulties in collecting revenue this year, to impress upon cattle owners that unless they have other means of obtaining money to meet their obligations, of the necessity of accepting reasonable offers for the cattle they have for sale. (National Archives 1924)

This eagerness to raise revenues for the state was understandable, given the directives to which the local Commissioner was subject. His alternative was to imprison defaulters and this had to be paid for out of his local budget. Sometimes, the dilemma led him to bend the rules, particularly on compulsory cattle dipping:

Europeans are still buying heavily from Natives and I am allowing these cattle . . . to leave the district without saying anything about payment of dipping fees. In the ordinary course this might appear to be doubtful policy but, with the urgent necessity of decreasing the number of native-owned cattle in the district, the money and food shortage which obtains, the view I have taken appears to be the best one. (National Archives 1933)

But it was not only tax revenue that prompted cattle sales. Another factor was the relationship between cattle sales and white settlement in the province. Among the host of requests to enter the reserve and buy cattle, one letter states the position vividly:

I want to ask if you will allow me permission to buy about thirty or forty head of cattle in Chibi District. Then I want to leave them with the natives until I collect them, within a few weeks, then I will brand them, the brand will read NVZ. . . . I am getting a farm on the Lundi river on the Shabanie Mashaba road and I want to buy the cattle for the farm, and I am not buying to sell again for profits. (National Archives 1934)

The general picture of Chibi in the interwar years – and it is a tentative picture not based on exhaustive research – is not one of intensive proletarianisation endemic in all strata of the society as Arrighi's analysis of the proletarianisation of the African peasantry seems to suggest. Rather, important groups of this peasantry manage to resist state pressure to drive them into the labour market, by selling cattle. The evidence further suggests that cattle were plentiful and that measures to enforce destocking provided a thin ideological justification for the revenue, profits and cattle that could be culled from the peasantry.

But clearly, too, these pressures on African society enormously strained the socio economic fabric. Overgrazing and tax demands exacerbated and strained the ecological balance between population and food entitlement. Chibi, on the edge of the low veld, has always been subject to low and intermittent rainfall. There are constant references in official correspondence to food shortages and the dangers of famine.

To my knowledge, the history of Chibi in the colonial period is not yet written. It would be fascinating to trace the history of drought and underdevelopment more scientifically, not least because Chibi was constantly in the news during the 1982–4 drought as one of the most hard-hit districts.

Differentiation: some analytical problems

The problems of conceptualisation and implementation of a study of patterns of inequality at the village level are legion. But before outlining some of these, let me state the central thesis which is that access to cash income, primarily derived from migrant labour, is the primary criterion of rural inequality within this type of migrant labour economy.

The primary conceptual problem is the absence of a set of adequate theoretical tools. The dominant theoretical paradigm in the analysis of the historical role played by the African reserves in the development of capitalism is the dependency school. But, put simply, the dependency school lacks the conceptual tools for the analysis of rural differentiation. This problem is exacerbated in southern African studies since the dependency school has tended to treat the effects of capitalist development on the African rural areas as essentially homogeneous. Once African peasant producers have been forcibly excluded from market competition with white settlers, then African peasant farmers subside into the mass of semi-proletarianised migrant worker households in a process of self-exacerbating and self-sustaining underdevelopment. Over time, the African reserves become an undifferentiated, marginalised mass. Clearly, such a theoretical perspective downplays the importance of patterns of differentiation within the African reserves. If inequality does exist, it is unimportant since such inequalities are 'overdetermined' by those that exist between the African reserves and the capitalist sectors of the economy.

Within the broader analysis of political economy, this problem relates to another problem which is that the mode of analysis for the analysis of differentiation within the peasantry – inspired by classical peasant studies – is relatively useless for the analysis of migrant labour economies. At the micro-level, classical analysis distinguishes between 'rich', 'middle' and 'poor' peasant households on the basis of criteria that distinguish between different patterns of labour utilisation in household production. Schematically, 'rich peasants' hire non-household labour, 'middle peasants' use exclusively household labour and 'poor peasants' hire out family labour.

Such a methodology is relatively impotent in the context of migrant labour economies and no use for the study of such economies in conditions of drought. First because, with few exceptions, in migrant labour economies most households hire out family labour to the wider economy (to which they are functionally related) and there is relatively little interchange of labour between households at the village level. Secondly, and particularly in conditions of prolonged drought, there is no obvious locus of household production for most families. There is simply no locus of production of subsistence and market crops within which the pattern of labour exchange can be used as a method of grasping the structural patterns of differentiation. Hence the terms of analysis obscure and confuse rather than clarify the patterns of differential access to resources we seek to expose. For, if the households most engaged in selling labour to the wider economy – at the highest rate of return and with the most permanent relationship to the labour market – if such households have the greatest access to resources and are the least susceptible to drought, then we turn the basic criteria for differentiation on their head. The 'poor peasants' become the 'rich peasants' and the 'rich peasants' become the 'poor peasants'.

In addition to the theoretical problems, there are also more strictly methodological ones concerning the household survey method used in this study. One concerns the unit of analysis – the household. It is obvious that household survey practice runs the risk of being blind to a variety of transactions *between* households.

Conceptually, such analysis posits a kind of nuclear family as the unit of production, distribution and exchange. Such a conception is at variance with a whole tradition of anthropological enquiry, within and without the broad rubric of political economy. The justification for the use of the household as the unit of analysis as offered here can only be partial. It is in line with the whole tradition of peasant studies which has made not inconsiderable inroads into the historiography of southern Africa. And this, in turn, reflects the historical experience of colonialism and underdevelopment in southern Africa: an experience which led to the rise and fall of African peasantries linked to a wider nation-state and world market.

A second type of justification is of a more practical kind. It reflects on and makes use of the political experience of colonial Zimbabwe in which the household was used by the colonial administration as a unit of measurement, exaction and control. For example, since the Land Husbandry Act of 1951, land allocations are recorded only to married African men. Another type of control, quite important in the predominantly cattle culture of these districts, was that records of cattle dipping only listed male ownership. But despite these justifications, there are valid objections to the use of household survey methods, though attempts were made to corroborate recorded information by interview.

Yet another qualification on the survey method concerns the relation between households 'domiciled' in the village, and domiciled elsewhere. The essence of the problem is that not all families formally registered as living in a village actually do live there. Furthermore, it is often the wealthier families – particularly in the cluster of the rural salariat – who can command the resources to live elsewhere. Hence some of the wealthier families may have neither cattle nor farming equipment in the village where they are formally registered. And the drought and the economic crisis have greatly exacerbated the drift out of the villages. Time and again, we were told that this particular family had moved away and might, or might not, return when the rains fell.

Four village studies

Summary findings

The results of the household surveys will be examined in the next sub-section and a tabulation of some findings is provided in an appendix. Here it will be useful to summarise the results. Measured in terms of household income and cattleholdings, four clear clusters emerge from the data.

The first cluster consists of those households in which the male breadwinner (usually but not always the head of the household) receives a regular monthly salary from a job requiring some education in a post which carries some security of tenure and other benefits such as pension rights. The core of the group consists of schoolteachers, but it also includes other civil servants of central provincial and district government plus the occasional clerical worker in the private and parastatal sectors. Measured in terms of cash income, this cluster – a kind of 'rural salariat' – is quite distinct and a considerable gap separates their income from other households. They also rate higher scores as regards cattleholdings and agricultural equipment.

The second cluster consists of households which contain at least one migrant worker – e.g. mineworkers, plantation workers on low veld sugar estates, and soldiers in the national army. While some of these migrants have been working many years for the same employer, they have far less job security than the first cluster. Rates of pay, pensions and fringe benefits tend to be also lower.

The third cluster consists of households without formal-sector employment. It is a much more heterogeneous group. It includes both families in which the breadwinner has become unemployed – often as a direct result of the economic crisis – and those who, for a host of reasons, are not migrant workers. Within this sub-category are households which – measured in terms of cattleholdings and farming equipment – are among the richest families in their villages. They constitute, for want of a better word, a kind of 'peasantariat'. Many of these are elderly and, in the four villages surveyed, few had ever held a formal-sector job. A variety of informal jobs are held by adults in this cluster, e.g. builders, beer brewers, traditional doctors.

The fourth cluster is, in social composition, distinctly less heterogeneous. It consists of households of widows plus separated, abandoned and divorced mothers. Many of these are in a state of destitution since they have lost the property and cash accumulated by the household to the family of the children's father (Mpofu 1982). Without cattle or cash income, eking out survival on such informal sector jobs as brewing beer and prostitution these households are closest to total destitution. And, since the twin impact of the drought and the economic crisis has severely damaged those redistributive systems in traditional culture, e.g. traditional forms of food-sharing and giving credit, which previously provided such households with a minimum of subsistence, they constitute the poorest of the rural poor.

Wealth and poverty in four villages

This sub-section will report the survey results for each village in some detail. First some basic data will be presented for each village in aggregate and summary form. Then for each village the clusters will be delineated and a range of general issues and specific features – mostly recorded from interviews – will be discussed.

Village A

Village A is a Business Community (a small township) situated some two kilometres from a Catholic Mission. The township is situated on a graded road and is an important bus stop on the road to the district capital, Chibi. However, none of the four stores in the township are owned by local people. The township has 52 households with a total population of 305, giving an average household size of 5.9.

In all, 21 adults had jobs in the formal sector: an average of 0.4 per household. Of those with such jobs: 7 were mineworkers, 3 worked at the Catholic Mission and 5 were clerks or schoolteachers. Of those with jobs in the informal sector, two were petty traders and two were bricklayers. The total cattleherd of the village was 191, making an average of 3.7 per household. Seventy-five head of cattle, i.e. 28 per cent of the total herd, had died in the last 12 months (mostly from the drought but also from other causes).

The total allocated land area of the village was approximately 308 acres, i.e. an average of 5.9 acres per household. In all four villages surveyed, shortage of land was not regarded as an acute problem and the incidence of landless households was very low. In interviews with kraalheads and village chairmen the problem was regarded as minor for two reasons. Firstly that after two years of drought, many families had effectively abandoned their land which could be used by others. Secondly, that while it was increasingly a problem to find unallocated land for young married men who had a legal entitlement to land, the problem was not yet acute.

No crops had been harvested in Village A in the last 12 months (apart from the vegetables grown in a communal, fenced vegetable garden watered from the nearby dam constructed by the Mission). Forty-one households (78 per cent) owned a plough and 19 households owned a scotch cart (36 per cent). The total disposable cash income of all households in Village A was 3,285 Zimbabwean dollars, making an average of 64 per household. Thirty-two households were receiving government drought relief. Under the government drought relief programme, all households earning less than the minimum wage (then Z$105) were entitled to 20 kilos per month per person of unmilled maize. In addition, the local Catholic Mission ran its own drought relief programme whereby each nearby village in turn chose two destitute families to send an adult to work on a construction project for one week in return for a 90 kg. bag of milled maize.

VILLAGE A: THE CLUSTERS

In Village A, five households can be identified as belonging to the cluster of the 'rural salariat' as defined in the introductory section. Of these five households, three household heads were primary school teachers employed locally and two were migrant workers – office employees in Hwankie and Harare (one, according to other villagers, had effectively abandoned his wife and three children although he pays school fees for one son). All three primary schoolteachers owned farming assets: all had scotch carts, two had planters and all were ploughing their land in the hope that the rains would come.

The second cluster, the 'employed families' who are not part of the rural salariat, were mostly families of mineworkers who worked at Shabane and travelled home frequently. The Mission provided jobs for three families, one of which, with Mission support, had bought a mill and was fairly prosperous – though charging only 30 cents for milling 20 kgs of maize – a price well below average.

The third cluster, the unemployed, was by far the biggest (22 families) and extremely heterogeneous. Many of these households received some cash from relatives – particularly for school fees and payments. One elderly man, who had only once held a formal sector job (as a sugarcane cutter in the 1960s) was supported by a son working as headmaster in a secondary school. Another, unemployed with three wives and supported by a son who worked at Mashaba, had the largest single herd of cattle (12) in the village (and, perhaps because he had three wives and 10 children to help with the cattle) none of his cattle had died in the drought.

The fourth cluster, widows and their families, numbered 11 families, almost all of whom had virtually no cash income at all. All received government drought relief, when available, and several who had young children received an additional monthly kilo of dried peas under a supplementary feeding programme run by the local Mission.

Village B
Village B is situated some four kilometres northwest of the same Catholic Mission as Village A in the Nyaningwe district of the Masvingo Province. The district straddles the descent from the middle veld (3–4,000 feet) to the low veld in the south. The district has mostly sandy soils of low fertility and has a mean average rainfall of under 600 millimetres a year. Suitable, at best, to extensive dryland farming, the district has, historically, been a cattle culture which, right until the Second World War exported large numbers of cattle (and many of the commercial farms in the province were originally stocked by purchases of cattle in this 'Native Reserve'). Subject to an intensive process of proletarianisation and underdevelopment since early colonial times, the district is today massively overcrowded with a population pressure varying from 'desperate' to 'extreme'.

Village B has 36 households with a total population of 216, giving an average household size of six. In all, 24 adults held jobs in the formal sector, i.e. an average of 0.67 per household. Of those with jobs, eight were mineworkers, five worked in the sugar estates of the low veld, five were soldiers in the national army and one was a clerk at the nearby Mission secondary school. Of those with jobs in the informal sector, two were bricklayers, two herded cattle and two women worked at a nearby foreign-aid-funded jersey knitting project.

The total cattle of the village numbered 118, i.e. an average of 3.3 per household. Sixty-two head of cattle had died in the last twelve months, i.e. 34 per cent of the total herd. The total allocated acreage of the village was 258 acres, i.e. an average of 7.8 acres per household. No crops had been harvested in the last twelve months and there was no vegetable garden since all water had to be fetched from the river bed some 6 kilometres away. The land resembles a desert and, at the time the survey was conducted ,there was hardly a blade of grass to be seen. The surviving cattle lived off the leaves of small trees.

While 27 households (75 per cent) owned a plough, only 8 households (22.5 per cent) owned a scotch cart. The total cash income of the village for September 1983 was 1,982 Zimbabwe dollars, making an average of $64 per household. Twenty-three households (64 per cent) were on drought relief.

VILLAGE B: THE CLUSTERS

In Village B, only two households are identified as belonging to the 'rural salariat'. One is headed by a school clerk and the other by a relatively uneducated sugarcane cutter who had worked 15 years at the Triangle Sugar Estate and is now a supervisor with a pension entitlement.

The majority of families in the second cluster, the unskilled unemployed, have a male breadwinner and, through interviews, appear to remit an unusually high percentage of their earnings to their families in the village. A relatively high proportion were soldiers in the national army. As with all the villages described in this survey, the influence of the years of guerrilla struggle (1976–9) is very marked. Here the struggle between the colonial security forces and the armed forces of the Zimbabwe African National Liberation Army (ZANLA) was long and intense. Many of the young men and women had worked as messengers for the ZANLA forces and some had been sent via Mozambique for military training in Tanzania. Those who returned before the ceasefire had been recruited into the army.

The boundary between the cluster of the employed and the unemployed is less distinct in Village B than Village A. For example, by far the largest herd of cattle (25) is owned by a family where the head of the household is unemployed. Typical too is that the elected village chairman of ZANU is also one of the unemployed. From many conversations we learnt that there was a definite prejudice against the election of both members of the rural salariat and of widows (and women generally) to the post of village chairman. In practice, most village chairmen are chosen from among unemployed men since they permanently reside in the village and are on hand to settle disputes and to officiate at the meetings of the village committee, the Youth League and the Women's League.

Only four families in Village B are identified as part of the fourth cluster, the widows. None of these had elected to transfer back to their home villages after the death of their husbands. There was no evidence of prostitution in Village B.

Village C

Village C is situated just to the west of the main road linking Chiredzi in the south to the district capital of Zaka. The district of Zaka, which is also within the Masvingo Province, lies some 100 kilometres due east of Nyaningwe. Zaka District, like Nyaningwe, straddles the middle and low veld. With sandy soils but a somewhat higher mean annual rainfall Zaka is classified as ecologically suitable for semi-intensive farming (natural regions three and four). With a slightly lower population density and, proportionately, a lower ratio of land alienated to commercial (European) farming, the Zaka District was also subjected to massive underdevelopment and proletarianisation. The effects of the two-year drought – 1981–3 – have not been quite as drastic in Zaka as in Nyaningwe. According to AGRITEX figures of the Ministry of Agriculture, some 10 per cent of the total cattle herd in the district had died in the previous twelve months (this compares with a district average for the Nyaningwe District of slightly over 30 per cent.

Village C consists of 44 households with a total population of 256, giving an average household size of 5.8. In all, 22 adults held jobs in the formal sector, i.e. an average of

0.5 per household. Of those with jobs, four were teachers and clerical officers, three worked in the low veld sugar estates, four were factory workers in Harare and two were soldiers in the national army. Of those with 'informal' sector jobs, two made and sold sleeping mats and one was a Nganga (traditional doctor).

The total herd was 121 cattle (an average of 2.7 per household). Fifty-six head of cattle had died in the drought – 32 per cent of the total herd. The total allocated acreage was 253 acres, i.e. an average of 5.7 per household. Twenty-five households (57 per cent) owned a plough and three households a scotch cart (9 per cent). The total cash income of the village was $930, an average of $27 per household. Thirty households (68 per cent) were on drought relief.

VILLAGE C: THE CLUSTERS

In Village C, four families are identified as being part of the rural salariat. Of these, two were schoolteachers and two (brothers) held senior administrative posts – one with a mining company and the other with central government. These last two seemed to have abandoned the village as a base for their economic activities. Neither had land, cattle nor farming equipment.

Relatively few families could be identified as part of the second cluster, the employed (in all ten families), and it was clear that several of these families were 'straddling' their home villages and the towns where the men worked. For example, two brothers are employed, together with their wives, in a tailoring factory in Harare. While formally registered with the kraalhead with land allotments, neither household had cattle nor the wherewithal to farm.

Within the cluster of the unemployed families, the role of the 'peasantariat' was marked. Many of the men had not worked for 10 to 15 years and were not actively seeking employment. The two men renowned as the best farmers in the village, one a master-farmer, both belonged to this cluster. The former master-farmer, who owned 25 head of cattle and employed two boys to herd them, was regarded as the richest man in the village – this despite the fact that he had no current source of cash income. The other two men with high status, though formally unemployed, were the sub-chief (of in all fourteen villages) and a Nganga.

In village C, the relative destitution of the widows was very marked. One old widow, whose husband had been a master farmer was, at the time of the survey, preparing to plant her maize. She had a hoe – but no cattle or plough – and was hacking small holes in the baked earth for each seed individually.

The pattern of life and economic activity in Village C was heavily influenced by the nearby primary (and attached rural secondary) school and by the adjacent townships. The township consisted of seven stores – two of which had grinding mills. One of the stores (owned by the former master-farmer described above as the richest man in the village) had gone out of business. All the other stores, with one exception, were owned by schoolteachers and managed by their wives or by close relatives. The one store not owned by a teacher was owned by a local building contractor and entrepreneur. He told us that since business was so bad and those families who had cash preferred to trade in the much larger township – a local, designated 'Growth Point' and prospective site of the district capital – some three kilometres away, he was now selling his bottlestore to a local teacher. One primary school teacher was the owner of a ten-year-old tractor which was contract-ploughing to local villagers for about $20 an acre.

The interrelationship between school and township was very marked. All of the primary schoolteachers were engaged in one or other form of urban trade. One teacher commented that he looked forward to the start of school on Monday mornings as the weekend's trading activities exhausted him. However, neither of the teachers resident in Village C worked at the adjacent school nor owned property nearby.

Village D

Village D borders on Village B – some six kilometres northwest of the same Mission. Village B consists of 39 households with a total population of 242 – i.e. an average household size of 6.2. Twenty-one adults held jobs in the formal sector – an average of 0.54 per household. Seven of these were mineworkers, four worked on the sugar estates, two were soldiers and one was a clerk. The total cattleherd was 62 – an average of 0.54 per household. Fifty-five head of cattle had died in the last twelve months, i.e. 47 per cent of the total herd.

The total allocated acreage of the village was 342 acres – an average of 8.8 per household. Twenty-nine households owned a plough and five households owned a scotch cart (13 per cent). The total cash income for the village for the month was $2,126, an average of $57 per household. Twenty-one families (54 per cent) were on drought relief.

VILLAGE D: THE CLUSTERS

Village D largely repeats the pattern of clusters we have already described. It is, however, different in two interesting aspects. One is that the village is a kind of 'satellite village' which was originally part of Village B. Secondly, the pattern of cluster-differentiation is relatively weaker.

The rural salariat is hardly represented – one family – and there is only one widow in the village. The boundaries between cluster two (the unskilled employed) and cluster three (the unemployed) are more blurred. The migrant labour force and the peasantariat blend and merge into each other.

The ZANU Village chairman is, here, also the local kraalhead. This phenomenon – far from unique – indicates a certain continuity between colonial and post-colonial political authority. It was explained to us in Village D that, in the final years of the War and the first years of independence, it had been customary to separate the posts of village headman (kraalhead – responsible to the sub-chief and, ultimately, the Native Administration, for public order, tax collection etc.) from the post of the chairman of ZANU. At the time, it was argued that the headman, whatever role he personally played in the struggle between ZANLA and the security forces, was too identified with the colonial administration to serve as an adequate spokesman of the aspirations of the villagers. However, although local taxes and licence fees were largely abolished after independence, the role of the village headman continued – particularly his functions of allocating land, ensuring that conservation measures were observed (e.g. not ploughing up the banks of streams and dongas) etc. This continuity of function made the separation of powers somewhat bureaucratic and likely to cause friction. On the important function of land allocation, for example, if the party chairman took over this job he had to rely on the kraalhead who had both the written records of entitlement and the memory of the process and the problems to which it gave rise). This was an explanation frequently advanced to explain the overlap of state and party posts at the village level.

Drought relief in southern Zimbabwe

Introduction

In the first section I argued that neither the phenomenon of drought nor the interplay between drought and rural differentiation can be analysed without examining the historical framework of drought. And, in discussing cattle and colonial policy, I suggested that state policy to promote cattle sales within a predominantly cattle culture had a connection – though an indirect one – to food availability.

The same is true, *pari passu*, of state response to drought. For just as state policies can either ameliorate or exacerbate a drought or famine, so the pattern of differential access to food-commanding resources – the pattern of food entitlements – is affected by state policies towards drought.

One such factor in post-independence state policy in Zimbabwe – the government drought relief programme – will be briefly discussed in this section. First the organisation of government drought relief is described. There follows a brief assessment of its impact on the four villages under study. The final sub-section raises two general issues pertaining to the paper as a whole. The first issue is the interplay of drought and rural differentiation in the specific context of this province. The second issue concerns the conceptualisation of drought and entitlement.

Drought relief in communal areas of Masvingo Province

Drought relief in the province was part of a national programme that commenced in early 1983. The scheme was principally financed by central government. Voluntary agencies and external donors financed a number of other programmes, e.g. a supplementary feeding scheme for nursing mothers and children under five.

Under the government programme, maize was purchased from the stores of the Grain Marketing Board. In the Masvingo Province, the maize was then trucked from the provincial capital, via the district capitals to distribution points – principally mission stations and schools.

Local distribution was the responsibility of the Ministry of Social Services. The district staff of the Ministry – about four officers – could not possibly administer the programme alone in a district numbering over one hundred thousand people. This task was impossible for them since very specific criteria had to be applied as to which households were eligible for drought relief. Hence lists had to be compiled at village and sub-district levels. Even the task of vetting these lists was in practice impossible without the co-operation of the people's own organisations. The main criterion for eligibility was that only the members of households in which the head of the household earned an income under the statutory minimum wage – which varies for different types of employment but was then 105 Zimbabwean dollars a month for industrial workers – were eligible for drought relief. And the ration consisted of a 'bucket' of unmilled maize. A 'bucket' is a large tin, widely used as a unit of measurement, and holds roughly 20 kilos of unmilled maize.

In practice, the drawing up of the lists of households eligible for drought relief was the responsibility of the local party organisations of the Zimbabwe African National Union and it is important to note that the Masvingo Province is in effect a one-party state of the ruling ZANU (Patriotic Front). The organisational structure of the party in the province is complicated and does not correspond in division or nomenclature to the layers of local government organisation. But in practice what seemed to happen was that the party chairman of each village submitted lists to the ward chairman of the party and the lists were jointly checked by the local district councillor of the ward and the officers of the Ministry of Social Services. The physical distribution of the maize took place in large gatherings of the villagers – led by the chairmen and other officers of the party at the village level.

The application of the drought relief programme was designed to mitigate the suffering of the rural poor in the communal areas. It involved distinguishing between those households where the head of household held a formal sector job (our clusters one and two) which did not receive drought relief, and those households (our clusters three and four) which did. (It should be remembered here that the maize is supplied unmilled and it was universal that maize is milled at local petrol and diesel driven grinding mills and not by hand. The cost of this varied from a low of 0.30 Zimbabwe dollars per bucket to a high of 50 cents – a not inconsiderable sum for destitute households.)

As far as I could assess, these criteria were applied fairly and, at the sub-district level, were felt to be fair (though there were frequent allegations that other districts received more favourable treatment). There were small exceptions that seemed to prove the rule. In one village, a debate had started as to whether a widow and her two daughters were eligible for drought relief. One of the daughters was a prostitute and it had been decided to review her case at the next revision of the lists. Those who had been recently sacked or quit formal sector jobs sometimes complained that they did not receive the ration to which they were entitled. The petty nature of these exceptions seemed to testify to the general perception of the fairness of the system. (But even this had its exceptions: several local traders complained of the effect of free hand-out on their business and hinted darkly that many of the families receiving drought relief were in fact quite rich – a frequent allegation about peasants everywhere.)

Generally, the fact that the lists were originally compiled by elected village chairmen – with intimate knowledge of the 30 to 50 families in their village – meant that such exceptions were few. It was, further, my impression that the degree of corruption and pilfering was very low at the point of distribution but increased up the distribution ladder from the point of distribution to the central government. As to whether each man, woman and child actually consumed the 20 kilos maize (less, roughly, 15 per cent weight lost in milling) to which he or she was entitled, this was impossible for me to control. Many claimed that the ration – and for those without access to cash and other entitlements it was their only food intake – was insufficient to last one month, especially since there was no fixed monthly distribution date.

A more basic fault of the system was its dependence on higher-level administration and a complex distribution system. According to my informants, supplies of maize had been fairly regular and sufficient from the inception of the system in February 1983 until early September that year. But from September, the frequency of maize deliveries became more erratic.

A variety of explanations were advanced for this. One was that in September 1983 the government decided to change the system of distribution. Until then, the physical delivery of the maize was handled by private truck companies who contracted with central government. The high cost of this – at a time of massive cuts in state expenditure – had led to the decision to use government transport for district distribution. But this was insufficient and used for a variety of other purposes. Hence the delays. Another explanation was that government delayed distribution in order to cut state expenditure. Corruption and massive stealing by government employees and contractors was another expectation frequently advanced.[2]

It is vital that these assessments are not applied indiscriminately to Zimbabwe nationally. I would be extremely reluctant to generalise about the drought relief programme outside the communal areas of Masvingo Province. First of all, the urban population was not eligible for drought relief. Nor, to my knowledge was the African population of the areas of commercial farming and the African Purchase Areas. The system was applied and administered quite differently in the Settlement Schemes. Nor would I be prepared to generalise on how the system is applied in the communal areas of other provinces of Mashonaland.

An even more important exception was the drought relief programme in the two provinces of Matebeleland. These two provinces were virtually closed to the investigator without the specific authorisation of the Ministry of Home Affairs and the government had taken Emergency Powers in these provinces to deal with the dissidents and 'super dissidents' of sections of the Zimbabwe African Peoples Union – whose chairman is Joshua Nkomo. From local press reports and information, it was well known that the drought relief programme was exceedingly patchy and, where it did exist, it was under the direct supervision of the police and the army. Further, it was official government policy to 'interdict' the food supplies of dissidents. This extended to the punishment of villagers for supplying food to dissidents.

Drought and rural differentiation

It is often argued that drought is really a natural phenomenon and that people cannot control the rainfall. However, it is an open question (to many climatologists for example) as to whether the incidence and regularity of rainfall is influenced by the pattern of land utilisation. Many would argue that widespread misuse of land – leading to overgrazing, soil erosion, the cutting down of trees for fuel – the 'prisoner's dilemma' of peasants and nomads caught within this vicious circle – does tend to decrease the rate of rainfall and few doubt its catastrophic effects on water utilisation. However, it is difficult to employ this type of analysis to a specific incidence of drought. For example, many climatologists would argue that the 1982–4 drought in Zimbabwe was related to global shifts in wind and weather patterns rather than to long-term changes in patterns of land utilisation.

When the focus shifts from drought as such, to food availability and hunger, then the rate of precipitation is only one of a number of climactic conditions that are relevant. For example, too much rainfall (flooding), or rainfall at the wrong time, can have just as deleterious effects on food production as drought.

Turning to the recent Zimbabwean drought and the findings of this survey it is important to emphasise that the methodology used here cannot 'prove' a correlation between differentiation and drought. The problem is essentially methodological given the limitations of household survey and the absence of time-series data. A useful illustration of the problem is the relationship between the clusters of differentiation and one source of wealth, cattle. In the villages surveyed, there is no clear correlation between different clusters and the number and proportion of cattle that died. Such a correlation would first require a hypothesis, e.g. that since poorer households have fewer cattle and, for many reasons, tend to look after them better, they would lose fewer cattle, proportionately, than richer households with more cattle where the men are away at jobs and the children are in school. But there is no clear correlation that emerges from the data. Indeed, the reverse hypothesis 'guiding' the correlation might be more plausible, that wealth from other sources can be employed to find better grazing, to hire herd boys, etc. But the evidence does not support this hypothesis as even a cursory examination of the data in Table 20.1 of the Appendix would reveal. Hence, in the specific context of this survey, no firm conclusion can be drawn on the relationship between differentiation and cattle.

On the direct correlation between drought and household income, the data is also inconclusive. Clearly, those households with greater cash income had access to food and other consumption items, an access denied those families dependent on traditional systems of redistribution and on government drought relief. But, and this applies particularly to the rural salariat, whether such families could use their command of cash income to consolidate their 'class' position at the expense of other village families, would require further study of other factors. One such factor would be the relationship of the rural salariat to the state: specifically to the local state apparatus that dispenses a variety of resources within the area, particularly the district and provincial state administration. This is the subject of a subsequent paper.

At a more abstract level, this chapter raises the question of the applicability of the 'entitlement approach' to the study of drought. Sen's provoking study of poverty and famine (Sen 1981) has inspired many to explore the issue of food entitlement at the micro level. In summary form, Sen argues that:

It is the totality of entitlement relations that governs whether a person will have the ability to acquire enough food to avoid starvation, and food supply is only one influence among many affecting his entitlement relations. It is sometimes said that starvation may be caused not by food shortage but by shortage of income and purchasing power. This can be seen as a rudimentary way of trying to catch the essence of the entitlement approach. (Sen 1981: 155)

The focus of Sen's study is on drought and famine and not on drought relief. Given this focus it is natural that the households studied tend to appear as both the objects of analysis and the victims of historical processes rather than its actual or potential agents.

This raises the further question of what exactly is an 'entitlement' and of how widely the concept can be applied without losing analytical precision. For, ultimately, the survival of the poorest families in these villages during the 1982–4 drought rested on the government drought relief programme. This, in turn, rested on a diffuse political entitlement to state resources – an entitlement which seems to have been absent for the villagers of northern Ethiopia both in the current drought and in the 1973 drought. In any total analysis surely this 'political entitlement' – or its absence – must be taken into account? Specifically in any total analysis of the drought as it affected the villagers within Masvingo Province, the role of the state and of state-party relationships within what is essentially a one-party state of the ruling Zimbabwe African National Union (ZANU) would have to be taken into account. It would be analytically incorrect to ignore them. It might also be politically unwise.

Appendix

TABLE 20.1 Compilation of clusters in the four villages surveyed

	Average cattle per household	*Average land per household*	*Average scotchcarts per household*	*Average cash income per household*
Village A				
Cluster One	4.5	8.5	0.5	107.5
Cluster Two	3.9	7.2	0.2	88.8
Cluster Three	2.4	8.4	0.1	39.0
Cluster Four	2.4	7.2	0.2	16.4

Table 20.1 continued

Village B

Cluster One	7.6	8.4	0.6	270.0
Cluster Two	3.3	4.8	0.4	120.0
Cluster Three	3.5	6.4	0.4	2.7
Cluster Four	2.2	4.3	0.1	14.5

Village C

Cluster One	7.2	8.4	0.2	150.0
Cluster Two	3.3	5.9	0.1	76.6
Cluster Three	2.1	6.5	0.05	13.2
Cluster Four	0.7	3.4	0.0	0.4

Village D

Cluster One	2.0	8.0	0.0	100.0
Cluster Two	0.5	7.9	0.1	74.4
Cluster Three	2.6	9.3	0.15	36.8
Cluster Four	0.0	6.0	0.0	30.0

TABLE 20.2 Differentiation, cattle and cattle deaths

	Average number of surviving cattle per household	Total cattle deaths (all causes) in 12 month period (Oct 82 – Oct 84)	Average cattle deaths in 12 month period per household
Village A			
Cluster One	4.5	11.0	2.2
Cluster Two	3.9	12.0	0.9
Cluster Three	2.4	37.0	1.9
Cluster Four	2.4	15.0	1.4
Village B			
Cluster One	7.6	8.0	4.0
Cluster Two	3.3	29.0	1.6
Cluster Three	3.5	14.0	1.3
Cluster Four	2.2	11.0	2.2
Village C			
Cluster One	7.2	1.0	0.2
Cluster Two	3.3	8.0	0.8
Cluster Three	2.1	43.0	2.4
Cluster Four	0.7	4.0	0.0
Village D			
Cluster One	2.0	2.0	2.0
Cluster Two	0.5	12.0	0.7
Cluster Three	2.6	41.0	1.9
Cluster Four	0.0	0.0	0.0

NOTES

1. This argument is generic to the dependency school (e.g. Amin 1972) and to reformist historiography in southern Africa (e.g. Wolpe 1972; Legassick 1974; Palmer 1977; Palmer and Parsons 1977; Arrighi 1967; Arrighi 1970; Clarke 1974).
2. Quite a reasonable explanation given later public trials and sentences for fraud. See Andre Meldrum 'Food Relief Fraud in Zimbabwe', *Guardian* 5 June 1984.

21

Food and hunger in the Ciskei[1]

Meredeth Turshen

Drought is significant only in situations of marginal or subsistence existence. As South Africa is neither a marginal nor a subsistence economy, the fact that widespread hunger was reported during the recent drought raises questions about distribution and deprivation in the bantustans. By analysing the situation in one bantustan, the Ciskei, this paper shows that the drought, although it exacerbated hunger, was not its cause; nor was the problem one of food shortages. Rather, the South African government's political strategy of creating 'independent homelands' reduced people's ability to obtain sufficient food by depriving them of a wide range of entitlements.

The drought that affected large areas of Africa entered its fourth year in 1984 in the so-called 'independent homeland' of Ciskei, an 8,000–9,000 square kilometre wedge of land on the eastern coast of South Africa. The South African government pieced together the Ciskei bantustan and 'colonised' it by massive population removals and relocations, making it one of the most densely settled parts of the country with perhaps 100 people per square kilometre.[2] One third of the estimated population of one million Xhosa-speaking blacks is concentrated in the dormitory town of Mdantsane. The inhabitants of Mdantsane provide daily labour for the nearby port of East London and contract labour for the mines. Few jobs are available within the bantustan's borders.

The drought reduced the demand for seasonal labour on white farms in the vicinity, the major source of casual employment for women and children. But the drought is not the main reason for extensive joblessness. Unemployment is widespread in the Ciskei as in other bantustans for a number of economic reasons. Within South Africa one may cite changes in the contract system for migrant labour,[3] the need for skilled rather than unskilled labour in the new high-tech industries, the decision to create a stable urban black labour force which reduces opportunities for migrant labour, the expansion of capital intensive agriculture which needs fewer workers,[4] and the current recession, in addition to the drought, all of which caused the demand for labour to fall. Within the Ciskei the promised development has failed to materialise. In 1982 Green and Hirsch estimated that fewer than five thousand jobs had been created for blacks. In 1983, at the start of the current recession, unemployment rates were an estimated 40 per cent in the Ciskei (*Sunday Tribune* 24 July 1983).

While unemployment rises in the bantustans, it has been reduced in white areas in an attempt to lessen the threat of urban unrest. The political strategy of creating 'independent homelands' enables the South African government to increase its control of labour. Whereas before blacks were merely disenfranchised, now they are aliens, stripped of their citizenship, and must acquire passports, in addition to passbooks. This change is more than symbolic; it alters people's entitlements[5] and legitimates new labour recruitment practices.[6]

Currently, South Africa recruits men from the bantustans for unskilled work (for example, as labourers, night watchmen, and to remove night-soil), for 'dirty' work (for example, at the foundries of ISCOR, the giant South African iron and steel corporation), for 'unpopular' work (for example, farmwork), or for 'unpopular' firms. Women are recruited for nursing and domestic work, but most find jobs only in casual and daily farm work, at sawmills, on roadworks, with very small firms, or on the sugar estates of Natal.

The new political strategy implies a new magnitude of economic manipulation. There are no labour laws in the Ciskei, no minimum wages, and trade unions are banned (*Sunday Tribune* 24 July 1983). The ban applies to commuters living in Mdantsane and working in East London. According to Hirsch and Kooy, wages in East London are generally lower than in other industrial centres such as Cape Town and Durban, and substantially lower than the national average: in 1976 African monthly wages in East London factories ranged from R40 to R100. Residents of Mdantsane who find work in East London are better off than the rural population. Farm workers earn an average of R45 per month (*Rand Daily Mail* 5 March 1984). The minimum living level for an average household was R250 per month at the beginning of 1983, according to the Swart Commission (*Daily Dispatch* 10 January 1984). The Surplus People Project estimated that in 1980, 59 per cent of rural households and 20 per cent of urban households earned less than R133 per month, well below the 1980 household subsistence levels of R170 in rural and R196 in urban areas.

Food prices soared during the drought: maize rose 25 per cent, imported rice 16 per cent, poultry 10–15 per cent, eggs 5 per cent, breakfast cereals 10 per cent, biscuits 9 per cent, tea 25 per cent, coffee 7.5 per cent, and sugar 3 per cent (*Star* 12 March 1984). The Ciskei imports over half of its maize and wheat, as well as milk and vegetables (Myrdal and Thomson 1983: 11). The falling value of the rand is likely to push the price of imported foodstuffs even higher.

In the past, subsistence farming absorbed the worst shocks of economic recession. This last resort is no longer available in the Ciskei. Much of the land is too mountainous or dry for productive use, and Hewu district in the northwest is semi-desert; only 13 per cent of the area to which hundreds of thousands of people have been removed is arable. Land scarcity was artificially created by the South African government when it allocated so little territory to the new 'state'. This absolute constraint is made worse by the Ciskei government, which bars so much land from habitation, reserving it for large commercial ranching and irrigation schemes. The remaining soil is overworked, overstocked, and eroded because of overcrowding; these conditions cannot be ascribed to poor farming practices.

Because subsistence farming yields so little, even families with access to land depend on the earnings of migrant workers. The extent of migration from the Ciskei is evident in imbalanced population ratios and age distributions: in the general population there are 86 males for every 100 females; in the rural population aged 25–64 years the ratio is 49 males for every 100 females. Children under 15 together with adults over 65 make up more than 50 per cent of the population (Surplus People Project 1983). The large proportion of young and elderly dependants places a heavy burden on wage-earners.

The impression that few Africans are farming is confirmed by reports from the labour bureaux. As recently as ten years ago, droughts and floods would bring forth more job-seekers. But during 1982, a drought year, there was no difference in the number of workers seeking jobs, presumably because few Africans were affected as so few now farm. According to one estimate, only 8 per cent of inhabitants of the Ciskei can actually be called subsistence farmers (*Financial Mail* 2 March 1984), and according to the South African Institute for Race Relations (1984: 377) 30,000 of them were destitute in 1983. Rural residents removed to settlement camps like Sada, which are considered townships or urban areas, were forced to sell their livestock and were not allocated farm land or grazing.

Only 36 per cent of income earned by Ciskei residents is generated inside the Ciskei; 64 per cent is earned outside by commuters and migrant workers (*Cape Times* 10 January 1984). Thus most people in the Ciskei depend on the income of commuters and the remittances of migrants; other sources of income are pensions and the daily earnings of those who find casual work. Labour recruiters no longer have to scour the countryside for workers; hundreds of applicants besiege their offices when rumours of jobs circulate.

The effect on women

In the old pattern of migration from the labour reserves, women remained in the rural areas working the farms, bearing and rearing children, and caring for the elderly, the ill, and the disabled, while men worked in the mines and on plantations and, later, in the factories. Apartheid carried the reserve system to an extreme in South Africa, requiring first men and then women to carry passbooks in which their places of origin were stamped and residence elsewhere was linked to a valid labour contract. Anyone remaining in a white area longer than 12 hours without a permit risked imprisonment; women were not given permits to accompany men to their worksites. The only employment available to women that would legalise their presence in the cities was live-in domestic work, which separated them not only from their men but also from their children.

This pattern has changed in the last two decades and with it, women's entitlements. Under sexually discriminatory laws, women have no rights to land in the bantustans and are often refused any land allocation by the government-appointed headmen. Even when they have access to land, rural women do not spend their days tending fields; the overcrowding and escalating poverty of the bantustans drive them off the land. Paradoxically, overcrowding has not overcome the labour constraints of subsistence agriculture, which are aggravated by the absence of migrant workers from individual families. The women, children, and the elderly who are dumped in the rural areas do not, in most instances, form a natural farming community with traditions of mutual assistance. Instead women are occupied in trying to earn money to support themselves and their families by working in the informal sector or on white farms (Yawitch 1983). Women must either find employment in the bantustans or join the stream of workers who migrate illegally to the cities (International Defence and Aid Fund 1981).

Once women could depend on remittances from migrants, but the new system of renewable annual contracts strains family relationships. In the past many men extended the break between spells away as much as three months to a year, especially if leave coincided with ploughing or harvesting. But now some men do not return at all, particularly those who have established a second home and family where they work. In these circumstances, remittances are sporadic and unpredictable, so women restricted to the bantustans must fend for themselves.

Customary law demands that men take all the major decisions in the family: even married African women are minors in the eyes of South African law. For many women, the demand that custom be upheld, or the unwillingness to flout convention in a situation where they are dependent and alone for eleven months out of every twelve, becomes highly oppressive and contradictory. The maintenance of male authority is entrenched in the tribal system, which is legitimated by the structure of 'independent homelands'. Only men are members of the tribal authority. Women are thus effectively shut out from access to the institutions that control their lives (ibid.).

The impact on health and nutrition

As the drought dragged on, the incidence of tuberculosis increased sharply in South Africa and newspapers reported epidemics of diseases like cholera and measles with growing frequency. There was a 50 per cent increase in adults and teenagers of pellagra dementia, an advanced stage of vitamin B deficiency probably induced by diets consisting solely of mealie meal (*Star* 7 November 1983; *Washington Post* 9 October 1983). A survey of childhood malnutrition in the Ciskei (Richter et al. 1984) found that 62 per cent of school children did not meet World Health Organisation developmental standards. In 1983, Operation Hunger, a project of the South African Institute of Race Relations, was said to be feeding 150,000 people daily in the Ciskei (*Star* 7 November 1983); and a year later, 80,000 were said to receive daily rations (*Daily Dispatch* 18 December 1984).

But long before the current drought the Institute of Race Relations warned that 75 per cent of urban and 80 per cent of rural children in the Ciskei were malnourished, and that 10 per cent of urban and 16 per cent of rural children two to three years old had kwashiorkor or marasmus (*Rand Daily Mail* 6 December 1980). Despite extensive press coverage, no deaths have been attributed directly to the drought, that is, no deaths in excess of the high mortality that prevails in bantustans like the Ciskei. The estimate of deaths from the drought in Mozambique runs as high as 100,000 with 700,000 people affected and 200,000 in refugee camps (*Star* 16 January 1984).

South Africa published no national mortality statistics by race, so there are no baseline data for purposes of comparison over time. In 1982 when Dr L. A. Munnik, then Minister of Health, was questioned about reports of high death rates among children and the elderly in Elukhanyweni, an area in the Ciskei to which 5,000 people were removed, many at gunpoint, he replied that the Ciskei 'does not fall within the jurisdiction of the Republic' (*Guardian* 14 May 1983). Thus, along with unemployment, illness and death have been 'relocated' in the bantustans.

The public attitude of South African officials is that the people bring hunger and death on themselves by overbreeding. Dr Nak van der Merwe, Minister of Health, attributed the high death rate among children suffering from malnutrition to too little food and too many people. 'People cannot simply continue to multiply uncontrollably', he said (*Daily News* 13 April 1983). That there are too many people is a direct consequence of forced removals. Average annual population growth in the Ciskei is a staggering 5.83 per cent, but most of that is due to resettlement; the rate of natural increase is 2.7 per cent, well below the sub-Saharan average of 3.1. That there is too little food is simply untrue.

Food availability

Although subsistence farming is no longer practised, capital-intensive commercial agriculture is expanding. Irrigation schemes are operating in Shilch, Keiskammahoek, and Tyefu under the management of South African consulting firms like Loxton Venn and Associates, using cheap seasonal labour from nearby resettlement camps (NUSAS

1983; Cooper 1983). Wages for workers on these schemes are very low: at Keiskammahoek women are paid R1.50 per day and men R3.00 (Myrdal and Thomson 1983: 10). During the worst period of drought and hunger, the schemes marketed agricultural products to the value of R3.4 million through the Ciskei Agricultural Corporation, which is directed by Don le Roux (*Daily Dispatch* 2 December 1983). Ciskei citrus is said to bring in foreign exchange; large quantities of fruit are produced for export to Europe through the South African Citrus Board in a project managed by Ciskei Agricultural Services under Ian Robertson (ibid.).

Surplus food is being destroyed rather than distributed to those in need. The South African press reports the destruction of citrus fruit and the dumping of hundreds of thousands of litres of milk on roadsides and down drains because no commercial market could be found (*Daily News* 4 January 1984; 11 May 1984). Other press reports note efforts to stop so-called 'illegal' shipments of food from overseas to relieve victims of drought-induced famine on the grounds that such imports undermine the market for South African agricultural products (*Financial Mail* 2 November 1983). In any case, as Sen (1981) has shown, starvation is not a function of food availability.

Sen's analysis of entitlements is useful because it permits a class analysis of hunger and poverty in place of the usual generalisations. Using data from a study of child nutrition in the Ciskei by Thomas (1981), one can trace the progressive loss of entitlements there. In extended families that are intact and multigenerational, with all units productive and contributing whether on the land or in employment, children are well nourished even if the family is poor. When economic necessity forces men out of their families, children remain well nourished so long as the migrants return at intervals for extended periods and send remittances regularly during their absences. But when the extended family is dissolved – through relocations and removals, through population pressure on land plots too small and exhausted to support large numbers, or through death or imprisonment – children are undernourished, their growth stunted, and their weight falls relative to norms for their age group. If penury shrinks the nuclear family, as for example when the father's migration becomes permanent, and if access to land and employment is curtailed, children will show signs of frank malnutrition. In families lacking both parents, as when the father is a permanent migrant and the mother leaves for town in search of work, the children left in the care of elderly relatives or aunts with children of their own are apt to be severely malnourished. Illegitimate children left in the care of impoverished elderly relatives may develop frank marasmus. Starving children are the remnants of fragmented families or of the discarded, unproductive fragments of families.

The South African government says that it spent US$1.9 billion in foreign exchange to import food in the summer of 1983 (*Wall Street Journal* 8 February 1984), but it is not possible to establish how much relief went to white farmers or to large commercial ranches in the bantustans and how much to feed hungry blacks. For example, US$60 million were spent to import 400,000 tons of wheat from Australia to alleviate the stock feed crisis (BBC 19 June 1984). Most likely government efforts focused on white farmers who were reported to be abandoning their farms at a record rate (*Rand Daily Mail* 3 March 1984). The cost of keeping a single farmer on the land is estimated to be R200,000 (*Rand Daily Mail* 8 June 1984). Relief sent to the bantustans consisted of fodder and other feeds, which reportedly saved livestock in the 1984 drought months (*Daily Dispatch* 12 April 1985).

According to the South African Institute of Race Relations (1984: 377) the South African government allocated R13 million in drought relief aid to the Ciskei in 1982–3 for public works jobs (digging trenches for cables and pipes, clearing silt from dams, and clearing land of brush at the rate of R2 per day), feeding schemes, and water and fodder distribution. One community charged that only card-carrying members of the Ciskei National Independence Party received food aid.

The beneficiaries

In a persuasive study based on field research in three Ciskei resettlement camps, Green and Hirsch (1983) show how the power structure of the bantustans operates: they show that the chiefs occupy a pivotal position because they control the allocation of land, labour contracts, housing, and other social security payments, yet they are dependent for their power on the state, which in the first instance is the Ciskei National Independence Party and ultimately is the government of South Africa.[7]

The way in which the Ciskei's dependency on South Africa operates may be illustrated by a small agricultural project in which land was distributed to African farmers. The chiefs have the power to reward loyal supporters with plots of land, but the public and private South African managers of the scheme controlled the African farmers who were not free to buy and sell as they liked; their purchases were directed to agricultural supply corporations and their produce to multinational traders (*Daily Dispatch* 16 May 1984). South African investors found it more efficient to operate through small farmers whom they supervised closely than to incur the risks of running a large plantation. The Ciskei government was able to bolster the position of the chiefs, promote the illusion of development and the advantages of the free market, and collect taxes to finance the national elites.

The elites of the Ciskei include the ruling Sebe family (rather reduced by arrests and trials in 1983–4) (*Times* 22 June 1984), top-level bureaucrats, and the tribal authorities. Agricultural schemes like the one just mentioned benefit the headmen in the tribal authorities (NUSAS 1983), and the land reform that Sebe introduced in 1984 strengthens their position by giving each tribal authority the power to control land tenure, land consolidation, subdivision and sale (*Rand Daily Mail* 30 July 1984). There is a small petty bourgeoisie, mainly employees of the state (which is the largest employer with 13,722 workers) (NUSAS 1983); it tends to be supportive of the Ciskei ruling class: 'its interests are rooted in a rigid patronage system that is based on the chiefs and institutionalised in the ruling Ciskei National Independence Party. Consequently its political responses tend to be conservative and at times violently anti-working class' (Swilling 1984).

The elites were placed in power by the South African government, which supports the Ciskei with annual transfer payments of R300 million (*Star* 8 May 1984). An additional sum of R1.5 million is collected through an annual per capita 'development tax' of R2.50, which was levied in 1984 but backdated to 1979. Each migrant worker pays R15 for 'development', in addition to R5 for a passport and R4 for photographs. Commuters also pay school fees (R16) (*Cape Times* 17 February 1984), rent (from R2.50), and health services (R2–4 per visit) (Myrdal and Thomson 1983: 27). While workers' burdens increase, investors' obligations are lightened: Sebe has turned the Ciskei into a tax haven to attract foreign investment by abolishing company taxes and reducing the personal income tax to a flat rate of 15 per cent on incomes over R8,000 (*Daily Dispatch* 15 November 1984). Child labour has been legalised, and whites can acquire land or operate businesses without restriction (*Rand Daily Mail* 30 July 1984). Whatever new schemes are devised, they are sure to benefit the Ciskei ruling class in the short run; in the long term, the beneficiary is South Africa.

Conclusion

Analyses of the Sahel famines of the early 1970s showed that drought is not a natural phenomenon nor famine its inevitable accompaniment (Franke and Chasin 1980). The same analysis holds for South Africa. The history of dispossession of blacks by whites in South Africa, of longer duration and deeper penetration than French colonial rule of the Sahel, suggests that the impact of the four-year drought will be disproportionate to its climatic significance. An explanation of the devastation is to be found not in climatology or demography but in the South African political economy. The government is using the drought to reach its own ends, which are to implement the homelands strategy. That strategy is crucial to the successful re-ordering of the South African economy, which is being restructured in the present crisis. The South African drought spread like an epidemic of disease, and the state's need to re-organise the labour force dictates its response – or failure to respond. In these circumstances, it is difficult to reach any conclusion other than that the South African government is consciously ridding itself of its surplus population. However, the militant resistance of black people will foil even a policy of genocide.

NOTES

1. The research for this paper was made possible by a grant from the Rutgers University Research Council. Admission to the libraries of the Institute of Commonwealth Studies, the International Defence and Aid Fund, the American Committee on Africa, and the Catholic Institute for International Relations, greatly facilitated this work.
2. All these figures are subject to political dispute. The Ciskei's boundaries are not yet fixed, the *de jure* population (Ciskei 'nationals') is twice the *de facto* population (Ciskei residents), and non-registration is a means of protest. Extrapolating from the government's 1980 data, the current population is 850,000, but this is widely acknowledged to be too low and an estimate of one million is used in this paper. All data calculated on a population base, for example population density, are necessarily estimates.
3. Migrant labourers are restricted to employment on one-year contracts. Whereas men used to remain at home between contracts, under the new system they renew before going on leave and must return in three weeks or lose their place. The employment of first-time mineworkers dropped from 70 to 25 per cent in recent years, suggesting that mineowners succeeded in creating a stable workforce.
4. In 1968 farmworkers could count on more than 90 jobs per hectare; in 1981 there were fewer than 20 jobs per hectare. A detailed analysis by the Surplus People Project identified as causes the abolition in 1980 of the labour tenancy system, mechanisation of agriculture, concentration of farm ownership in fewer hands leading to redundancies, farmers' action against elderly workers and 'troublemakers', and the eviction or voluntary departure of workers from land farmed for their own use when owners expanded cultivation (South African Institute of Race Relations 1984: 158). For more details see Green and Hirsch (1983: 17–26).
5. Relocation entails the loss of section 10 rights, which grant Africans permanent residency in white urban areas. Without this status, their presence is illegal after 72 hours, unless they have a one-year migrant labourer's contract and housing.
6. Officially, 'homeland' authorities manage their own affairs while the role of the South African state in the market declines. In practice, the bantustans exercise petty control over labour matters (for example, the distribution of contracts to CNIP supporters), while

South African bureaucracies, particularly administrative boards, play a growing role in rural labour markets (see Greenberg and Giliomee 1985 for a detailed field report). However, the South African government is not ignorant of the political advantage of homeland authorities appearing inefficient and corrupt.

7. While most members of the Ciskei cabinet are black, 12 of 16 'key men' (and they are all men) are white: Theo de Vries, Chancellor to the Presidency, D. G. Bouchier, Director-General of Internal Affairs, I. Melville, Director-General of Finance, I. M. Mullins, Auditor-General, Gary Godden, Director of Planning, Bobby Michau, Director-General of Manpower, Col Herbert Webster, Commissioner of Prisons, J. F. Venter, Director-General of Posts, P. J. Welman, Director-General of Transport, C. L. Atwell, Director-General of Public Works, and Reg Beavitt, Chief Traffic Officer. Key posts held by blacks are foreign affairs, agriculture, education, and health. (Despite considerable turnover, whites retain approximately the same number of posts.)

22

The crisis in the reproduction of migrant labour in southern Africa

Ray Bush, Lionel Cliffe, Valerey Jansen

Changes in the patterns and nature of migrant labour in South Africa have often been understood and linked to responses by the interests of capital to a crisis in the country's political economy. Indeed, it was precisely a crisis in South Africa's economy in the 1940s, a crisis for the needs of emerging industrial manufacturing capital and the demands of white workers – in short, secondary industrialisation of an economy hitherto based on gold and maize – which brought forth the National Party's ideology of racial supremacy (Legassick 1975).

South Africa's crisis of the 1940s and the ensuing transition from policies of 'segregation' to those of 'apartheid' is in many respects matched by the present crisis of accumulation in that country and recent constitutional changes and shifts in the pattern of migrant labour recruitment as a response to it. The debate about South Africa's crisis of capitalist accumulation is well known. South Africa's economy has a large structural imbalance between departments I and II, respectively the capital goods and consumer goods producing sectors. Agriculture and mining have generally low imports and high exports while manufacturing – now the leading sector over mining – has the reverse. The initial complementarity of the three sectors of manufacturing, mining and agriculture which underlay the growth of manufacturing in the late 1950s and early 1960s was undermined as gold exports stagnated and rapid growth in food and livestock was checked. Growth of the manufacturing sector has been impeded, moreover, by the problem of low domestic demand because of low black consumption – a problem inherent to apartheid. It is as a response to this crisis of underconsumption – of the need to sustain the interests of manufacturing capital – that recent constitutional reform in South Africa can be seen (Clarke 1978). It is also as a response to this crisis of capital accumulation that we can understand more fully South Africa's strategy of destabilisation in the region. South Africa needs ultimately to link countries in the region into a sub-imperialist economy based on a constellation of southern African states backed by the imperialist interests of Britain, North America and West Germany – investors who provide much of South Africa's high technology which is used to offset the low organic composition of capital in South Africa's manufacturing sector and help it to compete more effectively on the world market. Although the relative boom years of the 1960s seemed to reflect a temporary quiescent African working class the recession of the 1970s and 1980s has led to a further mounting conflict, at the point of production and in the urban areas, between the state and working class. Because of escalating costs in its strategy of regional destabilisation, and because of recession and balance of payments crisis, the South African state has recently sought to complement with political reform South African capitalists' attempts to intensify the rate of surplus value extraction in the manufacturing sector. On the one hand the state is operating in an increasingly repressive manner to prevent the formation of black political class struggle – nationally and regionally. On the other hand it has been seeking to divide and steer onto safe ground political forms which have emerged. It is in this context that the limited concessions of Wiehahn and Rieckert, the political 'independence' of the homelands and the encouragement of a subordinate black bourgeoisie, 'local government' in the townships and the President's Council referendum amongst whites, must be seen – a strategy of attempted disintegration of recent integrating struggles. Of course the South African state's strategy – if it can be seen as a homogeneous one at all – is not without contradictions. Not the least of these is the big capital/small capital divide and the notion that the continued racist hierarchical division of labour is still in the interest of the south African bourgeoisie or any significant fraction of it. Saul and Gelb (1981) recently added to this debate by suggesting that big capital is now ready to introduce new patterns of accumulation, a broadening of the range of commodities considered part of the living wage and thus ultimately a redefinition of urban black labour away from one based on the necessities of life in the bantustans. A prominent spokesman of this view has been Harry Oppenheimer who in his 1976 lecture to the London Stock Exchange saw systems of migrant labour less and less appropriate to the labour requirements of South African capital.

We have documented the recent political measures introduced by the South African state and the implications for these for the South African political economy elsewhere (Bush et al. 1984; Charney 1984; and Bush and Kibble 1985). We introduce a brief discussion of them here because they highlight the particular response of the South African state to the international and national economic and political crisis in the 1980s. Like much of the literature though which has charted the development of the structures of apartheid from the 1940s, current analyses of the crisis in South Africa say very little about its effect on the social reproduction of migrant labour – both in South Africa and elsewhere in the region. We need to focus on this particular aspect of the region's political economy to shift discussion away from either an economistic appraisal of the present conjuncture or a recognition of political reform *per se* to an understanding of the structures and social processes upon which most of the region's political economy is based. But before we examine some of the present empirical detail of what is actually happening in some of the countries in the region we need to raise questions about the theoretical tools at our disposal for analysing the reality of the present conjuncture. What concepts do we have with which we can adequately begin to grasp the complexity of social differentiation and class formation in the rural areas of the region?

Conceptualising labour, the household and their reproduction

The work of Wolpe has made a significant advance in understanding the nature of migrant labour in the context of apartheid (Wolpe 1980). In criticising Legassick, Wolpe rightly observed that the focus on secondary industrialisation assumed that rural political and economic structures remained unchanged. He displaced an explanation of the growth of migrant labour and apartheid in purely racial and ideological terms. He recognised instead that racial prescriptions are always articulated in any social formation with the mode or modes of production (Wolpe 1980: 294). He highlighted this interrelationship and that between an increasingly dominant capitalist mode of production and its impact on the declining viability of local indigenous forms of production. His basic thesis is that apartheid *'can best be understood as the mechanism specific to South Africa* in the period of secondary industrialisation, of maintaining a high rate of capitalist exploitation through a system which guarantees a cheap and controlled labour-force, under circumstances in which the conditions of that labour-force is rapidly disintegrating' (Wolpe 1980: 296).

For Wolpe, disintegration of the rural political economy emerged as the fragile equilibrium between production in the reserves and the adequacy of urban wages for migrants became imbalanced. In short the contradiction for apartheid is that in creating the conditions for cheap migrant labour it undermines the economic viability of pre-capitalist relations of production and the site where the labour is recruited. This is because at one and the same time the rural areas in southern Africa need to remain productive centres to 'renew' labourers' capabilities to return to the urban areas for work: the rural area must not however become sufficiently viable as to pose a real alternative to trekking to work in the town.

Wolpe offers very useful insights into the influence of migrant labour but his perspective does have certain limitations. First, his model is one of transition from pre-capitalist modes of production to capitalism in *South* Africa. However, even to explain the dynamics of the system in South Africa we clearly need to recognise the dynamics of those other societies outside of the Republic, the origin in 1970 of 80 per cent of the migrant labour for the key sector, gold. To do this we need to recognise and raise questions about the (colonial) states' roles in these neighbouring countries and see whether Wolpe's approach is applicable to those parts of the region and those countries too where considerable *internal* labour migration exists like Zimbabwe, Namibia, Angola and Zambia. Second, we need to examine more clearly a fuller specification of relations in the pre-capitalist mode of production (PCMP) including relations of *reproduction* in the articulation process. Finally, we need also to begin a more extensive exploration of the 'crisis' of disintegration of the rural economy and how it comes about. This paper, which focuses on southern Africa outside of the Republic of South Africa, will explore the applicability of Wolpe's thesis and in doing so seeks to use a framework that overcomes these limitations. In practice this will mean asking to the extent that southern Africa is experiencing 'crisis' is it (belatedly) going through a comparable crisis to that South Africa has already suffered and to which Wolpe alludes, or one which is different? To accomplish this task it is necessary to get greater purchase on the different elements in the *reproduction* of the system – i.e. the whole set of relations of production and reproduction (and its possible breakdown) and their complex articulation and in this section we shall explore some recent contributions to the debate to see how far they help us in this task.

The mechanism whereby the South African state reproduced the system of migrant labour is through what Burawoy has called 'the separation of the means of renewal from the areas of maintenance of a labour force' (Burawoy 1980: 43). For an economy to operate efficiently a labour force has to be both maintained – subsist from day to day – and renewed – vacancies filled by healthy new recruits. Under 'normal' conditions of capitalism the distinction between the two dimensions of this process of reproduction of labour power is concealed – often by the family. The organisation of migrant labour however distinguishes separate *geographical* sites for the two processes and may provide different *institutions* of maintenance and renewal or a single institution may continue to engage in both processes (Burawoy 1980: 138). Capital maintains migrant labour in the urban areas in the knowledge that it does not have to pay a wage large enough to contribute to the full cost of that labour renewal. This cost is borne by the reproductive worker in the reserves or bantustans. Burawoy makes this point very clearly:

On the one hand, renewal processes are dependent on income left over from maintenance, which is remitted home by the productive workers. On the other hand, productive workers require continued support from their families engaged in renewal at home, because they have no permanent legal or political status at the place of work. (Burawoy 1980: 134)

Burawoy in fact offers us a perspective that he calls 'reproduction analysis' for analysing different societies where migrant labour is common over time. This means specifying both the 'inherent structures' which systems of migrant labour always establish in the form of 'the separation of maintenance and renewal processes' and also the specific character of migrant labour to emerge from these structures (p. 164). Burawoy continues: 'the state organises the dependence of the productive worker on the reproductive worker, while the economy organises the dependence of the reproductive worker on the productive worker' (p. 139).

He omits discussion of the 'family' which we will see in a moment is a problematic set of relationships which are subject to transformation, for the state in these societies creates the circumstances for separation and renewal but these vary according to 'differing political, ideological and economic situations in which the separation of maintenance and renewal process is organised' (ibid.).

Burawoy offers a useful peg for extending analysis to the different social formations in the rest of the region but an understanding of the institutional mechanism whereby systems of migrant labour are reproduced only at this level is inadequate. This is because 'reproduction analysis' can only grasp the full effect of migrant labour and the crisis in the region's peasant agricultural political economy by being built upon a premise of an understanding of the mechanisms of social reproduction in rural communities from where migrants are drawn.

Beginning from quite different premises two recent contributions to the literature have touched on these issues (Meillassoux 1983; Wallerstein 1982). Wallerstein speaks of the mechanisms imposed by white settlers which helped create a labour force in southern Africa:

taxes to force the sale of the means of sustenance and to purchase male wage labour; denied of access to land . . . [and] availability only to white farmers of new seed strains, agricultural assistance, water, railways, and agricultural markets. (Wallerstein 1982: 444)

Although Wallerstein talks about patterns of resistance established in opposition to the processes of commoditisation of labour his main assertion is that the character of rural communities can best be understood through the process of their insertion in the capitalist world economy and in particular the systematic pressures from those acting in the interests of capital 'to create specific kinds of income-pooling-households'. The household as an income pooling unit is what Wallerstein offers as a way of conceptualising the development and influence of migrant labour in southern Africa and the unit which he recognises pursues specific economic strategies of gain. In this way he aims to both capture the impact of the global economy in transforming the rural community and the internal composition and change in the 'household'. This approach does indeed help us to understand the influence of migrant labour in the rural areas:

1. on the changing production processes within the household itself;

2. on shifts in the sexual division of labour; and
3. on the changing patterns of consumption and reproduction of the household.

We explore these themes in greater detail below but what is questionable about Wallerstein's approach is the concern he and others have with the reified concept of the 'household' and its definition as an income pooling unit. At a theoretical and indeed empirical level, the notion of household is problematic: like the 'family' it carries with it many assumptions about social organisation or the lack of it. Moreover it assumes not only that a household can be defined as an income pooling unit but that its form continues uninterrupted while male migrants live and work in urban areas – an assumption that is becoming more and more doubtful in the context of southern Africa.

Meillassoux offers further insight into understanding the impact of capitalist encroachment on rural economies and the crisis which it engendered. Instead of using the somewhat static notion of the household as an income pooling unit Meillassoux (p. 52) talks about the domestic unit of production – which in pre-capitalist social formations maintains a balanced 'organic composition' between its members, the level of production and consumption. Moreover, for the domestic mode of production to maintain itself:

A certain ratio must be kept between individuals at two levels: at the level of production, between the productive and the unproductive, at the level of reproduction, by the number of pubescent women compared to the whole group. (p. 52)

These ratios are maintained in the PCMP by the economic basis of demographic reproduction, or to be more precise, with the social relations on which the reproduction is based. Because 'sex and age are subject to randomness of fecundity and differential mortality' rural communities enter into social relations with each other to ensure the maintenance of indigenous social structures. These relations are based on the institutionalisation of kinship, the circulation of wives, and agricultural limits of production. Ultimately, for Meillassoux, 'demographic reproduction is . . . related to the current production of food' (p. 55). It is this which is disrupted as capitalism undermines the indigenous communities' ability to safeguard the mechanism of social reproduction.

Two social processes in particular are set in train as capitalism encroaches on the PCMP: the community either directs a part of its energy towards the production of commercial agricultural goods, or it directs a part of its manpower towards the wage-earning sector – in southern Africa obviously mainly the latter. The result of these transformations is for 'agricultural production of food to decline and that monetary income tends increasingly to be substituted for self produced food' (Meillassoux: 56). The introduction of cash undermines indigenous forms of collective labour. Kinship ties too lessen in importance as seasonal work, wage relations, leasing and commoditisation of land spread throughout the local economy. The community's ability to produce means of subsistence and also its mechanism for its social (and biological) reproduction are undermined. Greater dependence on labour migration, especially when time in urban areas outweighs the length of the off-season and therefore erodes the agricultural base leads to food deficits, the increased dependence upon the market and a further cycle of the undermining of the local community.

In short, the wage breaks down the domestic community: as the urban worker is severed from his/her domestic unit demography takes a new turn. Population growth and the reproduction of the domestic unit no longer depends upon indigenous agricultural productivity and on the ability of the community to store sufficient grain for the off season. Instead, the domestic unit depends for its survival upon 'access to cash, on the level of wages, on the duration of employment, on the price of food, and eventually on the rate of exchange between the country of the worker and of his employer' (Meillassoux: 7).

Meillassoux's work complements Burawoy's concern with political structures that the domestic states established to continue labour migration. Meillassoux helps clarify our understanding of the influence which migrant labour has on the demographic reproduction of the domestic unit. This is done by highlighting the social processes of commoditisation of land and labour and the disruption that this imposes. The local community is increasingly unable to maintain the circulation of subsistence goods, and the storage of sufficient grain for the whole year. This results from the transfer of labourers to the urban areas to work which will – in times of economic crisis – disrupt the ability of the local community to reproduce itself. In short, the migration of labour to the town contributes to depopulation and a deterioration of the condition of life in the rural areas (Meillassoux: 58).

These processes can indeed be clearly seen to be at work in the region, and, in South Africa itself, this latter stage has long been reached. But still the assumption is that the domestic unit continues, even though it is faced with difficulties. We shall in fact be arguing that increasingly men and women are pursuing strategies for survival which, given the manifold pressures and disintegrating context that they face, do not always include the contracting of institutional bonds that form the basis of the household or domestic unit of production.

The differing national patterns of reproduction

The political and economic connections between South Africa and the surrounding states vary from the extreme dependency of illegally occupied Namibia, still largely administered from Pretoria, to the confrontational relationships with Angola and Mozambique. The economies of Botswana, Lesotho and Swaziland, although ostensibly 'British Protectorates' have always been integrated into that of South Africa and little has changed since independence, although the precise form that their 'integration' takes has not been the same in all three. Zambia and Malawi, further from South Africa's borders, walk the tightrope of dependency unsteadily, making spasmodic gestures of political defiance. Zimbabwe must check every shift in policy, with one eye on the road to South Africa.

Moreover, these countries vary widely in the structures of their political economies and how these are reproduced. They differ in the extent of their productive sectors and in the nature of those sectors. Some have large-scale capitalist agriculture, 'settler' agriculture as in Zimbabwe and Namibia or an extension of South African capitalist agribusiness, as in Swaziland. Others, such as Lesotho, have no such sector. Some have other productive sectors, such as mining, and those with their own mining sectors tend to have adopted their own internal system of migrant labour, as in Zambia and Namibia. This has not precluded the flow of migrant labour to South Africa itself. A reverse flow of migrant labour, especially the more skilled grades, from South Africa to peripheral states is not uncommon – in Namibia and Botswana, for example. For some economies migrant labour to South Africa has itself developed into a major producer of domestic income, most notably in Mozambique for most of this century, and over-populated Lesotho, where there are few internal alternatives to the perpetuation of a system of oscillating migration. Whereas some states have attempted to reduce or eliminate labour migration, as Malawi did from 1974 to 1977 and Mozambique later, such a reduction, leading to widespread unemployment, is extremely difficult, and for Lesotho is well-nigh impossible. Thus, the internal economies of southern African states may be analysed in terms of the interrelationships between the various internal productive sectors and the flow of labour and consumption goods, and the further complexities inherited from long-term dependence on South Africa itself. These internal/external flows are different in different places. Zimbabwe alone has a significant manufacturing sector as well as work opportunities in mining and commercial agriculture. Swaziland and Lesotho are without mineral resources, but Swaziland's sugar plantations and fruit canning industry are thriving and offer work, albeit at pitiful wages.

Social differentiation, based on unequal allocation of land and unequal distribution of livestock, is a feature of all countries in the region, though it operates in different ways in different places. Historically, what Clarke (1977) calls 'the confiscation of assets' took place throughout the region, the indigenous African populations losing control over the means of production, not simply in terms of minerals, such as copper, diamonds or gold, but also in terms of access to land and water, for both growing crops and grazing livestock. Lesotho lost the most fertile lowlands to the Boers. In Namibia German settler agriculture confiscated cattle as well as land. At the same time, retention of land for personal use by chiefs, as in Swaziland or Botswana, and, more recently, the promotion of wealthy peasants as 'master farmers', as in Malawi and Zimbabwe, has improved some holdings at the expense of others.

The presence of large-scale commercial farming, largely for export, distorts the economy as a whole, the most fertile land, the best grazing, the greatest access to water and transport being already allocated. What remains is also unevenly distributed and poorer peasants lack cattle and other livestock: thus, the means of cultivation are lacking and the land deteriorates further. Many peasants, in Lesotho and Botswana particularly, no longer find it worthwhile to plough and plant, even when they have land. Many others, especially women, have no access to land anyway. Shortage of labour is a major reason for non-cultivation – together with shortage of livestock with which to plough. This inability to cultivate is common throughout the region, among the poorer strata of households, especially female-headed households.

In some places, as Murray has observed, remittances from migrant labour could be considered to have sharpened inequality in the labour reserves. Wage structures throughout the region have become more differentiated and complex, and there are trends towards increasing inequality everywhere throughout the region. Moreover, patterns of inequality have been reinforced by drought. Poorer peasants have often survived by sales of livestock to wealthier peasants, and such losses are often irretrievable. In Namibia it has been reported that white farmers rented pasture to African peasants, thus profiting from the drought in a small way.

Whatever differences there may be, the same structural similarities and similarities in trends of reproduction patterns are discernible throughout southern Africa. Most of the 'independent' states of southern Africa are in no way peripheral to the economic system operating in South Africa itself. The entire region is interconnected and the same kind of mechanisms operating in South Africa itself, whereby Africans have been restricted to the poorest land, excluded from agricultural commodity markets and forced into contract labour on plantations and farms, in mines and construction work, have been at work throughout southern Africa. Historically, all the peripheral economies were at one point involved in commodity production by peasant farmers with the exception of Swaziland, and even these peasant farmers were comfortably self-sufficient until the latter half of this century. Lesotho had a brief prosperity exporting grain to the diamond fields around Kimberley during the 1860s and 1870s, before the Boers appropriated much of the fertile lowlands and restricted the Basuto to the less fertile uplands. Even so, Lesotho remained self-sufficient in grain, and continued to export a surplus until drought and a drop in world prices brought a slump, and the long-term effects of lost labour on the land began to show with decreasing production levels. Botswana exported cattle until restrictions on the type of cattle acceptable closed the market to all except European-type cattle. The Ovambo in northern Namibia have only recently been reduced to poverty, as drought and war finally destroyed the flourishing system of agriculture on the flood plain, already weakened by a system of migrant labour which made it illegal for the expanding population to move south with the miners employed at Tsumeb, Oranjemund and smaller mines throughout the country.

Gradually, the capacity for communities to remain self-sufficient and even to engage in commodity production was undermined by a combination of pricing strategies, overpopulation (Ovamboland and Lesotho) state policies and pressure from South Africa for labour together with exploitation of labour in the peasant sectors as in Mozambique, urging men into the search for a cash wage. Thus the exodus from the land began, and the subsequent deterioration of the land and loss of control over the means of subsistence. The effects of migrant labour have reverberated throughout the region in terms of deterioration of land and disintegration of communities. For the greater part of this century three-quarters of migrant workers in South Africa were drawn from the periphery through recruiting agencies which kept a tight control on the terms of contract. Control over land has been the lever for controlling labour, and loss of control over land and labour has meant a decline towards sub-subsistence agriculture throughout the region.

Trends towards sub-subsistence agriculture developed throughout southern Africa. Peasant agricultural areas and reserves became net importers of basic foodstuffs, and those without access to a wage sank ever more deeply into poverty. At the same time, a significant output and export level of non-essentials was maintained. A feature of the region as a whole is that while the capitalist sector of agriculture produces a significant output and export of non-essentials, such as coffee and tobacco, there is at the same time a net import of basic foodstuffs. Sometimes both non-essentials and foodstuffs are exported – karakul pelts but also fish and beef from Namibia, sugar and a variety of canned fruit from Swaziland. The export from commercial agriculture is very often *to* South Africa, or *through* South Africa, and the import of food is largely from South Africa. Thus capitalist agriculture throughout the region is closely tied into the South African economy, and the subsistence needs of the region are largely met by South African produce. Namibia, it has been said, is self-sufficient in nothing and the same story repeats itself from Botswana to Lesotho, to Swaziland, all the former British Protectorates.

Meillassoux has stressed the significance of the commoditisation of land and labour, disrupting the capacity of rural households to reproduce themselves, the land being no longer viable as a means of production and the acquisition of food coming to depend on the wage.

Wallerstein has drawn attention to the mechanisms imposed by white settlers to force labour off the land and to prevent them from entering the commodity market, but also to patterns of resistance established in opposition to these mechanisms.

Different patterns of 'households'

If we use Wallerstein's notion of 'households' as 'income-pooling units', then we need to look at the flow of labour and the flow of consumer goods, the twin commoditisation. Wealthy peasant-farmers may produce food for the national market and for home consumption, generating capital for agricultural inputs or land purchases from other family members, possibly working in one of the professions as teachers or civil servants. Less wealthy households may have family members employed in migrant labour, either in South Africa itself or in the internal mining sector, if there is one, or even in capitalist agriculture, thus generating income from a variety of sources, but being dependent on cash wages, due to lack of land and livestock. Poor households, without sufficient access to wages and without access to land, livestock or even labour, to subsidise subsistence production, may be forced to generate income as best they can.

It would be useful here to consider various *models* of household, bearing in mind that there is a constant shift. The shifting pattern of social relationships is striking: men move back and forth as migrants' children are shunted from one relation to another, women move from rural to urban areas in search of work. As has been pointed out, Wallerstein's concept of 'household' and 'pooling of income' is too rigid. It is preferable to see households as constantly in flux and to look at flows of income and services (it is useful to think in terms of services and not just income) between kinship networks and within a given community, according to traditional patterns of rights and responsibilities, but also according to modern commercial transactions, e.g. renting rooms, selling beer, providing transport.

Spiegel's work in Lesotho examines the way in which money brought in to the community by migrant labour circulates through various households. In both Lesotho and Botswana returned migrants spend time with friends (Spiegel 1981), and beer-brewing is thus an activity by which those households without direct access to a migrant wage can gain access to the migrant wages of the returning men. This is obviously particularly important for female-headed households. In urban areas too beer-brewing and food-selling are strategies for making cash.[1] However, migrant wages may also be invested and used to generate further cash income. In isolated rural areas particularly, but in urban areas too, the possession of a truck enables some families to generate cash income. In Namibia, lack of a reliable public transport system makes such an investment profitable both for long journeys and short. Old-age pensioners who must collect their pension in person on the day it falls due thus pass some of that pension on to others in the community. Here, of course, the poor are made still poorer while petty entrepreneurs become richer at their expense.

Wealthy peasant households may own sufficient land and livestock to generate an income from agriculture alone, and even employ labourers. Such households often have links with the 'new petty-bourgeoisie', the teachers, nurses and civil servants whose salaries enable them to maintain a relatively high standard of living, including perhaps employing domestic servants like the white settler elite. Many of this salariat invest some of their earnings in land and livestock, so that the social differentiation that is visible throughout southern Africa permeates both rural and urban areas. In Botswana the urban elite is interested in ranching. In Namibia teachers spend their vacations supervising the cultivation of their land. In Malawi where there is a substantial peasant-based sector producing for the market, sons and daughters are educated for professional employment.

Such a household, with some members in the rural areas, but others perhaps in professional jobs, generates considerable income from agriculture but may also receive investment income from salaried relatives. Thus they would generate income and accumulate some capital from (i) agricultural commodity production; (ii) subsistence needs of households though it is likely that food and clothing will also be bought for cash, and that a certain amount of 'luxury' items will be included; and (iii) income from salaried relatives, as an investment, to purchase more land or livestock, or agricultural inputs.

Moderately wealthy households might have access to the wages of two or more migrant labourers, perhaps working in South Africa or perhaps engaged in internal migration. Parents in the rural areas, and unmarried daughters, remain behind to look after livestock and perhaps to produce sufficient food for everyday needs and a little surplus to sell at local markets. Wages provide enough capital for agricultural inputs and to buy new draught oxen – hiring out oxen generates a little more income. Thus their income consists of (i) migrant wages; (ii) subsistence production; (iii) money earned from selling crops, hiring out oxen, even hiring out a truck; (iv) pensions; and (v) beer-brewing and other casual activities. Here, the access to migrant wages contributes agricultural inputs and perhaps other investment that can be used to generate further income. As in Lesotho, as Murray (1981) points out, migrant labourers' families are not the poorest families – the migrant wage is essential for survival, and wages are used to invest for the future. Those without access to the wage must find other strategies for survival.

In contrast, there is the female-headed rural household where the female head is an older woman. This generation has remained in rural areas where children can be dumped. Grandmothers in rural areas accept responsibility for children while parents look for work in urban areas taking on responsibilities beyond their capacities. They manage on (i) subsistence production; (ii) old-age pensions; (iii) beer-brewing, basket-making, etc. and (iv) remittances. The pension is likely to be the most reliable source of income here, though even that is not entirely reliable. The household in which the grandmother and children live in the rural areas thus draws from the state in cash, subsistence food from agricultural production or from livestock, and spasmodically receives income from the children's parents or from other community members through beer-brewing etc. A substantial amound of food must be bought for cash, as subsistence production is very little. Such consumption needs are often met from local stores, imported food at high prices. The household is constantly changing as children come and go and adult members arrive for visits. People are often unsure exactly how many people are living in a given household from day to day.

Overcrowded urban households struggle to survive in other ways. They may in fact pool income because they are forced into proximity, sometimes as groups of kin sharing township houses, sometimes as groups of strangers, herded into the same adequate accommodation. Such pooling may be a temporary expediency rather than constituting any 'rights' or 'responsibilities'. More and more frequently two or three female relations are the nucleus of urban households with female 'household heads'. Children sent to stay with urban relatives are often unprovided for and exist as best they can, the only security being that they have a place to stay. Such urban households exist on some of the following possible sources of income: (i) cash income from wages, brought in by one or more members; (ii) rent, flowing *between* household members; (iii) pensions, from older members of the household or perhaps from disabled people or widows; (iv) intermittent money from such strategies as beer-brewing, food-selling, prostitution, craft-work; and (v) exchange of services between household members such as food-preparation and child-caring.

   In the next section discussion will focus on the poorest of these households, both those totally dependent on migrant labour, in the current situation where rising unemployment, rapid urbanisation and South Africa's policies of destabilisation, as well as the disastrous consequences of drought, have all contributed to what could be called a 'crisis in reproduction' (Edholm et al. 1979).

The nature of the reproduction crisis

Meillassoux has drawn attention to the loss of control over production which entails loss of control over reproduction. Pre-capitalist African societies were such that subsistence production by all members of the family, whatever the sexual division of labour, reproduced the worker and his family. Food produced was food consumed, and as we have shown most peasant economies were self-sufficient and even produced a surplus. Throughout southern Africa, however, the African population has gradually been confined to the least productive land and labour has been drained from the land into capitalist industry, the African population has gradually been confined to the least productive land and labour has been drained from the land into capitalist industry, the African peasant transformed into a worker-peasant, stretched between his wage relationship to the means of production and his intermittent relationship to the increasingly unproductive land, there being no security either at the workplace, where he has no residence rights, nor in the rural areas where the wage is needed to supplement agricultural production.

Thus, the employer pays only day-to-day maintenance money, because the man's family is invisible, and the worker, separated from immediate contact with his family may or may not finance the reproduction of his family, depending on a number of intervening variables, including his inability to send remittances, due to the inadequacy of the wage, and to the strength of the ties binding him to his family. Burawoy stresses the *interdependence* of productive and reproductive workers even under the migrant labour system, i.e. the dependence of men and women on each other. He suggests that this interdependence established the cohesion of the family and that when it breaks down the family breaks down. This is reminiscent of Wolpe's suggestion that there has been a 'conservation' of the 'reciprocal obligations' of the family, 'albeit in a restructured form' (Wolpe 1972). As Murray comments, it might be better to acknowledge that: 'A certain pattern of reciprocal obligations has broken down, and . . . the onus placed on certain relationships, particularly the conjugal one, has intensified (Murray 1981). Murray also draws attention to the way in which women are expected to carry out their responsiblities while still being accountable to men for the way in which they do so, giving examples from his Lesotho fieldwork where women's priority of feeding the family was not the priority of men far away in South Africa:

In the southern African periphery women very often assume the onus of managing the rural household but have very little control over the resources with which to manage it. (Murray 1981: 107)

As Moorsom has observed, the migrant wage is the man's wage and although there is an interdependence between productive and reproductive workers, Burawoy has perhaps underestimated the shift in power that has occurred:

What money migrant labour brings in has concentrated power in the hands of the men; only they have access to it. Women are tied hand and foot to the place where they live – men may escape their responsibilities in the towns. The migrant system therefor deepened the age-old exploitation of women and the weak. (Ideas and Action Series 1978)

Here we must note that women who are the reproductive workers[2] are also productive workers while the land continues to provide subsistence (for women in African peasant societies have always been producers) but once the land ceases to yield subsistence they become dependent on the production of the men and once dependency on men's wages has become established these women, separated from the means of production, *and* from direct access to the wage have no other resources. Once the productive labourer fails to subsidise reproduction, or, to put it more simply, once men fail to send remittances back home to the women, the reproducers have no alternative but to finance reproduction themselves, i.e. women must either watch their babies die or attempt to earn cash themselves.

Moreover, male unemployment is rising steadily throughout southern Africa, due to shifts to capital-intensive industry and mechanisation of agriculture and to technological improvements in the mining industry. Although South Africa is still taking large numbers of migrant workers, these are increasingly skilled workers and the unskilled are becoming an embarrassing encumbrance, rather than a useful pool of labour resources. In Malawi the number of registered unemployed doubled between 1969 and 1977, and unemployment continues to be a major problem in spite of the re-establishment of migrant labour flows to the Republic. In Namibia the townships are full of unemployed men, both seeking work and avoiding the hazards of war-torn Ovamboland.

The economic crisis in South Africa plus a politically-dictated shift to recruiting within the Republic has affected the labour supply countries drastically. According to official South African figures, the number of 'foreign black workers' has fallen from 475,000 in 1973 to 287,000 in 1982, although the actual numbers will be higher than this. Among mine labour, some 80 per cent was recruited from outside in 1973, now it is less than 40 per cent; Malawi has suffered a decline from 110,000 in 1973 to 15,000 in 1982; Mozambique from 91,000 in 1975 to 40,000 in 1982. The reductions have not been as marked from Botswana, Lesotho and Swaziland – which is just as well as these countries have hardly any significant, alternative sources of employment – but still means that no recruits who have not been miners before are given contracts.

Women and the 'household'

In these circumstances, unemployed men cannot offer women security and there is an increasing tendency for couples to live together without marriage, and even for women to refuse marriage, as in Botswana and Namibia. The number of children born out of wedlock is rising for marriage is expensive, and no longer offers the stability and security it traditionally ensured. In Namibia only 16 of 332 children baptised by the Catholic Church in Katutura were born out of wedlock, and 80 per cent of all children in school are illegitimate; in Botswana the number of illegitimate children is rising.

The postponement, and even rejection, of marriage has become a feature of some societies. Young men engaged in oscillating migration see little advantage in marrying (until they are too old to work) and young women are reluctant to tie themselves to an absent husband, leaving the security of their own family for the uncertainties of being a daughter-in-law. Moreover, parents are often happy to keep the earnings of sons rather than expend money on bride-price, and no longer necessarily find it worthwhile to press reluctant bridegrooms into marriage (Bulbrandsen 1984). Moreover, there has been a weakening of the marriage bond due to prolonged separation of husband and wife reported widely by researchers in southern Africa:

on the one hand, the economic viability of the conjugal relationship in practice requires the separation of the spouses. On the other hand, the prolonged separation of the spouses is most conducive to the destruction of the conjugal relationship. (Murray 1981)

This paradoxical situation has led to a growing number of female-headed households, both young women abandoned by lovers or husbands, or older women keeping together a household base for large numbers of children whose parents are working or seeking work. Large numbers of female-headed households, in both rural and urban areas have been noted in surveys across the region and these households are amongst the poorest everywhere. In rural areas women have been left to manage agricultural production and at the same time to care for young children, the sick and the elderly. In some places (South Africa itself, Zimbabwe, Malawi and Swaziland) women have themselves become agricultural labourers, even migrant labourers, harvesting and weeding for pathetically low wages. Moreover, women are increasingly being employed because they provide cheaper and more docile workers, as we have already noted, often on a seasonal or part-time basis. Due to mechanisation there is now need for fewer permanent workers and a large number of seasonal workers for weeding and harvesting. The number of casual agricultural workers in South Africa increased 100 per cent between 1965 and 1970. Many of these workers are now women. Indeed, a majority of casual workers are women.

Thus, women who were once *producers and reproducers* have been stripped of their productive roles and left to carry out the task of reproduction without the means of so doing. Their immediate reaction has been to go in search of jobs themselves, to gain direct access to the wage. Hence, the movement of women into the urban areas throughout southern Africa and, in some areas, the increasing employment of women as seasonal migrant farmworkers (Wilson et al. 1977; McFadden 1983).

Women in urban areas have three options open to them:

1. to enter wage work, where this is available, either in factories, or as domestics;
2. to generate income via strategies such as beer-brewing, food-selling, craft-work or perhaps even prostitution; or
3. to remain dependent, living on the wage of husbands, or other male or female relatives, or new lovers.

In situations of migrant labour women were reduced to dependency, and an insecure dependency at that, separated as they were from the menfolk who were working. But, today, widespread male unemployment has increased women's vulnerability, for even the men have lost access to cash income, and there are inadequate social welfare benefits to fill the gap. Rapid urbanisation of women who survive through a variety of strategies, employed in industry, as domestics, or surviving in the informal sector by beer-brewing, food-selling, craft-work and perhaps childcare for other family members, is accompanied by male marginalisation. Moreover, there are indications that employers are eager to take on women instead of men, because they can pay them even less. A convenient assumption by employers is that all women are married, so that their wage only supplements the wage of the breadwinner – an ironic assumption in southern Africa. This rationale for paying them less may be coupled with the fact that they are employed only as casual or seasonal workers and therefore unprotected by legislation protecting permanent workers

Why are women prepared to work for even less than men, and in appalling conditions? The answer lies partly in women's subordinate position in African society as well as under apartheid. Women are not accustomed to assert themselves in public against men even in African communities, so it is hardly likely that they will do so in white factories or plantations. Moreover, women are powerfully motivated to work because they have direct responsibility for preparing and cooking food, and for the care of children, the sick and the elderly. Women are closely involved with their children. This is what being responsible for reproduction means. It is difficult for them to watch babies starve, day by day, and any wage is better than none. This close connection between birth and death drives women to work for wages which even the exploited men would turn down.

The distinction between reproduction at the biological level and reproduction at the societal level must be remembered here, as Edholm et al. have reminded us. As Meillassoux observes:

When the working conditions of male adults compel them to live far from their families for long periods of time, or when they can only enjoy short stays with their family, the income of the wage-earners *tends to be directed outside of the conventional family framework* towards uses aimed at immediately attenuating the harshness of their urban living conditions. The instability of income due to unemployment, delinquency, police harassment, have the effect of interrupting and eventually stopping the transfer of income towards the wife and children, thus leading the women to look for a job and to abandon her children . . .. One then observes the decomposition of the family which goes along with a degradation of the population, both physical and social. . . . (Meillassoux 1983)

This is not the only possible scenario, but it is a common one.

Everywhere, rising unemployment and rapid urbanisation are occurring. Both men and women have entered the urban areas in large numbers, for women will no longer remain in the rural areas to starve and their illegal urbanisation constitutes an important political statement and mass resistance. Everywhere, the preponderance of women in urban areas is causing concern for the state because they are a source of potential unrest. In South Africa and Namibia they are constantly arrested, fined and shunted back to ethnic homelands. In Mozambique a form of influx control has been instituted, and in Zimbabwe women in the streets without men have been jailed as prostitutes. Women in urban areas exist precariously, often in shanty towns and squatter settlements, engaging in a range of desperate activities in order to raise cash to feed their families. Women are accustomed to operating in the informal sector and are unable to make an income through such activities as beer-brewing as easily as a man. In addition domestic service is often a possibility for women and, as we have seen, there is evidence that women might be preferred to men, in some industries and in agriculture.

Rapid population growth and population pressure in urban areas where families live in appalling conditions often without sanitation and access to clean water, present a whole set of problems. For babies, there is the increased likelihood of gastroenteritis as opposed to the malnutrition of the rural areas and susceptibility to measles and meningitis epidemics that kill many. For women, there is the vulnerability to rape, male violence, alcoholism and maybe the temptation to turn to prostitution. Even when they are rounded up and jailed, however, there is effectively nowhere else for them to go.

Poverty and high infant mortality rates in both rural and urban areas are a sign of breakdown in social reproduction, but have also given credence to the myth of overpopulation, and consequent population control policies, noticeable throughout southern Africa, except where deliberate reversals of such policy have been made, as in the banning of Depo-Provera in Zimbabwe and Banda's ban on all contraception. Clinics aimed at limiting family size are a priority even where the lack of clean water and sanitation endanger the lives of living babies and malnutrition leaves its inheritance of disease and stunted growth, both physical and mental, even when its victims survive.

The crisis of agricultural production and of access to subsistence

The structures where large a farm sector received preference over a neglected, labour-supplying peasant sector, together with the trends of commercialisation, to population pressure in the restricted reserves, and of class formation (even at low general levels of living) have now created a situation of crisis proportions in the peasant farming areas throughout southern Africa. Total production is nowhere near enough to feed the producers themselves, let alone the urban population; and certain large and growing minorities of the rural dwellers are becoming totally impoverished: denied access to any regular source of remittances from migrant labour, and denied the wherewithal to be independent producers. Levels of total production from the large farm and peasant sectors combined are now by and large what they were at the beginning of the 1970s in Botswana, Lesotho, Namibia, Zambia, Zimbabwe and even South Africa, which means per capita production is much lower than in the last decade – although the effect of three years of drought in all of these countries, with the partial exception of Zambia, must be remembered before too much is read into the statistical series. Mozambique and Angola suffered a marked decline in overall production following the white exodus after Independence from which they have yet to recover. Malawi and Swaziland are the two countries that show marked increases in farm production. The former, particularly, is distinct, not only in not experiencing drought but also in that its own large farm sector has seen a significant increase – unlike all the others where the former settler sector has lost land and its share in production to the peasant sector. So in Malawi, significant overall growth in agriculture may well cover up an even greater relative impoverishment of part of the labour reserves' population.

A clearer indication of the declining capacity of the southern African countries to meet their own food needs is given if we look at figures for the production but also imports of the basic staple of the region, maize:

TABLE 22.1

Country	Production ('000 metric tonnes)				Imports					
	1974–76	1981	1982	1983	1981		1982		1983	
Angola	433	250	250	275	84	34%	128	51	135	49
Botswana	60	n.a.	n.a.	25						
Malawi	1,127	1,245	1,415	1,500	56	4	63	4	65	4
Mozambique	383	275	270	200	150	55	92	34	120·	120
Zambia	1,424	1,007	735	935	117	12	50	7	40	4
Zimbabwe	1,886	2,814	1,767	1,000	242 exp	–	352 exp	–	250 imp 1,000 exp	
South Africa	9,186	14,660	8,344	3,910	4,400 exp	–	4,000 exp	–	1,200 imp	30
Lesotho	n.a.	n.a.	n.a.	n.a.	95		n.a.		n.a.	

Source: FAO

What these figures tell us is that, even before the drought, most of the SADCC countries with the exception of Zimbabwe had to import a greater or smaller part of their staple food needs, but obviously in part that is to meet urban food needs. Thus, even if there is no aggregate food surplus from agriculture, that does not necessarily mean 'subsistence' is not met through self-production of peasants. Two further adjustments need to be made to the analysis to see how the labour reserves are now, in most of the region, net food importers. First we need to recognise that imports to some countries, like Angola and Mozambique, and Lesotho and Botswana, are on such a level that they must be going to meet more than the demand from urban markets. But second, we have to discount the contribution of the large farm sector. In fact all of the countries in the region, with the exception of Lesotho, have significant large farm sectors, and in many cases maize and other foods, for the local market if not for export as well, are produced by this capitalist sector and sold not only to urban but rural dwellers also. Even if the peasant sector as a whole, the labour reserves, still offer some surplus of grain for sale, throughout the region the peasant sectors are net importers of food. In Swaziland, for instance, by the 1970s, the peasant sector produced only half of its basic food needs. To understand the real trends to impoverishment among the most vulnerable it is necessary, however, to disaggregate the picture. One of the more controversial papers (by C. Simkins) at the Carnegie Conference on Poverty in Cape Town in April 1984 reported 'real improvements in incomes of Homeland residents'. Whereas almost no households achieved minimum standards of living in 1960, now some 20 per cent do so. But the same report also revealed that there was an *increase in the number of destitutes*: The number of people receiving 'zero income' rose from 250,000 in 1960 to 1,450,000 in 1980.

The same pattern as in South Africa's bantustans – of fostering a better-off, commercially-oriented section of the peasantry – has been pursued in most countries of the region in recent years. But there has also been the same increasing minority of destitutes – poor peasants becoming virtually landless. In *Malawi*, where the large estates have taken away land in the last few years from the peasant sector, over 50 per cent of all rural households have *holdings too small to produce their basic food needs*. In *Lesotho*, over half the work-seekers have no arable land of their own. In *Zimbabwe*, estimates suggest that maybe as many as 20 per cent of households in the Communal Areas, as the reserves are now called, were landless at Independence. In *Botswana* even, with only 1 million people in a vast territory, there is evidence of the beginnings of *land scarcity*, reflected in a tendency for people to establish their own households later in life than before.

Impoverishment is reflected not only in limited access to land, but to another means of production crucial in the farming systems that characterise most of the region – *livestock*, crucial as a means of livelihood, a store of wealth, and a means of ploughing: In Botswana, half of rural families have no cattle. In Zimbabwe, likewise, almost half of Communal Area households have none. One of the basic, long-term effects of the current widespread *drought* is that it has not only led to great losses in livestock numbers, but will confirm growing numbers of the rural poor in their propertylessness – a process graphically illustrated by these figures about the homeland of Lebowa in South Africa: whereas the average family previously had 10 cattle, by 1983 the number was down to 5, and by the end of 1984 the average is expected to be 1. There is also a strong correlation between the destitute, 'poor peasant' families and the women-headed households who number roughly 30 per cent of rural households in most of southern Africa. Many of these are without regular remittances of earnings from elsewhere and their own production is massively constrained as they have less chance of access to land, and to oxen for ploughing, and are also short of *labour* at crucial seasons, with the result that, in *Botswana*, 80 per cent of all those 'working for rations' in drought relief projects were *women*.

Conclusion

When we talk about a crisis in reproduction we need to ask what it is that is not being reproduced. The capitalist mode of production in southern Africa seems to be in little immediate danger, although we need to see other developments in the light of a crisis in capital accumulation. However, the relations of production and reproduction are shifting and the system of migrant labour is undergoing transformation. The current crisis in capital accumulation in southern Africa is accompanied by a massive restructuring of the social system and a restructuring of the gender construction of that system, entailing the proletarianisation of women and children. The rapid growth in unemployment has brought about male marginalisation on an unprecedented scale so that the significant gap in future may be between those in employment and the unemployed, a split in the class which until now has variously been referred to as a 'rural proletariat', 'peasantariat' or simply as 'worker peasants'.

The widespread urbanisation of whole populations is accompanied by disintegration of family structures, to the extent that the social reproduction of patterns of migrant labour could be considered in danger. If women will no longer stay in the rural areas where sub-subsistence conditions prevail, who will keep even the skeleton of agriculture together, especially when the older generation of grandmothers at present taking care of the next generation is dead and buried? The split between renewal and maintenance functions is now so complete that interdependence no longer exists and, as Clarke observes, 'not all households necessarily secure subsistence. As a result, higher mortality rates, lower life expectancy and greater malnutrition is evidenced.' (Clarke 1977).

What is not necessarily being reproduced is the labour force. It has already become commonplace to speak of South Africa's bantustan policies as 'genocidal'. However, if our analysis is correct, and the whole of southern Africa is following the same road, this genocide is not confined to the boundaries of South Africa itself.

NOTES

1. Boycotts of beer halls in South Africa and attacks on them are the result of women's anger when municipalities open such halls and siphon off one important source of revenue.
2. See Edholm et al. (1979). It is important to distinguish between three levels of reproduction: social, labour force and human biological. Here, we refer to 'biological reproduction of the labour force'.

Bibliography

Abba, A. (1983), 'An interim reply to the attacks on the PRP', Marx and Africa Conference, Zaria, March.

—— (1984), 'The roots of the Nigerian economic crisis and the alternative strategy for national independence and development', ASUU National Conference on the State of the Economy, Benin, April.

Abdullahi, Y. A. (1983), 'The state and agrarian crisis: rhetoric and substance of Nigerian agricultural development policy', State of the Economy Workshop, A.B.U., Zaria.

Abubakar, S. (1983), 'Imports policy and the crisis: a review of the 1981 import licensing exercise', State of the Economy Workshop, Ahmadu Bello University, Zaria.

Acharya, S. N. (1981), 'Perspectives and problems in sub-Saharan Africa', *World Development*, vol. 9, no. 2.

AERLS (1979), *Report on wheat production and marketing in Nigeria*, Ahmadu Bello University, Zaria.

Ahmed, A. E. M. and O. M. F Beshir, (1983), *A modelling approach to forecasting: a critique of some essential aspects of the Sudanese Six Year Plan*, Hamburg.

Ake, C. (1981), *A political economy of Africa*, London: Longman.

—— (1984), 'An alternative development strategy for Nigeria', ASUU National Conference on the State of the Economy, Benin, April.

Akomeso, A. (1984), *The role of multipurpose cooperative societies in economic development in Bendel State*. Unpublished dissertation, University of Port Harcourt.

Ali, T. (1982), *The cultivation of hunger: towards a political history of agricultural development in the Sudan, 1956–1964*, Ph.D. thesis, University of Toronto.

—— (1983), 'The road to Jouda', *Review of African Political Economy*, no. 26.

Allison, C. and R. H. Green (eds) (1983a), 'Accelerated development in sub-Saharan Africa: what agendas for action?', *Bulletin*, vol. 14, no. 1, Institute of Development Studies, Brighton.

—— (1983b), 'Stagnation and decay in sub-Saharan Africa: dialogues, dialectics and doubts', *Bulletin*, vol. 14, no. 1, Institute of Development Studies, Brighton, January.

Aluko, Sam A. (1974), Comments on the papers by Professor Helleiner and Mr Akintomide in Onitiri and Olatunbosun.

Amin, Samir (1972), 'Underdevelopment and dependence in black Africa: origins and contemporary forms', *Journal of Modern African Studies*, vol. 10, no. 4.

—— (1979), 'UNCTAD IV and the new international economic order', in H. Golbourne (ed.), *Politics and the state in the third world*, London: Macmillan.

Andrae, G. (1983), *Agro-based industry: forms of labour subordination*, Uppsala: Scandinavian Institute of African Studies, (mimeo.).

Andrae, G. and Beckman, B. (1984), 'Labour and industrial crisis in the third world: the case of Nigerian textiles and cotton', AKUT 30, Uppsala.

—— (1986), *The wheat trap: bread and underdevelopmnent in Nigeria*, London: Zed Press.

Anglo-American Corporation of South Africa (1983 and 1984), *Annual Reports*.

Anker, R. and J. Knowles, (n.d.), *Population, growth, employment and economic development: demographic interactions in Kenya: Bachue-Kenya*, New York: St Martins Press for the ILO.

Arrighi, G. (1967), *The political economy of Rhodesia*, Hague: Mouton.

—— (1970), 'Labour supplies in historical perspective, *Journal of Development Studies*, vol. 6, no. 3.

—— (1978), 'Towards a theory of capitalist crisis', *New Left Review*, no. 111.

—— (1982), 'A crisis of hegemony', in S. Amin *et al.*, *The dynamics of global crisis*, New York: Monthly Review Press.

Arrighi, G. and B. J. Silver (1984), 'Labour movements and capital migration: the United States and Western Europe in world-historical perspective', in C. Bergquist (ed.), *Labor in the capitalist world-economy*, Beverly Hills: Sage.

Astrow, A. (1983), *Zimbabwe: a revolution that lost its way?*, London: Zed Press.

Bibliography

Bangura, Y. (1983), *Britain and commonwealth Africa: the politics of economic relations between 1951 and 1975*, Manchester: Manchester University Press.

—— (1984), 'Overcoming some basic misconceptions of the Nigerian economic crisis', paper presented at meeting of the Nigerian Political Science Association, May.

Bates, R. H. (1981), *Markets and states in tropical Africa*, Berkeley: University of California Press.

Beckman, B. (1980), 'Imperialism and capitalist transformation: critique of a Kenyan debate', *Review of African Political Economy*, no. 19.

—— (1981), 'Imperialism and the national bourgeoisie', *Review of African Political Economy*, no. 22.

—— (1982), 'Whose state: state and capitalist development in Nigeria', *Ibid*, no. 23.

—— (1983), 'Marxism and underdevelopment: a critique of Ake', paper presented to Marx and Africa Conference, Zaria, March.

—— (1985), 'Public investment and agrarian transformation in northern Nigeria', in M. Watts (ed.), *State, oil and agriculture in Nigeria*, Berkeley: University of California Press.

Bello, S. (1983), 'Inherent limitations of petit-bourgeois political analysis', Faculty of Arts and Social Sciences seminar, Ahmadu Bello University, Zaria, 7 May.

Bernstein, H. (1981), 'Notes on the state and peasantry: the Tanzanian case', *Review of African Political Economy*, no. 21.

Bhagavan, M. R. (1981), 'Establishing the conditions for socialism: the case of Angola', in B. Munslow (ed.), *Africa: Problems in the Transition to Socialism*, London: Zed Press.

Bienefeld, M. (1983), 'Efficiency, expertise, NICs and the accelerated development report', *Bulletin*, vol. 14, no. 1, Institute of Development Studies, Brighton, January.

Biermann, W. (1985), 'Industrialisation and capital accumulation in Tanzania, 1967–1984', *Research Report*, Economic Research Bureau, University of Dar es Salaam.

Bird, G. (1983), 'Should developing countries use currency depreciation as a tool of balance of payments adjustment? a review of the theory and the evidence, and a guide for the policymaker', *Journal of Development Studies*, March.

Block, F. (1977), *The origins of international economic disorder*, Berkeley: University of California Press.

BMCE (Banque Marocaine de Commerce Exterieur), *Monthly Information Review*, no. 46.

Bobo, N. (1983), 'The Zimbabwe lesson', *Monthly Review*, September.

Bolton, Dianne (1985), *Nationalization: a road to socialism? the case of Tanzania*, London: Zed Press.

Bond, M. (1983), *Agricultural responses to prices in sub-Saharan Africa*, Washington: IMF Research Department, May.

Bratton, M. (1983), 'Farmer organisations in the communal areas of Zimbabwe: preliminary findings', University of Zimbabwe.

Brewer, A. (1980), *Marxist theories of imperialism*, London: Routledge & Kegan Paul.

Bundy, Colin (1972), 'The emergence and decline of a South African peasantry', *African Affairs*, vol. 71, no. 285.

—— (1979), *The rise and fall of the South African peasantry*, London: Heinemann.

Burawoy, M. (1980), 'Migrant labour in South Africa and in the United States', in T. Nichols (ed.), *Capital and labour: studies in the capitalist labour process*, London: Fontana.

Burniaux, J-M. and J. Wealbroeck (1984), 'Agricultural protection in Europe: its impact on developing countries', in C. Stevens (ed.), *Food aid and the developing world*, London: Croom Helm and Overseas Development Institute.

Bush, R., S. Kibble and G. Wright (1984), 'Destabilisation in South Africa: an overview', *Working paper*, no. 3, Southern Africa Research Project, Leeds University.

Bush, R. and S. Kibble (1985), 'Destabilisation in southern Africa', *Current African Issues*, no. 4, Scandinavian Institute of African Studies, Uppsala.

Callaghy, T. M. (1984a), 'Africa's debt crisis', *Journal of International Affairs*, Summer.

—— (1984b), *The state-society struggle: Zaire in co-operative perspective*, New York: Columbia University Press.

Callear, Diana (1983), 'Who wants to be a peasant? Food production in a labour exporting area of Zimbabwe', (mimeo.).

Bibliography

Carlsson, J. (ed.) (1983), *Recession in Africa*, Uppsala: Scandinavian Institute of African Studies.

Carvalho Somoes, J. Y. (ed.) (1984), *SADCC: energy and development to the year 2000*, Uppsala: Scandinavian Institute of African Studies.

Central Bank of Swaziland (1984), *Quarterly Review*, March.

Charney, C. (1984), 'The politics of changing partners: control and co-option in the new South African constitution', *Review of African Political Economy*, no. 29.

Clarke, D. G. (1974), *Contract workers and underdevelopment in Rhodesia*, Gwelo: Mambo Press.

—— (1977), *Foreign migrant labour in southern Africa: studies in accumulation in the labour reserves: demand determinants and supply relationships*, Working Employment Programme, working paper no. 16, Geneva: ILO.

Clarke, S. (1978), 'Capital, fractions of capital, and the state', *Capital and Class*, no. 5.

Cliffe, L. and B. Munslow (1985), 'The politics of agrarian transformation: the state, bureaucracy and participation', paper to the Annual Conference of the Political Studies Association, University of Manchester.

Clough, P. and G. Williams (1984), 'Decoding Berg: the World Bank in northern Nigeria', *Review of African Political Economy*, no. 31.

Colclough, C. (1983), 'Are African governments as unproductive as the accelerated development report implies?', *Bulletin*, vol. 14, no. 1, Institute of Development Studies, Brighton, January.

Commercial Farmers' Union (1984), Econ/84/823 4317/D2, 5th March.

Cooper, D. (1983), 'Looking at development projects', *Work in Progress*, no. 26.

Coulson, A. (1982), *Tanzania: a political economy*, Oxford: Clarendon Press.

Crockett, A. D. (1981), 'Stabilisation policies in developing countries: some policy considerations', *IMF staff papers*, vol. 28, no. 1, March.

Daniel, P. (1983), 'Accelerated development in sub-Saharan Africa: an agenda for structural adjustment lending?', *Bulletin*, vol. 14, no. 1, Institute of Development Studies, Brighton.

De Beers (1983 and 1984), *Annual Reports*, De Beers, Botswana Mining Co. (Pty) Ltd.

Dell, S. (1981), 'On being grandmotherly: the evolution of IMF conditionality', *Essays in International Finance*, no. 144, Princeton University, October.

Dell, S. and R. Lawrence (1980), *The balance of payments adjustment process in developing countries*, New York: Pergamon.

Demunter, P. (1975), *Masses rurales et luttes politiques au Zaire*, Paris: Anthropos.

Doucet, L. (1983), 'Tieboudienne at noon', *West Africa*, 7 November.

Dusey, B. (1984), Personal communication, Central Selling Organisation, London, August.

Economist Intelligence Unit (1984), *Quarterly Economic Review*, nos. 1 and 2.

—— Reports no. 82 (Namibia, Lesotho, Botswana, Swaziland); Report no. 76 (Zambia) and Report no. 75 (Angola).

Edholm, F., H. Harris and K. Young (1979), 'Conceptualising women', *Critique of Anthropology*, vols 9 and 10, no. 3.

Ekpo, A. H. (1984), *Food dependency and the Nigerian economy: an ex-post analysis*, Calabar: University of Calabar.

Ekuerhare, B. (1983), 'Orthodox models versus marxian models of economic analysis: a comparative appraisal', Public lecture, Nigerian Economic Studies Association, 13 March.

Ekuerhare, B. and A. Ihuoma (1984), 'Capital goods industry as essential ingredient in Nigeria's self-reliant industrialisation strategy', Nigerian Economic Society Conference, May.

Ellis, F. (1983), 'Agricultural marketing and peasant-state transfers in Tanzania', *Journal of Peasant Studies*, vol. 10, no. 4.

Emmanuel, A. (1972), *Unequal exchange*, London: New Left Books.

Engineering and Mining Journal (E & MJ) (1984), March.

European Community (1982), *Tanzania's economy 1981–2*, Economic and Commercial Officers of the European Community Member Countries, Dar es Salaam, (confidential).

Europe Outremer (1983), 'L'avenir des fermes composées', in special issue *Blé, Minoteries et Boulangeries en Afrique*, vol. 6, May-June.

Fadlalla, B. O. M. (1983), *Problems and perspectives of the socio-economic development of the Sudan*, Hamburg.

Bibliography

FIIRO (1974), 'Composite flour: its use for confectionery and breadmaking in Nigeria', *Technical Information Bulletin for Industry*, Federal Institute for Industrial Research, Oshodi, July.

Findlay, A. M. (1978), *Geographical patterns of Moroccan emigration*, M.A. thesis, University of Durham.

First, R. (1970), *Power in Africa*, New York: Random House.

—— (1983), *Black gold: the Mozambican miner, proletarian and peasant*, Hassocks: Harvester Press.

Food and Agricultural Organisation of the United Nations (FAO), *Production yearbooks*, Rome.

—— (1980), *The state of food and agriculture*, Rome.

—— (1983), *Food outlook: 1983 statistical supplement*, Rome.

—— (1984a), *Food aid in figures*, Rome.

—— (1984b), 'Agricultural price policies in Africa', 13th FAO Regional Conference for Africa, Harare, 16–25 July.

Franke, R. W. and B. Chasin (1980), *Seeds of famine*, Montdesir.

Frankel, G. (1984), 'An African success story', *The Guardian Weekly*, vol. 16, no. 12.

Gaidzanwa, R. B. (1981), *Promised land: towards a land policy for Zimbabwe*, unpublished MDS thesis, Institute of Social Studies, The Hague.

Garcia, R. V. and Escudeno J. C. (1981), *Drought and man: the 1972 case history: vol. 1: nature pleads not guilty*, Oxford: Pergamon.

Gardner, R. (1980), *Sterling dollar diplomacy in current perspective*, New York: Columbia University Press.

Girvan, N., R. Bernal and W. Hughes (1980), 'The IMF and the third world: the case of Jamaica 1974–1980', *Development Dialogue*, no. 2.

Glyn, A. and B. Sutcliffe (1972), *British capitalism, workers and the profits squeeze*, Harmondsworth: Penguin.

Godfrey, M. (1983), 'Export orientation and structural adjustment in sub-Saharan Africa', *Bulletin*, vol. 14, no. 1, Institute of Development Studies, Brighton, January.

—— (1985), 'Trade and exchange rate policy: a further contribution to the debate', in T. Rose (ed.), *Crisis and recovery in sub-Saharan Africa*, Paris: OECD.

Gough, I. (1979), *The political economy of the welfare state*, London: Macmillan.

Gran, G. (ed.) (1979), *Zaire: the political economy of underdevelopment*, New York: Praeger.

Green, P. and A. Hirsch (1982), 'Manufacturing industry in the Ciskei', in *Homeland tragedy: function and farce*, Johannesburg: University of the Witwatersrand.

Green, R.H. (1983a), 'Incentives, policies, participation and response: reflections on World Bank "policies and priorities in agriculture"', *Bulletin*, vol. 14, no. 1, Institute of Development Studies, Brighton, January.

—— (1983b), '"No worst is there none" Tanzania political economic crisis 1978-?????', in J. Carlsson (ed.) *Recession in Africa*, Uppsala: Scandinavian Institute of African Studies.

Green, R. H. *et al.* (1980), *Economic shocks and national policy making: Tanzania in the 1970s*, The Hague: Institute of Social Studies.

Griffiths-Jones, S. (1981), 'The evolution of external finance and development in Chile, 1973–78', Discussion paper no. 160, Institute of Development Studies, Brighton.

—— (1983), 'A Chilean perspective', *Bulletin*, vol. 14, no. 1, Institute of Development Studies, Brighton, January.

Grynberg, R. and J. Wagao (1983), 'The deterioration of the Tanzanian balance of trade', Economic Research Bureau staff seminar paper, University of Dar es Salaam.

Guitan, M. (1981), *Fund conditionality: evolution of principles and practice*, IMF Pamphlet no. 38, Washington.

Gulbrandsen, O. (1984), 'To marry or not to marry', Department of Social Anthropology, University of Bergen, (mimeo.).

Guyer, J. I. (1984), 'Women's work and production systems: a review of two reports on the agricultural crisis', *Review of African political economy*, nos. 27–28.

Hanak, E. (1982), *The Tanzanian balance of payments crisis: causes, consequences and lessons for a survival strategy*, paper no. 82.1, Economic Research Bureau, University of Dar es Salaam.

Hansohm, D. and H-E Woltersdorff (1984), *Determining factors of working behaviour in*

Bibliography

"traditional" societies – a case study from western Sudan: the fur and the Baggara, Bremen.

Haysom, N. (1983), 'Ruling with the whip: a report on the violation of human rights in the Ciskei', Johannesburg, University of the Witwatersrand.

Helleiner, G. K. (1983), 'The IMF and Africa in the 1980s', Essays in International Finance paper no. 152, Princeton University, July.

Hewitt, A. (1982), 'The European development fund and its function in the EEC's Development Aid Policy', Working paper no. 11, Overseas Development Institute, London, (mimeo.).

—— (1983), 'Stabex: analysing the effectiveness of an innovation', in C. Stevens (ed.), *The EEC and the third world: a survey*, London: Overseas Development Institute.

Heyer, J., P. Roberts and G. Williams (1981), *Rural development in tropical Africa*, London: Macmillan.

Heywood, C. (1981), 'The role of the peasantry in French industrialisation 1815–80', *Economic History Review*, vol. 34, no. 3.

Hinderink, J. and J. Sterkenburg (1983), 'Agricultural policy and production in Africa: the aims, methods and the means', *Journal of Modern African Studies*, vol. 21, no. 1.

Hirsch, A. and A. Kooy (1982), 'Industry and employment in East London', *South African Labour Bulletin*.

Hirschmann, A. (1977), 'A generated linkage approach to development, with special reference to staples', *Economic Development and Cultural Change*, Supplement, no. 25.

Hopkins, A. G. (1973), *An economic history of West Africa*, London: Longmans.

Horsefield, K. J. (1969), *The International Monetary Fund 1945–1965*, vol. 2, Washington D.C.: International Monetary Fund.

Ideas and Action (1978), Special issue on apartheid, no. 126 7–8, Annex.

Iduchaba, F. S. (1980), 'Letter to the Permanent Secretary, Ministry of Agriculture', in Ministry of Agriculture (Nigeria), *The green revolution: a food production plan for Nigeria*, Lagos.

Ihinga, K. (1984), 'Déroutante afrique ou la syncope d'un discours', *Canadian Journal of African Studies*, vol. 18, no. 1.

International Defence and Aid Fund (1981), *Women under apartheid*, London.

International Labour Office (ILO) (1976), *Growth employment and equity: a comprehensive strategy for the Sudan*, Geneva: ILO.

International Monetary Fund (IMF) (1981), *Memorandum on Tanzania*, Washington D.C., (confidential).

—— (1982 and 1983), *Annual reports*, Washington D.C.

—— (1984a), *World economic outlook*, Washington D.C.

—— (1984b), *Survey*, Washington D.C.

—— (1985), *World economic outlook*, Washington D.C.

—— (1986), *International financial statistics*, Washington: IMF, April.

Jackson, A. with D. Eade (1983), *Against the grain: the dilemma of project food aid*, Oxford: Oxfam.

Jaggi, M., R. Muller and S. Schmid (1977), *Red Bologna*, London: Writers & Readers.

Jamal, A. (1983), 'Development means structural adjustment', speech delivered at UNCTAD VI, Belgrade.

de Janvry, A. (1981), *The agrarian question and reformism in Latin America*, Baltimore: John Hopkins University Press.

JASPA/ILO (1982), *Tanzania: basic needs in danger*, Addis Ababa.

Jewsiewicki, B. (1979), 'Introduction to contributions to a history of agriculture and fishing in Central Africa', *African Economic History*, no. 7.

—— (1980), 'Political consciousness among African peasants', *Review of African Political Economy*, no. 19.

Joinet, B. (1981), *Tanzanie: manger d'abord*, Paris: Karthala.

Jones, J. V. S. (1983), *Resources and industry in Tanzania: use, misuse and abuse*, Dar es Salaam: Tanzania Publishing House.

Kaldor, N. (1982), 'The role of devaluation in the adjustment of balance of payments deficits', *Report to the Group of 24*, UNCTAD/MFD/TA16 GE. 82–55831.

Kanesa-Thasan, S. (1981), 'The fund adjustment policies in Africa', *Finance and Development*, September.

Bibliography

Kay, Geoffrey (1975), *Development and underdevelopment: a marxist approach*, London: Macmillan.

Kay, George (1972), 'The distribution and density of the African population in Rhodesia', Department of Geography, University of Hull, Miscellaneous Series, no. 12.

Kilby, P. (1969), *Industrialisation in an open economy 1945–1966*, Cambridge.

Killick, T. (1981), 'IMF stabilisation programmes in the third world', *Development Studies Association Paper*, July, Oxford.

—— (ed.) (1982), *Adjustment and financing in the developing world: the role of the IMF*, Washington: IMF.

Killick, T., G. Bird, J. Sharpley and M. Sutton (1984a), *The IMF and stabilisation*, London: Heinemann.

—— (1984b), *The quest for economic stabilisation*, London: Heinemann.

Kindleberger, C. P. (1973), *The world in depression 1929–1939*, Berkeley: University of California Press.

Kriesel, H. C. (1974), *Some economic performance problems in the primary marketing component of statutory marketing systems*, in I I. M. A. Onitiri and D. Olatunbosun, *The marketing board system*, Ibadan: NISER.

Laar, A. van der (1980), *The World Bank and the poor*, The Hague: Niejhoff.

Lal, D. (1983), *The poverty of "development economics"*, Hobart paperbacks no. 16, London: IEA.

Legassick, M. (1974), 'South Africa: capital accumulation and violence', *Economy and Society*, 3.

—— (1975), 'Forced labour, industrialisation and racial differentiation', in R. Harris (ed.), *The political economy of Africa*, Chichester: John Wiley.

Lemarchand, R. (1979), 'The politics of penury in rural Zaire', in Gran (ed.).

Lloyds Bank, 'Economic group reports on Botswana (1983), Tanzania (1984), Zambia (1983) and Zimbabwe (1984).

Loft *et al.* (1982), 'An evaluation of the Kigoma rural development project', ERB (restricted), paper no. 82, University of Dar es Salaam.

Loxley, J. (1984a), 'The Berg Report and the model of accumulation in sub-Saharan Africa', *Review of African Political Economy*, Nos. 27/28.

—— (1984b), *The IMF and the poorest countries*, Ottawa: North-South Institute.

—— (forthcoming), *External finance and structural adjustment in third world countries*, Ottawa: North-South Institute.

McCallum, J. and D. Vines (1981), 'Cambridge and Chicago on the balance of payments', *Economic Journal*, June.

McFadden, P. (1983), 'Women workers in South Africa', *Journal of African Marxists*, September.

MacGaffrey, W. (1982), 'The policy of national integration in Zaire', *Journal of Modern African Studies*, vol. 20, no. 1.

Maddison, A. (1982), *Phases of capitalist development*, New York: Oxford University Press.

Madunagu, E. (1983), *Nigeria: the economy and the people*, London: New Beacon Books.

Manghezi, A. (1983), 'Ku Thekela: strategies for survival against famine in southern Mozambique', *Estudos Mocambicos*, no. 4.

de Mas, P. (1978), 'The place of peripheral regions in Moroccan planning', *Tijdschrift voor Economische en Sociale Geografie*, vol. 69, nos. 1–2.

Matthews, A. (1985), 'The effects of agricultural trade liberalisation on less developed countries', in C. Stevens, *The EEC and the third world: a survey*, London: Overseas Development Institute.

Mawuli, A. (1984), 'The currency exchange, money supply and the dilemma of the Central Bank of Nigeria', CSER Workshop on the development role of the Nigerian banking system, no. 2.

Maxwell, S. and H. W. Singer (1979), 'Food aid to developing countries: a survey', *World Development*.

May, Jacques M. (1985), *The ecology of malnutrition in Middle Africa*, New York: Hafner Publishing Co.

Mbilinyi, M. (1973), 'Education for rural life or education for socialist transformation?', Universities of East Africa Social Science Conference, Dar es Salaam, December.

el Medani, K. A. (1978), *The impact of economic development on the ethnic groups inhabiting Al-Reuk*

Bibliography

region of the Upper Nile Province, M.Sc. thesis, University of Khartoum.

Meillassoux, Claude (1983), 'The economic bases of demographic reproduction: from domestic mode of production to wage earning', *Journal of Peasant Studies*, vol. 11, no. 1.

Metalgessellschaft Aktiengesellschaft (1983), *Metal statistics 1972–82*, (edited by Villy Bauer).

Ministry of Agriculture (Nigeria) (1980), *The green revolution: a food production plan for Nigeria*, Lagos.

Ministry of Economic Development (Nigeria) (1975), *Third national development plan 1975–80*, Lagos.

Ministry of Information (1970), *Second National Development Plan, 1970–1974*, Lagos.

Ministry of National Planning (Sudan) (1977), *The Six Year Plan of economic and social development*, Khartoum.

Ministry of Planning (Nigeria) (1981), *Outline of Fourth Development Plan 1981–1985*, Lagos.

Modibbo, M. A. (1984), *The future of education in Nigeria*, NANS Public Lecture, CAS.

Mohammed, A. S. (1983), 'The management of the economy and the current economic crisis', paper to conference on the state of the nation, Political Science Department, A.B.U., Zaria.

Moore Lappe, F. and J. Collins (1979), *Food first: beyond the myth of scarcity*, San Francisco: Institute of Food and Development Policy; Ballantine Books.

Moore, M. *et al.*, 'Smallholder food production in Tanzania', Report to SIDA and the Tanzanian government, IDS, University of Sussex.

Morocco, Republic of (1973), *Plan de développement économique et social 1973–1977*, vol. 1, Rabat.

Mozambique Information Office (MIO) (1984), *News Review*, no. 37.

Mozambique, Peoples Republic of (1984), 'National Planning Commission', *Economic Report*, January.

Mpofu, J. (1983), 'Some observable sources of women's subordination in Zimbabwe', Centre for Applied Social Sciences, University of Zimbabwe, Harare.

Msambichaka, L.A., B. J. Ndulu and H. K. R. Amani (1983), *Agricultural development in Tanzania*, Friedrich Ebert-Stiftung.

Muhtar, M. (1983), *Agricultural price policy in developing countries – groundnuts in Northern Nigeria*, M. Phil. dissertation, University of Cambridge.

Mukundala, R. (1983), 'Trends in civil service size and income in Tanzania 1967–82', *Canadian Journal of African Studies*, vol. 17, no. 2.

Munslow, B. and P. O'Keefe (1984), 'Energy and the southern African regional confrontation', *Third World Quarterly*, vol. 6, no. 1.

Murray, C. (1981), *Families divided*, Cambridge: Cambridge University Press.

Mustapha, R. (1984), 'The relevance of the NEPU/PRP heritage to the Nigerian revolution', *Studies in Politics and Society*, Issue no. 1, April.

—— (1983), *Foreign capital and class formation in Nigeria: case study of Kano*, M.Sc. dissertation, Ahmadu Bello University, Zaria.

Myrdal, S. and L. Thomson (1983), 'Health and health services in the Ciskei', Working paper no. 54, South Africa Labour and Development Research Unit, Cape Town.

NANS (1984), *Nigerian students and the struggle against commercialised education*, National Association of Nigerian Students.

National Archives (1924), Chibi: Native Commissioner Correspondence to Superintendent of Natives, Fort Victoria. S 606, 10 January.

—— (1933), Chibi: Native Commissioner Correspondence to Superintendent of Natives, Fort Victoria. S 1693, 30 August.

—— (1934), Chibi: Native Commissioner Correspondence to Superintendent of Natives, Fort Victoria. S 1693, 28 March.

National Economic Council (Nigeria) (1983), *Expert Committee Report on the state of the economy*, Lagos.

Newbury, C. (1984a), 'Ebutumwa bw'emiogo: the tyranny of cassava: a women's tax revolt in eastern Zaire', *Canadian Journal of African Studies*, vol. 18, no. 1.

—— (1984b), 'Dead and buried or just underground? the privatisation of the state of Zaire', *Canadian Journal of African Studies*, vol. 18, no. 1.

Nicholson, S. (1976), *A climatic geography for Africa: synthesis of geological, historical and geographical information and data*, Ph.D. thesis, Wisconsin.

Nigerian Labour Congress (1983) *Nigeria is not for sale*, NLC Information Department.

Nixson, F. I. (1982), 'Import-substituting industrialisation', in M. Fransman (ed.), *Industry and accumulation in Africa*, London: Heinemann.

Norman, D. (1984), 'Food security in SADCC', SADCC seminar, Commonwealth Institute, London, 19 July.

NUSAS (1983), *South Africa's bantustans: the pillars of apartheid*, National Union of South African Students, Cape Town.

Nwanko, G. O. (1984), *Managing Nigeria's external debt*, National Institute of Bankers seminar, Enugu.

Nzongola-Ntalaja (1982), *Class struggles and national liberation in Africa*, Roxbury, Mass: Omenama.

———— (1984), 'Bureaucracy elite: new class: who serves whom and why in Mobutu's Zaire?', *Canadian Journal of African Studies*, vol. 18, no. 1.

O'Brien, J. (1978), 'How traditional is "traditional" agriculture?', *Sudan Journal of Economic and Social Studies*, vol. 2, no. 1.

———— (1980), *Agricultural labour and development in Sudan*, Ph.D. thesis, University of Connecticut.

———— (1981), 'Sudan: an Arab breadbasket?', MERIP Reports, no. 99.

———— (1983a), 'The political economy of capitalist agriculture in the central rainlands of Sudan', *Labour, Capital and Society*, vol. 16, no. 1.

———— (1983b), 'The formation of the agricultural labour force in Sudan', *Review of African Political Economy*, no. 26.

Oesterdiekhoff, P. (1977), *Internal marketing conditions and distribution of foreign trade gains*, Bremen, (in German).

———— (1982), 'Problems with large-scale agro-industrial projects in the Sudan: the example of the Kenana Sugar Corporation', in G. Heinrits (ed.), *Problems of agricultural development in the Sudan*.

———— (1983), 'Industrial development, structural deficiencies, agro-industrial prospects and alternatives', in P. Oesterdiekhoff and K. Wohlmuth (eds), *The development perspectives of the Democratic Republic of Sudan*, Munchen/Koln.

O'Keefe, P. and B. Munslow (1984), *Energy and development in southern Africa*, 2 vols., Uppsala: Scandinavian Institute of African Studies.

Olatunbosun, D. and Olayide (1974), 'The effects of the Nigerian marketing boards on the output and income of primary producers', in H. M. A. Onitiri and D. Olatunbosun, *The marketing board system*, Ibadan: NISER.

Olumati, N. (1984), *Peasants and their problems in contemporary Nigeria*, unpublished dissertation, University of Port Harcourt.

Ong, B. N. (1984), 'Women and the transition to socialism in sub-Saharan Africa', in B. Munslow (ed.), *Africa: Problems in the Transition to Socialism*, London: Zed Press.

Onimode, B. (1982), *Imperialism and underdevelopment in Nigeria*, London: Zed Press.

Onitiri, H. M. A. and D. Olatunbosun (1974), *The marketing board system*, Ibadan: NISER.

Osoba, S. (1978), 'The deepening crisis of the Nigerian bourgeoisie', *Review of African Political Economy*, no. 13.

Ousey, B. (1984), Personal communication, Central Selling Organisation, London.

Palma, G. (1978), 'Dependency: a formal theory of underdevelopment or a methodology for the analysis of concrete situations in underdevelopment', *World Development*, vol. 6, no. 7/8.

Palmer, R. (1979), *Land and racial domination in Rhodesia*, London: Heinemann.

Palmer, R. and N. Parsons (1977), *The roots of rural poverty in central and southern Africa*, London: Heinemann.

Payer, C. (1982), *The World Bank: a critical analysis*, New York: Monthly Review Press.

———— (1983), 'Tanzania and the World Bank', *Third World Quarterly*, vol. 5, no. 4, October.

Peet, R. (1984), *Manufacturing, industry and economic development in the SADCC countries*, Scandinavian Institute of African Studies, Uppsala.

Phelps Brown, E. H. with M. H. Browne (1969), *A century of pay*, London: Macmillan.

Bibliography

———— (1973), 'New wine in old bottles: reflections on the changed working of collective bargaining in Great Britain', *British Journal of Industrial Relations*, vol. 9, no. 3.

———— (1975), 'A non-monetarist view of the pay explosion', *Three Banks Review*, no. 105.

Phimister, I. (1977), 'Peasant production and underdevelopment in southern Rhodesia 1890–1914, with particular reference to the Victoria district', in Palmer, R. and N. Parsons, *The roots of rural poverty in central and southern Africa*, London: Heinemann.

Polak, J. J. (1957), 'Monetary analysis of income formation and payments', *IMF staff papers*, November.

Raikes, P. (1984a), 'Stabex: offsetting shortfalls or distributing windfalls?', CDR project paper D.84.6, Copenhagen, (mimeo.).

———— (1984b), 'EEC aid in perspective: financial flows and development aid', CDR project paper, Copenhagen, (mimeo.).

———— (forthcoming), as yet untitled paper on EEC/EDF aid and the analysis of aid projects.

Resnick, I. N. (1981), *The long transition: building socialism in Tanzania*, New York and London: Monthly Review Press.

Review of African Political Economy (1980), Special issue on Zimbabwe, no. 18.

Richards, P. (1983), 'The politics of African land use', *African Studies Review*, vol. 26, no. 2.

Richter, M. J. C. (1984), 'Nutritional value of diets of blacks in Ciskei', *South African Medical Journal*.

Ruf, W. (1984), 'Tunisia in contemporary politics', in R. Lawless and A. Findlay (eds), *North Africa*, London and New York: Croom Helm and St. Martins Press.

Sachs, J. (1979), 'Wages, profits and macro-economic adjustment: a comparative study', Brookings paper on Economic Activity, no. 2.

SADCC (1981), 'Regional co-operation in the mining industry', Government of Zimbabwe to SADCC Council of Ministers Meeting, Blantyre, November.

———— (1984), *Annual progress report, 1983–4*, Gaborone.

———— (1985), *Annual progress report, 1984–5*, Gaborone.

Sano, H-O (1984), *Danmarks Fodevarebistand* (Denmark's food aid), Copenhagen: Den Ny Verden.

Sau, R. (1983), 'Africa's options in development strategy', *Economic and Political Weekly*, vol. 18, no. 44.

Saul, J. and S. Gelb (1981), *The crisis in South Africa: class defense, class revolution*, New York: Monthly Review Press.

Schatzberg, M. G. (1980), *Politics and class in Zaire: bureaucracy, beer and business in Lisala*, New York: Africana.

Schoepf, B. G. (1975a), 'Rural development in Zaire: conceptual models and historical perspective', paper presented to Society for Applied Anthropology, US and Netherlands Joint Meeting, Amsterdam, April.

———— (1975b), 'Family farming and green revolution in the Lufira Valley: a research proposal', presented to the Rockefeller Social Science Foundation, December.

———— (1980), 'Macro-system factors in farming systems research', discussion paper, second workshop on Sahelian agriculture, Department of Agricultural Economics, Purdue University.

———— (1983), 'Unintended consequences and structural predictability: man and biosphere in the Lufira Valley', *Human Organisation*, vol. 42, no. 4.

———— (1984), 'The political economy of agrarian research in Zaire: man and biosphere in the Lufira Valley', in J. Barker (ed.), *The politics of agriculture in tropical Africa: transnational and local perspectives*, Beverly Hills: Sage Publishers.

———— (1985), 'Food crisis and class formation: an example from Shaba', *Review of African Political Economy*, no. 33.

Schoepf, B. G. and C. Schoepf (1980), 'Beyond farming systems research', paper presented at the American Anthropological Association Annual Meeting, Washington D.C.

———— (1981), 'Zaire's rural development in perspective', in B. G. Schoepf (ed.), *The role of US universities in rural and agricultural development*, Centre for Rural Development, Tuskegee Institute.

Bibliography

—————— (1984), 'State, bureaucracy and peasants in the Lufira Valley', *Canadian Journal of African Studies*, vol. 18, no. 1.

Schoepf, C. (forthcoming), *Small farmer maize cultivation in southern Shaba: a linear programming analysis*, MS thesis, Auburn University.

Seddon, J. D. (1980), *Moroccan peasants*, Folkestone: William Dawson.

Sen, A. (1982), *Poverty and famines*, Oxford: Clarendon Press.

—————— (1983), 'Carrots, sticks and economics: perception problems in economics', *Indian Economic Review*, vol. 18, no. 1.

Senate (Nigeria) (1982), *Committee on banking and currency: reactions to Federal government measures and banking practices in Nigeria*, Lagos: National Assembly Press.

Shearson/American Express (1984), *The annual review of the metal markets, 1983–4*.

Shindo, E. (1985), 'Hunger and weapons: the entropy of militarisation', *Review of African Political Economy*, no. 33.

Singh, A. (1979), 'The basic needs approach to development versus the new international economic order: the significance of third world industrialisation', *World Development*, June.

—————— (1982), 'The structural disequilibrium of the Tanzanian economy: the strategic significance of industry in short and long-term adjustment', Tanzania Advisory Group and Department of Applied Economics, Cambridge.

—————— (1983), 'The present crisis of the Tanzanian economy: notes on the economics and politics of devaluation', Department of Applied Economics, Cambridge.

—————— (1984a), 'The IMF programme', *Daily News*, 24 February.

—————— (1984b), 'The continuing crisis of the Tanzanian economy: the political economy of alternative policy options', Department of Applied Economics, Cambridge.

Sjaastad, L. (1983), 'International debt quagmire: to whom do we owe it?', *The World Economy*, vol.6, no.3.

Sluglett, P. and M. Farouk-Sluglett (1984), 'Modern Morocco: political immobilism economic dependence', in R. Lawless and A. Findlay (eds), *North Africa*, London and New York: Croom Helm and St. Martins Press.

Sørbø, G. (1977), 'Nomads on the scheme: a study of irrigation agriculture and pastoralism in Eastern Sudan', in P. O'Keefe (ed.), *Land and development in Africa*, London: International Africa Institute.

Spiegel, A. D. C. (1981), 'Changing patterns of migrant labour and rural differentiation in Lesotho', *Social Dynamics*, vol, 6, no. 2.

Spraos, J. (1983), *Inequalising trade?*, Oxford: Clarendon Press.

Steel, W. F. (1984), 'Industrialisation experience in sub-Saharan Africa: objectives, strategies, results and issues', paper prepared for High Level Industrial Policy seminar for Africa, West Berlin (with the assistance of J. W. Evans).

Stern, E. (1982), 'World Bank financing of structural adjustment', in J. Williamson, *The lending policies of the International Monetary Fund*, Washington D.C.: Institute for International Economics.

Stevens, C. (1979), *Food aid and the developing world*, London: Croom Helm and O.D.I.

—————— (ed.) (annual), *The EEC and the third world: a survey*, London: O.D.I.

Stewart, F. and A. Sengupta (1982), *International financial co-operation: a framework for change*, London: Pinter.

Stoneman, C. (ed.) (1981), *Zimbabwe's inheritance*, London: Macmillan.

Sudanese Economist (1983), 'Sudan: a policy of increasing denationalisation of national wealth', *Review of African Political Economy*, no. 26.

Sunmonu, H. (1984), 'The state of the Nigerian economy', seminar, University of Benin.

Surplus People's Project (1983), *Forced removals in South Africa*, Cape Town.

Swilling, M. (1984), 'The buses smell of blood: the East London boycott', *South African Labour Bulletin*, vol. 9, no. 5.

Tangermann and Krostitz (1982), *Protectionism in the livestock sector, with particular reference to the international beef trade*, Goettlingen: Institut fuer Agrarwirtschaft.

Tanzania, United Republic of (various years), *Price policy recommendations: annexes*, Dar es Salaam: Ministry of Agriculture, Marketing Development Bureau.

Bibliography

—— (1982), *Structural adjustment programme*, Dar es Salaam: Ministry of Planning and Economic Affairs.

—— (1983a), *Tanzania national food strategy*, Dar es Salaam: Ministry of Agriculture.

—— (1983b), *The agricultural policy report*, Dar es Salaam: Ministry of Agriculture.

—— (1984a), *Budget speech*, Dar es Salaam: Ministry of Finance.

—— (1984b), *National economic survival programme*, Dar es Salaam: Government Printer.

Tarrant, J. R. (1980), *Food policy*, Chichester: John Wiley.

Taylor, L. (1982), 'Back to basics: theory for rhetoric in the North-South round', *World Development*, vol. 10.

Teriba, O., E. C. Edozien and M. O. Kayode (1981), *The structure of manufacturing industry in Nigeria*, Ibadan: University of Ibadan Press.

Tetzlaff, R. (1980), *The World Bank: power instrument of the USA or aid for developing countries?*, Munchen/Koln (in German).

Thomas, C. Y. (1974), *Dependence and transformation*, New York: Monthly Review Press.

Thomas, G. (1981), 'The social background of childhood nutrition in the Ciskei', *Social Science and Medicine*, vol. 15A, no. 5.

Titiloye, M. O. and A. A. Ismael (1974), 'A survey of the trends and problems in the domestic arrangements for the marketing of groundnuts and cotton', in H. M. A. Onitiri and D. Olatunbosun, *The marketing board system*, Ibadan: NISER.

Toyo, E. (1983), *The impact of multinationals on the development of Nigeria*, Kuru: National Institute of Policy and Strategic Studies, (mimeo.).

—— (1984), 'From export-led to democratic self-reliance: alternative economic orientations', ASUU National Conference on the State of the Economy, Benin, April.

—— (forthcoming), *The political economy of incomes policy in Nigeria*, Fourth Dimension.

Tschannerl, G. (1979), 'Rural water supply in Tanzania: is politics or technique in command?', in A. Coulson (ed.), *African socialism in practice*, Nottingham: Spokesman.

Turner, T. (1976), 'Multinational corporations and the instability of the Nigerian state', *Review of African Political Economy*, no. 5.

Umbadda, S. and E. Shaaeldin (1983), *IMF stabilisation policies: the experience of Sudan 1978–1982*, Hamburg.

UNDP/World Bank (1982), *Costs of production and comparative advantage of crops in the Sudan*, Khartoum.

UNDRO (1982), *Report of the United Nations Multi-agency fact finding mission to Angola 1981*, New York: United Nations.

UN Economic Commission for Africa (1981), *Survey of economic and social conditions in Africa, 1979–80*, E/CN.14/802, Addis Ababa.

UNIDO (1979), *World industry since 1960: progress and prospects*, New York: United Nations.

—— (1981), *World industry in 1980, UN biennial industrial development survey*, New York: United Nations.

—— (1982), *Industrial development decade for Africa*, Progress Report, ID/B/274, March.

—— (1983), *Industry in a changing world: special issue of the industrial development survey of the fourth general conference of UNIDO*, New York: United Nations.

—— (1984), *Country report on Mozambique*, UNIDO, March.

United States Department of Agriculture (1981), *Food problems and prospects in sub-Saharan Africa: the decade of the 1980s*, Washington D.C.

United States Department of the Interior (1982), *Bureau of Mines yearbook*, vol. 3, Washington.

—— (1984), *Mineral industries of Africa*, Bureau of Mines, Washington D.C.

Usman, Y. B. (1979), *For the liberation of Nigeria*, London: New Beacon Press.

—— (1982), 'Behind the oil smokescreen: the real causes of the current economic crisis', in Gaskiya, *Who is responsible?*.

—— (1984a), 'Middlemen, consultants, contractors and the solutions to the current economic crisis', *Studies in Politics and Society*, no. 2, October.

—— (1984b), 'Further misconceptions, misinterpretations and evasions: a rejoinder to Bangura', *Studies in Politics and Society*, no. 2, October.

Uzoaga, W. O. (1984), 'Managing Nigeria's external debt', National Institute of Bankers, seminar, Enugu.

Valdes, A and J. Zietz (1980), 'Agricultural protectionism in OECD countries: its cost to less developed countries', Washington D.C.; IFPRI.

Van Onselen, C. (1976), *Chibaro: African mine labour in southern Rhodesia 1900–1933*, London:

Wagstaff, H. (1981), 'Food imports of developing countries: trends and dilemmas', *Food policy*, autumn.

Wallerstein, I. (1982), 'Household structures and production processes: preliminary theses and findings', *Review*, no. 5, winter.

Wangwe, S. M. (1983), 'Industrial development strategies for Africa', Economic Research Bureau, University of Dar es Salaam, (mimeo.).

Warren, B. (1980), *Imperialism, pioneer of capitalism*, London: New Left Books.

Weinbaum, M. G. (1980), 'Food and political stability in the Middle East', *Studies in Comparative International Development*, no. 15, summer.

Weiner, D., S. Moyo, B. Munslow, P. O'Keefe (1985), 'Land use and agricultural productivity in Ziambabwe', *Journal of Modern African Studies*, vol. 23, no. 2.

Wheeler, D. (1984), 'Sources of stagnation in sub-Saharan Africa', *World Development*, vol. 12, no. 1.

Whitsun Foundation (1978), *The peasant sector*, Data Bank, no. 2.

Williams, G. (1977), 'Class relations in a neo-colony: the case of Nigeria', in P. Gutkind and P. Waterman (eds), *African social studies: a radical reader*, New York: Monthly Review Press.

Williamson, J. (1982), *The lending policies of the International Monetary Fund*, Washington D.C.: Institute for International Economics.

——— (ed.) (1983), *IMF conditionality*, Washington D.C.: Institute of International Economics.

Wilmot, P. F. (1983), 'Multinational corporations, indiscipline and corruption in the third world', paper presented to National Ethical Reorientation Seminar on Indiscipline and Corruption, Ahmadu Bello University, Zaria, April.

Wilson, F., A. Kooy and D. Henrie (eds) (1977), *Farm labour in South Africa*, Cape Town: David Philips.

Wohlmuth, K. (1983), 'The Kenana sugar project: a model of successful trilateral co-operation?', in P. Oesterdiekhoff and K. Wohlmuth (eds), *The development perspectives of the Democratic Republic of Sudan*, Munchen/Koln.

Wolpe, H. (1972), 'Capitalism and cheap labour power in South Africa: from segregation to apartheid', *Economy and Society*, no. 1.

World Bank (1978a), *Sudan agricultural review*, Report No. 1836a-SU, 10 August.

——— (1978b), *World development report 1978*, Washington D.C.

——— (1981a), *World development report 1981*, Washington D.C.

——— (1981b), *Accelerated development in sub-Saharan Africa*, (the 'Berg Report'), Washington.

——— (1981c), *Economic memorandum on Tanzania*, Report No. 3086-TA, Washington D.C.

——— (1982), *World development report 1982*, Washington D.C.

——— (1983a), *World development report 1983*, Washington D.C.

——— (1983b), *Sub-Saharan Africa: progress report on development prospects and programmes*, Washington D.C.

——— (1984a), *World development report 1984*, Washington D.C.

——— (1984b), *Towards sustained development in sub-Saharan Africa*, Washington D.C.

——— (1984c), *World debt tables, 1983–4*, Washington D.C.

——— (1985), *World development report 1985*, Washington D.C.

Yawitch, J. (1983), 'Apartheid and family life', *Work in Progress*, no. 27.

Young, M. C. (1978), 'Zaire: the unending crisis', *Foreign Affairs*, vol. 57, no. 1.

——— (1983), 'Zaire: the politics of penury', *SAIS Review*, vol. 3, no. 1.

Zambia Consolidated Copper Mines (ZCCM) Ltd (1983), *Annual report*.

Zghal, A. (1984), 'La Tunisie, dernièe république civile', *Jeune Afrique*, no. 1205.

Zulu, J. B. (1983), Lecture to Association of African Central Banks, Arusha, IMF Survey, Washington D.C., 22 August.

Zulu, J. B. and S. M. Nsouli (1984), 'Adjustment programmes in Africa: the experience of fund supported programmes 1980–81', *Finance and Development*, March.

Index

Index